STECK-VAUGHN

Spelling

Teacher's Edition
Level 2

John R. Pescosolido, Ph.D.
Professor Emeritus
Central Connecticut State University
New Britain, Connecticut

Consultants

Felice M. Rockoff
Reading Teacher
New York City Public Schools
New York, New York

Theodore J. Thibodeau
Assistant Superintendent
Attleboro Public Schools
Attleboro, Massachusetts

Anna L. Ulrich
Adjunct Professor
College of Santa Fe
Albuquerque, New Mexico

Anita Uphaus
Coordinator of Early Childhood Programs
Austin Independent School District
Austin, Texas

STECK-VAUGHN
COMPANY
ELEMENTARY • SECONDARY • ADULT • LIBRARY

Acknowledgments

Executive Editor: Diane Sharpe
Project Editor: Amanda Johnson
Design Manager: Richard Balsam
Designers: Jim Cauthron
Danielle Szabo

Product Development: Cottage Communications
Typesetting: Publishers' Design and Production Services, Inc.

Writers: Phyllis Keaton (pp. 18, 152); Mindy Menschell (pp. 6, 12, 24, 44, 50, 56, 62, 70, 76, 82, 88, 94, 102, 108, 114, 120, 134, 140, 146, 158, 166, 172, 184); Sally Paynter (pp. 30, 38, 126, 190)

Artists: Paige Billin-Frye, Maxie Chambliss, Brian Cody, Eulala Conner, Julie Durrell, Jon Friedman, Simon Galkin, Jon Goodell, Carol Grosvenor, Meryl Henderson, Ruth Hoffman, True Kelley, Tom Leonard, Jon McIntosh, Sal Murdocca, Ed Parker, Diane Paterson, Jan Pyk, Jerry Smath, N. Jo Smith, Pat Traub, Elaine Vogt, John Wallner, Kathy Wilburn, Lane Yerkes

---

ISBN 0-8114-9280-X

TABLE OF CONTENTS

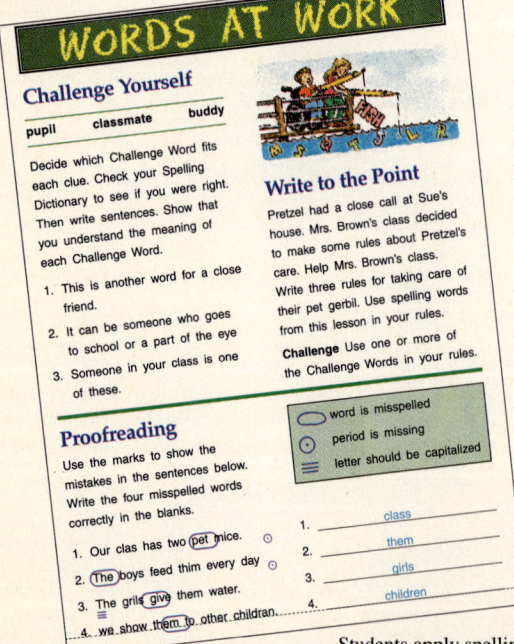

in is it with sick quit

Listen to the story. Circle the spelling words.

The New Girl

There is a new girl in my class. Her name is Kim. My best friend is Anna. She walked to school with Kim this morning. I had to walk to school alone. It made me feel sick.

Today we played kickball. Anna picked Kim for her team. She didn't pick me. It made me so angry that I quit! I sat on the ground and watched the game.

That new girl was up. I wanted her to miss the ball because she took my best friend away from me. She kicked the ball.

POW! She kicked a home run!

Maybe tomorrow I will ask Kim to walk to school with me!

in is it with sick quit

Write in the missing spelling words.

1. Kim i ___ a new girl
i ___ my class. 2. Anna
___ent with Kim. I
___ade me feel s ___.
___ ___ the team.
5. I'll go w ___ Kim
tomorrow.

85

Cloze selections allow students to use spelling words in meaningful context.

Steck-Vaughn
SPELLING

Integrates spelling with reading, writing, and language arts!

More favorite features for teachers!

The all-new *Steck-Vaughn Spelling* has more of the features teachers love. The holistic approach integrates spelling with reading, writing, and language arts. **Words at Work activities reinforce list words in context.** Word meaning, proofreading, and dictionary skills get extra emphasis. **Challenge Words extend each lesson!** It's an ideal environment for expanding vocabulary and improving spelling accuracy.

Consistent instruction, enrichment, maintenance, and review!

Steck-Vaughn Spelling builds skills through a consistent pattern of instruction, enrichment, maintenance, and review. Each new word is analyzed on the basis of structure, sound, and meaning, and then reinforced through reading, writing, proofreading, and dictionary activities. The colorful format, compelling stories, and creative exercises keep student motivation high.

- Word lists built around similar sounds and spelling patterns emphasize spelling rules.

WORDS AT WORK

Challenge Yourself

| pupil | classmate | buddy |

Decide which Challenge Word fits each clue. Check your Spelling Dictionary to see if you were right. Then write sentences. Show that you understand the meaning of each Challenge Word.

1. This is another word for a close friend.
2. It can be someone who goes to school or a part of the eye.
3. Someone in your class is one of these.

Write to the Point

Pretzel had a close call at Sue's house. Mrs. Brown's class decided to make some rules about Pretzel's care. Help Mrs. Brown's class. Write three rules for taking care of their pet gerbil. Use spelling words from this lesson in your rules.

Challenge Use one or more of the Challenge Words in your rules.

Proofreading

Use the marks to show the mistakes in the sentences below. Write the four misspelled words correctly in the blanks.

○ word is misspelled
⊙ period is missing
≡ letter should be capitalized

1. Our clas has two pet mice. ⊙
2. The boys feed thim every day ⊙
3. The grils give them water.
4. we show them to other children.

1. class
2. them
3. girls
4. children

Students apply spelling skills to challenge words and writing activities.

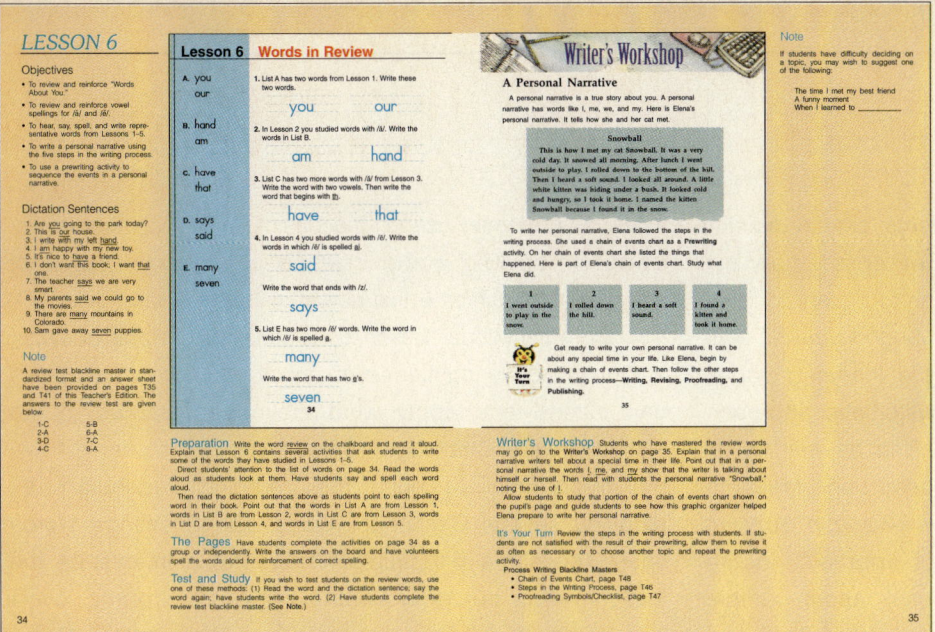

With each review lesson, students engage in a process writing activity. Student models provide a springboard to prewriting.

- *Checkpoint* activities using the bound-in dictionary encourage students to explore word meanings and origins, and invite interaction in multicultural classrooms.

- Two-page cloze reading selections encourage students to use spelling words in context.

- Language arts activities extend spelling into grammar, usage, mechanics, and dictionary skills.

- Challenge Words introduced in each lesson share the same phonetic sound or structural feature as list words but are more difficult in meaning.

- New *Words at Work* pages incorporate list words into thematically related writing and proofreading activities.

- A review every sixth lesson reinforces lessons and assesses progress.

- A *Writer's Workshops* with each review lesson challenges students to complete an extended writing activity using writing process skills.

Teaching resources at your fingertips!

Resourceful Teacher's Editions include reduced, annotated student pages, detailed lesson plans, word lists, handwriting models, record-keeping charts, a Scope and Sequence, and other new features.

- New strategic assessment section provides tools for error analysis and strategies to help students master frequently misspelled words.

- New blackline masters support family involvement and the writing process.

What you want is what you get!

We asked hundreds of teachers all over the country what they wanted in a spelling series.

Steck-Vaughn Spelling is the answer.

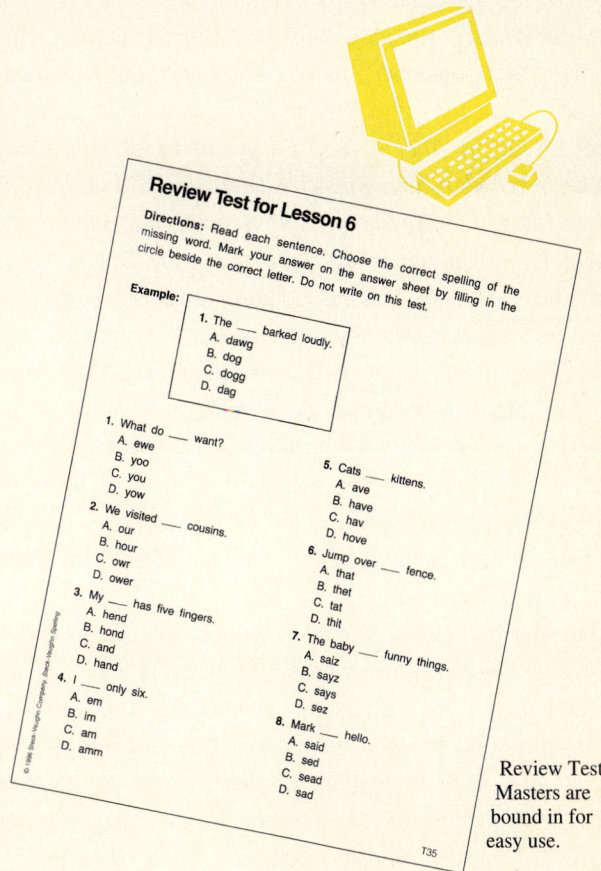

Review Test Masters are bound in for easy use.

SERIES OVERVIEW

Spelling is a skill that many students cannot master without hard work. Hard work alone, however, is usually not enough. Students need a well-constructed plan to help them gain strong spelling skills. *Steck-Vaughn Spelling* was created to offer such guidance. On the following pages you will find a comprehensive and systematic approach that recognizes the importance of spelling as well as its inherent connection to writing. Based on research conducted over several decades, *Steck-Vaughn Spelling* presents an integrated language arts approach to the study of spelling. Six-page lessons afford ample opportunities to use words in a variety of writing and language arts assignments.

The Lesson

Throughout the core of the program, each six-page instructional lesson begins with a word analysis page, which introduces a list of words derived from analysis of research on spelling difficulty and word frequency in students' writing. Sources consulted include *The American Heritage Word Frequency Book*, by Carroll, Davies, and Richman; *Computational Analysis of Present-Day American English*, by Kucera and Francis; *The New Iowa Spelling Scale*, by Green; *The Spelling Encyclopedia of Educational Research*, by Horn; and *Phoneme-Grapheme Correspondences as Clues to Spelling Improvement*, by Hanna and Hanna. Other studies used were those by Dolch, Horn, Dale and O'Rourke, Gates, Loomer, and Rinsland. The words are organized to facilitate analysis of sounds and letters as students study and write each word. The word analysis page is followed by **Checkpoint**, a series of meaning-based prompts in the forms of definitions, context clues, analogies, synonyms, antonyms, and word plays for writing each word a second time. At this point an optional and independent self-assessment tool, the **Checkpoint Study Plan**, is recommended.

The next two pages, the story pages, are devoted to a carefully structured reading passage. In levels 7 and 8, the passage is provided on blackline masters. The passage allows students to work with meaning in the cloze-style format often used in testing. Students must use context clues as they complete the passage using words from the lesson list, which is reprinted adjacent to the passage.

Attention is then given to the related language arts areas of grammar, usage, mechanics, and dictionary skills. Using the spelling words, students engage in a variety of activities that reinforce instruction in these areas.

Each instructional lesson concludes with **Words at Work**, a highly motivating series of activities in which students can extend and apply what they have learned in the lesson. In the **Challenge Yourself** section, students have the opportunity to build their reading vocabulary by studying several Challenge Words. The Challenge Words share the same phonetic or structural elements as the lesson words but range approximately two grade levels above the level of the list words. In **Write to the Point**, students have an opportunity to apply their spelling skills in a brief writing assignment thematically related to the earlier reading passage. Finally, students practice proofreading for spelling, capitalization, punctuation, and similar errors, using sentences or a paragraph that is also thematically tied to the reading passage.

Level 1 follows a special pattern. This level begins with a series of readiness lessons based on a story or poem and designed to help students master basic phoneme-grapheme relationships. The instructional lessons that follow include an activity page with an abbreviated word list, two story pages on which students identify list words and complete sentences about the story, and a final page that integrates spelling with language arts activities.

Maintenance and Review

The phonetic and structural principles that form the focus of the lessons are maintained and reviewed from level to level through increasingly difficult words, sometimes in an affixed form. In addition, beginning in level 2, every sixth lesson reviews representative words from previous lessons. Flexible blackline masters available in the **Activity Masters** booklets provide three options for use: review, maintenance, and enrichment. The **Teacher's Edition** also provides an additional review in standardized test format.

Writing and Enrichment

The **Challenge Yourself** feature of each concluding lesson page allows students to extend the phonetic and structural principles of the lesson to words with similar phonetic or structural elements. By combining the use of the **Spelling Dictionary** and a variety of context-related clues, students unlock the meanings of more challenging words and have the opportunity to use these words in a "quick write" assignment.

Each of the six review lessons provides a more formal writing assignment drawn from a variety of writing types: narratives, letters, description, explanation, evaluation, and persuasion. The type of writing as well as a prewriting activity is modeled for students. Students then follow the steps in the writing process to complete the writing assignment. The fully developed prewriting activities usually include the use of a graphic organizer.

Comprehensive Teacher Aids

Steck-Vaughn Spelling contains a wealth of material with which you can strengthen and enrich your lessons.

Pupil's Edition

- **Checkpoint Study Plan** for self-assessment allows students to study and practice spelling independently.
- **Spelling Dictionary** includes all lesson words and Challenge Words.

Teacher's Edition

- **Reduced annotated student pages** display correct answers and facilitate instruction.
- **Detailed lesson plans** feature a warm-up activity to introduce pages, guidelines for teaching, and suggestions for follow-up activities.
- **Clear objectives** for each part of the lesson state the concepts and skills that students should achieve.
- **Spelling Dictionary** facilitates teaching spelling and dictionary skills.
- **Word lists** include all lesson words and Challenge Words for a grade level as well as the words from the levels immediately above and below.
- **Scope and Sequence** chart displays the instructional content for a grade level, along with the content of the levels immediately above and below it.
- **Class Recordkeeping Chart** provides a convenient resource for tracking students' progress.

Blackline Masters

- **Review Tests** in standardized testing format provide a consumable alternative to the sentence dictation test.

- **Family Involvement Letters** in English and Spanish facilitate communication with students' families and offer specific activities for important at-home support.
- **Steps in the Writing Process** serves as a reference for students while they are working on writing assignments.
- **Proofreading Symbols/Checklist** guides students through the proofreading step of the writing process.
- **Graphic Organizers** help students generate and arrange ideas before they write a first draft.

Blackline Masters Booklets

- **Activity Masters** booklets for levels 2 through 8 include games, puzzles, and similar activities to motivate students to analyze words.
- **Comprehension Masters** booklets for levels 7 and 8 allow students to use the spelling words in a meaningful context.

Evaluation and Assessment

Specific self-assessment opportunities occur twice during each instructional lesson. In **Checkpoint** students check their work and determine which words need study.

The Teacher's Edition provides **Sample Sentences** for pre- and/or post-testing. Embedded in each sentence is a single spelling word. A second set of sentences, labeled **Dictation Sentences**, may incorporate several spelling words into each sentence. Because the vocabulary of these sentences has been controlled, teachers may require students to write the entire sentences. Dictation Sentences are also included in the review lessons. As mentioned above, alternative **Review Tests** in standardized format appear as blackline masters in the Teacher's Edition.

ESL and Special Needs

Steck-Vaughn Spelling offers several advantages for students for whom English is a second language and for students with special needs. The **Checkpoint** step in each lesson provides focused attention to word meaning. In addition the reading passage that follows each **Checkpoint** lends itself easily to oral practice with the spelling words in a meaningful and motivating context. In the Teacher's Edition, the **Spelling Strategy** for each instructional lesson discusses possible causes for misspelling and offers one or more activities to address the problem.

SAMPLE
TEACHER'S EDITION PAGE

An easy-to-use, helpful teacher's edition accompanies each student edition in *Steck-Vaughn Spelling*. These teacher's guides provide thorough, consistent lesson plans and supplementary activities to meet individual needs. Each teacher's edition contains the following features:

- Sample pages from the student edition with notes explaining the purpose of each page
- A section on testing and classroom management
- A recordkeeping chart for noting students' progress
- A scope and sequence chart listing the instructional content for a particular level, as well as for the levels immediately above and below it
- A word list including all the spelling words at that level, as well as the words in the levels immediately above and below it
- Blackline masters consisting of review tests in standardized testing format, family involvement letters (English and Spanish), and writing process aids (five steps, graphic organizers, and proofreading)

Lesson pages include these features:

(1) Each student page is shown in reduced form.

(2) Correct responses are printed in blue on the student page.

(3) Clear, consistently placed objectives specify exactly what students should accomplish for each lesson.

(4) Sample sentences are provided for every lesson.

(5) A lesson plan for each page is presented beneath the reduced student page. Lessons are presented in three sections: Preparation, The Page, and Follow-Up. These sections include warm-up exercises to help the teacher introduce the activities, guidelines for page instruction, and suggestions for extension activities. At the conclusion of each lesson, helpful advice is provided for checking student progress and assigning short writing and proofreading activities thematically tied to the story pages, as well as an optional Challenge Word activity.

Lesson 1   Words About You   ①

Say these words.
Then do the exercises.

her
him
boys
our
girls
you
the
them
had
child
children
class

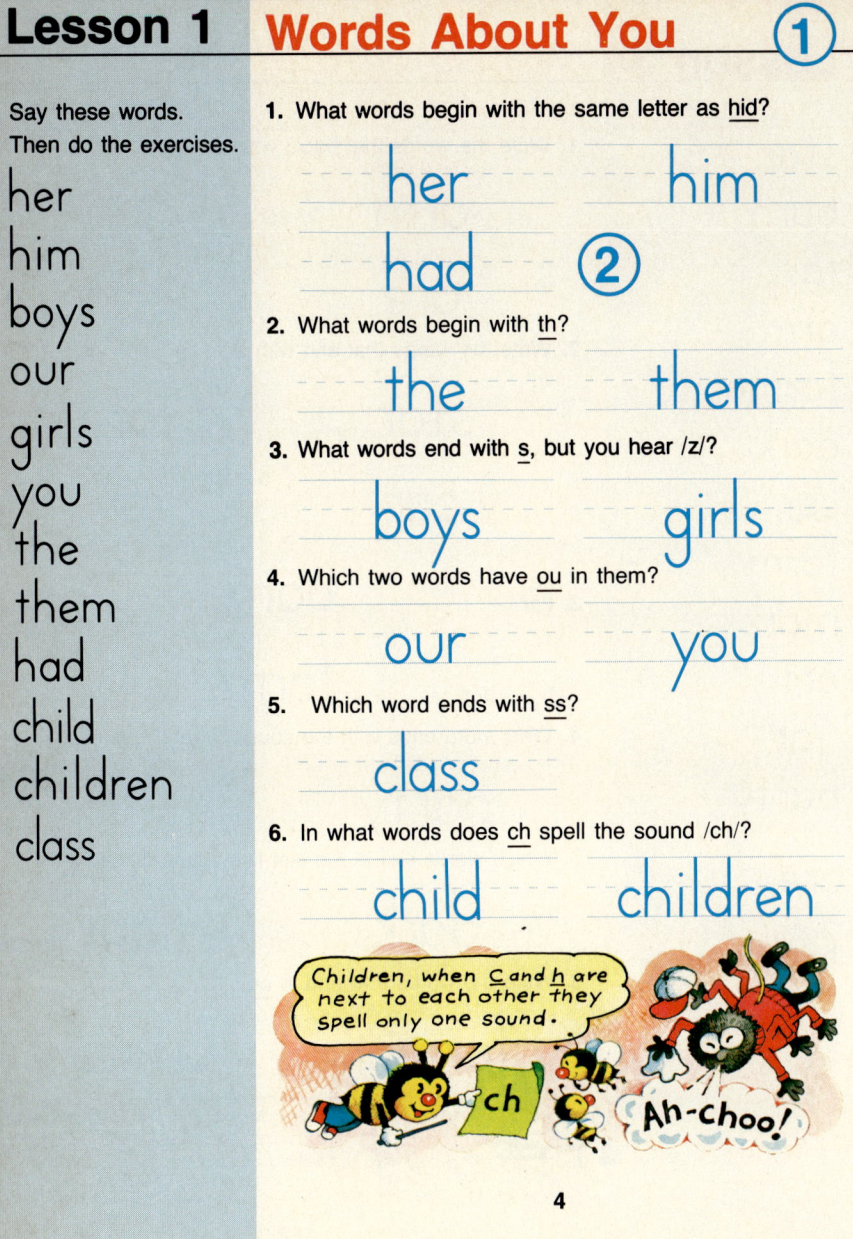

1. What words begin with the same letter as hid?

her   him

had   ②

2. What words begin with th?

the   them

3. What words end with s, but you hear /z/?

boys   girls

4. Which two words have ou in them?

our   you

5. Which word ends with ss?

class

6. In what words does ch spell the sound /ch/?

child   children

Children, when C and h are next to each other they spell only one sound.

ch   Ah-choo!

4

Objectives   ③

- To hear and say ten spelling words.
- To write the spelling words with attention to letter sequence and sound/symbol relationships.
- To write each spelling word once.

Sample Sentences   ④

1. I know <u>her</u> brother is very tall.
2. We gave <u>him</u> the soccer ball.
3. The <u>boys</u> remembered their gym shoes.
4. They were excited by <u>our</u> news.
5. The <u>girls</u> are going on a hike.
6. Would <u>you</u> lend me your new bike?
7. There's a slide on <u>the</u> playground.
8. I asked <u>them</u> all to come inside.
9. My sister Janie <u>had</u> a cold.
10. The <u>children</u> are all eight years old.

⑤

Preparation   Review <u>vowels</u> and <u>consonants</u>. Write the five vowels <u>a,e,i,o,u</u> on the board. Mention that there is a sixth vowel, <u>y</u>. Tell students that <u>y</u> is special. It is a consonant when it appears at the beginning of a word and a vowel when it comes at the end of a word. Every word except <u>I</u> and <u>a</u> contains consonants and at least one vowel.

Tell students that in Lesson 1 they are going to spell words that they use frequently in speaking and in writing. Turn to page 4 and have students repeat and spell each list word after you. Ask which word begins with the consonant <u>y</u>. *(you)* Note that the cartoon calls attention to the consonant digraph <u>ch</u>. Write <u>ch</u> and <u>th</u> on the board and review their sounds. Have students find the spelling words that contain these digraphs. *(child, children, the, them)*

Ask the students to point to the spelling word as you read each sample sentence aloud.

The Page   Do page 4 with the students. Have them take turns reading each activity aloud. Allow time for them to write the answers. Then have volunteers write the answers on the board so students may check their work.

Follow-Up   Ask students how they plan to study their spelling words. Suggest these methods: Students may write the words several times and review them carefully, or they may spell the words aloud with a partner.

SAMPLE STUDENT LESSON

First Page

The first page of every level 2 lesson has these features:

① A title introduces the lesson and identifies the sound.

② The words for the lesson are grouped according to the different spellings of the sound. The first twelve of the level 2 lessons contain twelve words each. The last twenty-four of the lessons contained in level 2 feature fourteen words each.

③ Exercises require students to examine sound/symbol relationships in list words.

④ Cartoons help students to note spelling generalizations.

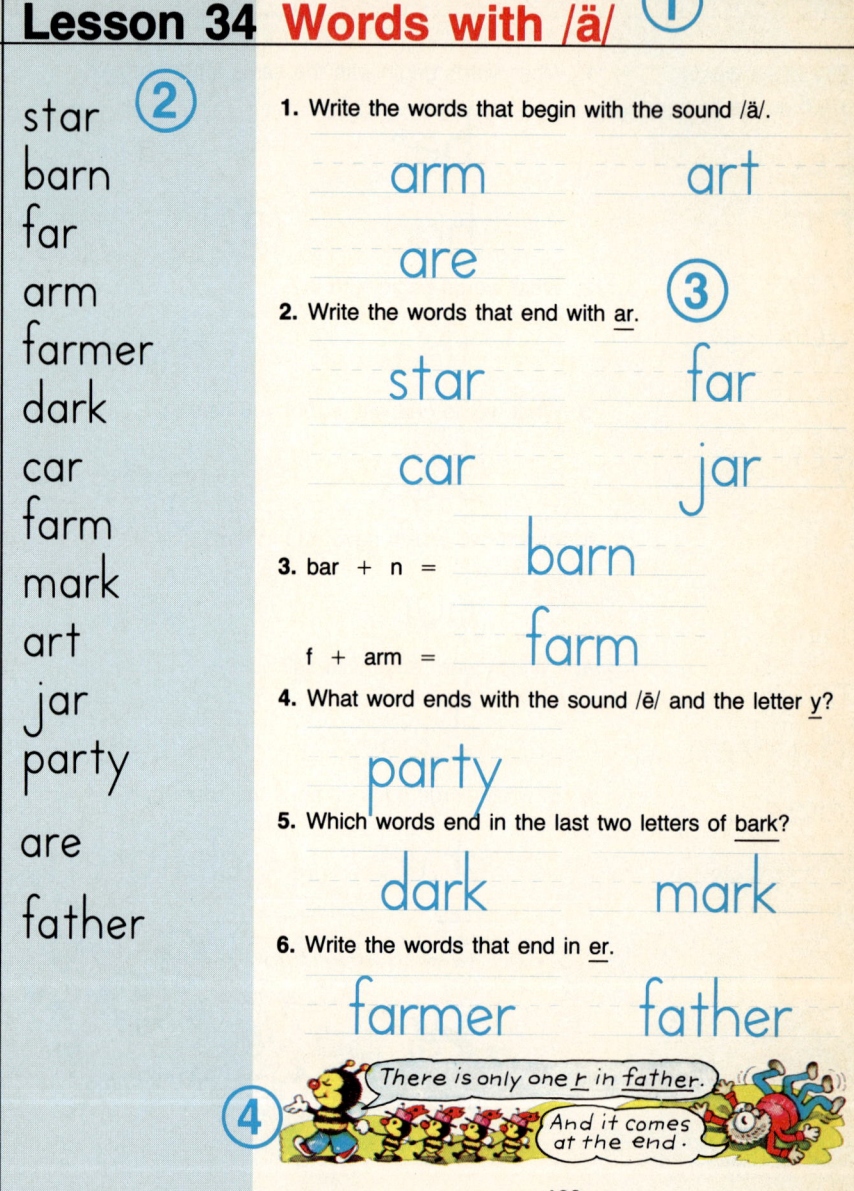

Lesson 34 Words with /ä/ ①

②
star
barn
far
arm
farmer
dark
car
farm
mark
art
jar
party
are
father

1. Write the words that begin with the sound /ä/.

arm   art

are   ③

2. Write the words that end with ar.

star   far

car   jar

3. bar + n =   barn

   f + arm =   farm

4. What word ends with the sound /ē/ and the letter y?

party

5. Which words end in the last two letters of bark?

dark   mark

6. Write the words that end in er.

farmer   father

④ There is only one r in father. And it comes at the end.

182

Word-Analysis Page

The first page of every lesson introduces the sound to be studied and list words containing that sound. The words are grouped according to different spellings of the sound.

Checkpoint

Write a spelling word for each clue. ①
Then use the Checkpoint Study Plan on page 224.

1. Gina's painting was a work of ___.

2. Twinkle, twinkle little ___.

3. A dad is a ___.

4. Does this sentence end with a question ___? ②

5. A cow lives in a ___.

6. Mom said to be home before ___.

7. If it's not near, it's ___.

8. He grows corn on his ___.

9. Bill is coming to my birthday ___.

10. You find jam in a ___.

11. We are funnier than they ___.

12. Your hand is part of your ___.

13. Someone who grows crops is a ___.

③

14. This mystery word named the kind of wagon you
    see in the picture. In some countries, it was
    spelled <u>carrus</u>. In other countries, it was spelled
    <u>carre</u>. Today, it's another word for automobile.
    Write the mystery word. ___

183

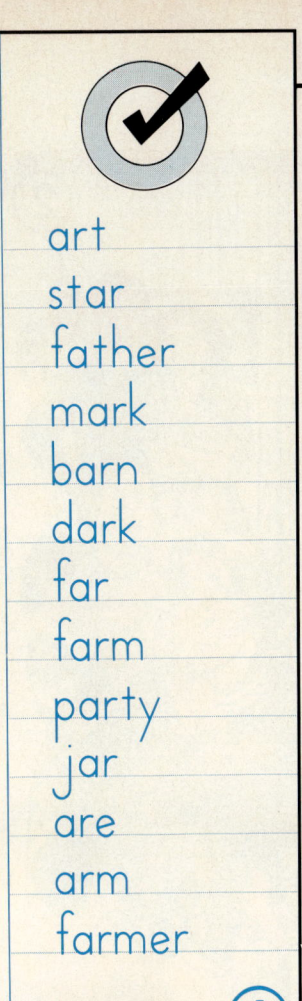

art
star
father
mark
barn
dark
far
farm
party
jar
are
arm
farmer

④

car

Second Page

The Checkpoint page has these features:

① Instructions direct students to choose
and write list words in response to
clues and then to use the Checkpoint Study Plan on the last page of
the book.

② Puzzle-like clues incorporate definitions, context clues, synonyms, antonyms, comparisons, word plays,
rhymes, and riddles. Students write
list words in response to these clues.

③ Each Checkpoint page relates the
etymology of a "mystery" list word.

④ The etymology clue is illustrated.

Checkpoint Page

The second page of each lesson, the Checkpoint page, has two important
purposes. First, it shifts the focus of the lesson from word structure to word
meaning and usage. Students write each spelling word in response to puzzle-
like clues and an etymology clue. This page· is also used with the Checkpoint
Study Plan on the last page of each student edition for self-testing and independent study.

SAMPLE STUDENT LESSON

Third and Fourth Pages

The story pages of every lesson have these features:

① Exercise directions are short and easy to understand.

② The story title is in large, appealing type.

③ The story uses all or most of the spelling words for each lesson. When all list words are not used in the story, the balance is used to complete questions at the end of the story.

④ Interesting, attractive art accompanies the story to hold students' interest and aid comprehension.

⑤ The list words are provided in manuscript form for students to use as a model for their own handwriting.

---

① **Fill in the blanks with spelling words.**

② # The Star Party

Four children lived with their parents and grandmother on a pretty _____. The _____ and his wife worked hard. They had many cows in the _____ to take care of every day.

One summer night the grandmother was very sad. "My eyes are bad," she said. "I can't see the stars anymore." ③

So, that night after dinner, the mother and _____ took the children for a ride in the _____. They made a plan to make the grandmother happy.

④ The next night the father said, "Tonight we are having a star party. The presents _____ all ready. Let the _____ begin!"

The first child gave the grandmother a kitten. It had a white _____ on its face just like a star. The

184

Story Pages

The third and fourth pages of each lesson integrate reading with spelling. Students choose and write spelling words to complete high-interest, continuous-text selections. In addition to providing another opportunity for students to practice writing and spelling list words, these pages also offer a change of pace and a chance for students to improve their understanding of word usage and meaning. The stories were checked for readability at an independent laboratory. The Spache, Fry, and Degrees of Reading Power formulas were applied.

second child had made a bracelet. The grandmother put

it on her _____. It was made of flowers just

like yellow stars. The third child had covered the garden

with a hundred paper stars! It was a work of _____.

Then the youngest child put a jar in the

grandmother's hands. It didn't seem to be a

_____ present at all. He told her to open

the jar in the dark.

Outdoors, the grandmother took the lid off the

_____. Everyone smiled. Fireflies flew all

around. They glowed in the _____.

"It's a jar of stars," said the youngest child.

The grandmother said, "I love the stars you gave

me. Now I don't need to see the stars that are so

_____ away."

185

star

barn

far

arm

farmer

dark

car

farm

mark

art

jar

party

are

father

⑤

Enrichment

A note in the teacher's edition indicates which activity master to assign to students to provide additional practice and enrichment.

Maintenance and Review

A note in the teacher's edition indicates which activity master to assign for review and maintenance of the previous week's lesson. In addition, a separate maintenance activity is included to review words from the previous lesson.

SAMPLE STUDENT LESSON

Fifth Page

The fifth page of every lesson has these features:

① The alphabet is provided for students to use as a reference for alphabetizing.

② A title identifies the language arts skill.

③ Text explains the language arts skill.

④ Exercises integrate the spelling words with the language arts activity.

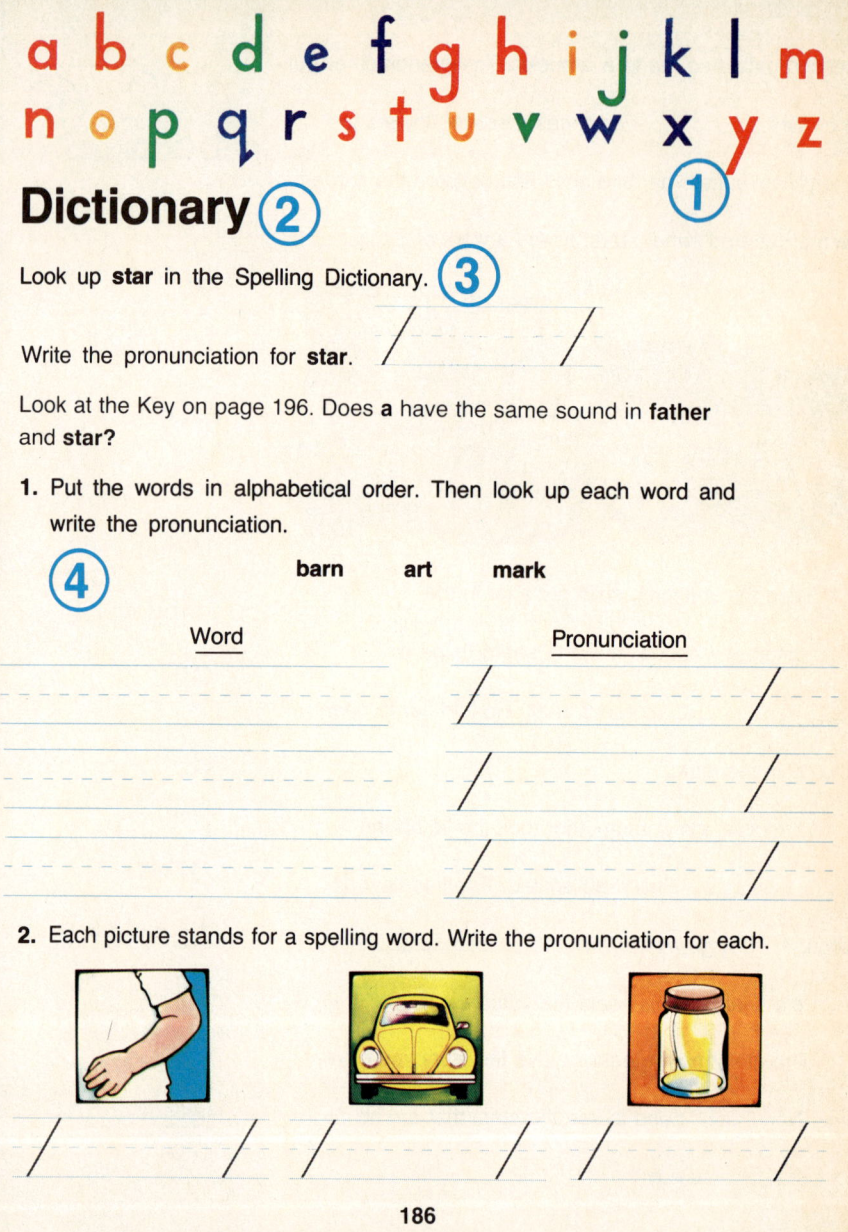

a b c d e f g h i j k l m
n o p q r s t u v w x y z ①

Dictionary ②

Look up **star** in the Spelling Dictionary. ③

Write the pronunciation for **star**. /   /

Look at the Key on page 196. Does **a** have the same sound in **father** and **star**?

1. Put the words in alphabetical order. Then look up each word and write the pronunciation.

④   barn   art   mark

Word   Pronunciation

2. Each picture stands for a spelling word. Write the pronunciation for each.

186

Language Arts Page

The fifth page of each lesson focuses on dictionary skills or other language arts skills, such as capitalization, punctuation, grammar, and usage. Students write their spelling words again as they practice these skills.

WORDS AT WORK

Challenge Yourself

barber   depart   harmful

Decide which Challenge Word fits each clue. Check your Spelling Dictionary to see if you were right. Then write sentences. Show that you understand the meaning of each Challenge Word.

1. You do this when you leave for school in the morning.

2. Something that hurts you is this.

3. This person cuts hair.

Write to the Point

Think of another good gift for the star party. Write a paragraph that tells about the gift. Use spelling words from this lesson in your paragraph.

Challenge Use one or more of the Challenge Words in your paragraph.

Proofreading ③

Use the marks to show the mistakes in the sentences below. Write the four misspelled words correctly in the blanks.

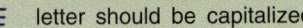

⬭	word is misspelled
⊙	period is missing
＝	letter should be capitalized

1. That night the stars lit up the daark sky.

2. The fireflies flew around the fairm

3. The father took the grandmother by the ahrm.

4. she thought it was a great pardy.

1. _____

2. _____

3. _____

4. _____

187

Sixth Page

The Words at Work page of every lesson includes these features:

① Three Challenge Words with the same sound or structural element as the list words are provided in an optional Challenge Yourself feature.

② A writing assignment provides students with an opportunity to use the list words and the Challenge Words in a brief writing activity on a topic thematically tied to the selection on the story pages.

③ The concluding exercise allows students to practice proofreading for spelling and appropriate language mechanics skills in sentences also thematically tied to the selection on the story pages.

Words at Work Page

Following a teacher-directed post-test, the Words at Work page of each lesson provides students with an opportunity to extend and apply the skills presented in the lesson.

An optional Challenge Yourself activity presents three new words with the same sound or structural element as the list words. Students use context and the **Spelling Dictionary** to unlock the meanings of these new words. In Write to the Point, students have an opportunity to use the list words and the Challenge Yourself words in a brief, informal writing assignment. This activity may be assigned to the entire class. All students also may be assigned the proofreading exercise that concludes this page.

SAMPLE REVIEW LESSON

First Page

Each review page includes these features:

① Lesson number and title are included.

② List words from the previous five lessons are grouped according to sounds.

③ Exercises require students to write list words in response to sound/symbol clues.

Lesson 36 Words in Review

A. town ②
   around

B. long
   saw
   talk
   small

C. short
   store
   floor

D. are
   car
   father

E. flatter
   writer

1. In Lesson 31, you studied two ways to spell /ou/: <u>ou</u> and <u>ow</u>. Write the words in List A.

2. Lesson 32 has words with /ô/. Write the words with /ô/ from List B.

3. In Lesson 33, you studied more words with /ô/. Write the words in List C.

③

4. Lesson 34 has words with /ä/. Write the words with /ä/ from List D.

5. Add <u>er</u> to <u>flat</u> and <u>write</u>. Use List E to check your words.

194

Review and Writer's Workshop Pages

Every sixth lesson in the student edition is a two-page review lesson. The first review page presents representative words from the previous lessons. The words were chosen because of their frequency of use and spelling difficulty.

Writer's Workshop

A Description ①

A description of a person tells how that person looks, moves, and sounds. Writers use details to make the person come alive in the reader's mind. Here is the beginning of Tara's description of her new baby brother.

The Baby

Yesterday Mom and Dad brought Corey home. At first I thought they left the baby at the hospital. The blanket looked empty. Then I saw a tiny pink hand pop out of the blanket. I knew he was in there. I got closer. I could hear little peeps. He sounded like a bird. He even looked like a bird. There was no hair on his little head. His skin was wrinkled.

Tara followed the steps in the writing process to describe her baby brother. She used a senses web as a **Prewriting** activity. On her web she wrote details that told about her baby brother. Part of Tara's web is shown here. Study what Tara did.

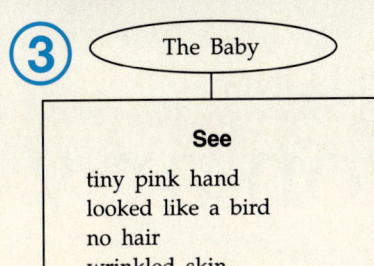

③

The Baby

See
tiny pink hand
looked like a bird
no hair
wrinkled skin

It's Your Turn

Get ready to write your own description. It may be of a friend or a relative. It may be a person in a story you have read. Like Tara, begin by making a senses web. Then follow the other steps in the writing process—**Writing, Revising, Proofreading,** and **Publishing.**

195

Second Page

The second page of every review lesson provides a carefully structured writing assignment with these features:

① The type of writing is identified and explained at the beginning of the lesson.

② A model student response to the writing assignment is provided.

③ A prewriting activity, usually incorporating a graphic organizer, is explained and modeled. In most cases a blackline master in the teacher's edition is provided for duplication and distribution to students.

Writer's Workshop Page

The second review page provides a carefully structured writing assignment keyed to the types of writing commonly studied at this level. The type of writing is clearly identified and explained. A model further assists students in drafting a response to the assignment.

DICTIONARY

Each student edition of *Steck-Vaughn Spelling* contains a Spelling Dictionary at the back of the text. It contains all the words taught in each level.

At level 1, a picture dictionary begins the developmental dictionary strand. An exemplifying sentence using the previously studied characters and words accompanies each boldface list word. When read in sequence, the sentences for each entry letter form a little story. The story is illustrated with colorful pictures.

The level 2 dictionary is an illustrated, beginning dictionary. Each boldface entry word has a pronunciation, one or more numbered definitions, and a simple, exemplifying sentence. Affixed forms are also given. Guide words and full-color illustrations are on each page.

The dictionary entries are more full in levels 3 through 6 and list pronunciations, parts of speech, common meanings, and when pertinent, affixed endings and irregular forms in a two-column format.

The entries in levels 7 and 8 are taken directly from *The American Heritage Student Dictionary* and contain more extensive definitions. All pronunciations and abbreviations in *Steck-Vaughn Spelling* are from *The American Heritage Dictionary*.

A page from the **Spelling Dictionary** in this level is shown.

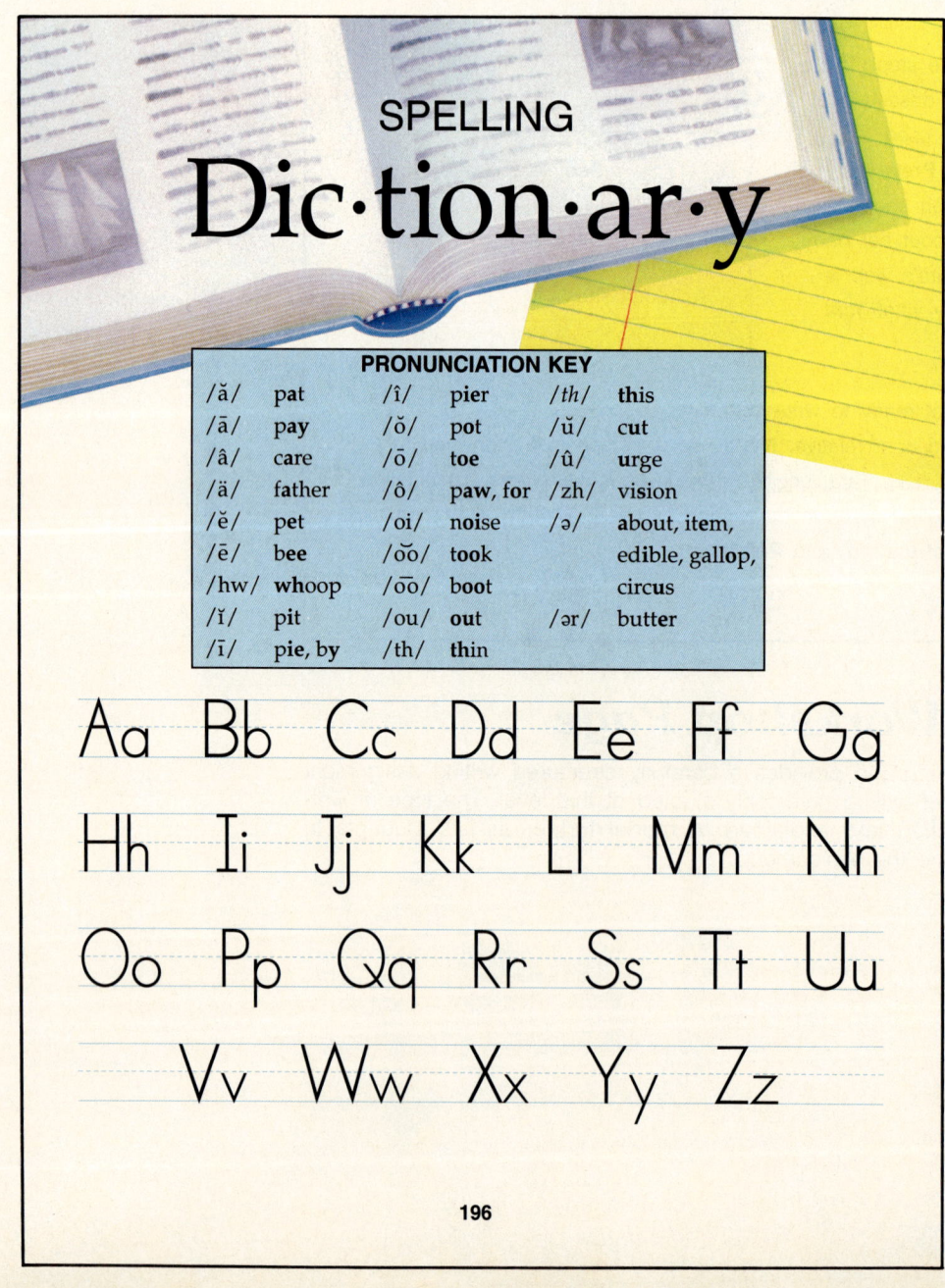

SPELLING

Dic·tion·ar·y

PRONUNCIATION KEY		
/ă/ pat	/î/ pier	/th/ this
/ā/ pay	/ŏ/ pot	/ŭ/ cut
/â/ care	/ō/ toe	/û/ urge
/ä/ father	/ô/ paw, for	/zh/ vision
/ĕ/ pet	/oi/ noise	/ə/ about, item,
/ē/ bee	/oŏ/ took	edible, gallop,
/hw/ whoop	/ōō/ boot	circus
/ĭ/ pit	/ou/ out	/ər/ butter
/ī/ pie, by	/th/ thin	

Aa Bb Cc Dd Ee Ff Gg

Hh Ii Jj Kk Ll Mm Nn

Oo Pp Qq Rr Ss Tt Uu

Vv Ww Xx Yy Zz

Steck-Vaughn Spelling encourages individualized study through the use of a special feature called the Checkpoint Study Plan. Students should use the plan in the following way:

- The second page of each lesson is called the Checkpoint page. Students write their spelling words in response to puzzle-like clues that involve definitions, synonyms, antonyms, analogies, context clues, and word plays. A final item asks students to write a list word after reading about its etymology or similar interesting information.

- Every Checkpoint page refers students to the Checkpoint Study Plan when they have correctly answered all the questions. The Checkpoint Study Plan is given on the last page in each student edition.

- Students number their papers according to the number of questions on the Checkpoint lesson page.

- Students read the clues on the Checkpoint lesson page, spell the answers aloud, and write the answers.
- Students then refer to their first set of answers.
- Students check their second answers against their first answers, circle the number beside any words they misspelled on their second set of answers, and write the correct spelling next to any misspelled words.
- Students then fold their papers so that only the numbers show. For each number that is circled, students go through the study process again.

The first few times that students are referred to the Checkpoint Study Plan, the teacher shows them how to use this study aid. Students need to realize that their answers to the Checkpoint lesson page must be correct before they can use the Checkpoint Study Plan. After the first week or two, this should become a self-directed activity.

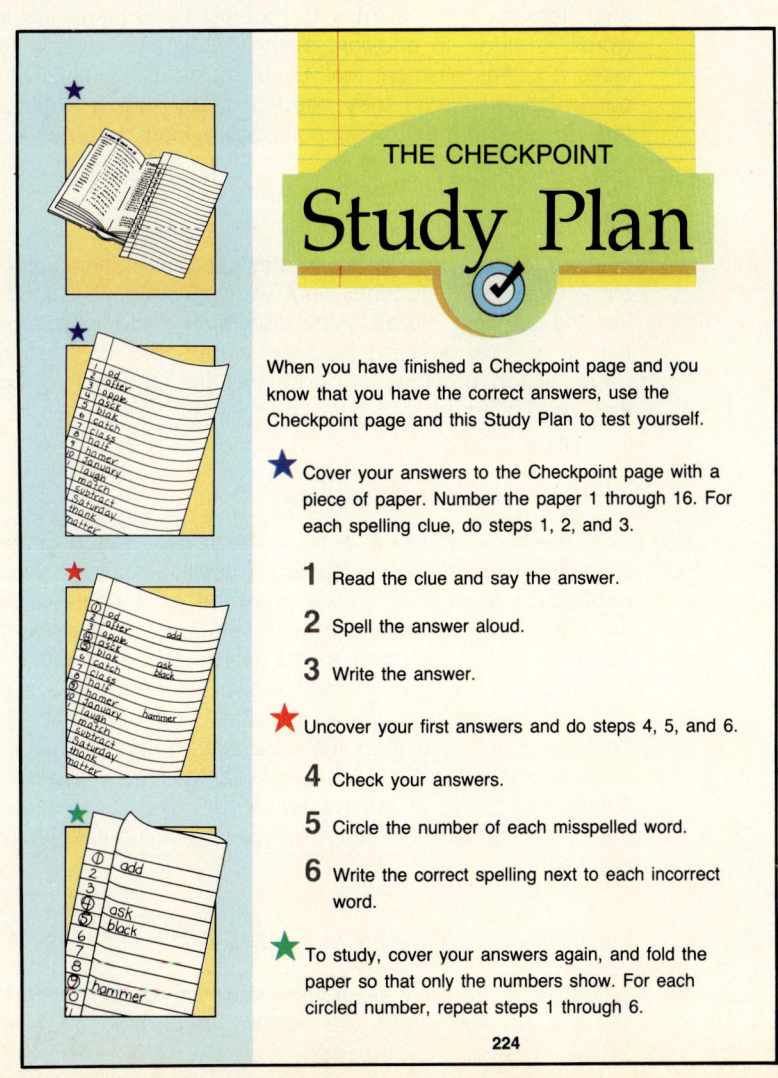

THE CHECKPOINT
Study Plan

When you have finished a Checkpoint page and you know that you have the correct answers, use the Checkpoint page and this Study Plan to test yourself.

★ Cover your answers to the Checkpoint page with a piece of paper. Number the paper 1 through 16. For each spelling clue, do steps 1, 2, and 3.

1 Read the clue and say the answer.

2 Spell the answer aloud.

3 Write the answer.

★ Uncover your first answers and do steps 4, 5, and 6.

4 Check your answers.

5 Circle the number of each misspelled word.

6 Write the correct spelling next to each incorrect word.

★ To study, cover your answers again, and fold the paper so that only the numbers show. For each circled number, repeat steps 1 through 6.

TESTING, CLASSROOM MANAGEMENT, AND RECORDKEEPING

Achieving spelling competency is a highly individual process. A responsible spelling program must ensure frequent and consistent checkpoints so that individual students can ascertain their own strengths and weaknesses on a regular basis. In levels 3 through 8 of *Steck-Vaughn Spelling*, each lesson provides options for pretesting, self-assessment, and post-testing. The six review lessons in each text at levels 3 through 8 also provide for maintenance, diagnostic evaluation, and reinforcement. (No formal testing is suggested in level 1; testing in review lessons is optional at level 2.)

TESTING

Steck-Vaughn Spelling incorporates test-study-test methods. Several options provide students and teachers with a means of measuring achievement and ascertaining which words to emphasize in their study and teaching.

Pretesting and Self-Assessment

Before assigning the first page of a lesson, teachers may administer an optional pretest using the sample sentences given in the teacher's edition for each lesson. The test may be scored by students so that they are aware of words to study. In addition, every Checkpoint page in levels 2 through 8 provides a self-assessment tool. By using the Checkpoint Study Plan, students find out which list words they need to study further. After the first few weeks of teacher direction, the Checkpoint Study Plan becomes a self-directed activity.

Post-testing

After the optional lesson pretest and the Checkpoint self-evaluation in levels 2 through 8, students work with other activities and gain practice in writing the spelling words. After completing the language arts page, students take a teacher-directed post-test. Then they proceed to the Words at Work page, which provides opportunities for students to extend and apply what they have learned.

Maintenance and Review

In levels 2 through 8, a two-page review lesson occurs after every fifth lesson. The teacher tests students on spelling mastery and then assigns students reinforcement or enrichment activities or a combination of these activities, according to individual progress. Students who missed words complete the activities that correspond to the words missed on the first review page. The format of the first review page allows teachers to have students work individually, completing only those activities that pertain to their individual needs. These students are then tested again to ensure that they have grasped the various spellings. When students demonstrate mastery, they can proceed to the second page of the review lesson. This page requires students to apply their spelling skills in a formal writing assignment using a process writing approach.

Midyear and End-of-Year Test

Midyear tests may be administered using list words from review lessons 6, 12, and 18. For end-of-year testing, words from all review lessons (6, 12, 18, 24, 30, and 36) may be used.

CLASSROOM MANAGEMENT

Steck-Vaughn Spelling is a highly flexible program, especially since pretesting and self-assessment assignments allow for a high degree of individualization. The following suggestions are offered for pacing:

Level 1

The first level is divided into two parts—readiness lessons and spelling lessons. The readiness lessons cover consonant and vowel recognition and discrimination. The spelling lessons consist of 20 four-page lessons. The order in which teachers use the consonant and vowel lessons is optional and may be determined by the order in which the letters are taught in the basal reading program. Pages are perforated so that lessons may be taught in a preferred order. Each vowel or consonant lesson is self-contained and not dependent on any specific lesson order. Students usually complete the consonant and vowel lessons by January or February.

The second part of level 1 contains formal spelling lessons. Most teachers find that one lesson a week is comfortable pacing.

Levels 2 Through 8

Since most schools operate on a thirty-six-week academic year, *Steck-Vaughn Spelling* bases its instructional format on thirty-six lessons. Each lesson can be covered in one week, using three, four, or five classroom periods per week. For example:

Levels 2 Through 8 Lesson Pacing

	Five-Day Plan	Four-Day Plan	Three-Day Plan
Word Analysis Page	One day	One day	One day
Checkpoint page	One day		
Story pages (or story masters)	One day	One day	One day
Language arts page	One day	One day	
Test and Words at Work Page	One day	One day	One day
Review pages	Ongoing after initial individual assignments		

RECORDKEEPING

A blackline master of a Class Recordkeeping Chart is provided on the following page. The chart has space for students' names and for recording the pretest and final post-test score for each lesson and review. Space is also provided for a midyear and a final score for teachers who wish to administer such tests.

CLASS RECORDKEEPING CHART

Lesson Number

Student Name	1	2	3	4	5	6	7	8	9	10	11	12	13	14	15	16	17	18	19	20	21	22	23	24	25	26	27	28	29	30	31	32	33	34	35	36

The skills identified in the Scope and Sequence may be found in the lessons indicated for each grade level.

Vowel Spellings	Level 1	Level 2	Level 3
/ă/			
a	1,2	2,3,6,11	1,6
au			1,6
/â/			
a			34,36
ai			34,36
e			34,36
/ā/			
a	11	15,18	2,3,6
a-e		15,18	2,6
ai		16,18	3,6
ay	12	15,18	2,6
ea			2,6
ei		16,18	3,6
ey	12	16,18	3,6
/ä/			
a		34,36	27,30
ea			27,30
/ĕ/			
a	3,4	5,6	7,12
ai	3	4,6	4,6
ay		4	4,6
e	3,4	4,5,6,11	4,6,7,12
ea			4,6
ie			7,12
ue			7,12
/ē/			
e	13	19,24	9,12
ea	13	20,24	8,12
ee	14	19,24	8,12

Vowel Spellings (cont.)	Level 1	Level 2	Level 3
e-e		19,24	
eo			8,12
ey			9,12
y		20,24	9,12
/ĭ/			
e			14,18
ee			14,18
i	5,6	7,8,12	14,18
ui	5		14,18
/ī/			
eye		21	15,18
i	16	21,22,24	15,16,18
ie		22,24	
i-e		21,24	15,18,34,36
ui-e			
uy			16,18
y	15	22,24	16
/î/			
ea			34,36
e			34,36
ee			34,36
/ŏ/			
a	7	9,10,12	19,24
o	7,8	9,10,12	19,24
/ō/			
o	17,18	25,26,30	20,21,24,29
oa	18	26,30	21,24
oe			20,24
o-e		25	20,24
ow		25,30	20,24

Vowel Spellings (cont.)	Level 1	Level 2	Level 3
/ô/			
a		32,36	31,32,36
au			31,32,36
aw		32,36	32,36
o		32,33,36	31,32,36
oo		33,36	31,36
ou		33	31,32,36
/oi/			
oi			28,30
oy			28,30
/ou/			
ou		31,36	33,36
ow		31,36	33,36
/o͝o/			
oo		27,30	22,24
ou		27,30	22,24
u		27,30	22,24
/o͞o/			
ew	20	28,30	25,30
o	20	28,30	25,30
oe	20		
oo	19,20	28,30	25,30
u			25,30
ue		28,30	25,30
/ŭ/			
o	9,10	13,14,18	10,12,13,18
oe			10,12
u	9,10	13,14,18	10,12,13,18
/û/			
e			26,30
ea			26,30
i			26,30
o			26,30
u			26,30
/yo͞o/			
ew			25,30
u-e			25,30
you	20		

Consonant Spellings	Level 1	Level 2	Level 3
/b/			
b		13	
/ch/			
ch		1	
/g/			
g		32	
/j/			
g			2
j		4,9	
/k/			
ck	5	14	1,14,19
k		14,17,19	1,9,14
/ks/			
ks	8		
x	8	7,10	
/kw/			
qu	5		8,31
/m/			
m		13	
/n/			
kn		25	
n		4	15
/p/			
p			20
/r/			
wr		21,29	
/s/			
c			2,7,9,15,28
s		11	7,15,33
z			
/sh/			
sh		17	
/sk/			
sc	19		
sk		5	
/t/			
ed		23	17,23
/v/			
v		12,29	13,25

Consonant Spellings (cont.)

Consonant Spellings (cont.)	Level 1	Level 2	Level 3
/z/			
s	4	1,2,6,11,12,19	8,9,10,19,25, 28,32
z			8,15

Vocabulary

Vocabulary	Level 1	Level 2	Level 3
Comparisons and Analogies			
Antonyms		1,2,3,4,5,8, 20,21,22,23, 25,26,27,28, 29,31,32,33, 35	1,2,4,7,9,10, 13,14,15,16, 17,19,20,21, 22,23,25,27, 31,32,33,34, 35
Compound Words		32	3
Etymologies and Word Facts	1	1,2,3,4,5,7, 8,9,10,11,13, 14,15,16,17, 19,20,21,22, 23,25,26,27, 28,29,31,32 33,34,35	1,2,3,4,5,7,8, 9,10,11,13,14, 15,16,17,19, 20,21,22,23, 25,26,27,28, 29,31,32,33, 34,35
Homographs and Homophones		19,25,27	13,27
Puzzles/Hidden Pictures	3,8,14,16,19, 20		
Rhymes and Word Plays		1,7,13,21	
Context		1,2,3,4,5,7, 8,9,10,11,13, 14,15,16,17, 19,20,21,22, 23,25,26,27, 28,29,31,32, 33,34,35	1,2,3,4,5,7,8, 9,10,11,13, 14,15,16,17, 19,20,21,22, 23,25,26,27, 28,29,31,32, 33,34,35
Special Vocabularies		1	
Synonyms		7,11,13,16,20, 21,28,32,33, 34	1,2,3,4,8,13, 14,20,21,23, 25,26,27,28, 31,33
Definitions		2,4,7,8,9,10, 11,14,15,16, 17,19,20,21, 22,23,25,26, 28,29,31,32, 33,34,35	1,2,3,4,5,7, 8,9,10,13,14, 15,16,17,19, 20,21,22,23, 25,26,27,28, 31,32,33,34, 35

Dictionary Skills

Dictionary Skills	Level 1	Level 2	Level 3
Base Words		29,35	5
Entry Words		10,22	4,5
Guide Words		20	15
Long and Short Sounds (Diacritical marks)	11,18	15,16	
Multiple Meanings		22	4,5,27,
Phonetic Spelling (Sound spelling)		16,34	25,34
Word Meanings		10	3,4,5,27

Proofreading

Proofreading	Level 1	Level 2	Level 3
Proofreading		1,2,3,4,5,7,8, 9,10,11,13,14, 15,16,17,19, 20,21,22,23, 25,26,27,28, 29,31,32,33, 34,35	1,2,3,4,5,7,8, 9,10,11,13,14, 15,16,17,19, 20,21,22,23, 25,26,27,28, 29,31,32,33, 34,35

Mechanics

Mechanics	Level 1	Level 2	Level 3
Abbreviations		27	
Alphabetizing	3,4,5,6,9, 11,18	1,5,8,10,11, 20,34	1,4,5,9,16,19, 31,34
Apostrophes			11,29
Capitals	2,5,7,10,12, 13,15,17	2,4,9,13,19, 23,27,31,	2,7,14,22, 28,33
Commas			23
Contractions			11,29
Exclamation Points		14,21,33	17
Periods	1,2,5,7,10, 12,13,15,17	3,4,21,33	2,17
Question Marks	7,15	7,21,33	10,17

Grammar and Usage

Grammar and Usage	Level 1	Level 2	Level 3
Adjectives			35
Inflected Forms (adding ed, ing, er) (plurals)		11,17,23, 29,35	17,23,35
Nouns			8

Grammar and Usage (cont.)	Level 1	Level 2	Level 3
Past Tense	17		
Predicates			32
Present Tense	17		
Recognition of Verbs			20
Subject of a Sentence			32
Subject/Verb Agreement	10		

Process Writing	Level 1	Level 2	Level 3
Personal narrative, narratives, friendly letters, descriptions, explanations		6, 12, 18, 24, 30, 36	6, 12, 18, 24, 30, 36

WORD LISTS

The following pages list the words for this grade level, as well as the words from the levels immediately above and below. The number after each word indicates the lesson in which the word appears. Words in bold type are the words from the Challenge Yourself activities on the Words at Work pages—they are not list words.

If you wish to keep a record of each student's mastery of words, reproduce a copy of the level word list for each student and cross off the words as the student learns them.

Level 1

A
am (1)
any (3)
at (1)

B
be (13)
big (6)
box (8)
bus (10)
but (10)
by (15)

C
can (1)
coat (18)
cold (17)
come (9)
cry (15)
cut (10)

D
day (12)
did (6)

E
eat (13)

F
fast (1)
feet (14)
five (16)
fly (15)
food (19)
fox (8)
from (10)
fun (9)

G
game (11)
get (4)
go (17)

H
hand (2)
has (2)
have (2)
he (13)
help (4)
hide (16)
home (18)
hop (7)
hope (18)
hot (8)

I
if (6)
in (5)
is (5)
it (5)

J
job (8)
jump (9)

K
keep (14)

L
last (1)

M
made (11)
make (11)
many (3)
may (12)
me (13)
mine (16)
moon (19)
my (15)

N
name (11)
new (20)
nine (16)
nose (18)
not (7)
note (18)

O
of (10)
old (17)
on (7)
one (9)
over (17)

P
pet (4)
play (12)

Q
quit (5)

R
ran (1)
red (3)
ride (16)
road (18)
room (19)
run (9)

S
said (3)
same (11)
sat (2)
say (12)
says (4)
school (19)
see (14)
seven (3)
she (13)
shoe (20)
sick (5)

sit (6)
six (6)
so (17)
socks (8)
soon (19)
stay (12)
stop (8)
street (14)

T
take (11)
ten (3)
that (2)
they (12)
this (6)
three (14)
time (16)
told (17)
too (20)
top (7)
tree (14)
try (15)
two (20)

U
up (10)
us (9)

V
van (2)

W
want (7)
we (13)
went (4)
what (7)
when (4)
who (20)
why (15)
with (5)

Y
you (20)

Z
zoo (19)

Level 2

A
active (2)
add (2)
adjust (13)
admit (7)
admitting (23)
adopt (9)
advice (21)
after (2)
alerting (17)
all (32)
am (2)
amusing (29)
an (2)
and (2)
any (5)
are (34)
arm (34)
around (31)
art (34)
ask (3)
asked (17)
ate (15)
athlete (19)

B
baby (15)
baby sitter (35)
back (3)
backs (11)
bacon (15)
bake (15)
baked (29)
baker (35)
baking (29)
ball (32)

bamboo (28)
barber (34)
barn (34)
batches (11)
bed (4)
bees (19)
beggar (5)
beginner (35)
being (19)
belief (19)
bell (5)
bells (11)
best (5)
big (7)
bigger (35)
bike (21)
biked (29)
bitter (8)
black (3)
blank (2)
blizzard (7)
block (9)
blue (28)
blush (14)
boat (26)
bonnet (10)
bony (25)
book (27)
booth (28)
boulder (26)
box (10)
boys (1)
brave (15)
braver (35)
bravery (16)
bring (8)
brother (14)
brow (31)
buckle (13)
buddy (1)
bug (13)
bulletin (27)
bus (13)
bushel (27)
but (13)
by (22)

C
call (32)
came (15)
cannon (3)
car (34)
cat (2)
catch (3)
catching (17)
cats (11)
chain (16)
cheap (20)
cheat (20)
child (1)
children (1)
chop (10)
city (20)
claimed (17)
class (1)
classmate (1)
clean (20)
climate (21)
clock (10)
clover (26)
clown (31)
club (13)
coat (26)
cocoon (28)
cold (26)
colder (35)
cook (27)
cookbook (27)
cookies (27)
corn (33)
could (27)
cow (31)
coward (31)
craft (3)
cry (22)
cut (13)
cutting (23)

D
dainty (16)
dark (34)
delay (15)
denying (17)
depart (34)
desk (5)

desks (11)
diet (22)
dipper (35)
disease (20)
disliked (29)
do (28)
dodge (10)
dog (32)
door (33)
dot (9)
dotted (23)
draw (32)
dream (20)
dress (5)
dresses (11)
dressing (17)
drop (10)
dropped (23)
dropping (23)
drought (31)
ducklings (11)

E
eat (20)
egg (5)
eggs (11)
eight (16)
end (4)
ended (17)
explode (25)
eye (21)

F
fade (15)
faithful (16)
false (32)
far (34)
farm (34)
farmer (34)
fast (3)
faster (35)
father (34)
faucet (32)
feet (19)
fill (7)
find (21)
fish (8)
fished (17)

fishing (17)
five (21)
flat (2)
flatter (35)
floor (33)
flower (31)
fly (22)
food (28)
foot (27)
for (33)
found (31)
four (33)
freeze (19)
frog (32)
from (13)
full (27)
fun (14)
funny (20)

G
gain (16)
game (15)
gave (15)
girls (1)
give (8)
giving (29)
glimpse (7)
go (25)
goat (26)
gold (26)
good (27)
got (9)
green (19)
grow (25)
guilt (8)

H
habit (2)
had (1)
hand (2)
handed (17)
hands (11)
happy (20)
harmful (34)
has (2)
haul (32)
have (3)
having (29)

he (19)
heat (20)
help (5)
helper (35)
helping (17)
her (1)
hid (7)
hide (21)
high (22)
hill (7)
him (1)
his (7)
hold (26)
hole (25)
home (25)
hop (9)
hope (25)
hoped (29)
hopeful (25)
hopped (23)
hopping (23)
horse (33)
hot (9)
house (31)
how (31)

I
ice (21)
inside (21)
insult (14)

J
jar (34)
jet (4)
jets (11)
job (9)
jobs (11)
jog (9)
jogged (23)
jogging (23)
joke (25)
joking (29)
jump (14)
jumper (35)
just (14)

K
keep (19)

kept (4)
know (25)

L
land (3)
last (3)
leap (20)
liberty (8)
license (21)
lie (22)
like (21)
liked (29)
lining (29)
lion (22)
live (8)
lived (29)
living (29)
lobster (9)
long (32)
longer (35)
look (27)
lost (32)
love (14)
loved (29)
lunch (14)

M
mail (16)
man (2)
many (5)
mark (34)
matter (3)
maybe (15)
mean (20)
melon (4)
memory (5)
men (11)
method (4)
mine (21)
mold (26)
monster (9)
moon (28)
more (33)
most (26)
mother (14)
mouse (31)
much (14)
mud (13)

must (14)
my (22)

N
nail (16)
name (15)
named (29)
napkin (3)
new (28)
next (4)
nine (21)
no (25)
nose (25)
not (9)
now (31)
numb (13)

O
of (13)
off (32)
old (26)
older (35)
on (9)
one (14)
open (26)
or (33)
orange (33)
orchard (33)
organ (33)
other (14)
our (1)
out (31)
over (26)
owl (31)
ox (10)

P
pail (16)
paint (16)
painter (35)
party (34)
peach (20)
pedal (4)
penny (20)
people (19)
pick (7)
picking (17)
pie (22)

play (15)
please (20)
pond (10)
profit (10)
propped (23)
pull (27)
pupil (1)
puppy (20)
put (27)

R
rain (16)
recesses (11)
rest (5)
rhyme (22)
ride (21)
riding (29)
ring (8)
road (26)
rock (10)
roll (26)
room (28)
rope (25)
round (31)
run (13)
runner (35)
running (23)

S
said (4)
sail (16)
sang (3)
saw (32)
say (15)
says (4)
school (28)
see (19)
send (5)
seven (5)
she (19)
shelf (4)
ship (7)
ships (11)
shop (10)
shopped (23)
shopper (35)
shopping (23)
short (33)

should (27)
side (21)
sister (8)
six (7)
skunk (14)
sky (22)
small (32)
snail (16)
snore (33)
snow (25)
so (25)
sold (26)
song (32)
soon (28)
sound (31)
sponge (14)
spot (10)
spotted (23)
spring (8)
star (34)
stay (15)
stone (25)
stood (27)
stop (10)
stopped (23)
stopping (23)
store (33)
storm (33)
story (33)
street (19)
strutting (23)
such (14)
summer (13)
sun (13)
swim (8)

T
tail (16)
talk (32)
ten (4)
than (2)
thank (3)
thanked (17)
that (3)
the (1)
them (1)
these (19)
they (16)

thing (8)
think (8)
thinking (17)
this (7)
three (19)
tie (22)
tiger (22)
tiny (22)
to (28)
today (15)
told (26)
too (28)
took (27)
tooth (28)
top (9)
torch (33)
town (31)
train (16)
tread (5)
trick (7)
tricked (17)
truck (14)
try (22)
two (28)
tying (22)

U
under (13)
up (13)
us (13)

V
van (2)
vans (11)
very (20)

W
wait (16)
walk (32)
want (10)
was (9)
wash (10)
we (19)
week (19)
well (5)
went (4)
whale (15)
what (9)

when (4)
white (21)
who (28)
why (22)
will (7)
wind (7)
wish (8)
wished (17)
wishing (17)
with (8)
would (27)
write (21)
writer (35)
writing (29)

Y

yellow (25)
yes (4)
you (1)

Z

zoo (28)

Level 3

A

able (3)
about (33)
add (1)
address (4)
addresses (5)
admire (15)
adobe (20)
afraid (3)
after (1)
again (4)
agent (3)
ago (21)
agony (1)
aid (3)
aim (3)
air (34)
alike (15)
almost (21)
alone (20)
along (32)
always (32)
apologize (19)
apple (1)

apples (5)
April (2)
arctic (14)
aren't (29)
arm (27)
around (33)
art (27)
artistic (27)
ask (1)
asked (17)
assure (22)
ate (2)
athletic (4)
attempt (4)
August (31)
autumn (31)
away (2)

B

barbecue (27)
bark (27)
barn (27)
because (32)
been (14)
before (31)
begin (14)
beginning (23)
behind (16)
belong (32)
best (7)
better (7)
bird (26)
black (1)
blend (7)
block (19)
blow (20)
blue (25)
boat (21)
body (19)
boil (28)
book (22)
born (31)
both (21)
bottle (19)
bottom (19)
bough (33)
bought (32)
boy (28)
break (2)

broil (28)
broth (32)
brought (32)
brown (33)
build (14)
bureau (22)
busy (9)
butter (13)
buy (16)
buzzard (10)
by (16)

C

cable (2)
came (2)
can't (29)
card (27)
care (34)
careless (34)
carry (9)
carton (27)
casual (25)
catch (1)
caverns (5)
celebration (4)
cemetery (9)
cents (7)
chair (34)
change (2)
child (16)
children (14)
chime (15)
choice (28)
circular (26)
city (9)
clank (1)
class (1)
classes (5)
clock (19)
close (20)
closed (23)
clowns (5)
coarse (31)
coat (21)
coax (21)
cocoa (21)
coin (28)
comb (21)

comment (19)
consented (17)
console (20)
contain (3)
cook (22)
cookies (22)
corner (31)
corridor (31)
could (22)
could've (11)
couldn't (29)
count (33)
cover (13)
crinkled (23)
cry (16)
curl (26)
cycle (16)

D

dairy (34)
danger (3)
dark (27)
dawdle (32)
dear (34)
debate (2)
deceive (8)
December (14)
deer (34)
define (15)
deposit (19)
designer (16)
dessert (26)
devour (33)
didn't (29)
dirt (26)
dirtier (35)
dirtiest (35)
dish (14)
dismay (2)
dispute (25)
does (10)
doesn't (29)
dome (20)
don't (29)
done (13)
door (31)
doubtful (33)
down (33)

draw (32)
dream (8)
dreamed (17)
dreary (34)
dress (4)
dresses (5)
drive (15)
driving (23)
dropped (23)
dropping (23)

E

each (8)
ear (34)
earth (26)
egg (4)
eggs (5)
eight (3)
end (4)
ending (17)
endure (22)
enjoy (28)
enjoyment (28)
error (7)
estimated (23)
even (9)
every (9)
eyes (15)

F

fable (3)
face (2)
faltering (17)
family (9)
father (27)
feat (8)
February (7)
few (25)
fill (14)
filled (17)
fire (34)
first (26)
floor (31)
flourish (26)
flower (33)
fly (16)
foot (22)
forget (4)

forgot (19)
fork (31)
found (33)
four (31)
fragile (1)
frail (3)
free (8)
Friday (16)
friend (7)
friendliness (7)
frog (32)
from (10)
front (10)
frontier (10)
fulfilling (17)
full (22)
funnier (35)
funniest (35)
funny (9)
fur (26)

G
garden (27)
genuine (4)
girl (26)
glider (16)
goes (20)
gold (21)
gourmet (22)
governed (17)
gray (2)
great (2)
greater (35)
greatest (35)
ground (33)
guess (7)
guessing (17)

H
hadn't (29)
hair (34)
half (1)
hammer (1)
hammers (5)
handed (17)
hands (5)
happy (9)
hard (27)

hasn't (29)
haven't (29)
he's (11)
head (4)
hear (34)
heart (27)
hello (21)
help (4)
here (34)
high (16)
hold (21)
hole (20)
hope (20)
hoped (23)
hopping (23)
hotter (35)
hottest (35)
hour (33)
house (33)
how'd (29)
huddle (10)
hundred (13)

I
I'd (11)
I'll (11)
I'm (11)
I've (11)
income (13)
index (7)
inside (15)
inspire (34)
install (32)
instruct (13)
isn't (29)
it's (11)

J
jabbing (23)
January (1)
jog (19)
jogged (23)
join (28)
joke (20)
joy (28)
July (25)
June (25)
just (13)

K
kept (7)
key (9)
kick (14)
kind (16)
knew (25)
know (20)

L
labor (2)
late (2)
laugh (1)
laughing (17)
learn (26)
light (16)
liked (23)
line (15)
lion (15)
little (14)
loaf (21)
long (32)
longer (35)
longest (35)
losses (5)
lovely (13)
luggage (14)
lunch (10)

M
maintain (3)
mall (32)
many (7)
March (27)
market (27)
match (1)
matches (5)
matter (1)
May (2)
meat (8)
meet (8)
meeting (17)
meteors (5)
miles (15)
mind (16)
mine (15)
misery (9)
moisten (28)
Monday (10)

money (10)
month (10)
morning (31)
most (21)
mother (10)
move (25)
much (10)
must (13)
mustn't (29)

N
near (34)
neckties (5)
need (8)
never (7)
news (25)
next (4)
nice (15)
night (16)
noise (28)
none (13)
noon (25)
north (31)
nothing (10)
November (20)
number (13)

O
o'clock (19)
October (19)
off (32)
oil (28)
one (13)
only (9)
open (21)
ornament (31)
other (10)
our (33)
over (21)
owl (33)

P
page (2)
pages (5)
paint (3)
painted (17)
paints (5)
paper (3)

papers (5)
patrol (21)
pay (2)
penny (9)
people (8)
place (2)
places (5)
plaid (1)
please (8)
pleased (23)
point (28)
poisonous (28)
poor (22)
popcorn (31)
pour (31)
power (33)
pretty (14)
problem (19)
pull (22)
pursue (25)
put (22)

Q
quart (31)
queen (8)

R
rain (3)
rained (17)
read (4)
read (8)
reading (17)
ready (4)
rejoice (28)
right (16)
river (14)
road (21)
rodent (20)
rodeo (21)
royal (28)

S
safe (2)
said (4)
sail (3)
Saturday (1)
sausage (32)
save (2)

says (4)
scheme (9)
school (25)
sea (8)
seam (8)
second (4)
sent (7)
September (7)
shakier (35)
shakiest (35)
sharp (27)
sharper (35)
sharpest (35)
she'll (11)
she's (11)
shine (15)
shining (23)
shook (22)
shop (19)
shopping (23)
should (22)
shouldn't (29)
shove (13)
show (20)
shrewd (25)
size (15)
sketch (7)
sky (16)
skyline (16)
sleep (8)
sleeping (17)
sleepy (9)

slept (7)
slow (20)
slump (13)
smiling (23)
smudge (13)
sneeze (8)
sneezed (23)
snow (20)
socks (19)
soggy (9)
soil (28)
solo (21)
some (13)
somebody (10)
something (13)
sorry (19)
sound (33)
spent (4)
spinach (14)
spoil (28)
sport (31)
spring (14)
stairs (34)
star (27)
starch (27)
start (27)
stood (22)
stopped (23)
storm (31)
story (9)
street (8)
strong (32)

stronger (35)
strongest (35)
stunned (23)
subtract (1)
subtracted (17)
such (10)
sum (13)
summer (10)
sun (10)
Sunday (10)
sunny (9)
supper (13)
sure (22)
surgeon (26)

T
table (3)
tables (5)
taking (23)
talk (32)
tall (32)
taller (35)
tallest (35)
team (8)
teenager (8)
test (4)
tests (5)
thank (1)
thanked (17)
them (7)
then (7)
there'd (29)

there'll (29)
these (9)
they (3)
they'd (11)
they'll (11)
they've (11)
thing (14)
think (14)
third (26)
Thursday (26)
times (15)
tiny (15)
tire (34)
toast (21)
toe (20)
too (25)
took (22)
tooth (25)
tower (33)
town (33)
toy (28)
train (3)
trains (5)
true (25)
try (16)
Tuesday (25)
turn (26)
two (25)

U
under (10)
used (25)

V
variety (15)
very (9)
voice (28)

W
waffle (19)
wait (3)
waited (17)
walk (32)
was (19)
wash (19)
wasn't (29)
water (32)
we'd (29)
we'll (11)
we've (11)
Wednesday (7)
weigh (3)
weirder (35)
weirdest (35)
were (26)
weren't (29)
wharf (31)
what (19)
wheel (8)
when (7)
where (34)
where'd (11)
which (14)
while (15)
white (15)

who (25)
who'll (11)
whole (20)
why (16)
width (14)
wildflower (33)
winter (14)
wire (34)
wished (17)
won (13)
won't (29)
wood (22)
word (26)
work (26)
world (26)
worm (26)
would (22)
would've (11)
wouldn't (29)
write (15)
wrote (20)

Y
yard (27)
year (34)
yellow (20)
you'd (11)
you'll (11)
you've (11)

ANNOTATED STUDENT PAGES
for
Lessons 1 - 36

LESSON 1

Objectives

- To hear and say twelve spelling words.
- To write the spelling words with attention to letter sequence and sound/symbol relationships.
- To write each spelling word once.

Sample Sentences

1. I know her brother is very tall.
2. We gave him the soccer ball.
3. The boys remembered their gym shoes.
4. They were excited by our news.
5. The girls are going on a hike.
6. Would you lend me your new bike?
7. There's a slide on the playground.
8. I asked them if they heard that loud sound.
9. My sister Janie had strawberries and cream.
10. Bob is the tallest child on the team.
11. The children are playing in the snow.
12. The class studied how plants grow.

Note

The sample sentences may be used for pretesting and post-testing.

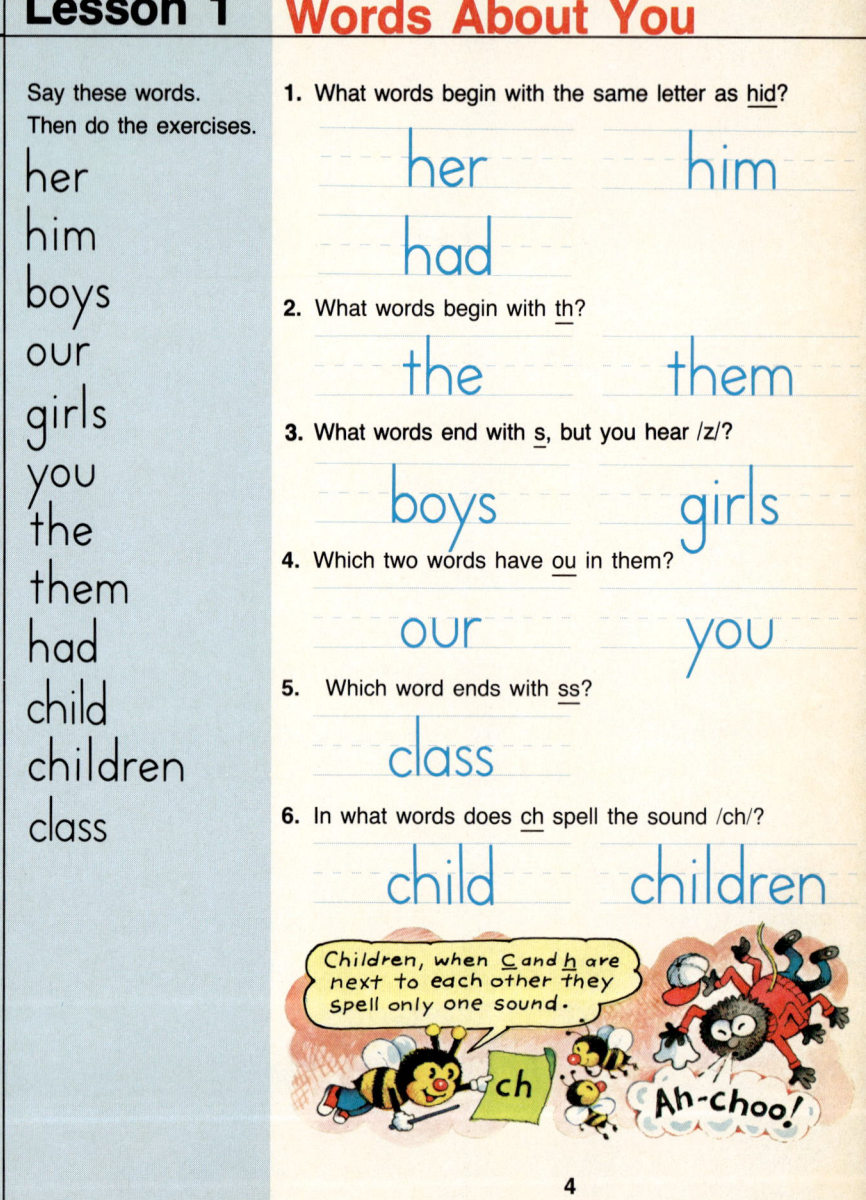

Lesson 1 — **Words About You**

Say these words. Then do the exercises.

her
him
boys
our
girls
you
the
them
had
child
children
class

1. What words begin with the same letter as hid?

her   him
had

2. What words begin with th?

the   them

3. What words end with s, but you hear /z/?

boys   girls

4. Which two words have ou in them?

our   you

5. Which word ends with ss?

class

6. In what words does ch spell the sound /ch/?

child   children

Children, when c and h are next to each other they spell only one sound.

ch   Ah-choo!

4

Preparation

Review vowels and consonants. Write the five vowels a,e,i,o,u on the board. Mention that there is a sixth vowel, y. Tell students that y is special. It is a consonant when it appears at the beginning of a word and a vowel when it comes at the end of a word. Every word except I and a contains consonants and at least one vowel.

Tell students that in Lesson 1 they are going to spell words that they use frequently in speaking and in writing. Turn to page 4 and have students repeat and spell each list word after you. Ask which word begins with the consonant y. *(you)* Note that the cartoon calls attention to the consonant digraph ch. Write ch and th on the board and review their sounds. Have students find the spelling words that contain these digraphs. *(child, children, the, them)*

Ask the students to point to the spelling word as you read each sample sentence aloud.

The Page

Do page 4 with the students. Have them take turns reading each activity aloud. Allow time for them to write the answers. Then have volunteers write the answers on the board so students may check their work.

Follow-Up

Ask students how they plan to study their spelling words. Suggest these methods: Students may write the words several times and review them carefully, or they may spell the words aloud with a partner.

Checkpoint

Write a spelling word for each clue. Then use the Checkpoint Study Plan on page 224.

1. In our class, there are ten girls and ten ___.

2. We looked for the balls but couldn't find ___.

3. I saw my mother and waved to ___.

4. My new neighbors have a two-year-old ___.

5. A word that sounds like sad and mad is ___.

6. We gave Tom's football back to ___.

7. There are twenty children in ___ class.

8. The school bus was full of laughing ___.

9. Happy birthday to ___.

10. I go to the school library with my ___.

11. We went to ___ zoo.

12. This mystery word is very old. Long ago, it had a different spelling. It was spelled <u>gerle</u>, <u>girle</u>, or <u>gurle</u>. It also had a different meaning. It meant "child." Now we use two words to mean "child." One of them is <u>boy</u>. What is the other word? Add <u>s</u> to get the mystery word. ___

5

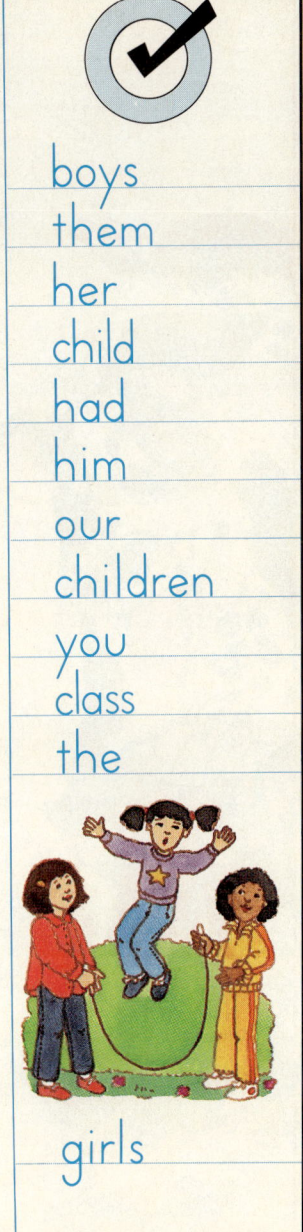

boys
them
her
child
had
him
our
children
you
class
the

girls

Objectives

- To write spelling words in response to clues: context and rhyme.
- To develop the critical thinking skills of analyzing and making inferences.
- To recognize that word meanings and spellings often change over time.

Spelling Strategy

Homophones can often cause spelling problems for children. Some students may substitute <u>hour</u> for the word <u>our</u>. Help students understand that <u>our</u> is used when talking about something we own; <u>hour</u> is used to talk about time.

Note

The **Checkpoint** page serves a dual purpose. In addition to the stated objectives, it also provides a test/study strategy: the **Checkpoint Study Plan**. This study plan provides a self-test and a method of ongoing independent study for the students. Directions for the **Checkpoint Study Plan** are on page 224 of the student book.

Before students use the **Checkpoint Study Plan**, help them check their pages for correct responses to clues and for spelling accuracy.

Preparation The clues on this page are like crossword puzzle clues. Explain to students that the response to each clue is a spelling word. Use the following examples to illustrate the types of clues used:

    Context Happy birthday to *(you)*.
    Rhyme A word that sounds like sad and mad is *(had)*.

The final clue explains that the word <u>girls</u> used to have a different meaning and spelling.

The Page Have students complete page 5 using the words on page 4. When students have finished, have them read each clue and spell the answer aloud. Check each response twice: once for the correct answer and a second time for spelling accuracy.

Follow-Up Guide students in using the **Checkpoint Study Plan** on page 224 to take a self-test. Have them use the plan for independent study. (See **Note**.)

Objectives

- To write the spelling words in continuous text and related sentences.
- To write each spelling word once.
- To integrate reading with spelling.

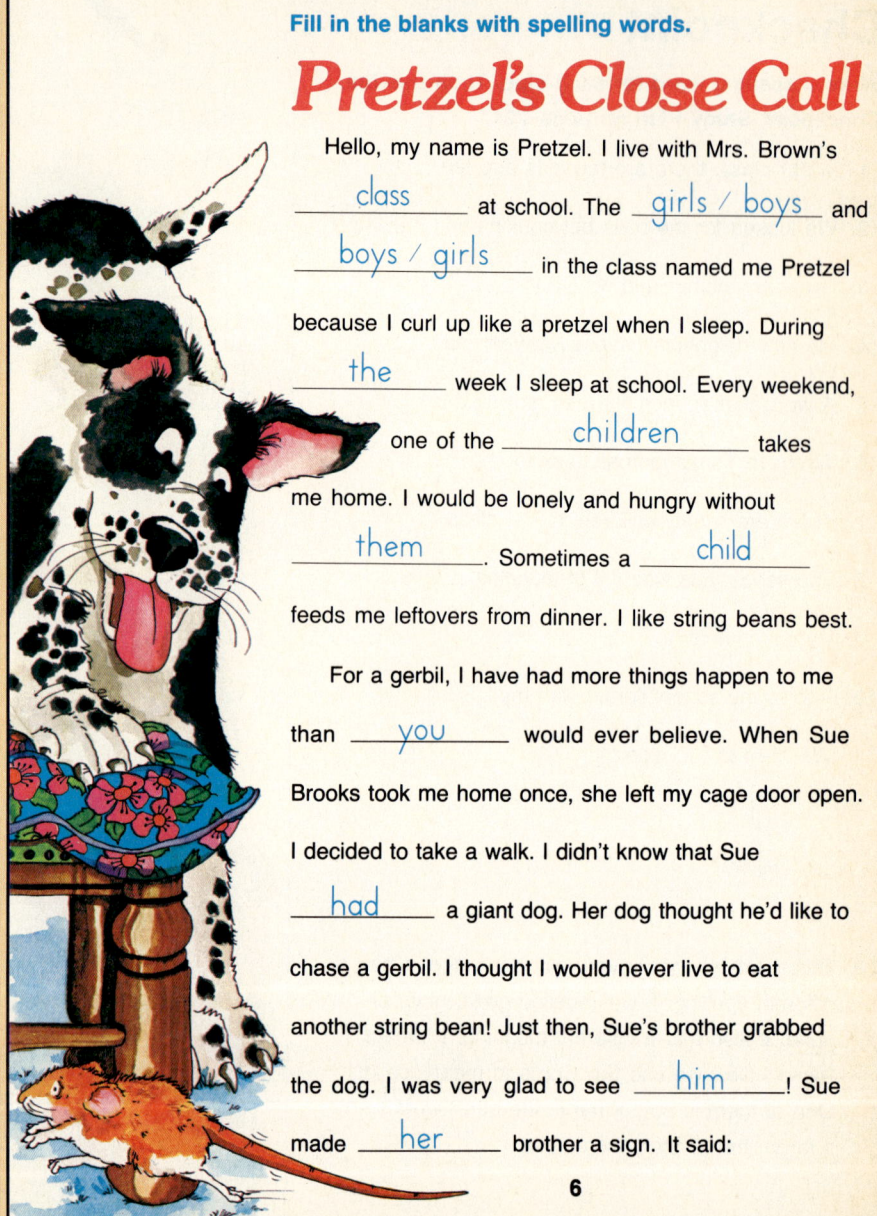

6

Fill in the blanks with spelling words.

Pretzel's Close Call

Hello, my name is Pretzel. I live with Mrs. Brown's _____class_____ at school. The ___girls / boys___ and ___boys / girls___ in the class named me Pretzel because I curl up like a pretzel when I sleep. During ___the___ week I sleep at school. Every weekend, one of the ___children___ takes me home. I would be lonely and hungry without ___them___. Sometimes a ___child___ feeds me leftovers from dinner. I like string beans best.

For a gerbil, I have had more things happen to me than ___you___ would ever believe. When Sue Brooks took me home once, she left my cage door open. I decided to take a walk. I didn't know that Sue ___had___ a giant dog. Her dog thought he'd like to chase a gerbil. I thought I would never live to eat another string bean! Just then, Sue's brother grabbed the dog. I was very glad to see ___him___! Sue made ___her___ brother a sign. It said:

6

Note

Some of the spelling words will be used twice on these two pages.

Preparation   Have students turn to pages 6 and 7. Call their attention to the word list. Have the students say the words. Then explain that each spelling word belongs in at least one of the blanks on pages 6 and 7. Some of the words will be used twice. Tell students that you will read the story aloud, supplying the missing words. Then they will write the missing spelling words as they complete the story on their own. You will repeat this procedure for the sentences on page 7.

Write the title "Pretzel's Close Call" on the board. Have a student read it. Explain that the story tells about a pet named Pretzel. Tell the students that they will find out what happened when Pretzel went home with one of the children.

The Pages   Read the story aloud, supplying the missing spelling words as the students follow along in their texts. When you have finished, you may wish to ask some questions about the story such as:

1. What kind of animal is Pretzel? *(a gerbil)*
2. What is a dog catcher? *(Someone who picks up stray dogs. The dogs may be returned to their owners or taken care of by the town.)*

Next, ask the students to reread the story to themselves and to complete it by writing the correct spelling word for each blank. Suggest that the students read the entire sentence before they write a word. The meaning of the sentence will help them to choose the right spelling word.

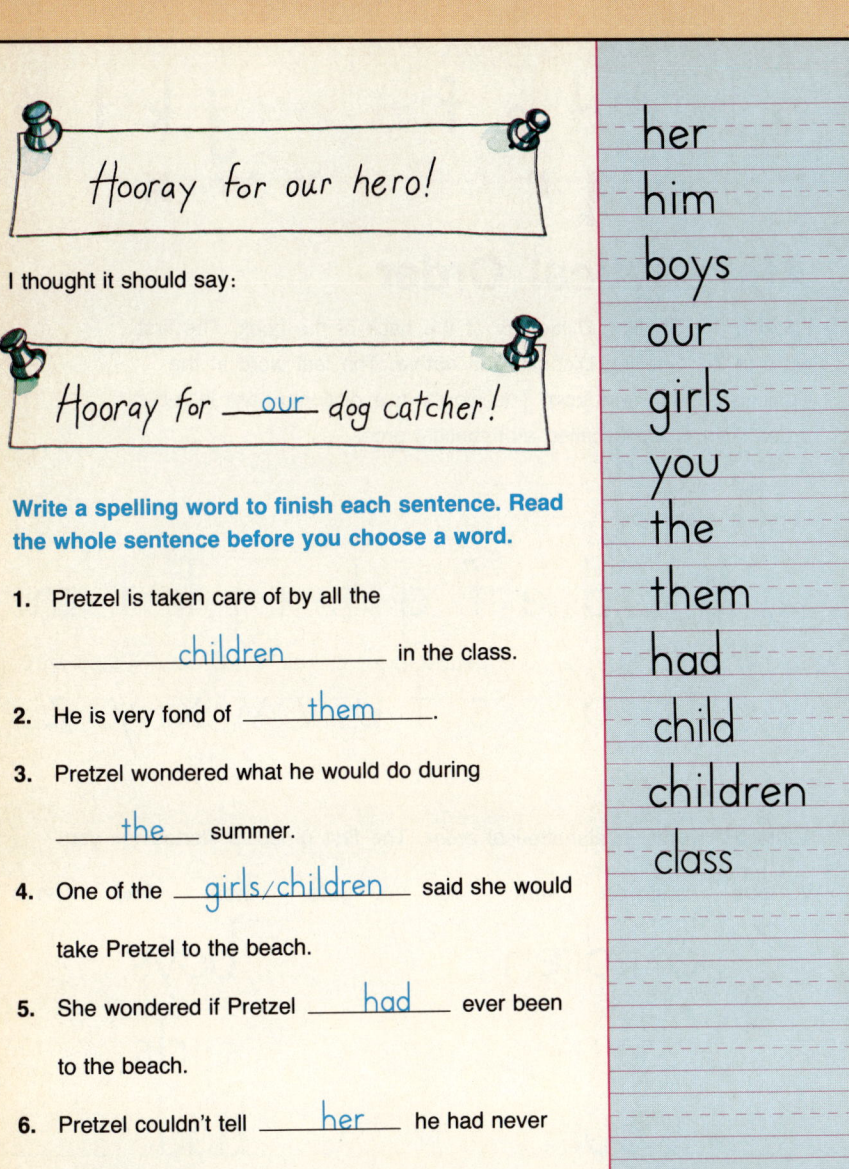

Hooray for our hero!

I thought it should say:

Hooray for ___our___ dog catcher!

Write a spelling word to finish each sentence. Read the whole sentence before you choose a word.

1. Pretzel is taken care of by all the

   _____children_____ in the class.

2. He is very fond of ___them___.

3. Pretzel wondered what he would do during

   ___the___ summer.

4. One of the ___girls/children___ said she would

   take Pretzel to the beach.

5. She wondered if Pretzel ___had___ ever been

   to the beach.

6. Pretzel couldn't tell ___her___ he had never

   seen a beach.

7. All that water scared ___him___!

7

her
him
boys
our
girls
you
the
them
had
child
children
class

Enrichment

If you want to use the blackline activity masters for enrichment and additional practice, assign Lesson 1 activities at this time.

Maintenance and Review

If you want to use the blackline activity masters for maintenance and review, wait until students have completed pages 12 and 13 of Lesson 2 before assigning the blackline activity masters for Lesson 1.

When students have finished, have volunteers write the answers on the board so students may check their own work. Then ask volunteers to read the story aloud, pausing before each blank. Have other students supply the missing spelling word by spelling it aloud. Ask volunteers to write the answers on the board so students may check their work.

Next, read aloud the sentences on page 7, supplying the answers. Then have the students read them independently and write the spelling words. Have volunteers read the sentences aloud, supplying the answers. Another student may write the answers on the board. Alternate answers from the spelling list may occasionally make sense, but suggest the word given as the preferred answer. Check the students' work for the accurate spelling of each answer.

Follow-Up Have students use each of the spelling words they missed in an original sentence.

As an additional follow-up activity, you may wish to organize the class into groups of three or four. Have each group choose a "pet," draw a picture of that pet, and give the pet a name. Then have each student in the group write one sentence about the pet, using a spelling word. Later, the sentences may be read aloud as the pictures of the pets are circulated. Other students may identify the spelling word in each sentence and spell it aloud.

Objectives

- To relate spelling words to a dictionary skill.
- To write the alphabet.
- To write spelling words in alphabetical order by the first letter.
- To use the **Spelling Dictionary.**
- To check handwriting for correct letter formation.

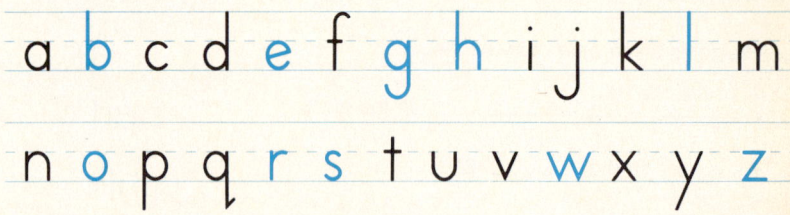

Alphabetical Order

Look at the Spelling Dictionary at the back of the book. The first word in the Spelling Dictionary is **active**. The last word in the Spelling Dictionary is **zoo**. The words in a dictionary are in a-b-c order. This order is called <u>alphabetical</u> <u>order</u>.

Finish this alphabet.

a b c d e f g h i j k l m
n o p q r s t u v w x y z

Write the words in alphabetical order. The first group is started for you.

1. **our   children   him   you**   2. **girls   them   had   boys**

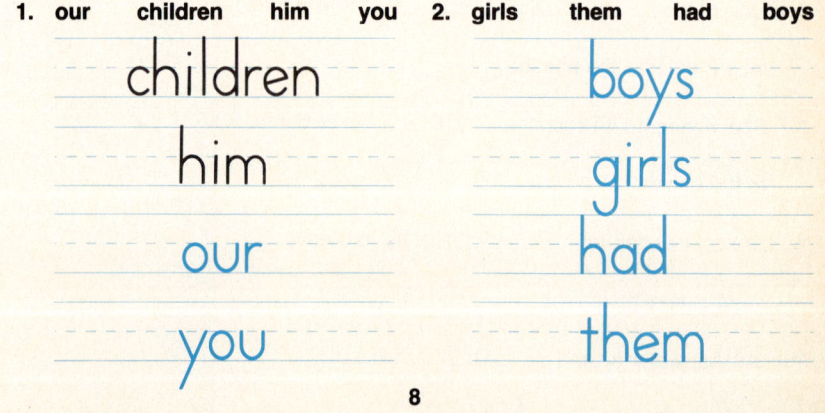

children	boys
him	girls
our	had
you	them

8

Preparation   Write the alphabet on the board in a horizontal line.

Write these words in a row: **the   you   girls**

Explain that to put words into alphabetical order, the students have to look at the first letter in each word. Have a volunteer underline the first letter in each word. Ask which letter comes first in the alphabet: <u>t</u>, <u>y</u>, or <u>g</u>. *(g)* Ask which word comes first in alphabetical order. *(girls)* Write <u>girls</u> on the board. Which word comes next? Write <u>the</u> under <u>girls</u> and <u>you</u> under <u>the</u>.

Introduce the **Spelling Dictionary.** Explain that it has all the spelling words arranged in alphabetical order. Allow students to look at the dictionary and ask questions about it.

The Page   Complete page 8 with the students. Remind them not to make spelling mistakes because of careless handwriting. Have students pay particular attention to the formation of the letter <u>h</u>, as in <u>had</u> and <u>her</u>. The strokes must touch the bottom line cleanly so <u>h</u> does not become confused with <u>b</u>, <u>k</u>, or <u>n</u>. Review the answers together.

Follow-Up   Write these words on the board: **the, you, had, children, our.** Have students write them on cards (or small pieces of paper) and alphabetize them. Then help them find the words in the **Spelling Dictionary.** Which word has a joke in its entry? *(you)*

8

WORDS AT WORK

Challenge Yourself

pupil   **classmate**   **buddy**

Decide which Challenge Word fits each clue. Check your Spelling Dictionary to see if you were right. Then write sentences. Show that you understand the meaning of each Challenge Word.

1. This is another word for a close friend.

2. It can be someone who goes to school or a part of the eye.

3. Someone in your class is one of these.

Write to the Point

Pretzel had a close call at Sue's house. Mrs. Brown's class decided to make some rules about Pretzel's care. Help Mrs. Brown's class. Write three rules for taking care of their pet gerbil. Use spelling words from this lesson in your rules.

Challenge Use one or more of the Challenge Words in your rules.

Proofreading

Use the marks to show the mistakes in the sentences below. Write the four misspelled words correctly in the blanks.

◯	word is misspelled
⊙	period is missing
☰	letter should be capitalized

1. Our ⬭clas⬭ has two pet mice.

2. The boys feed ⬭thim⬭ every day⊙

3. The ⬭grils⬭ give them water.

4. <u>we</u> show them to other ⬭childran.⬭

1. _____ class

2. _____ them

3. _____ girls

4. _____ children

9

Test Review the spelling of the twelve words. Test the spelling words, using one of these testing methods: (1) Say the word; read the sample sentence from page 4; say the word; have students write the word. (2) Read each dictation sentence above; have students write the sentence. Correct the test with students.

Challenge Yourself The optional Challenge Words may be assigned to the entire class or limited to those students who do well on the test. Have students note the spellings of the Challenge Words. Responses to this activity should be completed on separate paper. Answers to the questions are provided above.

Write to the Point Help students recall the selection "Pretzel's Close Call" on pages 6 and 7; then assign the three rules. Remind students to write their rules in complete sentences. This activity should be completed on separate paper.

Proofreading The proofreading practice includes misspellings of words from this lesson as well as a capitalization error and a punctuation error.

9

LESSON 2

Objectives

- To hear and say words with /ă/.
- To write words with /ă/ with attention to letter sequence and sound/symbol relationships.
- To write each spelling word once.
- To recognize that /ă/ may be spelled a.

Sample Sentences

1. Mom drives a big red van.
2. Sally is older than I am.
3. She rides an orange bike.
4. Her neighbor is a man named Mike.
5. We run and play in the sand.
6. I always write with my right hand.
7. Our cat, Fluffy, is all tan.
8. I fry eggs in a big, flat pan.
9. Billy has a cute pet lamb.
10. Do you know how strong I am?
11. To make the batter, add one cup of flour.
12. I'll come to your house after school for an hour.

Note

The sample sentences may be used for pretesting and post-testing.

Lesson 2 — Words with /ă/

Say these words. Listen for /ă/ in each one.

van
than
an
man
and
hand
cat
flat
has
am
add
after

1. Write the words that begin with the sound /ă/.

an   and
am   add
after

2. Which words end like the word bat?

cat   flat

3. Which words end like ten?

van   than
an   man

4. Which words begin with the sound /h/?

hand   has

The word has ends with an s, but you hear the sound /z/.
Z-z-z-z-z-z-z

10

Preparation

Write /ă/ on the chalkboard and have students repeat the sound /ă/ as in pat. Explain to students that the symbols within the brackets / / represent speech sounds, not letters. Then say the word pairs below. Ask students to raise their hands when they hear a word with the sound /ă/ in it.

then – than   and – end   pen – pan   man – men

Have students look at the spelling words on page 10. Say each word aloud. Then have students say and spell each word.

Point out that two words end with the letters nd. Ask the students to find the two words. (and, hand)

Now read the sample sentences. Ask the students to point to the spelling word in their books as you read the sentence for each one.

The Page

Do page 10 with the students. Have them take turns reading each activity aloud. Allow time to write the answers. The cartoon will help students answer question 4. Then have volunteers put the answers on the board so that students may check their own work.

Follow-Up

Suggest some study methods for this lesson: Students may work with a partner to spell the words aloud to each other, or they may write each word on a piece of paper, tape them up at home, and look at them during the week.

Checkpoint

Write a spelling word for each clue. Then use the Checkpoint Study Plan on page 224.

1. Part of an arm is a ___.

2. Carla runs faster ___ Joan.

3. A boy grows and becomes a ___.

4. A kitten grows into a ___.

5. The opposite of subtract is ___.

6. He isn't tall, but I ___.

7. I have one cat, but my friend ___ two.

8. I fed the horse ___ apple.

9. The opposite of before is ___.

10. Our car has a ___ tire.

11. Our flag is red, white, ___ blue.

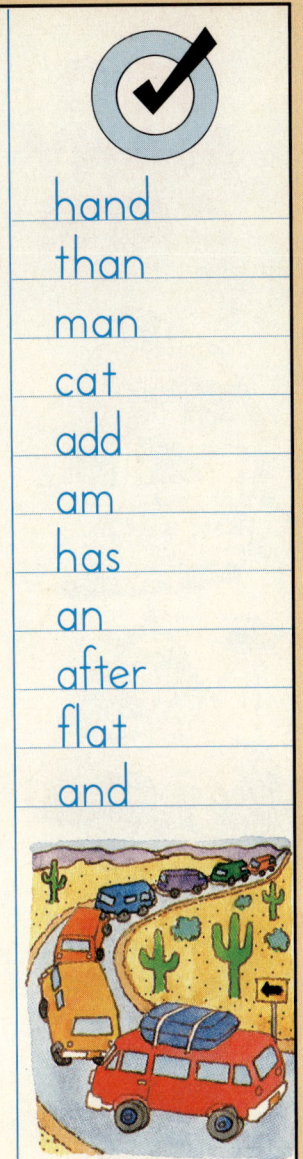

hand
than
man
cat
add
am
has
an
after
flat
and

van

12. This mystery word comes from the word <u>caravan</u>. A long time ago, a caravan was a covered carriage or cart. After the automobile was invented, we used the mystery word to mean a truck or station wagon. Can you guess the mystery word? ___

11

Objectives
- To write spelling words in response to clues: definitions, antonyms, and context.
- To develop the critical thinking skills of contrasting and predicting outcomes.
- To understand that word meanings often change over time.

Spelling Strategy

Students sometimes confuse <u>than</u> and <u>then</u> when writing. To help clarify the meaning and spelling for students, write the following sentences on the chalkboard:

I would rather read <u>than</u> sleep.

<u>Then</u> I can dream about the story I read.

Read the sentences aloud, emphasizing the words <u>then</u> and <u>than</u>.

Preparation The clues on this page are like crossword puzzle clues. Explain to students that the response to each clue is a spelling word. Use the following examples to illustrate the types of clues used:

Definition	Part of an arm is a *(hand)*.
Antonym	The opposite of subtract is *(add)*.
Context	I have one cat, but my friend *(has)* two.

The final clue explains how the word <u>van</u> came into the English language.

The Page Have students complete page 11 using the words on page 10. When students have finished, have them read each clue and spell the answer aloud. Check each response twice: once for the correct answer and a second time for spelling accuracy.

Follow-Up Guide students in using the **Checkpoint Study Plan** on page 224 to take a self-test. Have them use the plan for independent study.

Objectives

- To write words with /ă/ in continuous text.
- To write each spelling word once.
- To integrate reading with spelling.

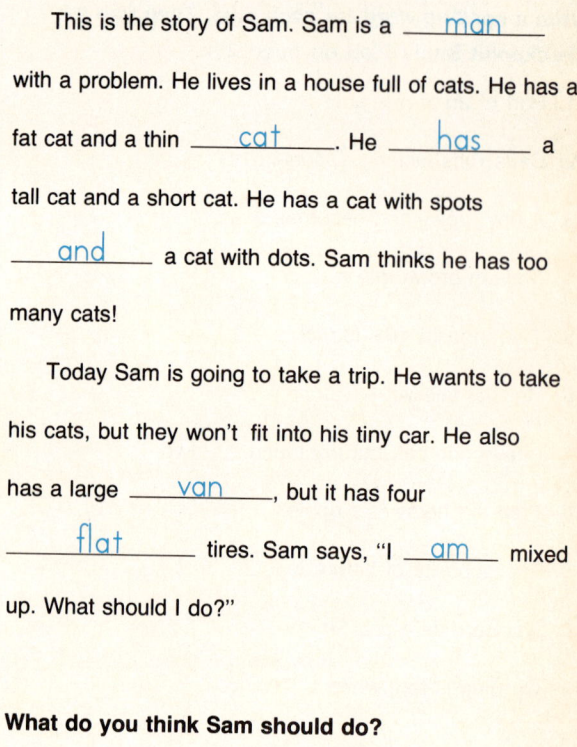

TOO MANY CATS!

Fill in the blanks with spelling words.

This is the story of Sam. Sam is a __man__ with a problem. He lives in a house full of cats. He has a fat cat and a thin __cat__. He __has__ a tall cat and a short cat. He has a cat with spots __and__ a cat with dots. Sam thinks he has too many cats!

Today Sam is going to take a trip. He wants to take his cats, but they won't fit into his tiny car. He also has a large __van__, but it has four __flat__ tires. Sam says, "I __am__ mixed up. What should I do?"

What do you think Sam should do?

Should he rent a bus?   Should he get a cat-sitter?

Should he stay home?   Should he rent a kennel?

Should he get new tires?

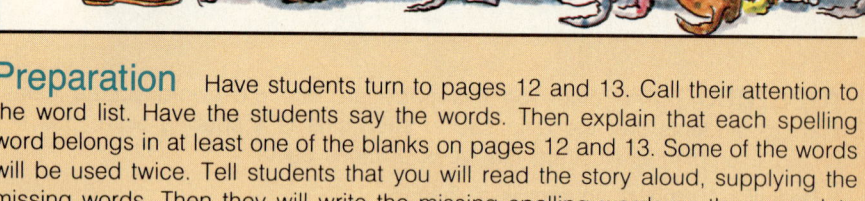

Note

- Some of the spelling words will be used twice on these two pages.
- The word hand is used as a verb on page 13. Ask someone to hand you a pencil with his or her right hand. Discuss these two meanings of hand.

Preparation Have students turn to pages 12 and 13. Call their attention to the word list. Have the students say the words. Then explain that each spelling word belongs in at least one of the blanks on pages 12 and 13. Some of the words will be used twice. Tell students that you will read the story aloud, supplying the missing words. Then they will write the missing spelling words as they complete the story on their own. Do the same with the letter on page 13.

Write the title "Too Many Cats!" on the board and have a student read it. Explain that the story is about a man named Sam who has a problem.

The Pages Read the story aloud, supplying the missing spelling words as the students follow along in their texts. When you have finished reading, you may wish to discuss the story. Ask the students what Sam's problem is. *(He has too many cats.)* Then read the questions at the bottom of page 12 to the class. Ask the students for ideas to help Sam solve his problem. *(Answers will vary.)*

Now have the students reread the story to themselves and complete it by writing the correct spelling word for each blank. When they have finished, volunteers may read the story aloud, spelling aloud the missing spelling word for each blank. Have other volunteers write the spelling word on the board so students may correct their work.

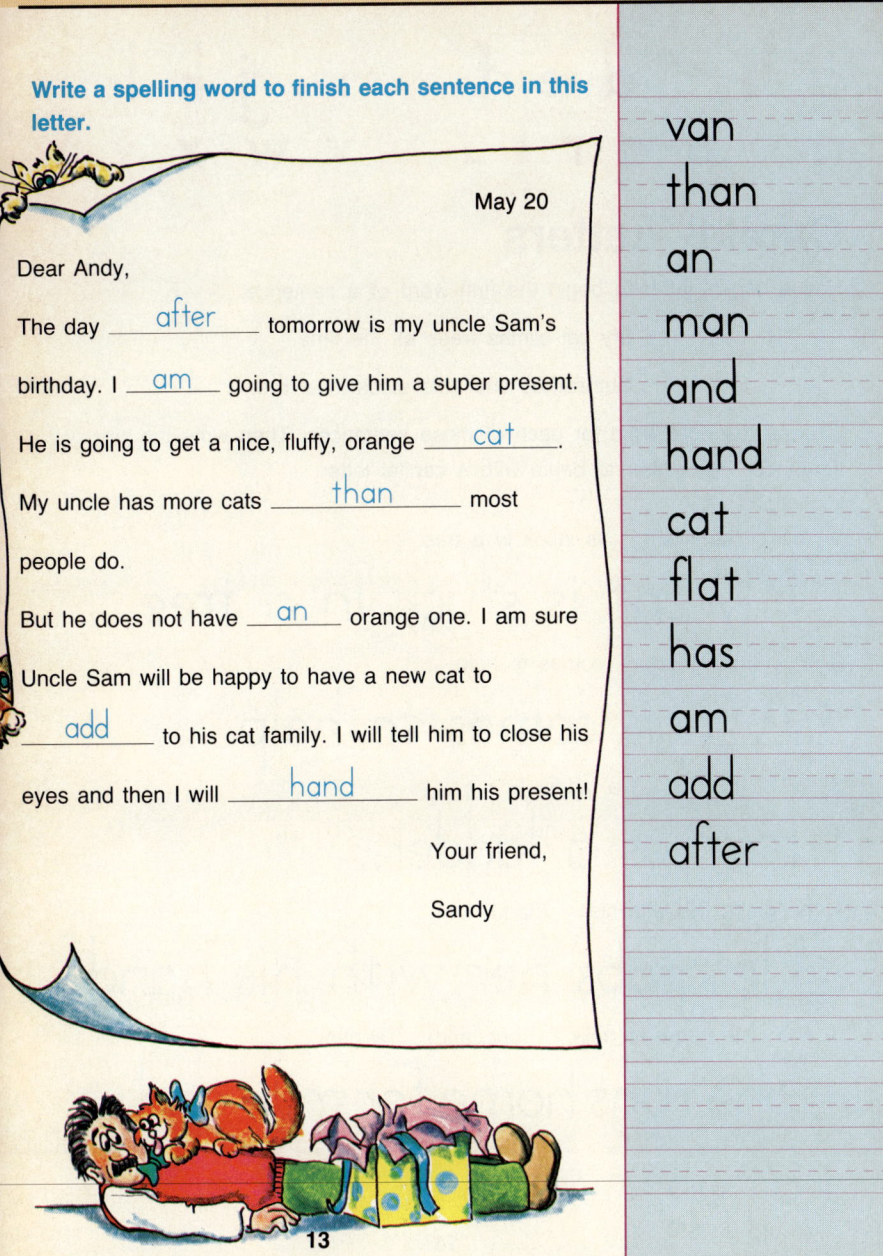

Write a spelling word to finish each sentence in this letter.

May 20

Dear Andy,

The day ____after____ tomorrow is my uncle Sam's

birthday. I ____am____ going to give him a super present.

He is going to get a nice, fluffy, orange ____cat____.

My uncle has more cats ____than____ most

people do.

But he does not have ____an____ orange one. I am sure

Uncle Sam will be happy to have a new cat to

____add____ to his cat family. I will tell him to close his

eyes and then I will ____hand____ him his present!

Your friend,

Sandy

13

van
than
an
man
and
hand
cat
flat
has
am
add
after

Enrichment

If you want to use the blackline activity masters for enrichment and additional practice, assign Lesson 2 activities at this time.

Maintenance and Review

OBJECTIVE

• To review "Words About You."

ACTIVITIES

If you want to use the blackline activity masters for maintenance and review, assign Lesson 1 activities at this time.

You can also use the activities below to review Lesson 1 with students.

Write the following words on the board:

| her | him | boys |
| girls | children | add |

Ask students to write each word and to illustrate it.

Then write these words on the board:

| our | you | the |
| them | had | after |

Have pupils write each word. Ask volunteers to suggest a sentence for each word.

Next, have the students look at the letter on page 13. Read the letter aloud, supplying the missing spelling words. Discuss the parts of the letter: date, greeting, body, closing, and name at the bottom. Ask who is getting this letter. *(Andy)* Who is sending it? *(Sandy)* You may also wish to ask what Sam's new problem is. *(Sam now has one more cat.)* Ask students if somebody can have too much of a good thing. *(Answers will vary.)*

Have students write the missing spelling words for the letter as they did in the story. Then check students' responses for the accurate spelling of each answer.

The Page
Have students use each of the spelling words they missed in an original sentence.

As an additional activity, you may wish to direct the following: Prepare a large cardboard cut-out of Sam's van, pictured on page 12. Make a slit in the van for each member of your class. Give each student a cardboard circle that will fit into a slit. Have students draw a cat on their circle, label their cat with a spelling word, and put their cat into Sam's van. Students will then take turns removing a cat from the van while reading and spelling its label.

Objectives

- To relate spelling to another language skill.
- To capitalize the first word in a sentence.
- To write spelling words in the context of sentences.
- To check handwriting for correct letter formation.

a b c d e f g h i j k l m
n o p q r s t u v w x y z

Capital Letters

Use a capital letter to begin the first word of a sentence.

My cat climbs trees all the time.

Sometimes she gets stuck in a tree.

Choose the right word for each of these sentences. Then write the sentence. Remember to begin with a capital letter.

1. my   (cat / fish)   is stuck in a tree.

My cat is stuck in a tree.

2. a   (bird / man)   comes to help.

A man comes to help.

3. he   (is / has)   a ladder.

He has a ladder.

4. he grabs her with his   (hand / foot).

He grabs her with his hand.

5. she runs home for milk   (but / and)   a nap.

She runs home for milk and a nap.

14

Preparation   Ask a volunteer to say a sentence for one of the spelling words. Write the sentence on the board, omitting the capital letter at the beginning. Ask students what is wrong. Have one student correct the error at the board. Continue writing sentences until several students have had a turn.

Then write this scrambled sentence on the board:

has   a   cat.   man   The

Ask what is special about the first word in any sentence. *(It begins with a capital letter.)* Then have a student circle the first word in the scrambled sentence. Ask students to unscramble the sentence and write it. *(The man has a cat.)*

The Page   Do page 14 with the students. Tell them to be careful not to make spelling mistakes because of careless handwriting. Remind them to be particularly careful that the letter <u>a</u> does not look like <u>o</u>, or else <u>cat</u> may become <u>cot</u>. Ask them to remember that the vertical bar on the <u>a</u> should descend to the bottom writing line but no farther. Review the answers together.

Follow-Up   Have students write their own sentences for these words: **van, than,** and **an**. Remind them about capitalization. Students may read their sentences aloud while others identify and spell the word.

WORDS AT WORK

Challenge Yourself

active   **blank**   **habit**

What do you think each underlined Challenge Word means? Check your Spelling Dictionary to see if you are right. Then write sentences. Show that you understand the meaning of each Challenge Word.

1. Some cats are lazy. But Eva's cats are very <u>active</u>.

2. Erase the chalkboard and leave it <u>blank</u>.

3. Always wearing your seat belt is a good <u>habit</u>.

Write to the Point

Read the story on pages 12 and 13 again. How can Sam take his trip? What can he do about his cats? Write a short letter to Sam. Tell him how he can take his trip. Use spelling words from this lesson in your letter.

Challenge Use one or more of the Challenge Words in your letter.

Proofreading

Use the marks to show the mistakes in the sentences below. Write the four misspelled words correctly in the blanks.

	word is misspelled
⊙	period is missing
≡	letter should be capitalized

1. One cat runs after our (ven)⊙

2. Uncle Sam (haz) to stop for it.

3. <u>he</u> puts the cat in my (han.)

4. We can (ad) one more cat⊙

1. _____ van

2. _____ has

3. _____ hand

4. _____ add

15

Objectives

- To extend the vowel spelling presented in Lesson 2 to the Challenge Words.

- To use context and the **Spelling Dictionary** to enlarge students' vocabulary.

- To apply the vowel spelling presented in Lesson 2 in a writing activity.

- To practice proofreading for spelling, punctuation, and capitalization.

Dictation Sentences

1. That <u>man</u> is my dad.
2. Our <u>cat</u> ran <u>after</u> the fly.
3. The <u>van</u> had <u>a</u> flat tire.
4. Can <u>you</u> <u>add</u> ten and ten?
5. Hold my <u>hand</u>.
6. The big tree <u>is</u> <u>an</u> old tree.
7. The boys <u>and</u> <u>girls</u> ride to school.
8. He <u>has</u> a <u>red</u> wagon.
9. I <u>am</u> older <u>than</u> he is.

Challenge Yourself Answers

Possible definitions:

1. busy
2. without anything on it
3. a repeated way of acting

Students' sentences will vary.

Test Review this way to spell /ă/: <u>a</u> as in <u>van</u>. Test words with /ă/. Use one of these testing methods: (1) Say the word; read the sample sentence from page 10; say the word; have students write the word. (2) Read each dictation sentence above; have students write the sentence. Correct the test with students.

Challenge Yourself The optional Challenge Words may be assigned to the entire class or limited to those students who do well on the test. Have students note the vowel spelling in the Challenge Words. Responses to this activity should be completed on separate paper. Answers to the questions are provided above.

Write to the Point Help students recall the selection "Too Many Cats!" on pages 12 and 13; then assign the letter. This activity should be completed on separate paper.

Proofreading The proofreading practice includes misspellings of words from this lesson as well as a capitalization error and two punctuation errors.

LESSON 3

Objectives

- To hear and say words with /ă/.
- To write words with /ă/ with attention to letter sequence and sound/symbol relationships.
- To write each spelling word once.
- To recognize that /ă/ may be spelled <u>a</u>.

Sample Sentences

1. I rode on the elephant's <u>back</u>.
2. We ran <u>fast</u> around the track.
3. The children <u>sang</u> a silly song.
4. They wanted to <u>ask</u> us to sing along.
5. The rabbit was <u>last</u> at the finish line.
6. The <u>land</u> around this house is mine.
7. I think I'll eat <u>that</u> apple pie.
8. She tried to <u>catch</u> a butterfly.
9. "<u>Thank</u> you," said the happy boy.
10. It's nice to <u>have</u> this little toy.
11. Michelle has long <u>black</u> hair.
12. What's the <u>matter</u> with your chair?

Lesson 3   Words with /ă/

Say these words. Listen for /ă/ in each one.

back
fast
sang
ask
last
land
that
catch
thank
have
black
matter

1. Write the word that begins with /ă/.

ask

2. Which words begin like the word <u>them</u>?

that   thank

3. Which words end with the last two letters in <u>past</u>?

fast   last

4. Which words end with the last two letters in <u>pack</u>?

back   black

5. l + and = land   s + ang = sang

    ca + tch = catch

    mat + ter = matter

6. What word has <u>a</u> and <u>e</u>, but you only hear /ă/?

have

I never remember the <u>e</u> in <u>have</u>, because I don't hear it.

It's easy for me. Words don't end with just <u>v</u>.

16

Preparation

Write /ă/ on the board. Have students repeat the sound /ă/ as in <u>pat</u>. Say these word pairs. If a word contains /ă/, students should stand.

     <u>have</u> – heave   <u>land</u> – lend   <u>last</u> – least   <u>sang</u> – sing

Have students look at the spelling words on page 16. Say each word aloud. Then have the students say and spell each one.

Note the spellings <u>tch</u> and <u>ng</u>. Write these on the board and review the sound that each spelling represents. Direct students' attention to the spelling words that contain them. (<i>catch, sang</i>) Discuss the three spellings of the sound /k/: <u>ck</u> as in <u>back</u> and <u>black</u>, <u>k</u> as in <u>ask</u>, <u>c</u> as in <u>catch</u>. Finally, call attention to Spelling Bee's reminder in the cartoon that the word <u>have</u> contains a silent <u>e</u>.

Ask the students to point to the spelling word as you read each sample sentence aloud.

The Page

Do page 16 together, allowing time for students to write the answers. Check their responses for immediate reinforcement of correct spelling. Volunteers may spell aloud or write their answers on the board.

Follow-Up

Discuss ways students will study their spelling words. Suggest these methods: Spell the words to someone else or write the words on a piece of paper and repeat them.

Checkpoint

Write a spelling word for each clue.

Then use the Checkpoint Study Plan on page 224.

1. I was late, so I walked very ___.

2. If you want to know something, you ___.

3. Jill looked sad, so I said, "What's the ___?"

4. I went to the airport to watch the planes ___.

5. My favorite colors are purple, red, and ___.

6. Everyone liked the song I ___.

7. What color hair does your brother ___?

8. Harry likes the present and wants to ___ us.

9. Do you want this one or ___ one?

10. The opposite of front is ___.

11. You need a ball to play ___.

12. Hundreds of years ago, this mystery word was spelled <u>latost</u>. It meant "latest." Now the word is spelled differently, but it means the same thing. It means "coming at the end." Can you guess the word? ___

17

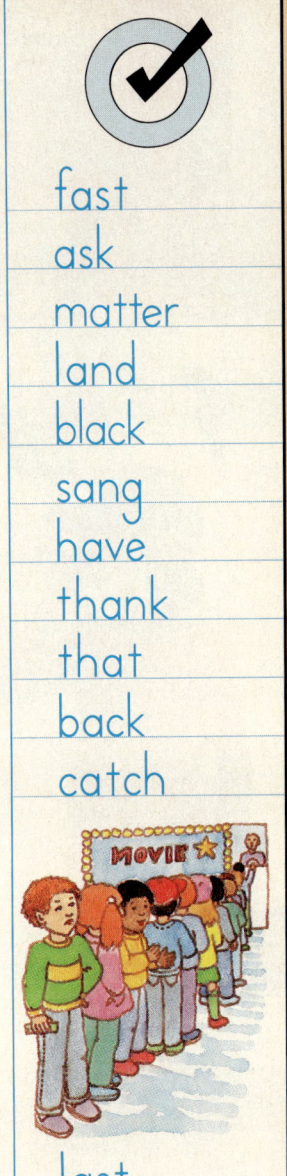

fast

ask

matter

land

black

sang

have

thank

that

back

catch

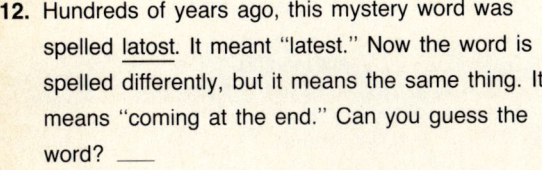

last

Objectives

- To write spelling words in response to clues: antonyms and context.

- To develop the critical thinking skills of making inferences and predicting outcomes.

- To understand that the spelling of words in the English language changes over time.

Spelling Strategy

Some students may omit the "silent t" in <u>catch</u>. This may be a good time to discuss the <u>tch</u> spelling of the /ch/ sound. Have students write the word <u>catch</u> and underline the <u>tch</u> spelling of the final /ch/ sound. Challenge students to substitute other letters for the initial <u>c</u> to form new words like <u>patch</u>, <u>match</u>, and <u>hatch</u>. Tell students that this <u>tch</u> spelling of /ch/ occurs only at the end of a word.

Preparation

The clues on this page are like crossword puzzle clues. Explain to students that the response to each clue is a spelling word. Use the following examples to illustrate the types of clues used:

Antonym	The opposite of front is *(back)*.
Context	I went to the airport to watch the planes *(land)*.

The final clue explains how the spelling of the word <u>last</u> has changed over time.

The Page

Have students complete page 17 using the words on page 16. When students have finished, have them read each clue and spell the answer aloud. Check each response twice: once for the correct answer and a second time for spelling accuracy.

Follow-Up

Guide students in using the **Checkpoint Study Plan** on page 224 to take a self-test. Have them use the plan for independent study.

Objectives

- To write words with /ă/ in continuous text.
- To write each spelling word once.
- To integrate reading with spellling.

**Fill in the blanks with spelling words.**

The Violin Lesson

"I'll be ___back___ at two o'clock," said her mother. Joan picked up her violin and got out of the car. She wanted to ___ask___ if she really had to take her lesson. But she knew that it wouldn't ___matter___. Her mom would say, "Yes."

Joan watched her mother drive off. Joan wasn't in any hurry. It was a beautiful day. A bird ___sang___ above her head. She watched it ___land___ near the feet of a girl. The girl was older than Joan. She was also carrying a ___black___ violin case.

"Hi!" Joan called. "I ___have___ never seen you here before," said Joan. "And I've been taking violin lessons from Mr. Crabbe for the ___last___ six months."

18

Note

- The word land is used in the story as a verb. Ask students to name some things that might land on the ground.
- The word catch is used as a noun. It is more commonly used as a verb. Have students make up sentences using catch as a verb.

Preparation   Have students turn to pages 18 and 19. Call their attention to the word list. Have the students say the words. Then explain that each spelling word belongs in one of the blanks in the story. Tell students that you will read the story aloud, supplying the missing words. Then they will write the missing spelling words as they complete the story on their own.

Write the title "The Violin Lesson" on the chalkboard and have a student read it. Tell your students that the story describes what happens to a girl on her way to a music lesson.

The Pages   Read the story aloud, supplying the missing spelling words as students follow along in their texts. When you have finished reading, you may wish to discuss the story by asking these questions:

1. Have you ever said something and then regretted saying it? *(Answers will vary.)*
2. How do you think Joan felt when she discovered who the tall girl was? *(embarrassed; frightened; sorry she'd said a mean thing)*

"I start today." The tall girl smiled. She showed Joan her violin case.

"Oh! Let me warn you about Mr. Crabbe. He's a good violin teacher. But he'll tell on you if you don't practice. My mother made me stop playing baseball and _____catch_____ with the kids after school. Now I have to go straight home and practice. I have Mr. Crabbe to _____thank_____ for that! Sometimes he really is an old crab!"

The tall girl stopped smiling. She said to Joan, "I guess you don't know who I am."

"No," Joan answered.

"I'm Ann Crabbe. That 'old crab' is my grandfather."

Joan thought _____fast_____. She knew _____that_____ she was in trouble. "Well, do you know who I am?"

"No."

"Good!" said Joan. She opened the door and shut it quickly behind her.

19

back
fast
sang
ask
last
land
that
catch
thank
have
black
matter

Enrichment

If you want to use the blackline activity masters for enrichment and additional practice, assign Lesson 3 activities at this time.

Maintenance and Review

OBJECTIVE

• To review words with /ă/ spelled a.

ACTIVITIES

If you want to use the blackline activity masters for maintenance and review, assign Lesson 2 activities at this time.

You can also use the activity below to review Lesson 2 with students:

Write the following words and riddles on the board. Read and discuss these riddles with the students. Have volunteers write the answers on the board. Then have students copy the answers or have them copy each riddle. (Answers are in parentheses.)

van   man   cat   hand   flat

1. You can find me on a car that cannot go fast. I am a tire, but I am _(flat)_.
2. You can find me curled up in the sun or up in a tree. I am a _(cat)_.
3. You can find me riding on the road. I carry lots of people. I am a _(van)_.
4. You can find me at the end of your arm. I am your _(hand)_.
5. You can find me almost everywhere — in a boat in the sea or a plane in the air! I am a _(man)_.

Then have students complete pages 18 and 19 by silently rereading the story and writing the correct spelling word for each blank. Have volunteers write the answers on the board as other students read the text aloud. Students should check their own answers. Finally, check students' responses for the accurate spelling of each answer.

Follow-Up Have students use each of the spelling words they missed in an original sentence that relates to the story.

As an additional follow-up activity, you may wish to have your students visualize Mr. Crabbe, the music teacher, and draw pictures of how he might look.

Objectives

- To relate spelling to another language skill.
- To use a period at the end of a statement.
- To write spelling words in the context of sentences.
- To check handwriting for correct letter formation.

a b c d e f g h i j k l m
n o p q r s t u v w x y z

Periods

Use a period(.) at the end of a sentence that tells something.

Camels live in the desert.   Some camels have two humps.

Write the sentences below. Choose a word from the list for the blank space. Remember to put a period at the end of the sentence.

catch   fast   that   back   have

1. Some camels ___ one hump

Some camels have one hump.

2. I know ___ camels are big

I know that camels are big.

3. A camel can carry you on its ___

A camel can carry you on its back.

4. You have to ___ it first

You have to catch it first.

5. Camels can run ___

Camels can run fast.

20

Preparation   Write this sentence on the board, omitting the period:

   The man at bat hit a fly ball

Ask students what is wrong with the sentence. *(no period)* A sentence that tells something ends with a period. Explain that in reading, the period signals the end of an idea and allows you to pause. Have a volunteer correct the punctuation and read the sentence aloud.

   Write this scrambled sentence on the board:

   to catch tried the football. The man

There is a clue for the last word in the sentence. Ask what it is. *(the period)* Have someone unscramble the sentence. *(The man tried to catch the football.)*

The Page   Read the examples on page 20. Then complete the page with the students. Have them write the sentences, reminding them about the period at the end. Be sure they are careful about their handwriting. Note that the letter c, as in back, must be formed carefully so it is not confused with o. Check students' responses.

Follow-Up   Write these words on the board: ask, thank, land, sang, last, black, matter. Have students write their own sentences for each word.

WORDS AT WORK

Challenge Yourself

napkin	craft	cannon

Use your Spelling Dictionary to answer these questions. Then write sentences. Show that you understand the meaning of each Challenge Word.

1. Does Emilio's beautiful painting of the horses show his craft?

2. Do people use a napkin to clean their hands and face after a meal?

3. Would you find a cannon in your kitchen?

Write to the Point

Joan had to think fast after her mistake. Would you have said something different to Ann Crabbe? Write sentences telling what you would have done in Joan's place. Use spelling words from this lesson in your sentences.

Challenge Use one or more of the Challenge Words in your sentences.

Proofreading

Use the marks to show the mistakes in the sentences below. Write the four misspelled words correctly in the blanks.

◯	word is misspelled
⊙	period is missing
≡	letter should be capitalized

1. Joan will have to (cach) the bus⊙

2. (Thet) bus takes her to a lesson⊙

3. will you (aske) Joan to play?

4. Joan plays (faste) and well.

1. _____catch_____

2. _____That_____

3. _____ask_____

4. _____fast_____

21

Objectives

- To extend the vowel spelling presented in Lesson 3 to the Challenge Words.
- To use context and the **Spelling Dictionary** to enlarge students' vocabulary.
- To apply the vowel spelling presented in Lesson 3 in a writing activity.
- To practice proofreading for spelling, punctuation, and capitalization.

Dictation Sentences

1. The land is flat.
2. We have to catch the bus.
3. Nancy can run fast.
4. Go back to school.
5. Am I the last to thank you?
6. He sang a song.
7. Ann has a black coat.
8. Is that my shoe?
9. The children ask for help.
10. What is the matter with the van?

Challenge Yourself Answers

1. yes
2. yes
3. no

Students' sentences will vary.

Test Review this way to spell /ă/: a as in back. Test words with /ă/. Use one of these testing methods: (1) Say the word; read the sample sentence from page 16; say the word; have students write the word. (2) Read each dictation sentence above; have students write the sentence. Correct the test with students.

Challenge Yourself The optional Challenge Words may be assigned to the entire class or limited to those students who do well on the test. Have students note the vowel spelling in the Challenge Words. Responses to this activity should be completed on separate paper. Answers to the questions are provided above.

Write to the Point Have students recall the selection "The Violin Lesson" on pages 18 and 19; then assign the sentences. You may wish to ask volunteers to read their sentences. This activity should be completed on separate paper.

Proofreading The proofreading practice includes misspellings of words from this lesson as well as a capitalization error and two punctuation errors.

LESSON 4

Objectives

- To hear and say words with /ĕ/.
- To write words with /ĕ/ with attention to letter sequence and sound/symbol relationships.
- To write each spelling word once.
- To recognize that /ĕ/ may be spelled e, ay, and ai.

Sample Sentences

1. At eight o'clock I go to bed.
2. The jet makes noise above my head.
3. Yes, the North Pole is really cold!
4. My brother Sam is ten years old.
5. I didn't want the play to end.
6. I went downtown with my best friend.
7. Sally kept her toys in a box.
8. I put my socks next to my shoes.
9. That shelf can hold a lot of books.
10. I love to help when my dad cooks.
11. The teacher says we must behave.
12. My father said, "I need a shave."

Note

Words are grouped according to spellings of /ĕ/:

    e
    ay
    ai

The sample sentences may be used for pretesting and post-testing.

Lesson 4   **Words with /ĕ/**

Say these words. Listen for /ĕ/ in each one.

bed
jet
yes
ten
end
went
kept
next
shelf
when
says
said

1. Write the word that begins like yellow.

yes

2. Write the words that end with the sound /n/.

ten   when

3. Which three-letter words end like had?

bed   end

4. What spelling word ends with the letters elf?

shelf

5. Write the words that end with the sound /t/.

jet   went
kept   next

6. Which words have the sound /ĕ/ but no letter e?

says   said

Are you surprised at the way said and says are spelled?

/ĕ/? Yĕs!

22

Preparation   Write /ĕ/ on the chalkboard and have students repeat the sound /ĕ/ as in pet. Then say the word pairs below. Ask students to put their hands on their heads if a word contains /ĕ/.

    ten – tan   bad – bed   see – says   said – seed

Have students repeat and spell each list word on page 22 as you say it.

Have a student write shelf and when on the board. Ask the students to say the sounds that the letters sh and wh represent. Also note that in the first group of ten words, /ĕ/ is spelled with the letter e.

Then call attention to the cartoon. Ask the students if they think the spelling of says and said is surprising. Do they hear the sound /ĕ/ in these words? *(yes)* What letters spell the sound /ĕ/ in says? *(ay)* What letters spell /ĕ/ in said? *(ai)* (See **Note**.)

Ask the students to point to the spelling word as you read each sample sentence aloud.

The Page   Do page 22 together, allowing time for students to write answers. Volunteers may put answers on the board.

Follow-Up   Ask students for a helpful way to study the spelling words. You might suggest that they try writing the words in large letters in crayon on sheets of newsprint, saying the words and spelling them aloud as they write.

Checkpoint

Write a spelling word for each clue. Then use the Checkpoint Study Plan on page 224.

1. A place to sleep is a ___.

2. The movie was so funny, we ___ laughing.

3. You can always believe what he ___.

4. The opposite of no is ___.

5. Did you hear what Ann ___?

6. The last part of something is the ___.

7. Jan will go first, and I will be ___.

8. Rob is coming home, but I don't know ___.

9. The number after nine is ___.

10. I keep my books on a ___.

11. A kind of plane is a ___.

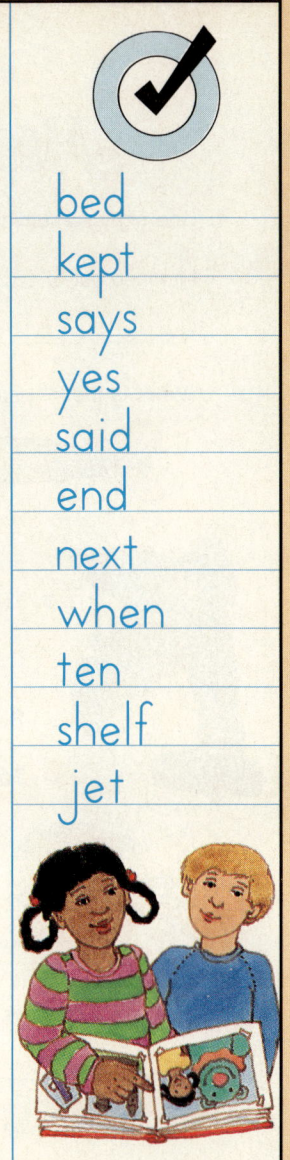

bed
kept
says
yes
said
end
next
when
ten
shelf
jet

went

12. This mystery word used to be spelled <u>wente</u>. At one time, <u>wente</u> meant "did turn." Then its meaning changed to "did go." That's what it means today. Can you guess the word? ___

23

Objectives

- To write spelling words in response to clues: definitions, antonyms, and context.
- To develop the critical thinking skills of sequencing and making inferences.
- To recognize that word meanings often change over time.

Spelling Strategy

Both <u>says</u> and <u>said</u> have unusual spellings for the /ĕ/ sound; therefore, some students may spell <u>says</u> as <u>seys</u> and <u>said</u> as <u>sed</u>. Have students work in pairs. One student can dictate a sentence using <u>says</u> or <u>said</u> while the other student writes the sentence. They can then check the spelling together.

Preparation The clues on this page are like crossword puzzle clues. Explain to students that the response to each clue is a spelling word. Use the following examples to illustrate the types of clues used:

Definition   A place to sleep is a *(bed)*.
Antonym   The opposite of no is *(yes)*.
Context   The movie was so funny, we *(kept)* laughing.

The final clue explains how the meaning and spelling of <u>went</u> has changed over time.

The Page Have students complete page 23 using the words on page 22. When students have finished, have them read each clue and spell the answer aloud. Check each response twice: once for the correct answer and a second time for spelling accuracy.

Follow-Up Guide students in using the **Checkpoint Study Plan** on page 224 to take a self-test. Have them use the plan for independent study.

Objectives

- To write words with /ĕ/ in continuous text and related sentences.
- To write each spelling word once.
- To integrate reading with spelling.

Note

Some of the spelling words will be used twice on these two pages.

Fill in the blanks with spelling words.

An Odd Dream

1. One night something woke me!

I jumped out of ___bed___

And ___went___ to the window.

"What is that?" I said.

2. A sky full of ___jet___ planes!

I must have seen ___ten___

They ___kept___ flying by,

And then back again.

3. "This cannot be true,"

I ___said___ to myself.

But then the noise shook

Toys and books off the ___shelf___!

4. And inside each jet,

Oh ___yes___, it was true,

Sat a funny fat pilot,

A blue kangaroo.

5. They ___went___ under, over,

And then all around.

And ___when___ it was over,

They flew upside down!

24

Preparation Have students turn to pages 24 and 25. Call their attention to the word list. Have the students say the words. Then explain that each spelling word belongs in at least one of the blanks on pages 24 and 25. Some of the words will be used twice. Tell students that you will read the poem aloud, supplying the missing words. Then they will write the missing spelling words as they complete the poem on their own. Use the same procedure for the questions on page 25.

Write the title "An Odd Dream" on the board and have a student read it. Point out that poetry is written in lines of verse rather than in sentences, and often contains rhyming words. Tell the class that the poem "An Odd Dream" has five stanzas of verse. Have students listen for the rhymes in the poem.

The Pages Read the poem aloud, supplying the missing spelling words as students follow along in their texts. When you have finished reading the poem, students may wish to tell about any odd dreams they have had.

Then ask students to reread the poem to themselves and to complete it by writing the correct spelling word for each blank. Note that the verse form sometimes offers clues about which word to choose. Have a volunteer write the answers on the board so students may check their own work. Then ask a student to read the poem to the class, pausing before each blank. The other students will say the missing spelling word at the appropriate time.

Use a spelling word to answer each question.

1. **Q.** What is each kangaroo riding in?

   A. Each kangaroo is riding in a ___jet___.

2. **Q.** How many jets does the boy see?

   A. He sees ___ten___ jets.

3. **Q.** Where does the boy keep his books?

   A. He keeps them on a ___shelf___.

   They are ___next___ to his toys.

4. **Q.** Where is the boy at the beginning of the poem?

   A. He is in ___bed___.

5. **Q.** What does he say when he sees the jets?

   A. He ___says___, "This cannot be true."

6. **Q.** When did the jets fly upside down?

   A. They flew upside down at the ___end___ of the dream.

7. **Q.** If you asked him if he liked his dream, what would the boy probably say?

   A. He would say, "___Yes___!"

bed
jet
yes
ten
end
went
kept
next
shelf
when
says
said

Next look at the paired sentences on page 25. Explain that each numbered question is followed by an answer. Read each question aloud. Then have students complete each answer with the correct spelling word. Have volunteers read each answer aloud, note the spelling word, and spell it. Finally, write the answers on the board so students may correct their own work. When both pages have been completed, check students' responses for the accurate spelling of each answer.

Follow-Up Have students use each of the spelling words they missed in an original sentence.

As an additional follow-up activity, you may wish to have students draw large outlines of twelve jets. A spelling word may then be written inside each jet.

Objectives

- To relate spelling to another language skill.
- To capitalize the first word in a sentence.
- To use a period at the end of a statement.
- To write sentences in correct word order.
- To write spelling words in the context of sentences.
- To check handwriting for correct letter formation.

---

a b c d e f g h i j k l m
n o p q r s t u v w x y z

Sentences

Unscramble the sentences. Remember capital letters and periods.

1. ten cats my pal has

My pal has ten cats.

2. hid they under the bed

They hid under the bed.

3. on a shelf they sat

They sat on a shelf.

4. they broke toy jet a

They broke a toy jet.

5. went up the chimney they

They went up the chimney.

Now write a sentence about the cats. Use one of these words:

yes   end   when   says   said

26

Preparation Write the following sentences on the board:

> dad took me fishing we went out on
> our boat soon I felt something
> tugging at my line

Ask the students to tell you what is wrong with these sentences. *(no capital letter at the beginning; no period at the end)* Read the sentences aloud without pausing, to emphasize the effect of omitting a period. Have a volunteer read the first sentence aloud and make the appropriate corrections at the board. *(Dad took me fishing.)* Continue until all three sentences are written correctly. Then have the whole class read each sentence, pausing at the period.

The Page Do page 26 with the students. Remind them to write each letter carefully. For instance, have them check to be sure the letter e in words like bed and end is written correctly. It should not extend far above the writing-line guide. Have volunteers write the unscrambled sentences with correct punctuation on the board so students may check their work.

Follow-Up Ask students to write some of their own sentences on the board for these words: **yes, end, said, when, kept, next,** and **says.** Have the students circle the spelling words in their sentences and spell the words aloud.

WORDS AT WORK

Challenge Yourself

melon   **pedal**   **method**

What do you think each underlined Challenge Word means? Check your Spelling Dictionary to see if you are right. Then write sentences. Show that you understand the meaning of each Challenge Word.

1. The best <u>method</u> of brushing your teeth is up and down.

2. My favorite fruit at the picnic was the <u>melon</u>.

3. My sister's bike needs a new <u>pedal</u>.

Write to the Point

The poem on page 24 tells about a very funny dream. Blue kangaroos flew upside down. Have you ever had a funny dream? Write a few sentences about your dream. Use spelling words from this lesson in your sentences.

Challenge Use one or more of the Challenge Words in your sentences.

Proofreading

Use the marks to show the mistakes in the sentences below. Write the four misspelled words correctly in the blanks.

⬭	word is misspelled
⊙	period is missing
≡	letter should be capitalized

1. I kept a toy jet (nekst) to my bed.

2. (Wen) i̲ got up, it was gone.

3. Mom said she put it on a (shef)⊙.

4. I dreamed it (wente) on a trip.

1. _____next_____

2. _____When_____

3. _____shelf_____

4. _____went_____

27

Objectives

- To extend the vowel spellings presented in Lesson 4 to the Challenge Words.
- To use context and the **Spelling Dictionary** to enlarge students' vocabulary.
- To apply the vowel spellings presented in Lesson 4 in a writing activity.
- To practice proofreading for spelling, punctuation, and capitalization.

Dictation Sentences

1. This is my <u>bed</u>.
2. My class ha̅s̅ <u>ten</u> boys and nine girls.
3. We <u>went</u> to the <u>end</u> of the street.
4. A <u>jet</u> can fly fast.
5. <u>When</u> is the <u>next</u> game?
6. The box is on the <u>shelf</u>.
7. We <u>kept</u> the cat in the barn.
8. Mom <u>said</u> to come home.
9. Luis <u>says</u> he runs fast.
10. <u>Yes</u>, <u>I</u> can jump up.

Challenge Yourself Answers

Possible definitions:

1. a way to do something
2. a kind of fruit
3. the place for your foot

Students' sentences will vary.

Test Review these ways to spell /ĕ/: <u>e</u> as in <u>bed</u>; <u>ay</u> as in <u>says</u>; <u>ai</u> as in <u>said</u>. Test words with /ĕ/. Use one of these testing methods: (1) Say the word; read the sample sentence from page 22; say the word; have students write the word. (2) Read each dictation sentence above; have students write the sentence. Correct the test with students.

Challenge Yourself The optional Challenge Words may be assigned to the entire class or limited to those students who do well on the test. Have students note the vowel spelling in the Challenge Words. Responses to this activity should be completed on separate paper. Answers to the questions are provided above.

Write to the Point Help students recall the selection "An Odd Dream" on pages 24 and 25; then assign the sentences. Encourage students to use descriptive words. This activity should be completed on separate paper.

Proofreading The proofreading practice includes misspellings of words from this lesson as well as a capitalization error and a punctuation error.

LESSON 5

Objectives

- To hear and say words with /ĕ/.
- To write words with /ĕ/ with attention to letter sequence and sound/symbol relationships.
- To write each spelling word once.
- To recognize that /ĕ/ may be spelled e and a.

Sample Sentences

1. My desk is made of wood.
2. I'll send you a book I think is good.
3. The rest of us will never tell.
4. I think I heard the recess bell.
5. He likes fresh water from our well.
6. I would help you if you fell.
7. Judy has that dress in blue.
8. My best friend is Sue.
9. I have an egg for breakfast each day.
10. We just gave seven puppies away.
11. Did you have any apple pie?
12. How many marbles can we buy?

Note

Words are grouped according to spellings of /ĕ/:

e
a

The sample sentences may be used for pretesting and post-testing.

Preparation Write /ĕ/ on the chalkboard. Have students repeat the sound /ĕ/ as in pet. Then say the word pairs below. Ask students to put their elbows on their desks when they hear a word with /ĕ/.

will – well   desk – disk   bill – bell   many – money

Have students look at the spelling words on page 28. Say each word aloud. Then have students repeat and spell each word.

Note the double consonants in bell and well. Ask students to find two more words with double consonants. *(egg, dress)* Explain that sometimes double consonants go together to represent only one sound: /g/, /l/, /s/.

Point out that in the first ten words, the sound /ĕ/ is spelled with the letter e. The last two words spell the sound /ĕ/ with the letter a. Call attention to the cartoon. Any and many have the sound /ĕ/, but there is no letter e in them. (See **Note**.)

Now read the sample sentences. Have the students point to each spelling word as you read the sentence for it.

The Page Do page 28 with the students. Allow time for them to write the answers. Then have volunteers put answers on the board.

Follow-Up Have students work in pairs, taking turns asking and spelling the words to each other.

Checkpoint

Write a spelling word for each clue.
Then use the Checkpoint Study Plan on page 224.

1. Please, may I ____ you?

2. I wrote her a letter, but I didn't ____ it.

3. The number after six is ____.

4. I went to the door and rang the ____.

5. I do my homework at my ____.

6. Andrea bought a skirt and a ____.

7. When you are sick, you don't feel ____.

8. I spent my money, so now I don't have ____.

9. The opposite of a few is ____.

10. After I jogged, I had to ____.

11. I like chocolate ice cream the ____.

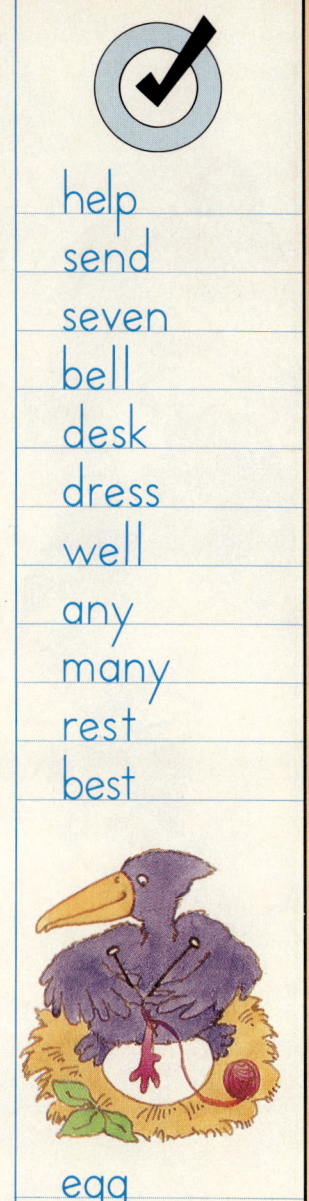

help
send
seven
bell
desk
dress
well
any
many
rest
best

12. This mystery word has a long history. It was first
used many, many years ago. At that time, it
meant "bird." Over the years, its meaning
changed. Now it tells what a bird hatches from.
Can you guess the word? ____

egg

29

Objectives

- To write spelling words in response to clues: antonyms and context.
- To develop the critical thinking skills of sequencing and predicting outcomes.
- To recognize that word meanings often change over time.

Spelling Strategy

Some students may spell <u>seven</u> as <u>sevin</u>, <u>sevan</u>, or <u>sevun</u>. This is because the unstressed vowel, or schwa, gives no audible clue to its spelling. Ask students to pronounce <u>seven</u> quietly to themselves, stressing both syllables so the vowel sound in the second syllable is more clearly heard.

Preparation The clues on this page are like crossword puzzle clues. Explain to students that the response to each clue is a spelling word. Use the following examples to illustrate the types of clues used:

Antonym   The opposite of a few is *(many)*.
Context   I do my homework at my *(desk)*.

The final clue explains how the meaning of <u>egg</u> has changed over time.

The Page Have students complete page 29 using the words on page 28. When students have finished, have them read each clue and spell the answer aloud. Check each response twice: once for the correct answer and a second time for spelling accuracy.

Follow-Up Guide students in using the **Checkpoint Study Plan** on page 224 to take a self-test. Have them use the plan for independent study.

Objectives

- To write words with /ĕ/ in continuous text.
- To write each spelling word once.
- To integrate reading with spelling.

Finish Meg's diary page with spelling words.

Meg's Chickens

October 20

Dear Diary,

Today is special. It's my birthday. My aunt and uncle sent me a pretty _____dress_____ to wear. They always _____send_____ me a nice gift.

Today was a special day in school, too. Last week my grandfather gave me eight eggs to bring to class. Everyone wanted to see baby chicks being born. The eggs hatched today. What a surprise we had!

It was exciting, Dear Diary. My _____desk_____ was right by the box with the eggs in it. Right after the _____bell_____ rang, I looked in the box. One _____egg_____ was beginning to crack.

Note

The story is about the <u>incubation</u> of eggs in a classroom. You might wish to explain that <u>incubation</u> involves keeping eggs in a box to control the temperature and dampness of the air. Once enough time has passed for the young to develop (20 days for chicks), the eggs will hatch.

Preparation   Have students turn to pages 30 and 31. Call their attention to the word list. Have the students say the words. Then explain that each spelling word belongs in one of the blanks in the story. Tell students that you will read the story aloud, supplying the missing words. Then they will write the missing spelling words as they complete the story on their own.

Have students look at the pages. Explain that this story is written as a diary entry. Tell students that a diary is a book in which you write what has happened to you. It is like a photo album; words instead of pictures help you to remember events. Ask students who has written the diary entry. *(Meg)* To whom is she writing? *(to her diary)* Why do they think a diary page always has a date? *(so you can remember when something happened)*

Write the title "Meg's Chickens" on the board and have a student read it. Call attention to the illustrations. Tell students that they are going to read about a girl who brings some eggs to school and about her big surprise when they finally hatch.

The Pages   Read the diary entry aloud, supplying the missing spelling words as students follow along in their texts. When you have finished reading, you may wish to discuss the story. Have students look at the illustrations on pages 30 and 31 and ask them which eggs might contain chickens. Which eggs might contain something else?

Everyone ran to see the new chick. One by one the

other _____seven_____ eggs began to crack. Soon

we could see all the babies. My friend Suzie said, "I

never saw ___any___ chickens like those before!"

"Where did you get the eggs?" my teacher asked.

"Grandfather gave them to me," I said. "He wants to

___help___ me learn about the animals on his farm."

"He likes to play jokes, too," laughed my teacher.

The _____rest_____ of the class also laughed. Not

___many___ things embarrass me, Dear Diary.

But eight tiny turtles were crawling around the box!

When I left school, the little baby turtles were doing

___well___ . Everyone calls them "Meg's

Chickens." I guess my grandfather wanted this to be

the ___best___ birthday surprise ever!

desk
send
rest
bell
well
help
dress
best
egg
seven
any
many

31

Enrichment

If you want to use the blackline activity masters for enrichment and additional practice, assign Lesson 5 activities at this time.

Maintenance and Review

OBJECTIVE

● To review words with /ĕ/ spelled: e, ay, ai.

ACTIVITIES

If you want to use the blackline activity masters for maintenance and review, assign Lesson 4 activities at this time.

You can also use the activity below to review Lesson 4 with students:

Write the following sentence fragments on the board (without underlining any words). Have students copy them and make up endings for them. Then ask the students to underline the spelling words. Students may wish to read their sentences aloud.

1. The radio says that it's
2. When it rains, we go to
3. Yesterday, we went
4. Mom said that
5. At the end of the day, we

Next ask students to complete the diary entry by rereading it silently and writing the correct spelling word for each blank. Then have volunteers read the pages aloud. Have other students write the correct words on the board so students can check their work. Be sure to check students' responses for correct word choice and for the accurate spelling of each answer.

Follow-Up Have students use each of the spelling words they missed in an original sentence that relates to the story.

As an additional follow-up activity, start with the first student in the first row and have him or her read the story until the first blank. Then have the next student say the missing spelling word for the blank and continue reading until the next blank appears. Then another student takes over. Continue until all students have had a turn or until the end of the story.

Objectives

- To relate spelling words to a dictionary skill.
- To alphabetize by the first letter in a word.
- To use the **Spelling Dictionary**.
- To check handwriting for correct letter formation.

a b c d e f g h i j k l m n o p q r s t u v w x y z

Alphabetical Order

Words in a dictionary are in alphabetical order.

Put these words in alphabetical order: **any rest many send**

Remember to look at the first letter of each word.

1. any
2. many
3. rest
4. send

Write the spelling words for these pictures. They will be in alphabetical order. Then find the words in the Spelling Dictionary. Write the page number of each of the four spelling words.

5. bell Page: 199
6. dress Page: 204
7. egg Page: 204
8. well Page: 222

32

Preparation Write these words on the board:

jet   bed   went   said

Have a volunteer underline the first letter in each word. Ask students which first letter in these words comes at the beginning of the alphabet. *(b)* Which word comes first in alphabetical order? *(bed)* Have students put the list in alphabetical order. *(bed, jet, said, went)*

Explain that it is easy to find words in a dictionary, because words are arranged in alphabetical order. Tell students that bed is near the beginning of the dictionary, just as the letter b is near the beginning of the alphabet. Ask them which word on the board will be found nearest to the end of the dictionary. *(went, because its first letter, w, comes nearest to the end of the alphabet)* Have students locate the word went in the Spelling Dictionary. (page 222)

The Page Do the activities on page 32 with the students. Tell them to be careful not to make a spelling mistake because of careless handwriting. For example, in the word many, the m has two bumps at the top and the n has just one bump. When students have finished, help them check their work.

Follow-Up Have students write spelling words on cards (or small pieces of paper) and alphabetize them. Then have them look up each word in the **Spelling Dictionary** and write its page number on the card.

32

WORDS AT WORK

Challenge Yourself

beggar   **tread**   **memory**

Decide which Challenge Word fits each clue. Check your Spelling Dictionary to see if you were right. Then write sentences. Show that you understand the meaning of each Challenge Word.

1. A good one will help you in school.

2. This is someone who begs.

3. When you walk on something, you do this.

Write to the Point

Meg wrote about her special day in a diary. Start your own diary. Write three or four sentences about a special day you have had. Begin with "Dear Diary, _____." Use spelling words from this lesson.

Challenge Use one or more of the Challenge Words in your sentences.

Proofreading

Use the marks to show the mistakes in the sentences below. Write the four misspelled words correctly in the blanks.

⬭	word is misspelled
⊙	period is missing
≡	letter should be capitalized

1. What will m<u>e</u>g do with so ⬭meny turtles?

2. Grandfather can take ⬭sevan⊙

3. Send the ⬭rist of them to Suzie.

4. Meg will not keep ⬭eny⊙

1. _____many_____

2. _____seven_____

3. _____rest_____

4. _____any_____

33

Objectives

- To extend the vowel spellings presented in Lesson 5 to the Challenge Words.
- To use clues and the **Spelling Dictionary** to enlarge students' vocabulary.
- To apply the vowel spellings presented in Lesson 5 in a writing activity.
- To practice proofreading for spelling, punctuation, and capitalization.

Dictation Sentences

1. The pen is on his desk.
2. Send her a get well note.
3. You can help me any time.
4. Did you want an egg?
5. I have a red dress.
6. Did you eat the rest of the food?
7. Many of us can play this game.
8. They did the best job.
9. Seven of us can help you.
10. The cat can play with the bell.

Challenge Yourself Answers

1. memory
2. beggar
3. tread

Students' sentences will vary.

Test
Review these ways to spell /ĕ/: e as in desk; a as in many. Test words with /ĕ/. Use one of these testing methods: (1) Say the word; read the sample sentence from page 28; say the word; have students write the word. (2) Read each dictation sentence above; have students write the sentence. Correct the test with students.

Challenge Yourself
The optional Challenge Words may be assigned to the entire class or limited to those students who do well on the test. Have students note the vowel spellings in the Challenge Words, especially the following new spelling: ea, as in tread. Responses to this activity should be completed on separate paper. Answers to the questions are provided above.

Write to the Point
Have students recall the selection "Meg's Chickens" on pages 30 and 31; then assign the diary sentences. Remind students to use the greeting, "Dear Diary," in their first sentence. This activity should be completed on separate paper.

Proofreading
The proofreading practice includes misspellings of words from this lesson as well as a capitalization error and a punctuation error.

LESSON 6

Objectives

- To review and reinforce "Words About You."

- To review and reinforce vowel spellings for /ă/ and /ĕ/.

- To hear, say, spell, and write representative words from Lessons 1–5.

- To write a personal narrative using the five steps in the writing process.

- To use a prewriting activity to sequence the events in a personal narrative.

Dictation Sentences

1. Are you going to the park today?
2. This is our house.
3. I write with my left hand.
4. I am happy with my new toy.
5. It's nice to have a friend.
6. I don't want this book; I want that one.
7. The teacher says we are very smart.
8. My parents said we could go to the movies.
9. There are many mountains in Colorado.
10. Sam gave away seven puppies.

Note

A review test blackline master in standardized format and an answer sheet have been provided on pages T35 and T41 of this Teacher's Edition. The answers to the review test are given below.

1-C	5-B
2-A	6-A
3-D	7-C
4-C	8-A

Lesson 6　Words in Review

A. you
   our

B. hand
   am

C. have
   that

D. says
   said

E. many
   seven

1. List A has two words from Lesson 1. Write these two words.

   you   our

2. In Lesson 2 you studied words with /ă/. Write the words in List B.

   am   hand

3. List C has two more words with /ă/ from Lesson 3. Write the word with two vowels. Then write the word that begins with th.

   have   that

4. In Lesson 4 you studied words with /ĕ/. Write the word in which /ĕ/ is spelled ai.

   said

   Write the word that ends with /z/.

   says

5. List E has two more /ĕ/ words. Write the word in which /ĕ/ is spelled a.

   many

   Write the word that has two e's.

   seven

34

Preparation Write the word review on the chalkboard and read it aloud. Explain that Lesson 6 contains several activities that ask students to write some of the words they have studied in Lessons 1–5.

Direct students' attention to the list of words on page 34. Read the words aloud as students look at them. Have students say and spell each word aloud.

Then read the dictation sentences above as students point to each spelling word in their book. Point out that the words in List A are from Lesson 1, words in List B are from Lesson 2, words in List C are from Lesson 3, words in List D are from Lesson 4, and words in List E are from Lesson 5.

The Pages Have students complete the activities on page 34 as a group or independently. Write the answers on the board and have volunteers spell the words aloud for reinforcement of correct spelling.

Test and Study If you wish to test students on the review words, use one of these methods: (1) Read the word and the dictation sentence; say the word again; have students write the word. (2) Have students complete the review test blackline master. (See **Note**.)

Writer's Workshop

A Personal Narrative

A personal narrative is a true story about you. A personal narrative has words like I, me, we, and my. Here is Elena's personal narrative. It tells how she and her cat met.

Snowball

This is how I met my cat Snowball. It was a very cold day. It snowed all morning. After lunch I went outside to play. I rolled down to the bottom of the hill. Then I heard a soft sound. I looked all around. A little white kitten was hiding under a bush. It looked cold and hungry, so I took it home. I named the kitten Snowball because I found it in the snow.

To write her personal narrative, Elena followed the steps in the writing process. She used a chain of events chart as a **Prewriting** activity. On her chain of events chart, she listed the things that happened. Here is part of Elena's chain of events chart. Study what Elena did.

1	2	3	4
I went outside to play in the snow.	I rolled down the hill.	I heard a soft sound.	I found a kitten and took it home.

It's Your Turn

Get ready to write your own personal narrative. It can be about any special time in your life. Like Elena, begin by making a chain of events chart. Then follow the other steps in the writing process—**Writing, Revising, Proofreading,** and **Publishing.**

35

Note

If students have difficulty deciding on a topic, you may wish to suggest one of the following:

    The time I met my best friend
    A funny moment
    When I learned to _____

Writer's Workshop Students who have mastered the review words may go on to the **Writer's Workshop** on page 35. Explain that in a personal narrative writers tell about a special time in their life. Point out that in a personal narrative the words I, me, and my show that the writer is talking about himself or herself. Then read with students the personal narrative "Snowball," noting the use of I.

Allow students to study that portion of the chain of events chart shown on the pupil's page and guide students to see how this graphic organizer helped Elena prepare to write her personal narrative.

It's Your Turn Review the steps in the writing process with students. If students are not satisfied with the result of their prewriting, allow them to revise it as often as necessary or to choose another topic and repeat the prewriting activity.

Process Writing Blackline Masters
• Chain of Events Chart, page T48
• Steps in the Writing Process, page T46
• Proofreading Symbols/Checklist, page T47

LESSON 7

Objectives

- To hear and say words with /ĭ/.
- To write words with /ĭ/ with attention to letter sequence and sound/symbol relationships.
- To write each spelling word once.
- To recognize that /ĭ/ may be spelled i.

Sample Sentences

1. My cat will chase that little mouse.
2. They all live in a great big house.
3. The ship will sail across the sea.
4. I have six bandages on my knee!
5. The wind is making our kite fly.
6. Who hid the last piece of apple pie?
7. Please pick up your toys.
8. A magic trick is hard to do.
9. He says his brother is only two.
10. The cider in this glass won't spill.
11. A rocky road goes up that hill.
12. Did you fill the tub with water?

Lesson 7 — Words with /ĭ/

Say these words. Listen for /ĭ/ in each one.

will
big
ship
six
wind
hid
pick
trick
his
this
hill
fill

1. Which words end like track?

pick   trick

2. What word begins and ends like beg?

big

3. Which word ends with x and the sound /ks/?

six

4. Which words end in the double consonant ll?

will   hill
fill

5. sh + ip = ship

th + is = this

h + is = his

6. Write the words that end with d.

wind   hid

36

Preparation Write /ĭ/ on the chalkboard. Have students repeat the sound /ĭ/ as in pit. Ask students to stand beside their desks as you say the word pairs. They are to sit down when they hear a word with /ĭ/.

hid – head   will – well   big – beg   shop – ship

Have students look at the spelling words on page 36. Say each word aloud. Then have the students say and spell each word.

Note the consonant digraphs sh in ship, th in this, ck in trick and pick. Ask volunteers to say the sound the digraph represents in each word. Ask students to find three words that have double letters. (will, hill, fill) Remind students of the two sounds s can spell at the end of a word: /s/ as in this and /z/ as in his.

Read each sample sentence and have the students point to the appropriate spelling word in their books.

The Page Do the activities together. Then have volunteers put the answers on the board so students may check their work.

Follow-Up Suggest that students plan how they are going to study their spelling words. Ask questions such as: When is a good time to study? Is it helpful to study with someone else or alone? Where do you like to study? Suggest these methods: Students may write the words several times and review them, or they may spell the words aloud with a partner.

Checkpoint

Write a spelling word for each clue.
Then use the Checkpoint Study Plan on page 224.

1. A big boat is a ___.

2. Give Jim the bat that is ___.

3. I flew my kite in the ___.

4. Another word for large is ___.

5. A word that sounds like kiss and miss is ___.

6. When I pour water into my glass, I ___ it.

7. The number before seven is ___.

8. To choose is to ___.

9. Tomorrow I ___ play.

10. Jack and Jill went up the ___.

11. I learned how to do a magic ___.

12. Long ago in England, the word hīdan meant "to cover over." If the word had not changed, today you'd be playing hīdan-and-seek! The mystery word comes from hīdan. It means "kept out of sight." Can you guess the word? ___

37

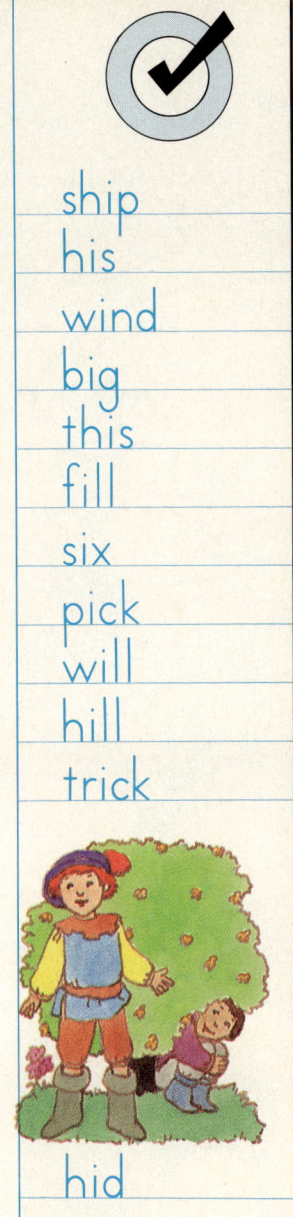

ship
his
wind
big
this
fill
six
pick
will
hill
trick

hid

Objectives

- To write spelling words in response to clues: definitions, synonyms, rhyme, and context.
- To develop the critical thinking skills of analyzing and comparing.
- To understand that word meanings and spellings often change over time.

Spelling Strategy

Some students may misspell trick and pick as trik and pik. Explain that a final /k/ sound in short, one-syllable words is sometimes spelled ck. Students may find it helpful to write trick and pick, underlining the final ck. Some students might be encouraged to find other words with the same spelling for the final /k/ sound.

Preparation The clues on this page are like crossword puzzle clues. Explain to students that the response to each clue is a spelling word. Use the following examples to illustrate the types of clues used:

Definition   A big boat is a *(ship)*.
Synonym   Another word for large is *(big)*.
Rhyme   A word that sounds like kiss and miss is *(this)*.
Context   I flew my kite in the *(wind)*.

The final clue explains how the spelling and meaning of the word hid changed over time.

The Page Have students complete page 37 using the words on page 36. When students have finished, have them read each clue and spell the answer aloud. Check each response twice: once for the correct answer and a second time for spelling accuracy.

Follow-Up Guide students in using the **Checkpoint Study Plan** on page 224 to take a self-test. Have them use the plan for independent study.

Objectives

- To write words with /ĭ/ in continuous text.
- To use the spelling words as rhyming words.
- To write each spelling word once.
- To integrate reading with spelling.

Note

Some of the spelling words will be used twice on these two pages.

Fill in the blanks with spelling words.

The Surprise on the Hill

Rick and his friend Anna raced to the top of the _____hill_____ . Anna got there first. She looked around. Suddenly she yelled, "Rick, hurry! You won't believe _____this_____ . A spaceship is up here."

Rick ran up to join _____his_____ friend. "Wow," he said. "Have you ever seen anything that _____big_____ before?"

The strange spaceship was very bright. In the sun it shone silver and gold. The children saw _____six_____ large jet engines on one side. The engines started up. A very strong blast of _____wind_____ struck the children. They could hardly stand up. All of a sudden, with a large s-w-o-o-s-h, the _____ship_____ took off. It rose straight up into the air. Then it was gone.

The boy and girl walked quietly back down the hill.

Then Anna said, "Did we really see that?"

"Yes," said Rick. "But who will ever believe us?"

38

Preparation Have students turn to pages 38 and 39. Call their attention to the word list. Have the students say the words. Then explain that each spelling word belongs in at least one of the blanks on pages 38 and 39. Tell students that you will read the story aloud, supplying the missing words. Then they will write the missing spelling words as they complete the story on their own. They will then complete the rhymes on page 39.

Write the title "The Surprise on the Hill" on the board and have a student read it. Tell your students that the story is about a very unusual adventure. Have them look at the picture and guess what the adventure involves.

The Pages Read the story aloud, supplying the missing spelling words as the students follow along in their texts. When you have finished, you may wish to discuss the story with the class. Ask the students whether they believe Anna's and Rick's story. Ask them to explain their reasons. *(Answers will vary.)*

Then ask students to complete the story by writing the correct spelling word for each blank. When everyone has finished, have a student read the story aloud, pausing before each blank. The other students will say the missing spelling word at the appropriate time. Have volunteers spell the answers on the board so students may check their work.

Fill in the blanks with words from the list.

1. Sid is a spaceman who takes a trip.

    A word that rhymes with <u>Sid</u> is ___hid___.

    A word that rhymes with <u>trip</u> is ___ship___.

2. Rick is an Earthling who fell down a hill.

    Words that rhyme with <u>Rick</u> are

    ___pick___ and ___trick___.

    Words that rhyme with <u>hill</u> are ___will___

    and ___fill___.

3. Mizz is a Martian who's in a fix.

    A word that rhymes with <u>Mizz</u> is ___his___.

    A word that rhymes with <u>fix</u> is ___six___.

will
big
ship
six
wind
hid
pick
trick
his
this
hill
fill

39

Enrichment

If you want to use the blackline activity masters for enrichment and additional practice, assign Lesson 7 activities at this time.

Maintenance and Review

OBJECTIVE

● To review words with /ĕ/ spelled: <u>e</u>, <u>a</u>.

ACTIVITIES

If you want to use the blackline activity masters for maintenance and review, assign Lesson 5 activities at this time.

You can also use the activities below to review Lesson 5 with students:

Write the following word list on the board and have students copy it. Then write the Lesson 5 word list on the board. Have students write a rhyming word (or words) from Lesson 5 for each word they have copied. Finally, have a volunteer write the answers on the board and check students' responses. (Answers are in parentheses.)

1.	tell	(bell, well)
2.	beg	(egg)
3.	test	(rest, best)
4.	end	(send)
5.	mess	(dress)

You may choose one of the rhyming pairs above to use to write a couplet or poem as a whole class activity. You might suggest a first line and have volunteers supply the second line. For example:

Even though I have a test
(I think I'll take a little <u>rest</u>.)

Next, direct students' attention to page 39. Have them look at the pictures. Then have them take turns reading the sentences aloud and suggesting rhyming words from the word list for each blank. Have them write the correct word. Then have volunteers put the answers on the board. When both pages have been completed, check students' responses for the accurate spelling of each answer.

Follow-Up Have students use each of the spelling words they missed in an original sentence.

As an additional follow-up activity, have the students look at the three illustrations on page 39 and write one or two sentences about each picture. They should use at least one spelling word in each sentence.

Objectives

- To relate spelling to another language skill.
- To use a question mark at the end of a question.
- To write spelling words in the context of sentences.
- To use the **Spelling Dictionary**.
- To check handwriting for correct letter formation.

---

a b c d e f g h i j k l m
n o p q r s t u v w x y z

Question Marks

Use a question mark (?) at the end of a question.

What is the biggest animal in the world**?**   Where is it found**?**

Write some question marks. **? ? ? ?**

Choose the right spelling word for each of these questions. Then write the question. Remember to end with a question mark.

1. How   (big / beg)   is the blue whale

How big is the blue whale?

2. What does   (this / there)   animal eat

What does this animal eat?

3. Can you see   (him / his)   tail

Can you see his tail?

4. Can you teach him a   (trick / track)

Can you teach him a trick?

5. (Well / Will)   a whale talk

Will a whale talk?

6. Look on page 222 in the Dictionary for the name of this animal.

It is a   whale

40

Preparation   Write these questions on the board, omitting the question mark:

Who saw a surprise on top of the hill   What did they see

Read the questions and ask what is wrong. *(no punctuation at the end)* Explain that a sentence that asks a question must end with a question mark. Ask a volunteer to correct the punctuation at the board.
   Now put these "answers" on the board:

They saw a giant spaceship   Rick and Anna saw it

Ask volunteers to read each sentence aloud and to correct the punctuation. *(Each sentence needs a period.)* Have a volunteer read each question above (with voice inflection) and answer it with the correct sentence.

The Page   Do the activities on page 40 with the students. Be sure that they are careful about their handwriting. Remind students always to dot a lower-case i.

Follow-Up   Ask the students to write their own questions using these words: **hid, ship, six, pick, hill, fill, wind**. The questions may be read aloud in class for volunteers to answer.

40

WORDS AT WORK

Challenge Yourself

admit   **blizzard**   **glimpse**

What do you think each underlined Challenge Word means? Check your Spelling Dictionary to see if you are right. Then write sentences. Show that you understand the meaning of each Challenge Word.

1. We got a glimpse of the baby deer. Then it was gone.

2. She must admit that she left the door open.

3. School was closed because of the blizzard.

Write to the Point

Rich asked, "But who will ever believe us?" Have you ever had trouble getting someone to believe you? Write several sentences telling what you said. Use spelling words from this lesson in your sentences.

Challenge Use one or more of the Challenge Words in your sentences.

Proofreading

Use the marks to show the mistakes in the sentences below. Write the four misspelled words correctly in the blanks.

⬭	word is misspelled
⊙	period is missing
≡	letter should be capitalized

1. This story is not a (trik) ⊙

2. a spaceship landed on the (hil.)
   ≡

3. A spaceman (hidd) in the ship.

4. (Hiz) suit had six silver snaps.

1. _____ trick
2. _____ hill
3. _____ hid
4. _____ His

41

Objectives

- To extend the vowel spelling presented in Lesson 7 to the Challenge Words.
- To use context and the **Spelling Dictionary** to enlarge students' vocabulary.
- To apply the vowel spelling presented in Lesson 7 in a writing activity.
- To practice proofreading for spelling, punctuation, and capitalization.

Dictation Sentences

1. This is his class.
2. The six children hid next to the tree.
3. Can I sit at the big desk?
4. I like to play with my ship in the tub.
5. We can see the wind in the trees.
6. Pick two girls to play this game.
7. I can do a trick with an egg and a hat.
8. Go up the hill on Fox Street to get to the zoo.
9. Joe will fill the box with toys.

Challenge Yourself Answers

Possible definitions:

1. a quick look
2. to say that something is true
3. large snowstorm

Students' sentences will vary.

Test Review this way to spell /ĭ/: i as in will. Test words with /ĭ/. Use one of these testing methods: (1) Say the word; read the sample sentence from page 36; say the word; have students write the word. (2) Read each dictation sentence above; have students write the sentence. Correct the test with students.

Challenge Yourself The optional Challenge Words may be assigned to the entire class or limited to those students who do well on the test. Have students note the vowel spelling in the Challenge Words. You may wish to have students work in pairs. Responses to this activity should be completed on separate paper. Answers to the questions are provided above.

Write to the Point Have students recall the selection "The Surprise on the Hill" on pages 38 and 39; then assign the sentences. Remind students to tell exactly what it was that someone wouldn't believe. This activity should be completed on separate paper.

Proofreading The proofreading practice includes misspellings of words from this lesson as well as a capitalization error and a punctuation error.

LESSON 8

Objectives

- To hear and say words with /ĭ/.
- To write words with /ĭ/ with attention to letter sequence and sound/symbol relationships.
- To write each spelling word once.
- To recognize that /ĭ/ may be spelled i.

Sample Sentences

1. Can you catch that slippery fish?
2. Close your eyes and make a wish.
3. Many flowers bloom in the spring.
4. I can bring some fruit to eat.
5. She likes spaghetti sauce with meat.
6. Can you swim across the lake?
7. My sister Sue loves carrot cake.
8. The princess wears a magic ring.
9. It's so foggy, I can't see a thing.
10. I think that robin likes to sing.
11. We live on a quiet street.
12. The sun can give us lots of heat.

Note

The sample sentences may be used for pretesting and post-testing.

Lesson 8 — Words with /ĭ/

Say these words. Listen for /ĭ/ in each one.

fish
wish
spring
bring
with
swim
sister
ring
thing
think
live
give

1. Write the words that end like wing.

bring   ring
spring   thing

2. Which words end with the sound /sh/?

fish   wish

3. th + ink = think

wi + th = with

4. Which word begins with s and has s in the middle?

sister

5. What words have i and e, but you only hear /ĭ/?

live   give

6. Which word begins and ends like swam?

swim

Can you hear an e in give or live?

No. You just have to remember them.

42

Preparation   Write /ĭ/ on the chalkboard and have students repeat the sound /ĭ/ as in pit. Say these word pairs. If a word contains /ĭ/, ask the students to raise their pencils in the air.

think – thank   wash – wish   five – give   bring – brought

Have students look at the spelling words on page 42. Say each word aloud. Then have students say and spell each word.

Note Spelling Bee's reminder in the cartoon that the words give and live contain the silent letter e. Ask the students to spell these words aloud, pronouncing the first three sounds distinctly and not voicing the silent e at the end.

Read the sample sentences. Have the students point to the spelling word as you read each sentence.

The Page   Do the activities with the students. Then have volunteers write their answers on the board or spell them aloud for immediate reinforcement of the correct spelling.

Follow-Up   Ask the students how they plan to study the spelling words. Suggest these methods: Students may write a word three times and then spell it without looking, or they may spell the words aloud to a partner.

Checkpoint

Write a spelling word for each clue.
Then use the Checkpoint Study Plan on page 224.

1. An animal with fins and gills is a ___.

2. An elephant is an animal ___ a trunk.

3. If it's not a person or a place, it's a ___.

4. The opposite of take is ___.

5. When I visit you, may I ___ my dog?

6. When you use your brain, you ___.

7. We go to the beach to ___.

8. To hope for something is to ___.

9. I have a brother and a ___.

10. The season after winter is ___.

11. A band on your finger is a ___.

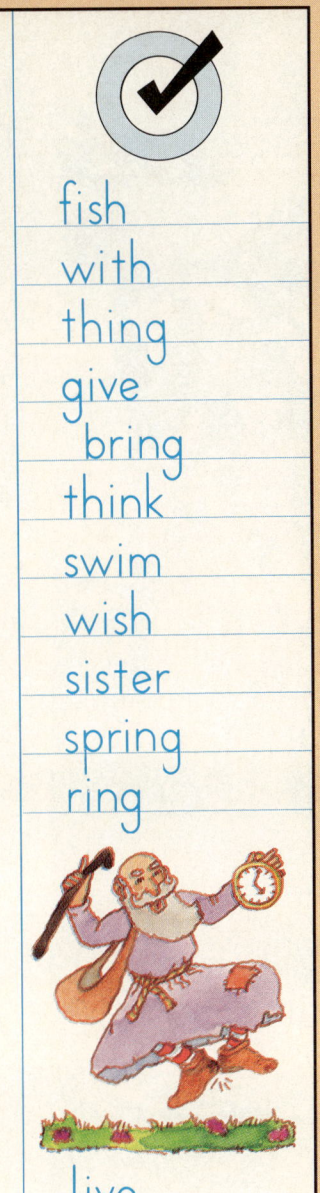

fish
with
thing
give
bring
think
swim
wish
sister
spring
ring

live

12. In England long ago, there was a word <u>lifian</u> that meant "to keep going." The mystery word comes from <u>lifian</u>. It means "to be alive." Can you guess what it is? ___

43

Objectives

- To write spelling words in response to clues: definitions, antonyms, and context.

- To develop the critical thinking skills of sequencing and contrasting.

- To understand that the meaning and spelling of words in the English language often change over time.

Spelling Strategy

Some students may spell <u>give</u> and <u>live</u> as <u>giv</u> and <u>liv</u> because the i_e spelling is usually associated with the /ī/ sound. Students having difficulty may benefit from writing these words and circling the <u>i</u> and the <u>e</u>.

Preparation The clues on this page are like crossword puzzle clues. Explain to students that the response to each clue is a spelling word. Use the following examples to illustrate the types of clues used:

Definition	To hope for something is to *(wish)*.
Antonym	The opposite of take is *(give)*.
Context	I have a brother and a *(sister)*.

The final clue explains how the meaning and spelling of the word <u>live</u> have changed over time.

The Page Have students complete page 43 using the words on page 42. When the students have finished, have them read each clue and spell the answer aloud. Check each response twice: once for the correct answer and a second time for spelling accuracy.

Follow-Up Guide students in using the **Checkpoint Study Plan** on page 224 to take a self-test. Have them use the plan for independent study.

Objectives

- To write words with /i/ in continuous text.
- To identify a nonsense word in a sentence and replace it with a spelling word.
- To write each spelling word once.
- To integrate reading with spelling.

Fill in the blanks with spelling words.

The Magic Fish

It was a warm _____spring_____ day. Mellie and

her _____sister_____ Clara went fishing.

They wanted to catch a _____fish_____ for supper.

"Oh, dear! We forgot to _____bring_____

the worms!" cried Mellie.

Clara said, "Never mind. Fish like things that shine. I

_____think_____ they will like my gold ring."

They put the ring on the fishing line and tossed it into

the river. In a flash there was a fish on their line! They

had caught a beautiful purple fish _____with_____ a

golden tail.

"Please," said the fish. "Let me live. If you do let me

_____live_____, I will _____give_____ you each

a wish. I promise!"

"Well," said Clara. "I wish I had my ring back."

"And I _____wish_____ we had some fish,"

said Mellie.

44

Note

Some of the spelling words will be used twice on these two pages.

Preparation   Ask the students to turn to pages 44 and 45. Call attention to the pictures and the word list. Have the students say the words. Then explain that each spelling word belongs in at least one of the blanks on pages 44 and 45.

Write the title "The Magic Fish" on the board and have a student read it. Ask your students how they go about getting something they want very badly. Do they ask for it? Do they work for it? Do they wish for it? Tell the class that they are going to read a story about two girls who want a fish for dinner.

The Pages   Read the story, supplying the missing spelling words as the students follow along in their texts. When you have finished reading, you may wish to discuss the story. Ask the class if they think the magic fish was wise. Why? *(Although it granted both wishes, it also required the girls to do some work; all things do not come easlly!)*

Now have students reread the story to themselves and complete it by writing the correct spelling word for each blank. When they have finished, ask a student to read the story aloud, pausing before each blank. Have the other students say the missing spelling word at the appropriate time. Have volunteers write the answers on the board.

"Done!" said the beautiful fish. And it began to

_____ swim _____ away.

When Clara looked down at her finger, she saw her

gold _____ ring _____.

Then Mellie saw one _____ thing _____ that was

not there before. It was a can of worms! "I guess we

have to work for the second wish," she sighed.

Each of these sentences has one nonsense word in it. Find the nonsense word. Change it to a spelling word that does make sense.

1. The framble was purple with a golden tail.

   _____ fish _____

2. The girls used a gold rumq for bait.

   _____ ring _____

3. The fish said it would give a wimble.

   _____ wish _____

4. The fish wanted the girls to let it lorq.

   _____ live _____

5. Clara was Mellie's sitzel.

   _____ sister _____

45

fish
wish
spring
bring
with
swim
sister
ring
thing
think
give
live

Maintenance and Review

OBJECTIVE
- To review words with /i/ spelled i.

ACTIVITIES
If you want to use the blackline activity masters for maintenance and review, assign Lesson 7 activities at this time.

You can also use the activity below to review Lesson 7 with students:

Write these sentence fragments on the board (without underlining any words). Have students copy and complete each sentence fragment. Then ask them to underline the spelling word (or words) in each completed sentence.

1. There is a big ship
2. It will take us to
3. This ship has six
4. A big wind came
5. As a trick, I hid

Direct students' attention to page 45 and read the sentences aloud with them. Tell students to find the spelling word to replace the nonsense word in each sentence. (Hint: The spelling word starts with the same letter as the nonsense word.) Allow time for the students to write the answers. Then have volunteers write the words on the board so students may check their own work. Check both of these pages for correct word choice and for the accurate spelling of each answer.

Follow-Up Have students use each of the spelling words they missed in an original sentence.

As an additional follow-up activity, you may wish to divide the class into groups of four so they may act out the story of "The Magic Fish." Assign the roles of the narrator, Mellie, Clara, and the fish in each group. As they read their lines, the actors should spell the spelling words that belong in the blanks.

Objectives

- To relate spelling words to a dictionary skill.
- To write spelling words in alphabetical order.
- To alphabetize by the first and second letters in a word.
- To use the **Spelling Dictionary**.
- To check handwriting for correct letter formation.

a b c d e f g h i j k l m
n o p q r s t u v w x y z

Alphabetical Order

Write these words in alphabetical order. Then look in the Spelling Dictionary and find each word. Write the number of its Dictionary page beside the word.

give ring live with

Word	Dictionary page
1. give	207
2. live	211
3. ring	216
4. with	223

When two words begin with the same letter, look at the second letter to put the words in alphabetical order. **bell big** The letter e comes before the letter i, so b<u>e</u>ll comes before b<u>i</u>g in the dictionary.

5. Which of these two words would come first in a dictionary, <u>swim</u> or <u>sister</u>?

sister

Check your answer in the Spelling Dictionary.

46

Preparation Write these words on the board: **wish sister think** Ask a student to put them in alphabetical order. *(sister, think, wish)*

Then write these words on the board: **sister swim said** Explain that when the first letter is the same in a group of words, the students have to look at the second letter to alphabetize the words. Have a student underline the second letter in each word. Have another student alphabetize the words. *(said, sister, swim)*

Then ask where in the **Spelling Dictionary** the words <u>sister</u>, <u>swim</u>, and <u>said</u> will be found. *(under the letter s)* Which of the three words will come first? (<u>said</u>, *because words in the dictionary are arranged in alphabetical order*) Have students locate all three words in the Spelling Dictionary and write the page number for each. *(said, page 216; sister, page 217; swim, page 219)*

The Page Do page 46 with the students. Tell the students to be careful when they form their letters. Make sure they form the letter <u>v</u> in <u>give</u> and <u>live</u> with a sharp point. Have volunteers write the answers on the chalkboard.

Follow-Up Have students alphabetize the words <u>spring</u>, <u>bring</u>, <u>thing</u>, <u>wish</u>, <u>think</u>, and <u>fish</u>, look them up in the **Spelling Dictionary**, and write the page number for each. *(bring, page 200; fish, page 205; spring, page 218; thing, page 220; think, page 220; wish, page 223)*

46

WORDS AT WORK

Challenge Yourself

bitter	guilt	liberty

What do you think each underlined Challenge Word means? Check your Spelling Dictionary to see if you are right. Then write sentences. Show that you understand the meaning of each Challenge Word.

1. This coffee tastes <u>bitter</u>.
2. The police proved his <u>guilt</u>.
3. You should give the snake its <u>liberty</u> after you take it to Show and Tell.

Write to the Point

The magic fish gave Clara and Mellie one wish each. Write two or three sentences telling what your wish would be. Use spelling words from this lesson in your sentences.

Challenge Use one or more of the Challenge Words in your sentences.

Proofreading

Use the marks to show the mistakes in the sentences below. Write the four misspelled words correctly in the blanks.

⬭	word is misspelled
⊙	period is missing
≡	letter should be capitalized

1. They will (breng) some fish home⊙
2. It is easy to catch fish (wit) worms.
3. their (sistar) will cook them.
4. Everyone will (whish) for more.

1. _____ bring _____
2. _____ with _____
3. _____ sister _____
4. _____ wish _____

47

Objectives

- To extend the vowel spellings in Lesson 8 to the Challenge Words.
- To use context and the **Spelling Dictionary** to enlarge students' vocabulary.
- To apply the vowel spellings in Lesson 8 in a writing activity.
- To practice proofreading for spelling, punctuation, and capitalization.

Dictation Sentences

1. I <u>think</u> my big <u>sister</u> is fun.
2. I <u>will</u> <u>wish</u> for a new pet.
3. Can <u>we</u> <u>swim</u> with the <u>fish</u>?
4. Olga and <u>Ping</u> <u>live</u> over <u>that</u> hill.
5. <u>Give</u> me that red dress.
6. The school bell will <u>ring</u> at three.
7. Mom can <u>bring</u> the food.
8. In the <u>spring</u> it is not cold.
9. What is that <u>thing</u> in my shoe?

Challenge Yourself Answers

Possible definitions:

1. sharp and unpleasant
2. knowing that you have done something wrong
3. freedom

Students' sentences will vary.

Test Review these two ways to spell /ĭ/: i as in <u>fish</u>; i_e as in <u>live</u>. Test words with /ĭ/. Use one of these testing methods: (1) Say the word; read the sample sentence from page 42; say the word; have students write the word. (2) Read each dictation sentence above; have students write the sentence. Correct the test with students.

Challenge Yourself The optional Challenge Words may be assigned to the entire class or limited to those students who do well on the test. Have students note the vowel spellings in the Challenge Words, especially the following new spelling: ui, as in <u>guilt</u>. Responses to this activity should be completed on separate paper. Answers to the questions are provided above.

Write to the Point Have students recall the selection "The Magic Fish" on pages 44 and 45; then assign the sentences. This activity should be completed on separate paper.

Proofreading The proofreading practice includes misspellings of words from this lesson as well as a capitalization error and a punctuation error.

LESSON 9

Objectives

- To hear and say words with /ŏ/.
- To write words with /ŏ/ with attention to letter sequence and sound/symbol relationships.
- To write each spelling word once.
- To recognize that /ŏ/ may be spelled o and a.

Sample Sentences

1. Remember, always dot your i's.
2. He got a job delivering pies.
3. His job is quite an easy one.
4. Some people jog, but I like to run.
5. I sometimes jump on waves for fun.
6. We hop and run away from waves.
7. It's often hot on summer days.
8. Your milkshake has cherries on top.
9. Be careful not to spill a drop.
10. Joe is the mail carrier on our block.
11. Can you tell me what is wrong?
12. That TV show was much too long!

Note

Words are grouped according to spellings of /ŏ/:

o

a

The sample sentences may be used for pretesting and post-testing.

Lesson 9 Words with /ŏ/

Say these words. Listen for /ŏ/ in each one.

dot
got
job
jog
on
hop
hot
top
not
block

what
was

1. Write the word that begins with /ŏ/.

on

2. Write the words that begin with the sound /j/.

job   jog

3. Write the words that end like mop.

hop   top

block

4. bl + ock = block

5. Write the words that end with ot.

dot   got

hot   not

6. What words have the sound /ŏ/ but no letter o?

what   was

Bee! Why are you wearing that top hat?

Well, a hat helps me to remember how to spell the word what.

48

Preparation Write /ŏ/ on the chalkboard and have students repeat the sound /ŏ/ as in pot. Say these word pairs. When they hear the /ŏ/ sound, the students should put their hands on top of their heads.

got – get   tap – top   hip – hop   what – wet

Read the words on page 48 as students follow along in their texts. Then have students say and spell each word.

Note Spelling Bee's mnemonic suggestion in the cartoon to remember to write the word hat inside the word what. Point out to the students that in the first ten words, the sound /ŏ/ is spelled with the letter o. Then call attention to the words what and was. Ask students if they hear the sound /ŏ/ in what and was. (yes) Do they see the letter o? (no) Which letter spells /ŏ/ in what and was? (the letter a) (See Note.)

Read the sample sentences as students point to the spelling words in their books.

The Page Do page 48 together. Then have volunteers write the answers on the board. Help students check their work.

Follow-Up Make study plans for the week. The students may practice their words in small groups by spelling them aloud.

Checkpoint

Write a spelling word for each clue. Then use the Checkpoint Study Plan on page 224.

1. The work you do is your ___.

2. When you move like a bunny, you ___.

3. When you run slowly, you ___.

4. A tiny spot is a ___.

5. Something that is old is ___ new.

6. I put my books ___ the desk.

7. The campfire was ___.

8. Tell me what you ___ at the store.

9. My toy box looks like a big red ___.

10. I don't know ___ to do.

11. I asked Dad where he ___ going.

12. This mystery word comes from an old word, topp. Topp meant "highest point." The word has not changed very much. Today, it still means the highest point of something, such as a ladder. Write the word. ___

49

job
hop
jog
dot
not
on
hot
got
block
what
was

top

Objectives

- To write spelling words in response to clues: definitions and context.
- To develop the critical thinking skills of making inferences and comparing.
- To learn that the spelling of a word can change over time while the meaning remains the same.

Spelling Strategy

The word <u>was</u> is frequently misspelled <u>wuz</u> because the vowel may be pronounced /ŏ/ or /ŭ/, and the final <u>s</u> is pronounced /z/. Students needing extra practice with this word might practice writing it in large, colorful letters as a memory aid.

Preparation The clues on this page are like crossword puzzle clues. Explain to students that the response to each clue is a spelling word. Use the following examples to illustrate the types of clues used:

    Definition   The work you do is your *(job).*
    Context   I put my books *(on)* the desk.

The final clue explains how the spelling of the word <u>top</u> has changed over time.

The Page Have students complete page 49 using the words on page 48. When students have finished, have them read each clue and spell the answer aloud. Check each response twice: once for the correct answer and a second time for spelling accuracy.

Follow-Up Guide students in using the **Checkpoint Study Plan** on page 224 to take a self-test. Have them use the plan for independent study.

Objectives

- To write words with /ŏ/ in continuous text and related sentences.
- To write each spelling word once.
- To integrate reading with spelling.

Fill in the blanks with spelling words.

HOT SNEAKS

Billy has a job that is lots of fun. His ___job___ is different from most people's work. Billy works for a company named HOT SNEAKS. Billy ___got___ his job because he is good at sports. He likes to run, jump, _jog / hop_, and _hop / jog_. Do you know what Billy gets paid for doing? He just wears HOT SNEAKS sneakers! First, he puts ___on___ a new pair of sneakers. Then he wears them everywhere. He runs and hops with them. He runs at top speed and hops at ___top___ speed. He goes block after ___block___.

Do you know why Billy gets paid for wearing sneakers? To find out, unscramble the sentence below.

how long they last . Billy tests sneakers to see

___Billy tests sneakers to see how long they last.___

50

Preparation

Ask your class to turn to pages 50 and 51. Call attention to the pictures and the word list. Read the words and have the students repeat them. Then explain that each spelling word belongs in one of the blanks on pages 50 and 51.

Write the title "Hot Sneaks" on the board. Ask students what this story might be about.

The Pages

Read the story aloud, supplying the missing spelling words as the students follow along in their texts. Ask students to unscramble the sentence at the bottom of the page to find out why Hot Sneaks pays Billy to wear their sneakers.

Have students complete the story by writing the correct spelling word for each blank. Call on a volunteer to read the complete story aloud. Then have the class spell each answer aloud as you write it on the board.

Next look at the pictures and the questions on page 51. Read the questions with the group and have students write the correct spelling word to complete each answer. Then have volunteers read each answer aloud, note the spelling word, and spell it. Write the answers on the board so that the students may check their work. Be sure to correct students' responses for the accurate spelling of each answer.

Fill in the blanks with spelling words.

1. What was Billy's job?

   His job ___was___ to test sneakers.

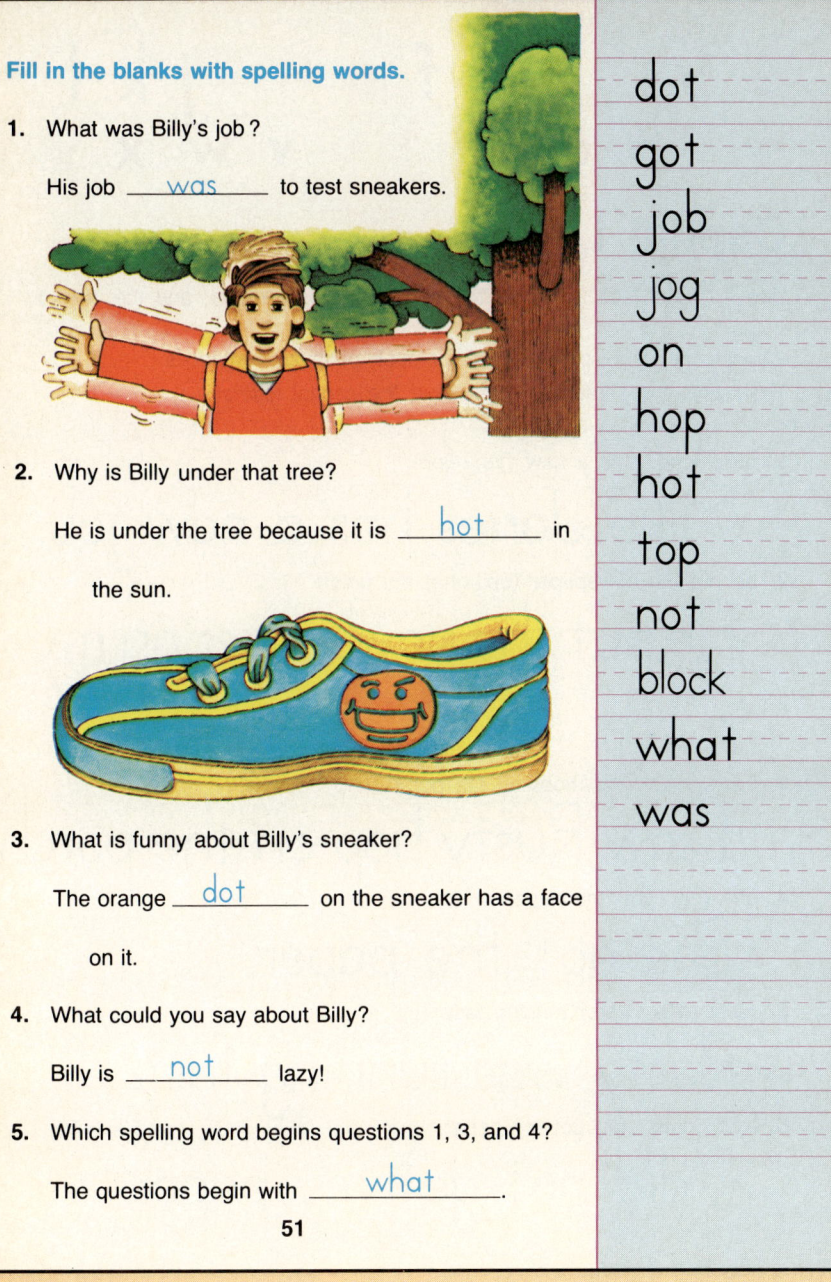

2. Why is Billy under that tree?

   He is under the tree because it is ___hot___ in

   the sun.

3. What is funny about Billy's sneaker?

   The orange ___dot___ on the sneaker has a face

   on it.

4. What could you say about Billy?

   Billy is ___not___ lazy!

5. Which spelling word begins questions 1, 3, and 4?

   The questions begin with ___what___.

51

dot

got

job

jog

on

hop

hot

top

not

block

what

was

Enrichment

If you want to use the blackline activity masters for enrichment and additional practice, assign Lesson 9 activities at this time.

Maintenance and Review

OBJECTIVE

● To review words with /ĭ/ spelled i.

ACTIVITIES

If you want to use the blackline activity masters for maintenance and review, assign Lesson 8 activities at this time.

You can also use the activity below to review Lesson 8 with students:

Write the following word pairs on the board. Have the students write a sentence for each pair. Then ask volunteers to read their sentences. Have other students identify the spelling words in the sentences and spell them aloud.

  give – ring
  bring – with
  fish – swim
  think – sister
  wish – live
  spring – thing

Follow-Up Have students use each of the spelling words they missed in an original sentence.

As an additional follow-up activity, have the students draw a mural of the different types of sneakers.

Objectives

- To relate spelling to another language skill.
- To capitalize the names of people, pets, and the word I.
- To write spelling words in the context of sentences.
- To check handwriting for correct letter formation.

a b c d e f g h i j k l m
n o p q r s t u v w x y z

Capital Letters

Use a capital letter to begin the names of people, pets, and the word I.

Choose the right spelling word for each of these sentences.
Then write the sentence. Remember the capital letters!

1. mike jones has a new (job / gob).

Mike Jones has a new job.

2. he put the newspaper (on / one) my porch.

He put the newspaper on my porch.

3. i saw rusty (hip / hop) on the porch.

I saw Rusty hop on the porch.

4. she (get / got) the paper.

She got the paper.

5. rusty (was / were) running fast.

Rusty was running fast.

6. i did (note / not) get my paper.

I did not get my paper.

52

Preparation Write these sentences on the board and read them aloud:

My dog patches is ten years old.   Our cat is called peanuts.

Explain that names always begin with a capital letter. Direct students' attention to the first sentence. Ask which word should be capitalized, dog or patches. (Patches, because it is the dog's name.) Have a student capitalize the p in Patches. Continue this drill. Then write the following on the board:

Why do i like to cook?   i like to eat!

Ask students what is wrong with these sentences. Have volunteers correct the capitalization errors, after explaining the capitalization of the word I.

The Page As you do this page together, remind students of the relative sizes of uppercase and lowercase letters. Review the answers with your class.

Follow-Up Have students write these sentences, circling spelling words (was, got) and filling in names of people they know. (Remind them to capitalize the names!)

_____ was my teacher last year.
_____ got a new pair of sneakers.

WORDS AT WORK

Challenge Yourself

lobster   **adopt**   **monster**

Use your Spelling Dictionary to answer these questions. Then write sentences. Show that you understand the meaning of each Challenge Word.

1. Does a <u>lobster</u> wear sneakers on its feet?

2. Would a grownup <u>adopt</u> another grownup?

3. Do scary movies sometimes have a <u>monster</u> in them?

Write to the Point

Billy has a job that is fun. What job do you think might be fun? Write a few sentences telling about a job you would like to have. Use spelling words from this lesson in your sentences.

Challenge Use one or more of the Challenge Words in your sentences.

Proofreading

Use the marks to show the mistakes in the sentences below. Write the four misspelled words correctly in the blanks.

⬭	word is misspelled
⊙	period is missing
≡	letter should be capitalized

1. Billy liked to jog down our ⬭blok⬭⊙

2. It ⬭waz⬭ a very hot job for him⊙

3. ≡he got to the ⬭topp⬭ of a hill.

4. Can you guess ⬭whut⬭ he saw there?

1. _____ block

2. _____ was

3. _____ top

4. _____ what

53

Objectives

- To extend the vowel spellings presented in Lesson 9 to the Challenge Words.

- To use context and the **Spelling Dictionary** to enlarge students' vocabulary.

- To apply the vowel spellings presented in Lesson 9 in a writing activity.

- To practice proofreading for spelling, punctuation, and capitalization.

Dictation Sentences

1. She <u>got</u> a <u>job</u> at my school.
2. Did you <u>dot</u> the i in big?
3. I will <u>jog</u> up the hill.
4. Jamal can <u>hop</u> very fast.
5. This is a <u>hot</u> day.
6. The box is <u>on top</u> of my desk.
7. My sister is <u>not</u> home.
8. <u>What</u> is the name of her cat?
9. It <u>was</u> time for school.
10. I <u>play</u> with the children on my <u>block</u>.

Challenge Yourself Answers

1. no
2. no
3. yes

Students' sentences will vary.

Test Review these two ways to spell /ŏ/: o as in <u>dot</u>; a as in <u>what</u>. Test words with /ŏ/. Use one of these testing methods: (1) Say the word; read the sample sentence from page 48; say the word; have students write the word. (2) Read each dictation sentence above; have students write the sentence. Correct the test with students.

Challenge Yourself The optional Challenge Words may be assigned to the entire class or limited to those students who do well on the test. Have students note the vowel spelling in the Challenge Words. You may wish to have students work in pairs. Responses to this activity should be completed on separate paper. Answers to the questions are provided above.

Write to the Point Have students recall the selection "Hot Sneaks" on pages 50 and 51; then assign the sentences. Encourage students to think of things they do well or things they enjoy doing before they begin writing. This activity should be completed on separate paper.

Proofreading The proofreading practice includes misspellings of words from this lesson as well as a capitalization error and a punctuation error.

LESSON 10

Objectives

- To hear and say words with /ŏ/.
- To write words with /ŏ/ with attention to letter sequence and sound/symbol relationships.
- To write each spelling word once.
- To recognize that /ŏ/ may be spelled o and a.

Sample Sentences

1. I always sit on this <u>rock</u> near the shore.
2. We feed the <u>ox</u>, but it always wants more.
3. There's a <u>spot</u> of dirt on the window-pane.
4. Did you feel a <u>drop</u> of rain?
5. I have to <u>shop</u> for shoes and socks.
6. Will you <u>chop</u> the onions and peppers?
7. I keep my marbles in a <u>box</u>.
8. Let's sit by the <u>pond</u> and watch frogs hop.
9. A red light means that cars must <u>stop</u>.
10. Our grandfather <u>clock</u> chimes on the hour.
11. I <u>want</u> a red and a yellow flower.
12. Tom will <u>wash</u> the dishes.

Note

Words are grouped according to spellings of /ŏ/:

o

a

The sample sentences may be used for pretesting and post-testing.

Lesson 10 Words with /ŏ/

Say these words. Listen for /ŏ/ in each one.

rock

ox

spot

drop

shop

chop

box

pond

stop

clock

want

wash

1. Write the spelling words that end like <u>crop</u>.

drop   shop

chop   stop

2. What spelling words end like <u>dock</u>?

rock   clock

3. Write the words that end with <u>x</u> and the sound /ks/.

ox   box

4. sp + ot = ____ spot

p + ond = ____ pond

5. What words have the sound /ŏ/ but no letter <u>o</u>?

want   wash

Spi! The word <u>want</u> is spelled with an <u>a</u>: w<u>a</u>nt.

Thanks for dropping by.

54

Preparation
Write /ŏ/ on the chalkboard and have the students repeat the sound /ŏ/ as in <u>pot</u>. Say these word pairs. Ask the students to put both hands on top of their desks when they hear a word with /ŏ/.

rock – wreck   ship – <u>shop</u>   <u>clock</u> – click   <u>want</u> – went

Have students look at the spelling words on page 54. Say each word aloud. Then have the students say and spell each word.

Note the ending sound /ks/ spelled <u>x</u> in the words <u>ox</u> and <u>box</u>. Have students identify the words that contain the consonant digraphs <u>sh</u> and <u>ck</u>. (shop, rock, clock) Finally, point out that in the first ten words, the sound /ŏ/ is spelled with the letter <u>o</u>. Have the students look at the word <u>want</u> and look at the cartoon. Ask a volunteer to write <u>want</u> and <u>wash</u> on the chalkboard and to underline the letter that spells /ŏ/. (<u>a</u>) (See <u>Note</u>.)

Have students point to the spelling words as you read the sample sentences.

The Page
Do the activities with the students. Have volunteers spell the answers aloud for reinforcement as others write the words on the board.

Follow-Up
Have several students tell their study plans for the week. Suggest that students use a crayon to write the words in large letters. Then they can trace over the letters with their fingers as they spell each word aloud.

Checkpoint

Write a spelling word for each clue.
Then use the Checkpoint Study Plan on page 224.

1. When the light is red, cars ___.

2. To cut with an ax is to ___.

3. You can see the time on a ___.

4. You wish for something that you ___.

5. You use soap and water when you ___.

6. When you buy things in a store, you ___.

7. The cart was pulled by a big ___.

8. The dog was white with one brown ___.

9. A stone is a small ___.

10. A frog lives in a ___.

11. Don't let the glass ___.

12. This mystery word comes from a word that was the name of a tree with very hard wood. People used the wood from the tree to make something that was strong and could hold things. Can you guess what they made? Write the mystery word. ___

55

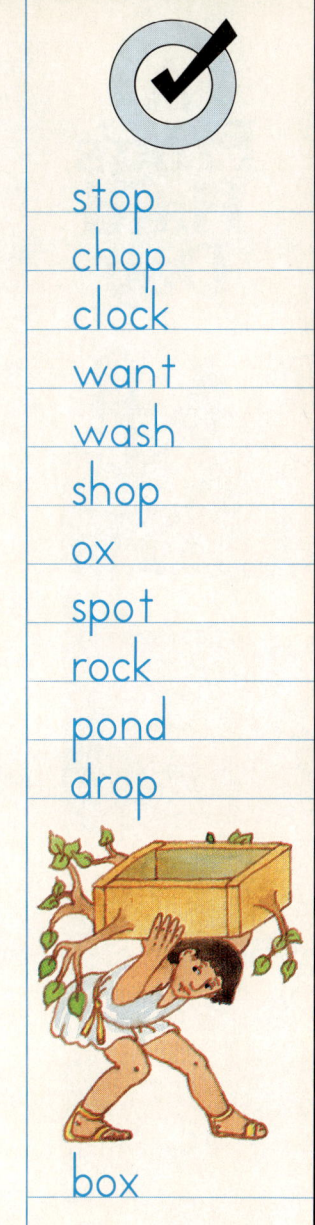

stop
chop
clock
want
wash
shop
ox
spot
rock
pond
drop

box

Objectives

- To write spelling words in response to clues: definitions and context.

- To develop the critical thinking skills of predicting outcomes and making inferences.

- To recognize that word meanings often change over time.

Spelling Strategy

When spelling a word that begins with a consonant cluster, some students may omit the second letter in the cluster or reverse the second and third letters. As a result stop, drop, and spot might be misspelled sop, dop, or sopt. It may help students having difficulty to pronounce the word slowly and sound out each consonant as they write the word several times.

Preparation The clues on this page are like crossword puzzle clues. Explain to students that the response to each clue is a spelling word. Use the following examples to illustrate the types of clues used:

Definition When you buy things in a store, you *(shop)*.
Context You can see the time on a *(clock)*.

The final clue explains how the word <u>box</u> came to have its current meaning.

The Page Have students complete page 55 using the words on page 54. When students have finished, have them read each clue and spell the answer aloud. Check each response twice: once for the correct answer and a second time for spelling accuracy.

Follow-Up Guide students in using the **Checkpoint Study Plan** on page 224 to take a self-test. Have them use the plan for independent study.

Objectives

- To write words with /ŏ/ in continuous text and related sentences.
- To write each spelling word at least once.
- To integrate reading with spelling.

Note

Some of the spelling words will be used twice on these two pages.

A Frog's Hard Day

Fill in the blanks with spelling words.

T. Green Frog was sitting on his favorite hard rock. He had been quietly sunning himself at the same ____spot____ for hours. His eyelids began to ____drop____. He was almost asleep when he heard a loud noise. Nearby, a large brown __ox__ was drinking water from the ____pond____. His soft dark eyes stared at T. Green's big yellow eyes.

"Don't ____stop____ sleeping," the ox said politely. "I didn't ____want____ to wake you up from your nap."

"I was not sleeping," T. Green replied slowly. "I was just thinking about moving from this rock to that warmer ____rock____ over there."

"I must be moving myself," said the ox. "I'm on my way to ____shop____ for food for dinner. I'm late, if that ____clock____ has the right time. Is there anything you need at the store?"

"Yes, please," said T. Green as he yawned. "A ____box____ of fresh flies and some suntan cream!"

56

Preparation   Have students turn to pages 56 and 57. Call their attention to the pictures and the word list. Have the students say the words. Then explain that each spelling word belongs in at least one of the blanks on pages 56 and 57. Some of the words will be used twice.

Then write the title "A Frog's Hard Day" on the board. Ask students what kinds of animals might live in and around a pond. *(frogs, worms, birds, cows, snakes, etc.)* Explain that this story describes a day in the life of a frog and his friend.

The Pages   Read the story aloud, supplying the missing spelling words as the children follow along in their texts. When you have finished reading, you may wish to discuss T. Green's way of life. Ask students what they think might be a hard day for a frog. *(Answers will vary.)*

Then have the students complete the story on their own by writing the correct spelling word for each blank. When they are finished, ask a volunteer to read the story aloud. Have others write the answers on the board so that students may check their own work.

Now read aloud the sentences on page 57, supplying the answers. Have students read the sentences independently and write the missing spelling words. Then ask volunteers to read the sentences aloud, saying the spelling word in each and spelling the word aloud. Write the answers on the board. Be sure to check students' responses for the accurate spelling of each answer.

Fill in the blanks with spelling words.

1. T. Green's flies come in a _____box_____.

2. The ox is careful not to _____drop_____ T. Green's groceries.

3. By the time the ox returned, the _____clock_____ said six o'clock.

4. Sometimes it is hard to _____shop_____ for groceries for someone else.

5. A farmyard is a good place for an _____ox_____ to live.

6. The ox will _____wash_____ his face before dinner.

7. Then he will _____chop_____ his food into small pieces.

57

rock
ox
spot
drop
shop
chop
box
pond
stop
clock
want
wash

Enrichment

If you want to use the blackline activity masters for enrichment and additional practice, assign Lesson 10 activities at this time.

Maintenance and Review

OBJECTIVE

• To review words with /ŏ/ spelled: o, a.

ACTIVITIES

If you want to use the blackline activity masters for maintenance and review, assign Lesson 9 activities at this time.

You can also use the activities below to review Lesson 9 with students:

Write the following words and riddles on the board. Read each riddle aloud. Have students copy the riddles and complete them. *(Answers are in parentheses.)*

| job | dot | hot | top | hop |

1. I'm not cold.
   I'm _(hot)_ .

2. I'm at the top of an i.
   I'm a _(dot)_ .

3. I'm usually done on one foot.
   I'm a _(hop)_ .

4. I'm the highest you can climb.
   I'm the _(top)_ .

5. I'm work.
   I'm not play.
   I'm a _(job)_ .

Remind students that the sound /ŏ/ can also be spelled with the letter a. Review the spelling of what and was. Have students write one sentence using both words.

Follow-Up Have students use each of the spelling words they missed in an original sentence.

As an additional follow-up activity, you may wish to divide the class into groups of three so that students may act out the story "A Frog's Hard Day." Assign the roles of narrator, T. Green Frog, and the ox. Have the actors pause and spell each spelling word aloud as they read through the story. Encourage them to adopt the characteristics and voice inflections of the characters they portray.

Objectives

- To relate spelling words to a dictionary skill.
- To read dictionary entries.
- To write words in alphabetical order.
- To use the **Spelling Dictionary**.
- To check handwriting for correct letter formation.

a b c d e f g h i j k l m
n o p q r s t u v w x y z

Dictionary

Look in a dictionary to find the meaning of a word.

ox /ŏks/—*plural* **oxen.** A male animal of the cattle family.
A strong **ox** *is a useful farm animal.*

The word **ox** is called an <u>entry</u> <u>word</u>. An entry in a dictionary shows the word, how to say the word, and its meaning.

Write the words in alphabetical order. Look in the Spelling Dictionary for the entry of each word. Finish the meaning for each word.

pond   clock   box

Word		Meaning
1. box		1. something used to hold things
2. clock		2. something that tells the time
3. pond		3. a small body of water

58

Preparation Write this word on the board and read it: rock
    Have students look up the word <u>rock</u> in the **Spelling Dictionary**. *(page 216)* Explain that each word listed in a dictionary is called an entry word. Review each part of the entry for <u>rock</u>. Have students point to the sound spelling, /rŏk/, and remind them that the letters within the brackets are speech sounds. Have them point to the plural, <u>rocks</u>. Explain that the plural form shows how to write a word to mean more than one. Then have a volunteer read the meanings and the sample sentences. The last part of the entry shows the word with the <u>ed</u> and <u>ing</u> endings: <u>rocked</u>, <u>rocking</u>.

The Page Do the activities on page 58 with the students. Be sure that students do not make a spelling mistake because of careless handwriting. This lesson offers practice in forming the letter <u>o</u>—a perfect circle, drawn around to the left and carefully closed at the top. After students have written the words and their meanings, have volunteers write the answers on the board. Help students correct their work.

Follow-Up Have the students write a sentence illustrating each of the three meanings they have written. Have them read their sentences aloud, note the spelling word in each, and spell the word aloud.

58

WORDS AT WORK

Challenge Yourself

profit	dodge	bonnet

Decide which Challenge Word fits each clue. Check your Spelling Dictionary to see if you were right. Then write sentences. Show that you understand the meaning of each Challenge Word.

1. This word means to move quickly.

2. It is the money that a store makes.

3. This kind of hat can be worn on a windy day.

Write to the Point

T. Green Frog needed some funny things from the store. Make your own shopping list. Write four or five things you need from the store. Put some funny things on your list, too. Use spelling words from this lesson in your list.

Challenge Use one or more of the Challenge Words in your list.

Proofreading

Use the marks to show the mistakes in the sentences below. Write the four misspelled words correctly in the blanks.

◯	word is misspelled
⊙	period is missing
≡	letter should be capitalized

1. Let's stop by the (pand.)

2. i see a box near that (rok.)

3. Did T. Green Frog (drap) it?

4. Only the brown (aux) knows ⊙

1. _____ pond

2. _____ rock

3. _____ drop

4. _____ ox

59

Objectives

- To extend the vowel spellings presented in Lesson 10 to the Challenge Words.

- To use clues and the **Spelling Dictionary** to enlarge students' vocabulary.

- To apply the vowel spellings presented in Lesson 10 in a writing activity.

- To practice proofreading for spelling, punctuation, and capitalization.

Dictation Sentences

1. I can sit on the <u>rock</u> in our <u>pond</u>.
2. The <u>ox</u> sat next to the goat.
3. Do <u>not</u> <u>drop</u> the <u>clock</u>.
4. They <u>want</u> blue <u>socks</u>.
5. We will help you <u>wash</u> the car.
6. Why did he <u>chop</u> that tree?
7. I think this bus will <u>stop</u> at her street.
8. What is in that <u>box</u>?
9. He has a black <u>spot</u> on his shoe.
10. She will <u>shop</u> for food.

Challenge Yourself Answers

1. dodge
2. profit
3. bonnet

Students' sentences will vary.

Test Review these ways to spell /ŏ/: <u>o</u> as in <u>rock</u>; <u>a</u> as in <u>want</u>. Test words with /ŏ/. Use one of these testing methods: (1) Say the word; read the sample sentence from page 54; say the word; have students write the word. (2) Read each dictation sentence above; have students write the sentence. Correct the test with students.

Challenge Yourself The optional Challenge Words may be assigned to the entire class or limited to those students who do well on the test. Have students note the vowel spellings of the Challenge Words. Responses to this activity should be completed on separate paper. Answers to the questions are provided above.

Write to the Point Have students recall the selection "A Frog's Hard Day" on pages 56 and 57; then assign the list. Encourage students to include things that might be on their family's shopping list. This activity should be completed on separate paper.

Proofreading The proofreading practice includes misspellings of words from this lesson as well as a capitalization error and a punctuation error.

LESSON 11

Objectives

- To hear and say plurals.
- To write plurals with attention to letter sequence and sound/symbol relationships.
- To write each spelling word once.
- To recognize that plurals may be formed by adding s and es.
- To note that some plurals are irregular.

Sample Sentences

1. We have five dogs and seven cats.
2. Those vans deliver big straw hats.
3. Clap your hands and throw the ball.
4. Turn your backs until I call.
5. We will clean our desks whenever you say.
6. School bells ring at the end of the day.
7. Jets require a lot of gas!
8. Watering the plants is one of the jobs in our classroom.
9. All the ships went out to sea.
10. Two eggs are hatching in the grass.
11. Those dresses come in blue and gray.
12. These men will help us move today.

Note

The sample sentences may be used for pretesting and post-testing.

Lesson 11 Plurals

Say these words. Listen for final /s/ or /z/ in each one.

cats
vans
hands
backs
desks
bells
jets
jobs
ships
eggs

dresses

men

1. Make these words mean more than one:

cat	hand	van	back	desk
bell	jet	job	ship	egg

cats   hands
vans   backs
desks   bells
jets   jobs
ships   eggs

2. Make this word mean more than one:

dress   dresses

3. Make this word mean more than one:

man   men

Hi, Spi! This is C. Bee. What has 12 legs and 8 eyes?

Hi, C. Bee! This is Spi. Two men and two cats?

Preparation Write these words on the board: hill clock desk Have volunteers read them and give a sentence for each. Point out that their sentences are about only one object. Have volunteers come to the board and add an s to each word. (hills, clocks, desks) Then have the plural words read and sentences suggested for them.

Read the spelling words on page 60 and have students repeat each word.

Note the /z/ sound of the s at the end of vans. Have students find other words that end with /z/. (hands, bells, jobs, eggs, dresses) Explain that es is used to form plurals of words that already end in s. Ask in which word es forms the plural. (dresses) Why? (Dress ends with an s.) Explain that some plurals don't have s or es. These words we just have to remember. Call attention to the cartoon. Which plural word does not end in s or es? (men)

Have students point to the spelling word as you read each sample sentence.

The Page Do the activities with the students and check their responses immediately. Volunteers may write the answers on the board or spell them aloud.

Follow-Up As a study method, ask students to form teams of two. Have one student say the singular form of a spelling word. Have the partner say and spell the plural form.

Checkpoint

Write a spelling word for each clue. Then use the Checkpoint Study Plan on page 224.

1. A clothing store sells skirts and ___.

2. Grown-ups are women and ___.

3. Some trucks are called ___.

4. I could hear the ringing of ___.

5. When you meet someone, you shake ___.

6. At the pier, you see ___.

7. At the airport, you see ___.

8. In a classroom, there are many ___.

9. Watering the plants is one of my ___.

10. Chicks hatch from ___.

11. We like to swim and float on our ___.

12. This mystery word comes from Latin, a very old language. The Latin word was <u>cattus</u>. In German, the word is <u>katze</u>. In French, it is <u>chat</u>. In Spanish, it is <u>gato</u>. In Italian, it is <u>gatto</u>. In Russian, it is <u>kot</u>. Guess what it is in English. Now add an <u>s</u>. What is the word? ___

61

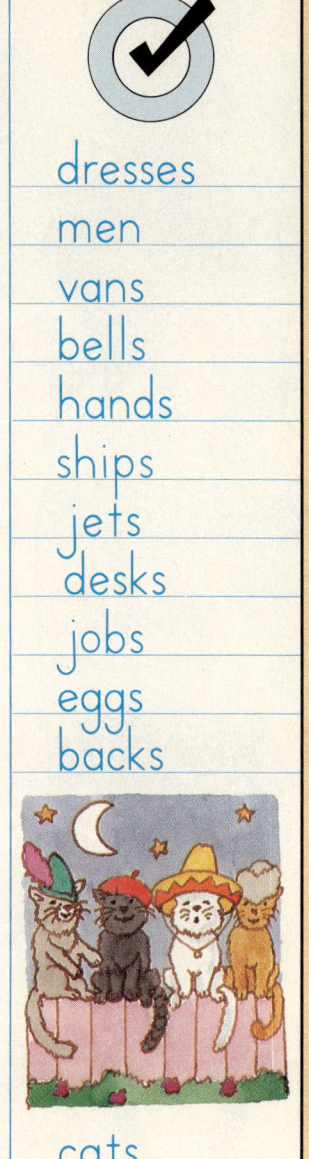

dresses

men

vans

bells

hands

ships

jets

desks

jobs

eggs

backs

cats

Objectives

- To write spelling words in response to clues: definitions, synonyms, and context.

- To develop the critical thinking skills of classifying and making inferences.

- To learn some similarities and differences between an English word and the same word in Latin and several contemporary languages.

Spelling Strategy

Some students may add an <u>s</u> to <u>men</u> to form the plural. These students <u>may</u> benefit from oral practice with the following sentences:

   Dan is a man.

   Ken and Ben are two men.

   One man can drive a van.

   It takes ten men to catch a hen.

Preparation The clues on this page are like crossword puzzle clues. Explain to students that the response to each clue is a spelling word. Use the following examples to illustrate the types of clues used:

   Definition Grown-ups are women and *(men)*.
   Synonym Some trucks are called *(vans)*.
   Context I could hear the ringing of *(bells)*.

The final clue compares the English word <u>cat</u> with the word for <u>cat</u> in several other languages.

The Page Have students complete page 61 using the words on page 60. When students have finished, have them read each clue and spell the answer aloud. Check each response twice: once for the correct answer and a second time for spelling accuracy.

Follow-Up Guide students in using the **Checkpoint Study Plan** on page 224 to take a self-test. Have them use the plan for independent study.

Objectives

- To write plurals in continuous text.
- To write each spelling word once.
- To integrate reading with spelling.

Fill in the blanks with spelling words.

A LIFE IN THE CIRCUS

When you think of working for the circus, do you

think of being a clown or an acrobat? There are lots of

other _____jobs_____ at the circus, too. Look at the

Rough and Tumble Circus.

There are people who train the lions and tigers. They

practice with the _____cats_____ every day. They

teach the lions to shake _____hands_____ with their

paws. There are also people who sew things for

the circus. They make pretty _____dresses_____

for the women to wear in the circus parade.

Sometimes they sew _____bells_____ on the

clowns' shirts that ring when they walk.

Preparation   Have students turn to pages 62 and 63. Call their attention to the pictures and the word list. Have the students say the words. Then explain that each spelling word belongs in one of the blanks in the story.

Write the title "A Life in the Circus" on the board and have a student read it. Ask students what is the first thing that comes to mind when they hear the word circus. Explain that there are many people who work for the circus who are never seen by circus audiences. The story will tell who these people are and what they do.

The Pages   Read the story aloud, supplying the missing spelling words as students follow along in their texts. When you have finished reading, you may wish to discuss the story. Have students list jobs they would like to have if they were a part of the circus. Have them explain the reasons for their preferences.

Have students complete the story by silently rereading it and writing the correct spelling word for each blank. Then ask a volunteer to read the pages aloud, pausing before each blank. Have other volunteers say each missing spelling word and write it on the board. Check students' responses for the accurate spelling of each answer.

Some people drive the circus ____vans____ that go from town to town. There are also women and ____men____ who don't travel with the circus at all. They sit in offices at ____desks____ and plan where the Rough and Tumble Circus will go next. Sometimes the circus must go to another country. Some circus people must sail on ____ships____. Others must fly in ____jets____.

Maybe the most important people at the circus are the cooks. They make sure the performers have a good breakfast every day. Sometimes, when the cooks' ____backs____ are turned, the clowns try their juggling act. Those are the mornings the cooks have to serve scrambled ____eggs____!

63

cats
vans
hands
backs
desks
bells
jets
jobs
ships
eggs
dresses
men

Enrichment

If you want to use the blackline activity masters for enrichment and additional practice, assign Lesson 11 activities at this time.

Maintenance and Review

OBJECTIVE

• To review words with /ŏ/ spelled: o, a.

ACTIVITIES

If you want to use the blackline activity masters for maintenance and review, assign Lesson 10 activities at this time.

You can also use the activity below to review Lesson 10 with students:

Write the following words and definitions on the board. Have volunteers read each definition and tell the word it defines. Then have students copy each definition and write the appropriate spelling word. (Answers are in parentheses.)

| rock | want | stop | shop |
| | spot | | drop |

1. To wish for. (want)
2. A round-shaped bit of water. (drop)
3. Solid stone. (rock)
4. To finish. (stop)
5. A place to buy things. (shop)
6. A small mark. (spot)

Follow-Up Have students use each of the spelling words they missed in an original sentence that relates to the story.

As an additional follow-up activity, you may wish to assign five groups to represent each of the five jobs mentioned in the story: animal trainers, costume designers, drivers, circus managers, and cooks. Have each group draw a mural for its circus job. Assign two spelling words to each mural and have the mural teams quiz one another on their words.

- To relate spelling words to a dictionary skill.
- To locate plural words in the **Spelling Dictionary**.
- To write spelling words in alphabetical order.
- To check handwriting for correct letter formation.

a b c d e f g h i j k l m
n o p q r s t u v w x y z

Dictionary

Plural words are usually found under their singular form in a dictionary. To find **cats**, look under **cat**.

> **cat** /kăt/—*plural* **cats.** A small furry animal. *Why is a cat a good pet? (Because it is purr-fect!)*

Write these words in alphabetical order. Then look them up in the Spelling Dictionary. Write the entry word and the page number next to each word. The first one is done for you.

men   jets   bells   eggs   dresses   desks

	Plural	Entry Word	Page
1.	bells	bell	199
2.	desks	desk	203
3.	dresses	dress	204
4.	eggs	egg	204
5.	jets	jet	209
6.	men	men	212
		man	211

64

Preparation Write these words on the board:

jobs   vans   cats   backs   hands   ships

Ask students to put them in alphabetical order. *(backs, cats, hands, jobs, ships, vans)* Explain that in order to find the plural form of a word in the dictionary, the students have to look at the entry for the singular form of the word. Call on volunteers to write the singular form of each word next to its plural form. *(back, cat, hand, job, ship, van)*

Then have students look up each word in the **Spelling Dictionary**. Have students point to the plural forms in the dictionary entries. The plurals appear after the sound spelling and before the first meaning.

The Page Do the activities on page 64 with the class. Remind students not to make spelling mistakes because of poor handwriting. This lesson provides practice writing the lowercase s, which curves evenly around to the left and back and around to the right. Tell students to make sure that both curves are the same size.

Follow-Up Have students write sentences for the singular and plural forms of these words: **bell, desk,** and **hand.** They may exchange papers and read one another's sentences aloud.

WORDS AT WORK

Challenge Yourself

ducklings   batches   recesses

What do you think each underlined Challenge Word means? Check your Spelling Dictionary to see if you are right. Then write sentences. Show that you understand the meaning of each Challenge Word.

1. Max made three <u>batches</u> of cookies.

2. The little <u>ducklings</u> swam near their mother.

3. My class gets two <u>recesses</u> every day.

Write to the Point

Which circus job would you like to have? You may pick a job from the story or think of one on your own. Write three or four sentences about the job. Tell what you would like about it. Use spelling words from this lesson in your sentences.

Challenge Use one or more of the Challenge Words in your sentences.

Proofreading

Use the marks to show the mistakes in the sentences below. Write the four misspelled words correctly in the blanks.

⬭	word is misspelled
⊙	period is missing
≡	letter should be capitalized

1. (Min) put the big cats in cages ⊙

2. They carry boxes on their (baks.)

3. <u>in</u> the boxes are (dreses.)

4. They work hard at their (jobz.)

1. _____Men_____

2. _____backs_____

3. _____dresses_____

4. _____jobs_____

65

Objectives

- To extend the study of the spelling patterns presented in Lesson 11 to the Challenge Words.

- To use context and the **Spelling Dictionary** to enlarge students' vocabulary.

- To apply the spelling patterns presented in Lesson 11 in a writing activity.

- To practice proofreading for spelling, punctuation, and capitalization.

Dictation Sentences

1. We have three <u>cats</u>.
2. The <u>hands</u> of the clock tell the time.
3. The school <u>bells</u> ring at the end of the class.
4. The pet shop has three red <u>vans</u>.
5. The <u>men</u> on the <u>ships</u> catch fish.
6. We can swim on our <u>backs</u>.
7. I will not drop the <u>eggs</u>.
8. She has two new <u>dresses</u>.
9. He said that <u>jets</u> go fast.
10. One of our <u>jobs</u> in school is to wash the <u>desks</u>.

Challenge Yourself Answers

Possible definitions:

1. groups
2. baby ducks
3. times to have fun

Students' sentences will vary.

Test Review these ways to form plurals: adding <u>s</u> as in <u>cats</u>; adding <u>es</u> as in <u>dresses</u>; and the irregular form of the plural as in <u>men</u>. Test the plural words from Lesson 11. Use one of these testing methods: (1) Say the word; read the sample sentence from page 60; say the word; have students write the word. (2) Read each dictation sentence above; have students write the sentence. Correct the test with students.

Challenge Yourself The optional Challenge Words may be assigned to the entire class or limited to those students who do well on the test. Have students note the spelling patterns in the Challenge Words. Responses to this activity should be completed on separate paper. Answers to the questions are provided above.

Write to the Point Have students recall the selection "A Life in the Circus" on pages 62 and 63; then assign the sentences. Remind students to look carefully at the pictures for ideas. This activity should be completed on separate paper.

Proofreading The proofreading practice includes misspellings of words from this lesson as well as a capitalization error and a punctuation error.

LESSON 12

Objectives

- To review and reinforce vowel spellings for /ĭ/ and /ŏ/.
- To review and reinforce the spelling of plurals.
- To hear, say, spell, and write representative words from Lessons 7–11.
- To write a narrative using the five steps in the writing process.
- To use a prewriting activity to plot the story line in a narrative.

Dictation Sentences

1. My dad has six hats.
2. Do you like this old shirt?
3. I think Sarah likes me.
4. Billy will give me a ride on his bike today.
5. I was the last one in line.
6. Can you guess what is in the box?
7. Do you want to join our club?
8. I wonder when it will stop raining.
9. Are those men really from outer space?
10. Sally never wears dresses to school.

Note

A review test blackline master in standardized format and an answer sheet have been provided on pages T36 and T41 of this Teacher's Edition. The answers to the review test are given below.

1-C	5-D
2-B	6-A
3-D	7-B
4-B	8-D

Lesson 12 Words in Review

A. six
this

B. think
give

C. was
what

D. want
stop

E. men
dresses

1. In Lesson 7 you studied words with /ĭ/. Write the two words in List A.

six   this

2. List B has two more words with /ĭ/ from Lesson 8. Write the word that ends with /v/.

give

Now write the word that ends with nk.

think

3. In Lesson 9 you studied words with /ŏ/. Write the word from List C that ends with /z/.

was

Write the word that begins with wh.

what

4. In Lesson 10 you studied ways to spell /ŏ/. Write the word from List D in which /ŏ/ is spelled a. Then write the word that begins with st.

want   stop

5. List E has plural words from Lesson 11. Write the plurals of man and dress.

men   dresses

66

Preparation Tell students that Lesson 12 is a review lesson. Lesson 12 contains several activities that ask them to write some of the words they have studied in Lessons 7–11.

Direct students' attention to the list of words on page 66. Read the words aloud as students look at them. Have students say and spell each word aloud.

Then read the dictation sentences above as students point to each spelling word in their book. Point out that the words in List A are from Lesson 7, words in List B are from Lesson 8, words in List C are from Lesson 9, words in List D are from Lesson 10, and words in List E are from Lesson 11.

The Pages Have students complete the activities on page 66 as a group or independently. Write the answers on the board and have volunteers spell the words aloud for reinforcement of correct spelling.

Test and Study If you wish to test students on the review words, use one of these testing methods: (1) Read the word and the dictation sentence; say the word again; have students write the word. (2) Have students complete the review test blackline master. (See **Note**.)

Writer's Workshop

A Narrative

A narrative is a story. Every good story has a beginning, a middle, and an end. Writers use the beginning of the story to tell who the story characters are. They also tell where the story takes place. Here is the beginning of Jesse's story about Sammy the Skunk.

> ### Sammy Grows Up
>
> Sammy the Skunk sat in the woods. Sammy was sad. He had no one to play with. His sisters Suzi and Sally were at summer camp. Sammy was too young to go to camp. He was too young for everything. He wished he could grow up! Sammy started to cry. He thought he was alone, but he was not. Someone heard Sammy's wish.

To write his story, Jesse followed the steps in the writing process. He used a story map as a **Prewriting** activity. The map helped him plan the beginning, middle, and end of his story. Jesse's story map is shown here. Study what Jesse did.

Beginning
Sammy wished he could grow up.

Middle
An elf heard Sammy's wish. He made Sammy a grown-up.

End
Sammy wished to be young again.

It's Your Turn

Get ready to write your own story. It can be about make-believe animals like Sammy the Skunk, or it can be about real people. After you have decided what to write about, make a story map. Then follow the other steps in the writing process—**Writing, Revising, Proofreading,** and **Publishing.**

67

Writer's Workshop Students who have mastered the review words may go on to the **Writer's Workshop** on page 67. Explain that a narrative is a story. Point out that at the beginning of a story, the writer usually introduces the story characters and tells where and when the story takes place. The middle of the story is where most of the action takes place. The end tells how the story turns out. Then read the beginning of the narrative "Sammy Grows Up" with students, noting the main character and setting.

Allow students to study the story map shown on the pupil's page and guide them to see how this graphic organizer helped Jesse prepare to write his narrative.

It's Your Turn Review the steps in the writing process with students. If students are not satisfied with the result of their prewriting, allow them to revise it as often as necessary or to choose another topic and repeat the prewriting activity.

Process Writing Blackline Masters
• Story Map, page T49
• Steps in the Writing Process, page T46
• Proofreading Symbols/Checklist, page T47

Note

If students have difficulty deciding on a topic, you may wish to suggest one of the following:

A story about a treasure map
A story about a talking fish
A retelling of a favorite fairy tale with a new ending

LESSON 13

Objectives

- To hear and say words with /ŭ/.
- To write words with /ŭ/ with attention to letter sequence and sound/symbol relationships.
- To write each spelling word once.
- To recognize that /ŭ/ may be spelled u and o.

Sample Sentences

1. Jim cut his knee when he fell.
2. He slipped in the mud and let out a yell.
3. The sun rises in the east and sets in the west.
4. Getting up early is the best.
5. I take a bus to school each day.
6. At recess, I like to run and play.
7. Jill went to camp, but not overnight.
8. I hope that bug doesn't bite.
9. The shady tree will keep us cool.
10. I joined a sports club after school.
11. Can you swim under water?
12. My family takes a vacation in the summer.
13. Would you like a piece of cake?
14. They brought back fish from Walton Lake.

Lesson 13 Words with /ŭ/

cut
mud
sun
up
bus
run
but
bug
us
club
under
summer
of
from

1. Which two-letter words begin like uncle?

up   us

2. Write the words that end like bun.

sun   run

3. What words begin or end with the sound /b/?

bus   but
bug   club

4. c + ut = cut
   m + ud = mud

5. Which words end like mother?

under   summer

6. What words have the sound /ŭ/ but no letter u?

of   from

Of course!

from

68

Preparation Write /ŭ/ on the chalkboard. Have the students repeat the sound /ŭ/ as in cut. Say these word pairs. Ask students to put their thumbs up in the air when they hear a word with /ŭ/.

cat – cut   bug – beg   club – crib   friend – from

Read the spelling words on page 68 as the students look at them. Ask students to repeat and spell each word aloud.

Note such special sound/symbol relationships as the /v/ sound spelled f in the word of. Then point out that the first twelve words spell the sound /ŭ/ with a u. Note that the sound /ŭ/ is spelled with the letter o in of and from. The cartoon will help students answer question 6. There is no letter u in of and from even though there is the sound /ŭ/. (See Note.)

Read the sample sentences above. Have students point to each spelling word as you read the corresponding sentence.

The Page Do page 68 with the class. Then have students spell their words aloud as volunteers write the answers on the board. Help students correct their work.

Follow-Up Be sure that each student has a study plan for the week. Suggest that students make flash cards for each of the words and practice spelling with the cards every day.

Checkpoint

Write a spelling word for each clue. Then use the Checkpoint Study Plan on page 224.

1. A seesaw goes ___ and down.

2. You use scissors to ___.

3. I belong to a book ___.

4. She found her book ___ the table.

5. Do you ride to school on the ___?

6. Pigs like to roll in the ___.

7. An insect is a ___.

8. We have a long vacation in the ___.

9. Where did that noise come ___?

10. The lake was full ___ fish.

11. Grandmother gave the tickets to ___.

12. We get light and heat from the ___.

13. A word that sounds like hut is ___.

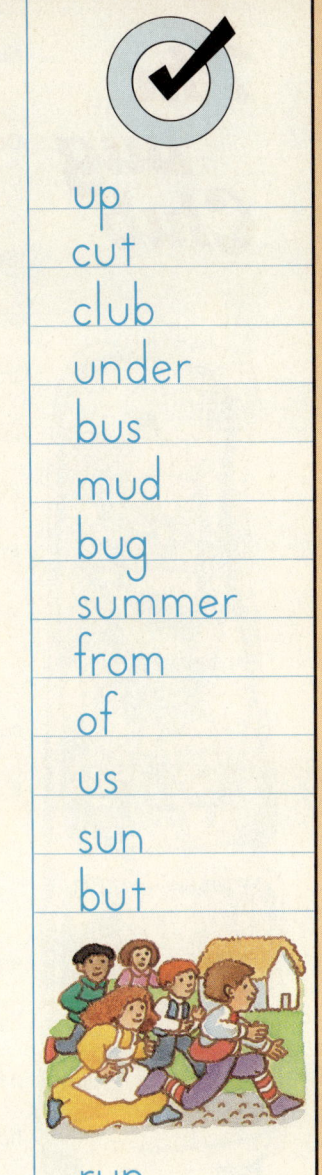

up
cut
club
under
bus
mud
bug
summer
from
of
us
sun
but

run

14. This mystery word comes from the Old German word <u>rinwan</u>. It was also spelled <u>rinnan</u>. It means "to move quickly." Guess the word. ___

69

Objectives

- To write spelling words in response to clues: rhyme and context.
- To develop the critical thinking skills of analyzing and contrasting.
- To appreciate the diversity of sources of the English language.

Spelling Strategy

The final, unstressed vowel sound in <u>summer</u> gives no clear clue to its spelling. Therefore, students may sometimes misspell this word as <u>sum-mar</u>, <u>summur</u>, or <u>summr</u>. In addition, it is not uncommon to spell <u>summer</u> with one <u>m</u>. Students experiencing these problems may benefit from writing the word, drawing a line between the syllables, and pronouncing each syllable as though it were a word.

Preparation The clues on this page are like crossword puzzle clues. Explain to students that the response to each clue is a spelling word. Use the following examples to illustrate the types of clues used:

    Rhyme   A word that sounds like hut is *(but).*
    Context   I belong to a book *(club).*

The final clue explains how the word <u>run</u> came into the English language.

The Page Have students complete page 69 using the words on page 68. When students have finished, have them read each clue and spell the answer aloud. Check each response twice: once for the correct answer and a second time for spelling accuracy.

Follow-Up Guide students in using the **Checkpoint Study Plan** on page 224 to take a self-test. Have them use the plan for independent study.

Objectives

- To write words with /ŭ/ in continuous text.
- To use the spelling words as rhyming words.
- To write each spelling word once.
- To integrate reading with spelling.

Note

- Some of the spelling words will be used twice on these two pages.
- Exercise 2 on page 71 is about a tarantula named Tut. Tell students that a tarantula is a large spider that usually lives in a very hot climate.

70

The Bug Club

Finish Kristin's letter with spelling words.

April 1

Dear Gus,

I'm sad you moved away _____from_____ here! Sometimes I'm still late and have to _____run_____ to catch the bus. Remember how we would race ___up___ the hill at the last minute? Remember the fun we had last _____summer_____? One morning we got up before the _____sun_____ rose. We went to the pond to see if frogs slept _____under_____ the rocks. All we found was wet and gooey _____mud_____!

I belong to a new _____club_____ at school. It's called the Creepy Crawlers. Every week we each find a large or small _____bug_____ and bring it to our meeting. No one will sit next to ___us___ riding on the _____bus_____. I think it is because of our boxes that are full ___of___ holes. Of course we _____cut_____ the holes so the bugs can breathe, _____but_____ some people think the bugs will crawl out. You wouldn't believe how scared some people are of bugs!

Love, Kristin

70

Preparation   Have students turn to pages 70 and 71. Call their attention to the word list. Have the students say the words. Then explain that each spelling word belongs in one of the blanks in the letter. Tell students that they are going to read a letter that a girl named Kristin wrote to a friend who has moved away.

Write the title "The Bug Club" on the board and have a student read the title aloud. Direct students' attention to the picture on page 70 and have them talk about what they see.

The Pages   Read the letter aloud, supplying the missing spelling words as the students follow along in their texts. When you have finished, you may wish to discuss the letter.

Then ask the students to complete the letter on their own by writing the correct spelling word for each blank. When they have finished, have a volunteer read the letter aloud, pausing before each blank. Other students will say and spell the missing spelling word at the appropriate time, and then write it on the board.

Then do the rhyming activities on page 71 with the group. Have students look at the pictures. Then read the sentences aloud. Say each underlined word and ask students to find the spelling word which rhymes with it. Call on students to say and spell the correct word aloud. Allow time for the students to write their answers. Then put the answers on the board so they may check their work. Be sure to check students' responses for the accurate spelling of each answer.

Fill in the blanks with rhyming words.

1. Bud is a bug that is kept in a cup.

   A word that rhymes with <u>Bud</u> is _____mud_____.

   A word that rhymes with <u>cup</u> is _____up_____.

2. Tut is a tarantula that likes to have fun.

   A word that rhymes with <u>Tut</u> is _____cut / but_____.

   A word that rhymes with <u>fun</u> is _____sun / run_____.

3. Gus is a grasshopper that soaks in a tub.

   A word that rhymes with <u>Gus</u> is _____bus / us_____.

   A word that rhymes with <u>tub</u> is _____club_____.

71

cut
mud
sun
up
bus
run
but
bug
us
club
under
summer
of
from

Enrichment

If you want to use the blackline activity masters for enrichment and additional practice, assign Lesson 13 activities at this time.

Maintenance and Review

OBJECTIVE

• To review the plural form.

ACTIVITIES

If you want to use the blackline activity masters for maintenance and review, assign Lesson 11 activities at this time.

You can also use the activity below to review Lesson 11 with students:

Write the following words and riddles on the board. Have students copy the riddles and complete them with spelling words. *(Answers are in parentheses.)*

| bells | desks | dresses |
| jets | men | |

1. You write on us yet you never leave a mark.
   We are your *(desks)* .

2. We make beautiful sounds but we have no throats.
   We are *(bells)* .

3. We fly through the air but we are not birds.
   We are *(jets)* .

4. We are all sons yet we are no longer boys.
   We are *(men)* .

5. We can be fancy or we can be plain. But we always have skirts.
   We are *(dresses)* .

Follow-Up Have students use each of the spelling words they missed in an original sentence.

You may also wish to use this additional follow-up activity. Have students work in pairs. Have one student choose a spelling word, say it, and spell it. Then the other one must say a word which rhymes with it. Have the students trade roles so that they are able to practice both skills.

Objectives

- To relate spelling to another language skill.
- To capitalize the names of streets.
- To write sentences in correct word order.
- To write spelling words in the context of sentences.
- To check handwriting for correct letter formation.

a b c d e f g h i j k l m
n o p q r s t u v w x y z

Capital Letters

Capitalize the names of streets.

Sharon lives at 31 **Main Street**.　The store is at 186 **First Avenue**.
My babysitter lives at 27 **Old Post Road**.

1. Write the number of a house and the name of a street.

_____

Unscramble the sentences. Remember capital letters and periods.

2. 10 oak street We moved from

We moved from 10 Oak Street.

3. us up The bus picks at 22 center street

The bus picks us up at 22 Center Street.

4. at 45 lee street The club is

The club is at 45 Lee Street.

5. 3 dale lane I run home to

I run home to 3 Dale Lane.

72

Preparation　Draw an envelope on the chalkboard. Add the name of the school and the street address, but write the name of the street in lowercase letters. Ask the students to tell you what is wrong with the address. *(Names of streets begin with a capital letter.)* Have a volunteer correct the error. Then have students take turns writing their names and street addresses in the corner of the envelope reserved for the return address. Be sure that each student knows his or her address and the correct form for writing it.

The Page　Do page 72 with the students. Remind students that spelling mistakes are sometimes due to careless handwriting. Lesson 13 offers practice in formation of uppercase letters. Check to make sure students know the relative sizes of uppercase and lowercase letters. When the class has completed the page, have volunteers write the corrected sentences on the board so students may check their own work.

Follow-Up　Ask students to copy the following sentences, capitalizing street names *(Mason Road, Pond Street, Oak Lane)* and underlining the three spelling words *(but, up, from).*

I live on mason road, but I ride my bike on pond street.
I think I'll ride up oak lane from now on.

WORDS AT WORK

Challenge Yourself

numb   **adjust**   **buckle**

What do you think each underlined Challenge Word means? Check your Spelling Dictionary to see if you are right. Then write sentences. Show that you understand the meaning of each Challenge Word.

1. Walking in the snow made my feet <u>numb</u>.

2. Please <u>adjust</u> the sound on your radio.

3. <u>Buckle</u> your seat belt before the car starts.

Write to the Point

Read "The Bug Club" on page 70 again. Draw a picture of a bug you would like to take to the Creepy Crawlers Club. Then write sentences that tell about your bug. Use spelling words from this lesson in your sentences.

Challenge Use one or more of the Challenge Words in your sentences.

Proofreading

Use the marks to show the mistakes in the sentences. Write the four misspelled words correctly in the blanks.

⬭	word is misspelled
⊙	period is missing
≡	letter should be capitalized

1. Have fun with us this (sumer⊙)

2. we can have a bug (clubb⊙)
   ≡

3. Some bugs live (undar) rocks.

4. They (rune) from the sun⊙

1. ___summer___

2. ___club___

3. ___under___

4. ___run___

73

LESSON 14

Objectives

- To hear and say words with /ŭ/.

- To write words with /ŭ/ with attention to letter sequence and sound/symbol relationships.

- To write each spelling word once.

- To recognize that /ŭ/ may be spelled u and o.

Sample Sentences

1. I must speak softly and try not to yell.
2. A skunk gives off a warning smell.
3. That ship seems much too large to dock.
4. The lunch bell rings at twelve o'clock.
5. We saw such a good movie.
6. I just saw a shooting star.
7. We'll need a truck to tow the car.
8. It's fun to slide on a snowy hill.
9. Can Greta jump as high as Jill?
10. There's one more piece of lemon cake.
11. I love to help my neighbor bake.
12. I would rather read the other book.
13. I have two sisters and a brother.
14. My uncle's sister is my mother!

Note

Words are grouped according to spellings of /ŭ/:

u

o

The sample sentences may be used for pretesting and post-testing.

Lesson 14 Words with /ŭ/

must
skunk
much
lunch
such
just
truck
fun
jump

one
love
other
brother
mother

1. What words end with the letters ch?

much   lunch   such

2. Write the words that end the same as dust.

must   just

3. f + un = fun

j + ump = jump

4. What spelling words have the sound /k/ in them?

skunk   truck

5. What words have the sound /ŭ/ but no letter u?

one   love

other   brother

mother

74

Preparation Write /ŭ/ on the board and have students repeat the sound /ŭ/ as in cut. Say these word pairs. If a word contains /ŭ/, the students should put their thumbs up in the air.

mist – must   skunk – sank   trick – truck   matter – mother

Have the students look at the spelling words on page 74. Say each word aloud. Then have the students repeat and spell each word.

Review the consonant digraphs ch and ck. Have students find the words that contain these spellings. (much, such, truck) Also note the consonant cluster nch in lunch. Ask someone to identify which word has the sound /w/ but has no letter w. (one) Ask the students to look at the first nine words. The sound /ŭ/ is spelled with the letter u in these words. Ask them to look at the last five words. What letter spells /ŭ/ in these words? (o) (See Note.) Allow time for students to read the cartoon.

Read the sample sentences as students point to the words in their books.

The Page Do the activities with the students. Then have volunteers put the answers on the board so students may check their own work.

Follow-Up Be sure that students have a study method. Suggest that they write the words on cards (or small pieces of paper). Then have them look at the word, close their eyes, spell the word aloud, and check the card.

Checkpoint

Write a spelling word for each clue.
Then use the Checkpoint Study Plan on page 224.

1. Mike has two sisters and a ___.

2. Those people are my father and my ___.

3. My dad drives a ___.

4. That game costs too ___.

5. I can hop, skip, and ___.

6. Peanut butter is a food I ___.

7. At twelve o'clock, we eat our ___.

8. The number before two is ___.

9. We went to the party and had ___.

10. I don't want to leave, but I ___.

11. Do you want this book or the ___?

12. These sneakers are ___ my size.

13. Flying a kite is ___ fun!

14. When the first people from Europe came to America, they saw many animals they had never seen. One animal had black-and-white fur and a bushy tail. American Indians called it a <u>segonku</u>. The new settlers tried to use its Indian name, but they couldn't say it very well. The mystery word is the name they used. What is it? ___

75

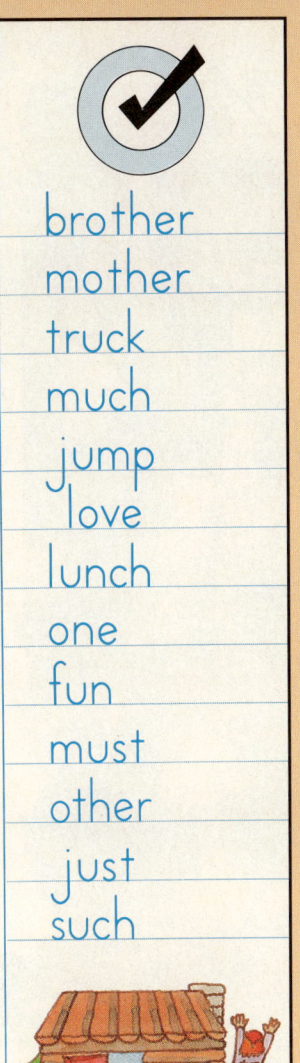

brother
mother
truck
much
jump
love
lunch
one
fun
must
other
just
such

skunk

Objectives

- To write spelling words in response to clues: definition and context.
- To develop the critical thinking skills of making inferences and sequencing.
- To learn that Native American languages are the source of some words in the English language.

Spelling Strategy

Some students may confuse the homophones <u>one</u> and <u>won</u>. Both words spell /ŭ/ with the letter <u>o</u>. Remind students that <u>one</u> is a number, while <u>won</u> is the opposite of <u>lost</u>. Some students may benefit from writing and reciting the phrase "My team <u>won</u> the game by <u>one</u> point."

Preparation The clues on this page are like crossword puzzle clues. Explain to students that the response to each clue is a spelling word. Use the following examples to illustrate the types of clues used:

Definition	The number before two is *(one)*.
Context	Flying a kite is *(such)* fun!

The final clue explains how the word <u>skunk</u> came into the English language.

The Page Have students complete page 75 using the words on page 74. When students have finished, have them read each clue and spell the answer aloud. Check each response twice: once for the correct answer and a second time for spelling accuracy.

Follow-Up Guide students in using the **Checkpoint Study Plan** on page 224 to take a self-test. Have them use the plan for independent study.

Objectives

- To write words with /ŭ/ in continuous text.
- To write each spelling word once.
- To integrate reading with spelling.

Fill in the blanks with spelling words.

A Pet of Our Own

My mother tries to grow a vegetable garden. It is _____much_____ harder than you might think. That is because of our neighbor Mr. Bonzo. He has six rabbits. They always make _____such_____ trouble in my mother's garden. They nibble on peas and _____other_____ vegetables for their _____lunch_____. They love to leap and _____jump_____ on the corn. They _____love_____ to sleep on the string beans. When my _____mother_____ talks to Mr. Bonzo about this, he says, "I love to see my rabbits have _____fun_____. It _____must_____ make you happy to see rabbits playing in your garden."

Preparation Have students turn to pages 76 and 77. Call their attention to the word list. Have the students say the words. Then explain that each spelling word belongs in one of the blanks in the story.

Write the title "A Pet of Our Own" on the board and have a student read it. Call attention to the picture on page 76, and explain that you are going to read a story about a family's problem with their vegetable garden. Have the students guess what the problem might be. Explain that the story will tell them what the mother did to solve the problem.

The Pages Read the story aloud, supplying the missing spelling words as the students follow along in their texts. When you get to the end, pause and have the students call out the last word in the story: skunk. Ask the students how a pet skunk would keep Mr. Bonzo's rabbits away.

Then ask the students to write the correct spelling word for each blank as they complete the story on their own. Have a volunteer read the story aloud, pausing before each blank. Other students will say the missing spelling word at the appropriate time and spell it aloud. Write the answers on the board so students may check their work. Check students' responses for the accurate spelling of each answer.

But rabbits having fun did not make my mother a bit

happy. "I ____just____ don't know what to do,"

she said. Then ____one____ day she had an idea.

"You kids come with me," she called. "Let's hop in

the ____truck____ and go to the pet store.

I think it's time you had a pet of your own."

My younger _____brother_____,

Sammy, and I were excited. We had never had a pet of

our own. "May we get a dog?" I asked.

"No, fiercer than a dog," said Mom.

"A tiger?" yelled Sammy.

"No, much smaller than a tiger," said Mom.

"A snake?" I asked in a brave voice.

"No, furrier than a snake," said Mom.

We bought the best pet there was in the store.

It's the funniest pet of all. And now there's never a

rabbit to be seen in our garden. Mr. Bonzo isn't to be

seen in our garden, either. What do you think we got?

Well, our new pet is a ____skunk____!

77

must
skunk
much
lunch
such
just
truck
fun
jump
one
love
other
brother
mother

Enrichment

If you want to use the blackline activity masters for enrichment and additional practice, assign Lesson 14 activities at this time.

Maintenance and Review

OBJECTIVE

● To review words with /ŭ/ spelled: u, o.

ACTIVITIES

If you want to use the blackline activity masters for maintenance and review, assign Lesson 13 activities at this time.

You can also use the activity below to review Lesson 13 with students:

Write the following words and sentences on the board. Have the students copy and complete each sentence by writing a spelling word. Then have the class suggest answers to the questions. (Answers are in parentheses.)

cut   run   up   bug

1. Children, kangaroos, and jack-in-the-boxes are all things that jump _(up)_.
   Can you think of more? (rabbits, frogs, grasshoppers)

2. Your hair, a cake, and a pie are all things that can be _(cut)_.
   Can you think of more? (ribbons, flowers, paper dolls)

3. A caterpillar, a mosquito, and a silverfish; each is an insect or a _(bug)_.
   Can you name more? (ladybug, ant, flea)

4. Athletes, joggers, cars, and buses are people or things that _(run)_.
   Can you think of more? (antelopes, furnaces, watches)

Remind the students that /ŭ/ may also be spelled with the letter o. Say the words of and from and have the class spell them aloud.

Follow-Up   Have students use each of the spelling words they missed in an original sentence that relates to the story.

As an additional follow-up activity, you may wish to play the following game. Divide the class into two teams — the skunks and the rabbits. Draw a vegetable garden on the board and practice spelling words aloud in a spelling-bee style. If the skunks spell a word correctly, circle a vegetable in the garden to show that it has been saved. If the rabbits spell a word correctly, cross out a vegetable to show that the rabbits have gotten into the garden. If there are more vegetables circled than crossed out, the skunks have won the spelling bee. If more vegetables have been crossed out, then the rabbits have won.

Objectives

- To relate spelling to another language skill.
- To use an exclamation point.
- To write sentences in correct word order.
- To write spelling words in the context of sentences.
- To check handwriting for correct letter formation.

a b c d e f g h i j k l m
n o p q r s t u v w x y z

Exclamation Points

Use an exclamation point (!) at the end of a sentence to show strong feeling or surprise.

My frog won a blue ribbon!

Write an exclamation point. !

Unscramble the sentences. Put an exclamation point at the end of each sentence.

1. are fun Frog contests

Frog contests are fun!

2. one has My brother frog

My brother has one frog!

3. can jump feet ten His frog

His frog can jump ten feet!

4. thinks win must he He

He thinks he must win!

5. much better was My frog

My frog was much better!

78

Preparation
Write the following sentences on the board:

Where did you go on your picnic
We had a picnic lunch at High Point
A great big skunk sat down beside me

Have volunteers read each sentence. Ask the students what is wrong with the sentences. *(no punctuation at the end)* Have students insert a question mark, period, and exclamation point, respectively. Tell students that an exclamation point ends a sentence that shows strong feeling or surprise.

The Page
Do page 78 with the students. Tell students to form their letters carefully. This lesson gives practice in forming the letter f. Remind students to be sure the top of the f, as in fun and frog, touches the top writing line and to cross the f in the middle. After they have unscrambled and written the sentences, have volunteers read each sentence aloud so students may check their own work.

Follow-Up
Have the students think of sentences that should end with an exclamation point, using the following spelling words: **lunch, fun, must.**

WORDS AT WORK

Challenge Yourself

insult   **blush**   **sponge**

What do you think each underlined Challenge Word means? Check your Spelling Dictionary to see if you are right. Then write sentences. Show that you understand the meaning of each Challenge Word.

1. Telling someone she smells like a skunk would be an <u>insult</u>.

2. I began to <u>blush</u> when I saw I had sat in gum.

3. Wash the sink with a <u>sponge</u>.

Write to the Point

Think about the story "A Pet of Our Own." Then write a letter to Mr. Bonzo. Ask him to keep his rabbits out of your garden. Tell why they are a problem. Use spelling words from this lesson.

Challenge Use one or more of the Challenge Words in your letter.

Proofreading

Use the marks to show the mistakes in the sentences below. Write the four misspelled words correctly in the blanks.

◯	word is misspelled
⊙	period is missing
≡	letter should be capitalized

1. My (bruther) and i love our garden⊙

2. It is (sach) fun to watch the skunk.

3. Mother (jist) came home for lunch.

4. she and I will jump in the (truk) and go to the garden.

1. _____brother_____

2. _____such_____

3. _____just_____

4. _____truck_____

79

Objectives

- To extend the vowel spellings presented in Lesson 14 to the Challenge Words.
- To use context and the **Spelling Dictionary** to enlarge students' vocabulary.
- To apply the vowel spellings presented in Lesson 14 in a writing activity.
- To practice proofreading for spelling, punctuation, and capitalization.

Dictation Sentences

1. The boys ran from the <u>skunk</u>.
2. I have a sister and a <u>brother</u>.
3. They had <u>such</u> fun at the zoo.
4. I <u>love</u> my pet so <u>much</u>.
5. My <u>mother</u> and I <u>went</u> home after lunch.
6. This <u>truck</u> is blue, but the <u>other</u> is red.
7. The school bus <u>just</u> went by.
8. We <u>must</u> go home soon.
9. Can <u>you</u> <u>jump</u> over this rock?
10. He has <u>one</u> cat and three fish in his room.

Challenge Yourself Answers

Possible definitions:

1. rude action
2. to turn red from embarrassment
3. something soft to clean with

Students' sentences will vary.

Test Review these ways to spell /ŭ/: <u>u</u> as in <u>must</u>; <u>o</u> as in <u>love</u>. Test words with /ŭ/. Use one of these testing methods: (1) Say the word; read the sample sentence from page 74; say the word; have students write the word. (2) Read each dictation sentence above; have students write the sentence. Correct the test with students.

Challenge Yourself The optional Challenge Words may be assigned to the entire class or limited to those students who do well on the test. Have students note the vowel spellings of the Challenge Words. Responses to this activity should be completed on separate paper. Answers to the questions are provided above.

Write to the Point Have students recall the selection "A Pet of Our Own" on pages 76 and 77; then assign the letter. Point out the importance of writing a polite letter. This activity should be completed on separate paper.

Proofreading The proofreading practice includes misspellings of words from this lesson as well as capitalization errors and a punctuation error.

LESSON 15

Objectives

- To hear and say words with /ā/.
- To write words with /ā/ with attention to letter sequence and sound/symbol relationships.
- To write each spelling word once.
- To recognize that /ā/ may be spelled a_e, ay, and a.

Sample Sentences

1. The team's best player was in last night's game.
2. We gave her a birthday party.
3. Our hero's name is Bobby Nye.
4. Everyone came on the trip.
5. We want to bake him a pecan pie.
6. The brave soldiers marched through wind and hail.
7. The ship chased the great white whale.
8. The horse ate the oats in the pail.
9. The newspapers say the forecast is for rain.
10. I'd like to play that song again.
11. Her tree house is a good place to stay.
12. We are going to the circus today.
13. The coach thought maybe the umpire was right.
14. The baby stayed up late last night.

Lesson 15 Words with /ā/

game
gave
name
came
bake
brave
whale
ate

say
play
stay
today
maybe

baby

1. Write the spelling words that end in ay.

say   play
stay   today

2. may + be = maybe

   ba + by = baby

3. What words have a and e, but you only hear /ā/?

game   gave
name   came
bake   brave
whale   ate

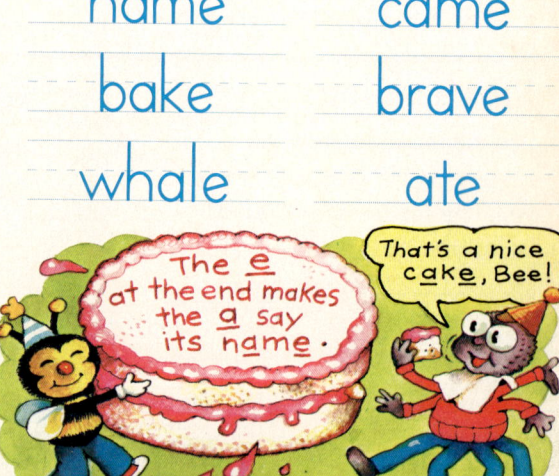

The e at the end makes the a say its name.

That's a nice cake, Bee!

80

Preparation

Write /ā/ on the board. Have students repeat the sound /ā/, as in pay. Say these word pairs. If the word contains /ā/, students should wave.

   while – whale   back – bake   baby – body   say – so   play – plaid

Read the spelling words on page 80 as students repeat and spell each one.

Call attention to the first eight words. Note that the final e signals the "long sound" of the vowel before it. Tell students that the "long a sound" is the same as the name a. Call attention to the cartoon.

Next, write these words on the board: mad   pan   tap

Have volunteers read each word. Then add the "signal e" and have students read the new words: made, pane, tape.

The next group of five words spells the sound /ā/ with the letters ay. In the last word, baby, the /ā/ sound is spelled with the letter a.

Have students point to the words as you read the sample sentences.

The Page

Do page 80 together and check the students' responses. For immediate reinforcement of correct spelling, ask volunteers to spell answers aloud.

Follow-Up

Discuss different ways students may study their spelling words. Suggest that they spell the words aloud with a spelling partner.

Checkpoint

Write a spelling word for each clue. Then use the Checkpoint Study Plan on page 224.

1. We put the pie in the oven to ___.

2. At noon, we ___ lunch.

3. I asked her if she could come, and she said ___.

4. It's raining, so I can't ___.

5. My sister took me to a baseball ___.

6. A very young child is a ___.

7. Can you come to visit ___?

8. Jim liked the present I ___ him.

9. Were you home when Grandpa ___ by?

10. The firefighter was very ___.

11. Softball is a game I like to ___.

12. What did you ___?

13. Sandy is my dog's ___.

14. Long ago, English sailors called this animal a hwael. The mystery word comes from that word. It names the biggest sea animal of all. Do you know what it is? ___

81

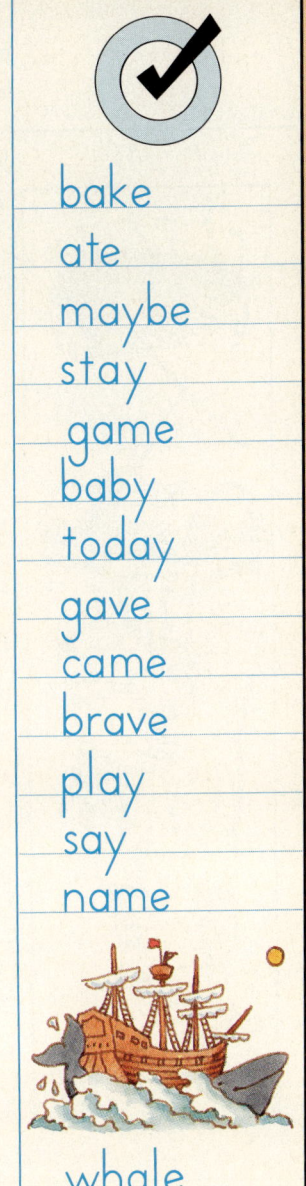

bake
ate
maybe
stay
game
baby
today
gave
came
brave
play
say
name

whale

Objectives

- To write spelling words in response to clues: definition and context.
- To develop the critical thinking skills of analyzing and making inferences.
- To understand that the spelling of words in the English language often changes over time.

Spelling Strategy

Some students may misspell the word baby as babe or babey. Ask students making this spelling error to remember the first line of the nursery rhyme "Rock-a-by-baby" as a means of recalling the correct spelling.

Preparation The clues on this page are like crossword puzzle clues. Explain to students that the response to each clue is a spelling word. Use the following examples to illustrate the types of clues used:

Definition   A very young child is a *(baby)*.
Context   Sandy is my dog's *(name)*.

The final clue explains how the word whale used to be spelled.

The Page Have students complete page 81 using the words on page 80. When students have finished, have them read each clue and spell the answer aloud. Check each response twice: once for the correct answer and a second time for spelling accuracy.

Follow-Up Guide students in using the **Checkpoint Study Plan** on page 224 to take a self-test. Have them use the plan for independent study.

Objectives

- To write words with /ā/ in continuous text.
- To write each spelling word once.
- To integrate reading with spelling.

THE WHALE

Has a Whale of a Day!

Monday was a very special day for Alex Tate and his fans. It was his twenty-first birthday! And he was playing in a very exciting ___game___ in Sage Field. The stands were packed with people shouting Alex Tate's name. But they weren't shouting, "Hurrah Alex!" They were yelling, "Hurrah Whale!"

If you ask him, Alex will ___say___ he doesn't know how he got the name " ___Whale___ ." But the true fans know that his teammates gave him that ___name___. It may be because Alex is rather large. In fact, Alex is about as large as a ___baby___ whale! Do you think that ___maybe___ one reason Alex is good at football is because he is so big?

82

Preparation

Have students turn to pages 82 and 83. Call their attention to the word list. Have students say the words. Then explain that each spelling word belongs in one of the blanks in the story.

Write the title "The Whale Has a Whale of a Day!" on the board. Tell students that this story is about a special day in the life of a star football player nicknamed the "Whale." The story is written in the form of a newspaper article. Ask the students why a football player might be called the "Whale."

The Pages

Read the newspaper article, supplying the missing spelling words as the students follow along in their texts. When you have finished, you may wish to discuss what happened to the Whale on his birthday. Ask students why he might eat so much birthday cake. *(To be polite. He loves birthday cake.)* Ask why the Whale might be so popular. *(He is a wonderful football player. He is a very nice person.)*

Then ask students to complete the article by silently reading it and writing the correct spelling word for each blank. When they are finished, have a volunteer read the article aloud, pausing before each blank. Have other volunteers say and spell the missing spelling word aloud at the appropriate time. Then have students write the answers on the board. Check students' responses for the accurate spelling of each answer.

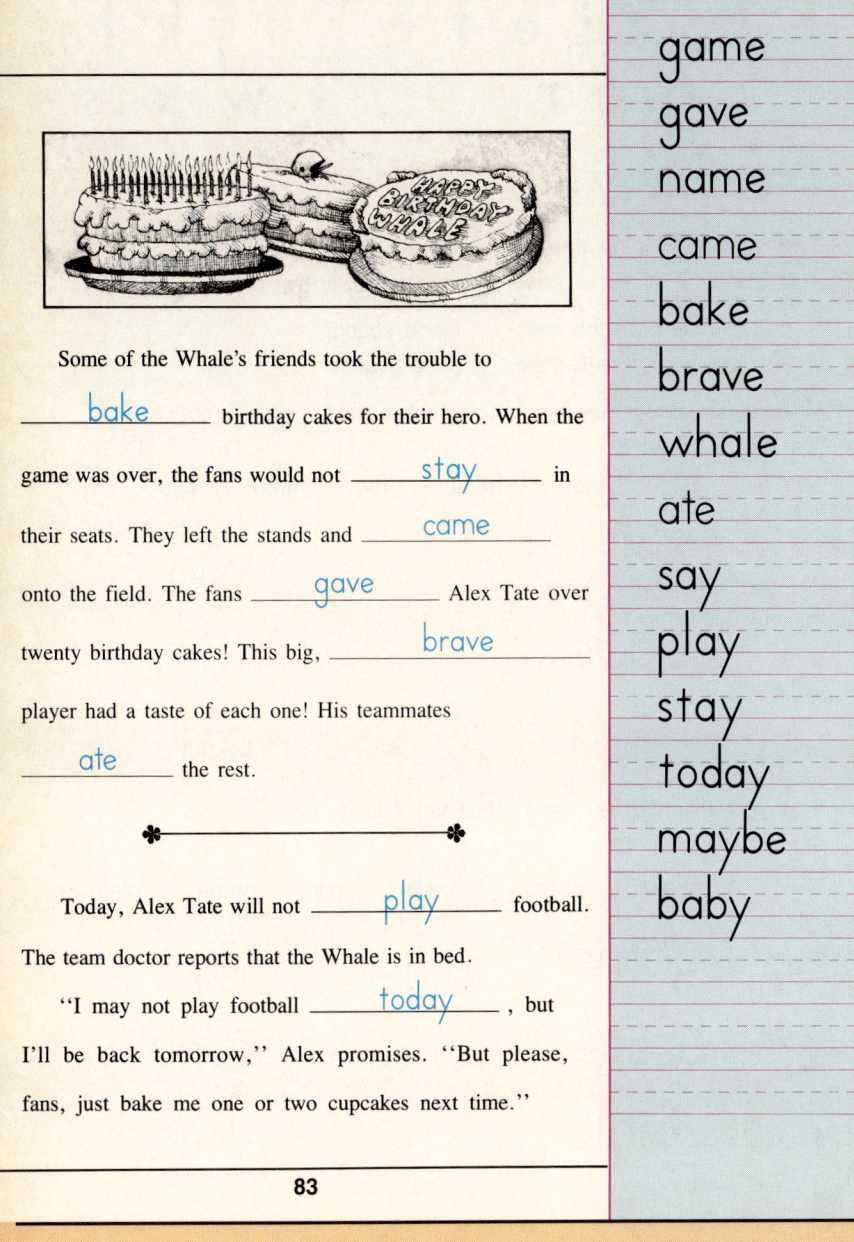

Some of the Whale's friends took the trouble to

_____bake_____ birthday cakes for their hero. When the

game was over, the fans would not _____stay_____ in

their seats. They left the stands and _____came_____

onto the field. The fans _____gave_____ Alex Tate over

twenty birthday cakes! This big, _____brave_____

player had a taste of each one! His teammates

_____ate_____ the rest.

❋————————————————❋

Today, Alex Tate will not _____play_____ football.
The team doctor reports that the Whale is in bed.

"I may not play football _____today_____ , but
I'll be back tomorrow," Alex promises. "But please,
fans, just bake me one or two cupcakes next time."

83

game
gave
name
came
bake
brave
whale
ate
say
play
stay
today
maybe
baby

Enrichment

If you want to use the blackline activity masters for enrichment and additional practice, assign Lesson 15 activities at this time.

Maintenance and Review

OBJECTIVE
- To review words with /ŭ/ spelled: u, o.

ACTIVITIES

If you want to use the blackline activity masters for maintenance and review, assign Lesson 14 activities at this time.

You can also use the activity below to review Lesson 14 with students:

Write the following sentence fragments on the board (without underlining any words). Have students copy the fragments and complete the sentences. Then have students underline the spelling words. They may read their sentences aloud, noting the spelling word in each and spelling it aloud.

1. My mother likes football better than
2. In fact, we just came from
3. My brother plays
4. At one game, he
5. He says there's too much
6. But I think it would be fun to

Follow-Up Have students use each of the spelling words they missed in an original sentence that relates to the story.

As an additional follow-up activity, you may wish to divide the class into two teams and draw a scoreboard. Practice spelling words aloud in a spelling-bee style. If one team spells a word correctly, score a "field goal" of 3 points. If a team scores 5 consecutive field goals with no errors, give them a bonus of 6 points. The winning team is the one to score the most points.

Objectives

- To relate spelling words to a dictionary skill.
- To recognize and use diacritical marks for short and long vowel sounds.
- To write spelling words with attention to pronunciation.
- To check handwriting for correct letter formation.

---

a b c d e f g h i j k l m
n o p q r s t u v w x y z

Dictionary

This mark ˘ over a vowel means the vowel has a short sound.
This mark ‾ over a vowel means the vowel has a long sound.

bătt   I bat the ball.   (short sound)
bāke   I bake a cake.   (long sound)

Write these words. Say them. Then put a short mark ˘ over the **a** in each word.

fat   back   hand   van   man   cat

1. făt
2. băck
3. hănd
4. văn
5. măn
6. căt

Write these words. Say them. Then put a long mark ‾ over the **a** in each word.

game   brave   whale   say   name   play

7. gāme
8. brāve
9. whāle
10. sāy
11. nāme
12. plāy

84

Preparation Write the following words on the board:

last   bake   hand   gave

Ask the students to listen for the vowel sound in each word as you read it aloud. What is different about the vowel sounds? (In last and hand, the letter a says /ă/; in bake and gave, the letter a says /ā/.)
Put these symbols on the board: /ā/ /ă/
Have students pronounce them. Then ask students to repeat after you: /ā/ as in bake, /ă/ as in last.

The Page Do page 84 with the students. Remind students to form their letters carefully. Pay particular attention to formation of the letter y in words like say and play. This letter slants from the center of the writing line to the bottom line and is crossed by another line to make a v at the base. Be sure the tail of the y extends below the writing line. When students have finished, ask volunteers to write their answers on the board.

Follow-Up Write the following words on the board: **gave, maybe, play, flat, baby, today.** Have students alphabetize the list and put the correct diacritical mark over the a in each word.

WORDS AT WORK

Challenge Yourself

delay   bacon   fade

Decide which Challenge Word fits each clue. Check your Spelling Dictionary to see if you were right. Then write sentences. Show that you understand the meaning of each Challenge Word.

1. Many people eat this food with eggs and toast.

2. Jeans do this after many washings.

3. When you put something off until later, you do this.

Write to the Point

Read "The Whale" on pages 82 and 83 again. Make a get-well card for Alex Tate. Draw a picture on the outside. Then write some sentences inside that will make Alex feel better. Use spelling words from this lesson on your card.

Challenge Use one or more of the Challenge Words on your card.

Proofreading

Use the marks to show the mistakes in the sentences below. Write the four misspelled words correctly in the blanks.

◯	word is misspelled
⊙	period is missing
≡	letter should be capitalized

1. Alex Tate (cam) to my home.

2. we talked about the (gane.)

3. The best (pley) was at the end⊙

4. I say (taday) was a great day!

1. _____ came _____

2. _____ game _____

3. _____ play _____

4. _____ today _____

85

Objectives

- To extend the vowel spellings presented in Lesson 15 to the Challenge Words.

- To use clues and the **Spelling Dictionary** to enlarge students' vocabulary.

- To apply the vowel spellings presented in Lesson 15 in a writing activity.

- To practice proofreading for spelling, punctuation, and capitalization.

Dictation Sentences

1. My class will bake a cake.
2. My baby brother can say his name.
3. Will you play this game with us?
4. He came home with me today.
5. You must stay home if you have a cold.
6. My sister gave me red socks.
7. Maybe I will see a whale at the zoo.
8. I ate a good lunch.
9. My brave cat ran after the fox.

Challenge Yourself Answers

1. bacon
2. fade
3. delay

Students' sentences will vary.

Test Review these ways to spell /ā/: a_e as in game; ay as in play; a as in baby. Test words with /ā/. Use one of these testing methods: (1) Say the word; read the sample sentence from page 80; say the word; have students write the word. (2) Read each dictation sentence above; have students write the sentence. Correct the test with students.

Challenge Yourself The optional Challenge Words may be assigned to the entire class or limited to those students who do well on the test. Have students note the vowel spellings in the Challenge Words. Responses to this activity should be completed on separate paper. Answers to the questions are provided above.

Write to the Point Have students recall the selection "The Whale" on pages 82 and 83; then assign the get-well card. Remind students to include a closing with their name at the end of the message. This activity should be completed on separate paper.

Proofreading The proofreading practice includes misspellings of words from this lesson as well as a capitalization error and a punctuation error.

LESSON 16

Objectives

- To hear and say words with /ā/.
- To write words with /ā/ with attention to letter sequence and sound/symbol relationships.
- To write each spelling word once.
- To recognize that /ā/ may be spelled ai, ei, and ey.

Sample Sentences

1. We hammered a nail to put up the weather vane.
2. The forecast says that it might rain.
3. How much weight did the baby gain?
4. We rode cross-country on a train.
5. She tied her bike with a chain.
6. When my dog is happy, he wags his tail.
7. Please paint a sign for the cake sale.
8. He went to the beach with his shovel and pail.
9. My sailboat had only one sail.
10. We found a snail on a leaf near the pond.
11. I can wait for you until three.
12. Did you mail the letters for me?
13. Her brother was just eight years old.
14. They live up north where it is cold.

Note

Words are grouped according to spellings of /ā/:

ai
ei
ey

The sample sentences may be used for pretesting and post-testing.

Lesson 16 Words with /ā/

nail
rain
gain
train
chain
tail
paint
pail
sail
snail
wait
mail

eight

they

1. Write the words that end like pain.

rain   gain
train   chain

2. What spelling word ends with /nt/?

paint

3. Write the words that end like trail.

nail   tail
pail   sail
snail   mail

4. What word begins with the first letter in we?

wait

5. Which word spells /ā/ with ey, as in obey?

they

6. Which word spells /ā/ with ei, as in neighbor?

eight

86

Preparation Write /ā/ on the board. Have students repeat the sound /ā/ as in pay. Say these word pairs. Ask students to wave when they hear a word with /ā/.

chin – chain   ran – rain   paint – pint   it – eight   they – the

Read the spelling words on page 86 and have the students repeat and spell each word.

Note the special sound/symbol relationships such as the consonant digraphs ch in chain, th in they, and the consonant blends tr in train, sn in snail. Then have the students look at the last two words, eight and they. Ask them if they see the letter a in eight or they. (no) Then ask if they hear /ā/. (yes) Explain that ei spells /ā/ in the word eight. What letters spell /ā/ in they? (ey) (See **Note**.)

Have the students point to the word in their spelling books as you read each sample sentence.

The Page Do the activities on page 86, allowing time for students to answer. Check students' responses for immediate reinforcement of correct spelling.

Follow-Up Be sure that each student has a study plan. Suggest that the students write each word on a card (or small piece of paper). Then have them tape the cards in different places and practice spelling a word every time they see the card.

Checkpoint

Write a spelling word for each clue. Then use the Checkpoint Study Plan on page 224.

1. A happy dog wags its ___.

2. When you walk slowly, you move like a ___.

3. We got to the movie early and had to ___.

4. The swing hangs from a ___.

5. Water that falls from clouds is ___.

6. Four and four are ___.

7. At the end of your finger is a ___.

8. How much weight did you ___?

9. A bucket is a ___.

10. In art class, I like to ___.

11. I made a paper boat to ___.

12. One way to travel is by ___.

13. Do you know who ___ are?

14. In France hundreds of years ago, a bag used to carry letters was called a <u>male</u>. The mystery word comes from this word. It sounds the same, but is spelled differently. Now the word means "letters and packages." Guess the mystery word. ___

87

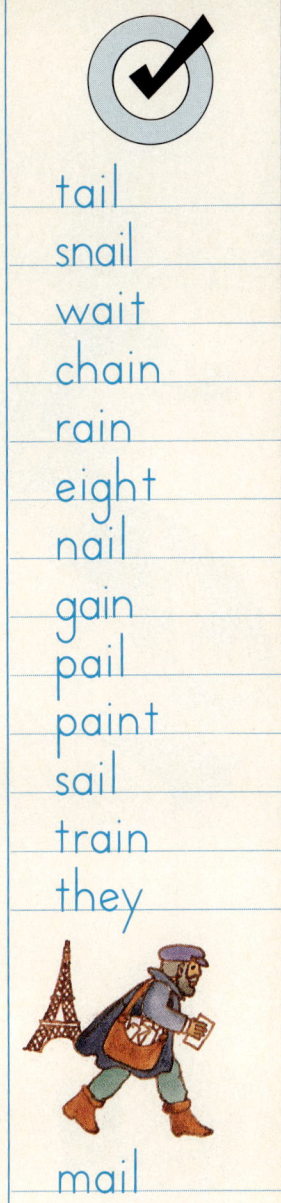

tail
snail
wait
chain
rain
eight
nail
gain
pail
paint
sail
train
they
mail

Objectives

- To write words with (ā) in continuous text.
- To write each spelling word once.
- To integrate reading with spelling.

Fill in the blanks with spelling words.

THE LETTER

What would you do if you saw a long tail

Sticking out of a letter you got in the ___mail___ ?

Would you yell, "This belongs in a ___pail___ !"

Would you feed it a worm, or even a ___snail___ ?

Would you jump in a boat and put up a ___sail___ ?

Would you nibble your finger and bite your

___nail___ ?

Would you ___paint___ it bright red?

Or might that cause a worry?

If you called the police,

Would ___they___ come in a hurry?

Preparation   Have students turn to pages 88 and 89. Call their attention to the pictures and the word list. Have the students say the words. Then explain that each spelling word belongs in one of the blanks in the poem.

Write the title "The Letter" on the board and have a student read it aloud. Next, ask the students to look at the five stanzas in their texts. Remind them that poetry is written in separate lines of verse rather than in sentences in a paragraph. Have them listen for rhyming words as you read this poem about a boy who receives something very peculiar in the mail.

The Pages   Read the poem aloud, supplying the missing spelling words as the students follow along in their texts. When you have finished, you may wish to discuss the poem. Ask students what they would do if they received a letter that had a tail sticking out of it!

Then have them complete the poem by writing the correct spelling word for each blank. When they have finished, ask half of the class to read the poem aloud, pausing before each blank. Have the other half of the class say the missing spelling word at the appropriate time. Write the answers on the board so students may check their own work. Be sure to check students' responses for the accurate spelling of each answer.

You could twist it all up

In the shape of an _____eight_____,

Then ask it to leave,

Not just sit there and _____wait_____!

Would you wrap it in paper that's plain?

Would you send it away on a _____train_____?

Would you leave it outside in the _____rain_____?

Would you tie it all up with a _____chain_____?

Would you weigh it?

How many pounds did it _____gain_____?

I know what I'd do if I saw a long _____tail_____

Sticking out of a letter I got in the mail.

I'd open the letter and then with a shout

I'd say, "Hi, there, Dragon! It's time to come out!"

89

nail
rain
gain
train
chain
tail
paint
pail
sail
snail
wait
mail
eight
they

Enrichment

If you want to use the blackline activity masters for enrichment and additional practice, assign Lesson 16 activities at this time.

Maintenance and Review

OBJECTIVE

• To review words with (ā) spelled: a_e, ay, a.

ACTIVITIES

If you want to use the blackline activity masters for maintenance and review, assign Lesson 15 activities at this time.

You can also use the activity below to review Lesson 15 with students:

Have students copy the words below and draw lines to match the rhyming words.

today	game
name	stay
say	maybe
baby	play

You may wish to have students choose one of the rhyming pairs and use it in a sentence.

(today – stay, name – game, say – stay, baby – maybe)

Follow-Up Have students use each of the spelling words they missed in an original sentence.

As an additional follow-up activity, have each student rewrite the poem and illustrate each stanza of "The Letter." Ask them to trace the spelling words in each stanza in a different color.

Objectives

- To relate spelling words to a dictionary skill.
- To locate and copy sound spellings from the **Spelling Dictionary**.
- To use the pronunciation key.
- To write spelling words with attention to pronunciation.
- To check handwriting for correct letter formation.

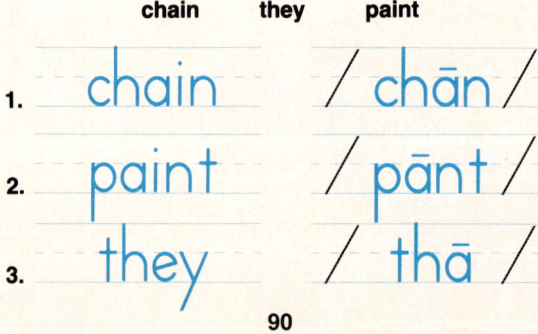

a b c d e f g h i j k l m
n o p q r s t u v w x y z

Dictionary

The dictionary gives a <u>sound spelling</u> for each word.
The <u>sound spelling</u> comes right after the word in the entry.

> **nail** /nāl/—*plural* **nails. 1.** The growth at the end of a
> finger or toe. *Fingernails protect the ends of your
> fingers.* **2.** A thin, pointed metal pin. *You can fasten
> pieces of wood together with a **nail**.*
> Jimmy: *I hit the **nail** with a hammer.*
> Dad: *Good work!*
> Jim: *No. It was my thumb**nail**.*

The word between the lines, /nāl/, is the same word as **nail**. It is
written with symbols so you will know how to say the word.
Look at the Key on page 196. It tells you that /ă/ sounds
like the **a** in p**a**t. It tells you that /ā/ sounds like the **a**
in p**a**y. Does **a** have the same sound in <u>nail</u> and in <u>pay</u>? yes

Write the words below in alphabetical order. Then look them up
in the Spelling Dictionary. Write each word in symbols.

	chain	they	paint
1.	chain	/ chān /	
2.	paint	/ pānt /	
3.	they	/ thā /	

90

Preparation Write these words on the board: ran   rain
Ask which word has the /ă/ sound *(ran)* and which has the /ā/ sound *(rain)*.
Have volunteers place the correct diacritical mark over each. Then ask students
to turn to the pronunciation key at the top of page 196 in the **Spelling Dictionary**. Explain that this key gives a sample word for each **vowel** sound. Have
students find the sound /ă/ and the sample word. *(pat)* Then have them find
the sample word for /ā/. *(pay)*

Write these words on the board: train   pail   mail   van
Have a volunteer alphabetize them. *(mail, pail, train, van)* Ask the students to
locate <u>mail</u> in the Spelling Dictionary. *(page 211)* Have a student write the
sound spelling for mail on the board *(/māl/)* Ask if <u>mail</u> has the sound of /ā/
as in <u>pay</u> or /ă/ as in <u>pat</u>. *(/ā/)* Continue the drill for the other three words.

The Page Do page 90 with the class. Remind students to pay attention
to handwriting. Be sure they dot their <u>i</u>'s and cross their <u>t</u>'s. Have students spell
each word aloud and then note the sound spelling with diacritical marks. Write
the answers on the board so the students may check their own work.

Follow-Up Have students take turns at the board writing the spelling words
with symbols. Have the rest of the class identify the words by saying them and
spelling them aloud.

90

WORDS AT WORK

Challenge Yourself

bravery	dainty	faithful

What do you think each underlined Challenge Word means? Check your Spelling Dictionary to see if you are right. Then write sentences. Show that you understand the meaning of each Challenge Word.

1. It took bravery to jump off the high diving board.

2. The dress was covered with dainty flowers.

3. A faithful pet will never run away from home.

Write to the Point

Think of a funny animal. It might be a dog with wings or a cat with six feet. It might even be a snail that talks! Write three or four sentences that tell about your animal. Use spelling words from this lesson in your sentences.

Challenge Use one or more of the Challenge Words in your sentences.

Proofreading

Use the marks to show the mistakes in the sentences below. Write the four misspelled words correctly in the blanks.

⬭	word is misspelled
⊙	period is missing
☰	letter should be capitalized

1. They are sending me a ⬭snale.⊙

2. it will take ⬭ate days.
   ☰

3. It will have a short ⬭tale⊙.

4. I can't ⬭waite until it comes!

1. _____ snail _____

2. _____ eight _____

3. _____ tail _____

4. _____ wait _____

91

Objectives

- To extend the vowel spellings presented in Lesson 16 to the Challenge Words.

- To use context and the **Spelling Dictionary** to enlarge students' vocabulary.

- To apply the vowel spellings in Lesson 16 in a writing activity.

- To practice proofreading for spelling, punctuation, and capitalization.

Dictation Sentences

1. You can get a nail from the box.
2. Will it rain today?
3. Ring the bell that is on the chain.
4. She will paint her train red.
5. Did they sail on the lake last summer?
6. I see eight cats in the pet shop.
7. The child has a snail in her pail.
8. I will wait and pick up the mail.
9. Did you dot the i in gain?
10. This fox has a red tail.

Challenge Yourself Answers

Possible definitions:

1. courage
2. delicate
3. loyal and true

Students' sentences will vary.

Test Review these ways to spell /ā/: ai as in train; ei as in eight; ey as in they. Test words with /ā/. Use one of these testing methods: (1) Say the word; read the sample sentence from page 86; say the word; have students write the word (2) Read each dictation sentence above; have students write the sentence. Correct the test with students.

Challenge Yourself The optional Challenge Words may be assigned to the entire class or limited to those students who do well on the test. Have students note the vowel spellings in the Challenge Words. Responses to this activity should be completed on separate paper. Answers to the questions are provided above.

Write to the Point Have students recall the selection "The Letter" on pages 88 and 89; then assign the sentences. This activity should be completed on separate paper.

Proofreading The proofreading practice includes misspellings of words from this lesson as well as a capitalization error and a punctuation error.

LESSON 17

Objectives

- To hear and say words with the suffixes ed and ing.
- To write words with the suffixes ed and ing with attention to letter sequence and sound/symbol relationships.
- To write each spelling word once.
- To recognize that the suffixes ed and ing may be added to verbs.

Sample Sentences

1. He handed the bone to the pup.
2. Day ended, but the pup is still up.
3. We thanked them for our meal.
4. I asked for a better deal.
5. We wished that we could stay.
6. We went out in a boat and fished.
7. The magician tricked the crowd.
8. We practiced catching the ball.
9. They were dressing for a party at Old Town Hall.
10. I was helping my neighbor bake a cake.
11. In the fall, we will go apple picking.
12. Sometimes I go fishing on Kingston Lake.
13. I've been thinking how tasty fish would be.
14. I've been wishing my sister and I would catch three.

Note

The sample sentences may be used for pretesting and post-testing.

Lesson 17 Adding ed and ing

handed
ended
thanked
asked
wished
fished
tricked

catching
dressing
helping
picking
fishing
thinking
wishing

1. end + ed = ended
2. hand + ed = handed
3. help + ing = helping

4. What words have the /k/ sound in them?

thanked   asked
tricked   catching
picking   thinking

5. Write the words in which you can hear /sh/.

wished   fished
fishing   wishing

6. What word has the double consonant ss in it?

dressing

Double consonants make only one sound.
Really?

92

Preparation Write ed and ing on the board. List these words on the board:
wish   trick   thank   ask
Then have a volunteer write wish, add ed, and then say the new word. Ask another student to use wished in a sentence. Do the same for trick, thank, and ask. Then have volunteers come to the board and add ing to wish, trick, thank, and ask. Have them say the new words and use them in sentences.

Have students look at the spelling words on page 92. Say each word aloud. Then have students say and spell each word.

Note the two sounds of ed: /ĕd/ and /t/. Ask students to find the words in which ed says /ĕd/. (handed, ended) Have them find the words in which ed says /t/. (thanked, asked, wished, fished, tricked) Ask the students to look at the cartoon and find the word with double consonants. (really)

Then read the sample sentences as students point to the spelling words.

The Page Do the page together. Then have students spell each answer aloud as one of them writes it on the board so they may check their work.

Follow-Up Suggest making two cards for each word: one for the spelling word, the other for the base word. Students may then shuffle the cards and play a game by matching the base word to the spelling word (hand and handed, for example).

Checkpoint

Write a spelling word for each clue.
Then use the Checkpoint Study Plan on page 224.

1. Every fall we go apple ___.

2. Are you right-handed or left-___?

3. I got the birthday present I ___ for!

4. Last June, we went to a lake and ___.

5. If you're hoping for something, you're ___.

6. When you put on clothes, you are ___.

7. I'll go home after the movie has ___.

8. I did what my teacher ___.

9. On April Fool's Day, I ___ Sam.

10. If you use your brain, you are ___.

11. Maria's family likes to go ___.

12. Grandma thanked me for ___.

13. When I left Jane's party, I ___ her.

14. The Latin word *capere* means "to get hold of."
The word *chase* comes from *capere*. The mystery
word means "getting hold of." All the letters
except the first two have changed. Can you
guess the word? ___

93

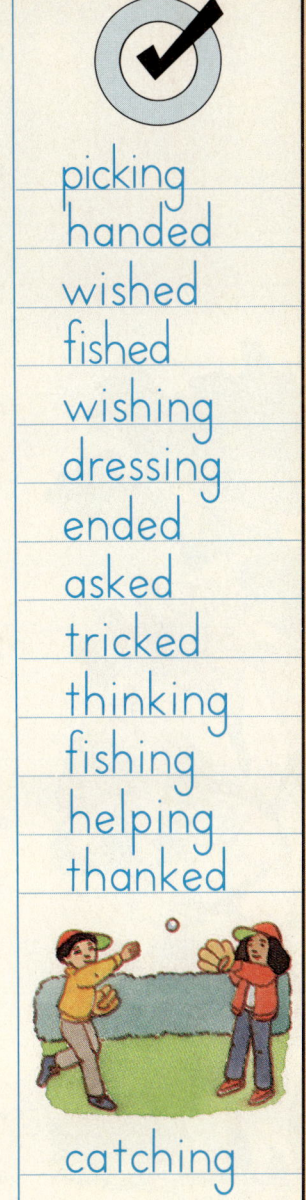

picking
handed
wished
fished
wishing
dressing
ended
asked
tricked
thinking
fishing
helping
thanked

catching

Objectives

• To write spelling words in response to clues: definitions and context.

• To develop the critical thinking skills of analyzing and making inferences.

• To understand that the spelling of words in the English language may change over time.

Spelling Strategy

Because the final *ed* sometimes sounds like /t/, some students may spell this ending *t*. Students experiencing this problem might find it helpful to write the word, draw a line between the base word and the *ed* ending, and pronounce it several times.

Preparation The clues on this page are like crossword puzzle clues. Explain to students that the response to each clue is a spelling word. Use the following examples to illustrate the types of clues used:

> **Definition**   When you put on clothes, you are *(dressing)*.
> **Context**   On April Fools' Day, I *(tricked)* Sam.

The final clue explains how the spelling of <u>catching</u> changed as it became a word in the English language.

The Page Have students complete page 93 using the words on page 92. When students have finished, have them read each clue and spell the answer aloud. Check each response twice: once for the correct answer and a second time for spelling accuracy.

Follow-Up Guide students in using the **Checkpoint Study Plan** on page 224 to take a self-test. Have them use the plan for independent study.

Objectives

- To write words with the suffixes <u>ed</u> and <u>ing</u> in continuous text
- To write each spelling word once.
- To integrate reading with spelling.

The Rabbit and the Slowpoke

Fill in the blanks with spelling words.

There once was a rabbit. He spent most of his time teasing a slowpoke turtle. The turtle wished and _____wished_____ he could run as fast as the rabbit. The turtle was _____wishing_____ he could beat the rabbit in a race. One day he wrote a note and _____handed_____ it to the rabbit.

> Meet me under the oak tree for a race to the river. The owl will be the judge.

The rabbit got all dressed up for the race. He wore his purple running shoes and a bright headband. He spent quite a long time _____dressing_____ himself. The turtle just wore his shell.

The race began at noon. The rabbit dashed past the turtle. Soon he was far ahead. He stopped and began _____picking_____ berries. Then he saw a pond and went _____fishing_____. He _____fished_____ for a long time.

94

Preparation

Have students turn to pages 94 and 95. Call their attention to the word list. Have the students say the words. Then explain that each spelling word belongs in one of the blanks in the story.

Write the title "The Rabbit and the Slowpoke" on the board and have a student read it. Then have students look at the pictures. Explain to the students that this story is about a turtle who challenges a rabbit to a race. Ask if students think a turtle could possibly outrace a rabbit.

The Pages

Read the story aloud, supplying the missing spelling words as the students follow along in their texts. When you have finished reading, you may wish to discuss the story. Ask the students if the turtle won the race because he was faster than the rabbit. *(no)* Why did the turtle win the race? *(He tried harder than the rabbit. Accept any reasonable response.)*

Then have students write the correct spelling word for each blank as they complete the story on their own. Ask a volunteer to read the story aloud, pausing before each blank. Have the other students spell the missing spelling word at the appropriate time while volunteers write the answers on the board. Be sure to check students' responses for the accurate spelling of each answer.

He did not know that the turtle was slowly

___catching___ up with him.

Soon the turtle passed the rabbit. But he was so quiet the rabbit never saw him. The turtle kept slowly walking. At last he saw the river and the finish line.

When the turtle crossed the finish line, the owl said that the race had ___ended___. She gave the turtle a blue ribbon, and the polite turtle ___thanked___ her.

A minute later the rabbit came running by holding the five fish he had caught. He ___asked___ the owl for his blue ribbon.

Then the rabbit saw that the turtle had the ribbon. "You fooled me. How could you win? I must have been ___tricked___! Did you have friends ___helping___ you?"

"No," said the turtle. "I had my own four feet. And I just kept ___thinking___ to myself: Slow but sure will win the race!"

95

handed
ended
thanked
asked
wished
fished
tricked
catching
dressing
helping
picking
fishing
thinking
wishing

Enrichment

If you want to use the blackline activity masters for enrichment and additional practice, assign Lesson 17 activities at this time.

Maintenance and Review

OBJECTIVE

- To review words with /ā/ spelled: ai, ei, ey.

ACTIVITIES

If you want to use the blackline activity masters for maintenance and review, assign Lesson 16 activities at this time.

You can also use the activity below to review Lesson 16 with students:

Write the following word pairs on the board and have the students copy them. Then ask students to write a sentence using each word pair.

1. paint – sail
2. wait – mail
3. pail – nail
4. they – eight
5. rain – train

Follow-Up Have students use each of the spelling words they missed in an original sentence that relates to the story.

As an additional follow-up activity, you may wish to divide the class into groups of four to act out the story. In each group, have one student serve as the narrator while the others act out the parts of the rabbit, the turtle, and the owl.

Objectives

- To relate spelling to another language skill.
- To use the ed or ing form of a word in context.
- To write spelling words in the context of sentences.
- To check handwriting for correct letter formation.

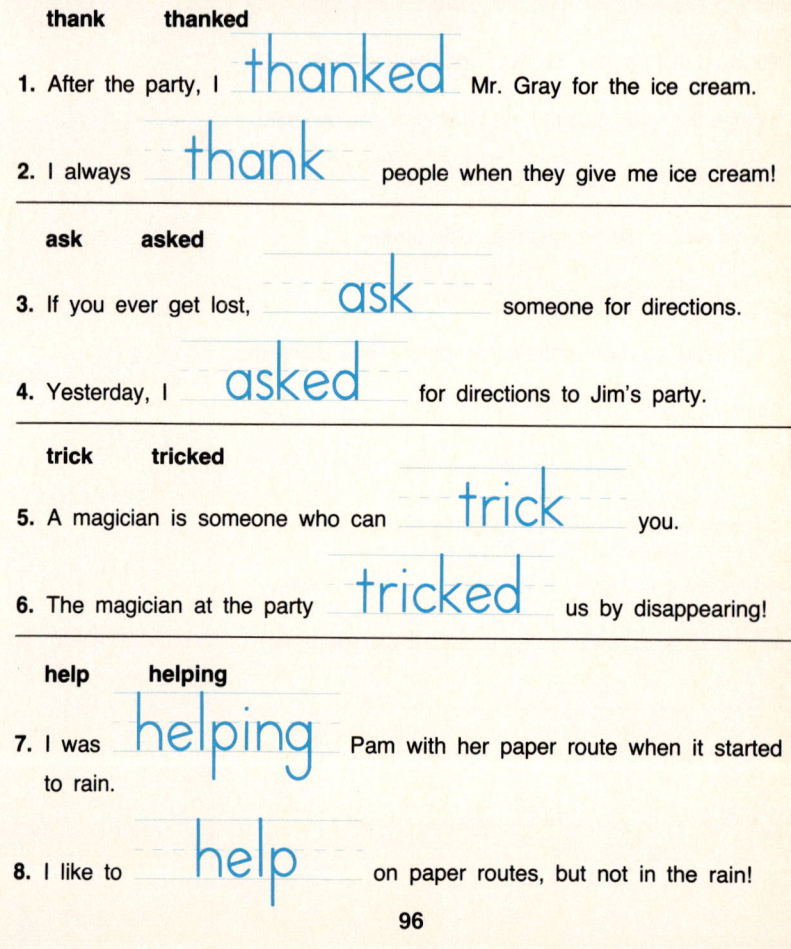

a b c d e f g h i j k l m
n o p q r s t u v w x y z

Using the Right Word

Choose the correct word to fill in the blank.

thank   thanked

1. After the party, I _thanked_ Mr. Gray for the ice cream.

2. I always _thank_ people when they give me ice cream!

ask   asked

3. If you ever get lost, _ask_ someone for directions.

4. Yesterday, I _asked_ for directions to Jim's party.

trick   tricked

5. A magician is someone who can _trick_ you.

6. The magician at the party _tricked_ us by disappearing!

help   helping

7. I was _helping_ Pam with her paper route when it started to rain.

8. I like to _help_ on paper routes, but not in the rain!

96

Preparation Tell students that to talk about something that happened in the past, we usually add ed to the action word. To talk about something that is happening right now, we usually add ing to the action word. Write the following words and sentences on the board:

wish   wished   wishing
1. I will _____ on a star tonight.
2. Last night I _____ that I had won the race.
3. Right now, I am _____ that it would stop raining.

Ask volunteers to read each sentence and write the correct form of wish. (1. wish; 2. wished; 3. wishing) Ask what clues in the sentences helped them to decide which word to use. (Last night is a clue for ed. Right now is the clue for ing.)

The Page Do page 96 together. Tell students not to make spelling mistakes because of poor handwriting. Remind them that the letter d should not be confused with the letter b. Have a volunteer write the words on the board so students may check their own work.

Follow-Up Write these words on the board: **dressing, ask, asking.** Have the students write their own sentences using these words.

WORDS AT WORK

Challenge Yourself

denying　　**claimed**　　**alerting**

What do you think each underlined Challenge Word means? Check your Spelling Dictionary to see if you are right. Then write sentences. Show that you understand the meaning of each Challenge Word.

1. My friend claimed she saw a purple cow.

2. Diego kept denying that he had eaten the cookies.

3. The alarm is alerting the police.

Write to the Point

The rabbit and the turtle had an exciting race. Write a short newspaper story about the race. Tell how the slower animal was able to win. Use spelling words from this lesson in your story.

Challenge Use one or more of the Challenge Words in your story.

Proofreading

Use the marks to show the mistakes in the sentences below. Write the four misspelled words correctly in the blanks.

	word is misspelled
⊙	period is missing
≡	letter should be capitalized

1. The race (endded) and the rabbit felt tricked⊙

2. He (wishd) that he had won!

3. ≡the rabbit was (fishin⊙)

4. The turtle is (pikin) up the prize!

1. _____ended_____

2. _____wished_____

3. _____fishing_____

4. _____picking_____

97

Objectives

- To extend the spelling patterns presented in Lesson 17 to the Challenge Words.
- To use context and the **Spelling Dictionary** to enlarge students' vocabulary.
- To apply the spellings presented in Lesson 17 in a writing activity.
- To practice proofreading for spelling, punctuation, and capitalization.

Dictation Sentences

1. I wished the game had ended at one.
2. I thanked my brother for helping me.
3. He asked if I went fishing.
4. What is he wishing?
5. My mother handed me a big box.
6. She is dressing up today.
7. Is the man catching many fish?
8. The boy tricked the fox.
9. My sister is thinking of picking me up at three.
10. I sat on the rock and fished.

Challenge Yourself Answers

Possible definitions:

1. said to be true
2. saying something is not true
3. warning

Students' sentences will vary.

Test Review these two suffixes: ed as in handed; ing as in thinking. Test words with ed and ing endings. Use one of these testing methods: (1) Say the word; read the sample sentence from page 92; say the word; have students write the word. (2) Read each dictation sentence above; have students write the sentence. Correct the test with students.

Challenge Yourself The optional Challenge Words may be assigned to the entire class or limited to those students who do well on the test. Have students note the spellings in the Challenge Words. Responses to this activity should be completed on separate paper. Answers to the questions are provided above.

Write to the Point Have students recall the selection "The Rabbit and the Slowpoke" on pages 94 and 95; then assign the newspaper story. This activity should be completed on separate paper.

Proofreading The proofreading practice includes misspellings of words from this lesson as well as a capitalization error and a punctuation error.

LESSON 18

Objectives

- To review and reinforce vowel spellings for /ŭ/ and /ā/.
- To review and reinforce the suffixes ed and ing.
- To hear, say, spell, and write representative words from Lessons 13–17.
- To write a friendly letter using the five steps in the writing process.
- To use a prewriting activity to explore things to say in a letter of invitation.

Dictation Sentences

1. My mother cut those flowers today.
2. This letter just came from Uncle Barney.
3. I am much younger than my sister.
4. We found only one blue shoe.
5. My dog's name is Iggie.
6. Did you say something?
7. My baby sister sleeps a lot.
8. Aunt Susan wears a silver chain.
9. Maria had eight balloons.
10. I think they want a biscuit.
11. Sandy is helping José deliver newspapers.
12. She asked if she could use my skates.

Note

A review test blackline master in standardized format and an answer sheet have been provided on pages T37 and T41 of this Teacher's Edition. The answers to the review test are given below.

1-C	5-B
2-A	6-D
3-D	7-C
4-C	8-A

Lesson 18   Words in Review

A. cut
   from

B. much
   one

C. name
   say
   baby

D. chain
   eight
   they

E. helping
   asked

1. In Lesson 13 you studied two ways to spell /ŭ/: u and o. Write the words in List A.

cut   from

2. List B has two more words with /ŭ/. Write the two words.

much   one

3. In Lesson 15 you studied three ways to spell /ā/. Write the words in List C.

name   say

baby

4. List D has three more words with /ā/. Write the three words.

chain   they

eight

5. In Lesson 17 you added ed and ing to some words. Add ing to help and ed to ask. Use List E to check your words.

helping   asked

98

Preparation Tell students that Lesson 18 is a review lesson. Lesson 18 contains several activities that ask them to write some of the words they have studied in Lessons 13–17.

Direct students' attention to the list of words on page 98. Read the words aloud as students look at them. Have students say and spell each word aloud.

Then read the dictation sentences above as students point to each spelling word in their book. Point out that the words in List A are from Lesson 13, words in List B are from Lesson 14, words in List C are from Lesson 15, words in List D are from Lesson 16, and words in List E are from Lesson 17.

The Pages Have students complete the activities on page 98 as a group or independently. Write the answers on the board and have volunteers spell the words aloud for reinforcement of correct spelling.

Test and Study If you wish to test students on the review words, use one of these testing methods: (1) Read the spelling word and the dictation sentence; say the word again; have students write the word. (2) Have students complete the review test blackline master. (See **Note**.)

Writer's Workshop

A Letter

People write to their friends for many reasons. They write to share feelings. They write to tell news about their lives. Sometimes they write to invite their friends somewhere. Here is part of Kara's letter to Ramón.

> **Dear Ramón,**
>
> Next Saturday is my birthday. I'm going to be eight years old. Mom said I can invite some friends to a party. I hope you can come! The party begins at 2:00 P.M. at 160 Elm Street. That is my house. Bring a bathing suit because we are going swimming at the pond. Later we will have lots of pizza. Call to let me know if you can come. My number is 555-0099.

Kara followed the steps in the writing process to write her letter. In a **Prewriting** activity, she made a list of things to say in her letter. Then she could be sure that she would not leave out any important facts. Part of Kara's list is shown here. Study what Kara did.

> Party for my birthday
>
> Saturday, 2:00 P.M.
>
> my address
>
> bring bathing suit
>
> my phone number

It's Your Turn

Get ready to write your own letter. You can invite someone to a party or to do something with you. First decide to whom you will write. Then decide what you will invite the person to. Make a list of things to say in your letter. Then follow the other steps in the writing process—**Writing, Revising, Proofreading,** and **Publishing.**

99

LESSON 19

Objectives

- To hear and say words with /ē/.
- To write words with /ē/ with attention to letter sequence and sound/symbol relationships.
- To write each spelling word once.
- To recognize that /ē/ may be spelled e, ee, e_e, and eo.

Sample Sentences

1. Is he your little brother?
2. Is she your aunt or your mother?
3. After school, we like to play.
4. It's nice to come home after being away.
5. I keep my socks in the drawer.
6. I didn't see the toy on the floor.
7. I took the wet shoes off my feet.
8. I gave green marbles to my friend Pete.
9. I like the houses on my street.
10. I want three raisin cookies to eat.
11. My birthday party is a week away.
12. The bees were buzzing around the yellow flowers.
13. Are these the pictures you painted today?
14. Those people are my neighbors.

Note

Lesson 19 Words with /ē/

he
she
we
being

keep
see
feet
green
street
three
bees
week

these
people

1. Which words end with one e and the sound /ē/?

he   she   we

2. What words end with two e's like the word free?

see   three

3. Write the words that have two e's in the middle.

keep   feet
green   street
bees   week

4. Write the words that end with the sound /z/.

bees   these
being

5. be + ing = _____

6. Which word has two p's?

people

I can't stand these /z/'s!

100

Preparation Write /ē/ on the board and have the students repeat /ē/ as in be. Say these word pairs. Ask the students to tap their feet when they hear a word with /ē/.

he – hat   being – bring   grin – green   these – those   threw – three

Have students look at the spelling words on page 100. Say each word aloud. Then have the students say and spell each word.

Note the two sounds of the letter s: /s/ and /z/. Ask the students to find the words in which s spells /s/. *(see, street)* The cartoon will help them identify the words in which s spells /z/. *(these, bees)* Then point out that in the first four words the sound /ē/ is spelled with the letter e. But in the next group of eight words, /ē/ is spelled with two letters. What are the two letters? *(ee)* Have students identify the spellings for /ē/ in the last two words. *(e_e, eo)* (See Note.)

Then read the sample sentences as students point to the spelling words.

The Page Do the page together, allowing time for students to write the answers. Then have volunteers write them on the board.

Follow-Up Suggest this study method. Have students write the words with a bright crayon. Tell them to spell each word aloud as they write it. Next, tell them to close their eyes, try to see the word, and to spell it aloud. Then they should open their eyes and check their spelling.

Checkpoint

Write a spelling word for each clue. Then use the Checkpoint Study Plan on page 224.

1. Men, women, girls, and boys are ___.

2. A word that sounds just like sea is ___.

3. They are going to the fair, and so are ___.

4. Blue and yellow make ___.

5. Linda runs faster than ___ does.

6. I don't want this, but I will ___ that.

7. I put the boots on my ___.

8. I like those apples but not ___.

9. Some insects that sting are ___.

10. A new family moved to our ___.

11. She is going, but ___ is not.

12. There are seven days in a ___.

13. I am a human ___.

14. This mystery word is a number. It started out as <u>trei</u>. It became <u>trī</u> in Irish, <u>trois</u> in French, and <u>tres</u> in Spanish. Can you tell what it became in English? It's the number after two. ___

101

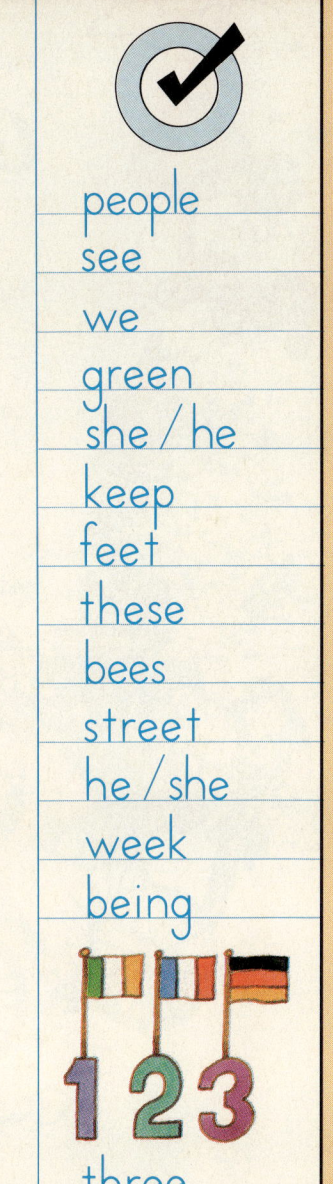

people
see
we
green
she / he
keep
feet
these
bees
street
he / she
week
being

three

Objectives

• To write spelling words in response to clues: homophones and context.

• To develop the critical thinking skills of classifying and analyzing.

• To recognize that the word for a concept may be quite similar across languages.

Spelling Strategy

Because of the unusual spelling of the /ē/ sound, some students may misspell <u>people</u> by either transposing the <u>e</u> and <u>o</u> or by doubling the <u>e</u> and dropping the <u>o</u>. Suggest that these students practice writing the sentence "Most <u>people</u> know that <u>e</u> comes before <u>o</u> in the alphabet."

Preparation The clues on this page are like crossword puzzle clues. Explain to students that the response to each clue is a spelling word. Use the following examples to illustrate the types of clues used:

Homophone   A word that sounds just like sea is *(see)*.
Context   She is going, but *(he)* is not.

The final clue explains similarities in the word for "three" across several languages.

The Page Have students complete page 101 using the words on page 100. When students have finished, have them read each clue and spell the answer aloud. Check each response twice: once for the correct answer and a second time for spelling accuracy.

Follow-Up Guide students in using the **Checkpoint Study Plan** on page 224 to take a self-test. Have them use the plan for independent study.

Objectives

- To write words with /ē/ in continuous text.
- To write each spelling word once.
- To integrate reading with spelling.

Fill in the blanks with spelling words.

Grandfather's Race

Robin and Tony went to ____see____ a bicycle

race last ____week____. The race was

____three____ miles long. Lots of ____people____

came to watch the race. Police were in the

____street____. They were asking people to

____keep____ back. Then the bicycles came. The

riders were wearing different colored shirts. A man in a

Preparation   Have students turn to pages 102 and 103. Call their attention to the word list. Have the students say the words. Then explain that each spelling word belongs in one of the blanks in the story.

Write the title "Grandfather's Race" on the board. Have students look at the picture. Tell students that this story is about a grandfather who is a terrific bicycle racer.

The Pages   Read the story aloud, supplying the missing spelling words as the students follow along in their texts. When you have finished reading, you may wish to discuss the story. Ask students why Grandfather was pedaling so fast. *(He was being chased by bees.)*

Have students complete the story by silently rereading it and writing the correct spelling word for each blank. Then have a volunteer read the story aloud, pausing before each blank. Have another volunteer say the missing spelling word at the appropriate time. Write the answers on the board so students may check their own work. Be sure to check students' responses for the accurate spelling of each answer.

bright _____green_____ shirt was in front.

"Hey! That's your grandfather!" yelled Tony. "I've

never seen him go so fast. How does __he__ do it?"

Robin laughed. "By pedaling with his two __feet__,

of course. On our bikes, __we__ could never be so

fast," __she__ said to Tony. "These racers

have racing bikes."

After the race, Robin ran up to her grandfather.

"You won!" she shouted.

Then she saw the __bees__. Her grandfather

was jumping around and ducking his head.

"These bees!" he said. "I'm afraid I wasn't

_____being_____ very careful. I bumped into their

hive. Then they chased me the whole way. I didn't

know how fast I could ride, until I tried to race

_____these_____ bees. And it looks like I lost that

race! Let's get out of here. The bees can have the

prize!"

103

he
she
we
being
keep
see
feet
green
street
three
bees
week
these
people

Enrichment

If you want to use the blackline activity masters for enrichment and additional practice, assign Lesson 19 activities at this time.

Maintenance and Review

OBJECTIVE

• To review words with the suffixes ed and ing.

ACTIVITIES

If you want to use the blackline activity masters for maintenance and review, assign Lesson 17 activities at this time.

You can also use the activity below to review Lesson 17 with students:

Write the following words on the board:

**hand   end   thank   ask   wish
dress   help   fish**

Ask the students to copy the words and to write two new words for each by adding the endings ed and ing. *(handed, handing; ended, ending; thanked, thanking; asked, asking; wished, wishing; dressed, dressing; helped, helping; fished, fishing)* Then have the students say sentences using the new words they have written while you write them on the board.

Follow-Up   Have students use each of the spelling words they missed in an original sentence that relates to the story.

As an additional follow-up activity, you may wish to have the students illustrate a scene from "Grandfather's Race." Ask students to caption their picture with sentences from the story. Then have them underline any spelling words in the captions.

Objectives

- To relate spelling to another language skill.
- To capitalize the names of cities, states, and streets.
- To write spelling words in the context of sentences.
- To practice proofreading.
- To check handwriting for correct letter formation.

---

a b c d e f g h i j k l m
n o p q r s t u v w x y z

Capital Letters

Capitalize the names of cities and states.

Denver	**Woodstock**
Colorado	**Vermont**

Write the name of your city.

Write the name of your state.

One word is spelled wrong in each sentence. Find the correct spelling in the words below. Write the sentence. Capitalize the names of states.

week   three   these

1. I went to ohio threa times.

I went to Ohio three times.

2. Theez apples come from new york.

These apples come from New York.

3. He is in texas this weke.

He is in Texas this week.

104

Preparation Write the following sentences on the board and read them:

My cousin lives in san diego, california.
He came to visit us in texas.

Ask the students what is wrong with these sentences. *(no capital letters to begin names of cities and states)* Have volunteers correct the errors at the board.

Then draw an envelope on the board. Address it to a fictitious character, omitting all capital letters. Ask a student to correct any errors. *(i.e., capitalizing names of people, streets, cities, and states)* Continue this drill, changing the person and address.

The Page Do the first part of page 104 with the students. Then read the directions aloud and have students complete the page, correcting the spelling mistakes and capitalizing as necessary. Remind them to pay particular attention to their handwriting when forming capital letters. Be sure these letters extend to the top line. To check the page, have volunteers write the corrected sentences on the board. Have other students find the spelling words and spell them aloud.

Follow-Up Have the students write their own sentences about streets in their neighborhood using these spelling words: **he, she, see, green.**

WORDS AT WORK

Challenge Yourself

athlete   **freeze**   **belief**

What do you think each underlined Challenge Word means? Check your Spelling Dictionary to see if you are right. Then write sentences. Show that you understand the meaning of each Challenge Word.

1. The best <u>athlete</u> was given a blue ribbon.
2. The ponds <u>freeze</u> every winter.
3. It's my <u>belief</u> that stealing is wrong.

Write to the Point

Read the story "Grandfather's Race" again. Write a letter to a friend. Tell how Robin's grandfather won the race. Use spelling words from this lesson in your letter.

Challenge Use one or more of the Challenge Words in your letter.

Proofreading

Use the marks to show the mistakes in the sentences below. Write the four misspelled words correctly in the blanks.

⬭	word is misspelled
⊙	period is missing
≡	letter should be capitalized

1. ⬭(Peopel) came to see the race.
2. They stood on their ⬭(feat) for hours⊙
3. Some ⬭(beez) flew into the crowd.
4. ≡one racer hid in a pond to ⬭(kepe) from being stung.

1. _____People_____
2. _____feet_____
3. _____bees_____
4. _____keep_____

105

Objectives

- To extend the vowel spellings presented in Lesson 19 to the Challenge Words.
- To use context and the **Spelling Dictionary** to enlarge students' vocabulary.
- To apply the vowel spellings presented in Lesson 19 in a writing activity.
- To practice proofreading for spelling, punctuation, and capitalization.

Dictation Sentences

1. My mother said <u>we</u> must be home by six.
2. The new socks are too big for my <u>feet</u>.
3. <u>I</u> think my mother will paint the room <u>green</u>.
4. Do <u>these</u> <u>people</u> live on her <u>street</u>?
5. Can <u>she</u> eat lunch with us?
6. The <u>children</u> ran from the <u>bees</u>.
7. I see that he can swim <u>well</u>.
8. Can <u>three</u> <u>children</u> play this game?
9. I <u>keep</u> my bike in my room.
10. I <u>went</u> back to school after <u>being</u> sick last <u>week</u>.

Challenge Yourself Answers

Possible definitions:

1. person who plays sports
2. harden into ice
3. faith

Students' sentences will vary.

Test Review these ways to spell /ē/: e as in <u>he</u>; ee as in <u>green</u>; e_e as in <u>these</u>; eo as in <u>people</u>. Test words with /ē/. Use one of these testing methods: (1) Say the word; read the sample sentence from page 100; say the word; have students write the word. (2) Read each dictation sentence above; have students write the sentence. Correct the test with students.

Challenge Yourself The optional Challenge Words may be assigned to the entire class or limited to those students who do well on the test. Have students note the vowel spellings in the Challenge Words, especially the following new spelling: ie as in <u>belief</u>. Responses to this activity should be completed on separate paper. Answers to the questions are provided above.

Write to the Point Have students recall the selection "Grandfather's Race" on pages 102 and 103; then assign the letter. This activity should be completed on separate paper.

Proofreading The proofreading practice includes misspellings of words from this lesson as well as a capitalization error and a punctuation error.

LESSON 20

Objectives

- To hear and say words with /ē/.
- To write words with /ē/ with attention to letter sequence and sound/symbol relationships.
- To write each spelling word once.
- To recognize that /ē/ may be spelled <u>ea</u> and <u>y</u>.

Sample Sentences

1. I love to <u>eat</u> vanilla ice cream.
2. When you sleep, do you <u>dream</u>?
3. Did you see that frog <u>leap</u> in the air?
4. What do you <u>mean</u> when you say you don't care?
5. A <u>peach</u> is a fruit with fuzzy skin.
6. I'll <u>clean</u> my room so it's as neat as a pin.
7. The <u>heat</u> is strong on a summer day.
8. Will <u>you</u> <u>please</u> pass me the bread?
9. The <u>happy</u> kitten loves to play.
10. The best circus act is the <u>funny</u> clown.
11. The little <u>puppy</u> is furry and brown.
12. A copper <u>penny</u> is small change.
13. That old house is <u>very</u> strange.
14. The <u>city</u> is a busy place.

Note

Words are grouped according to spellings of /ē/:

ea
y

The sample sentences may be used for pretesting and post-testing.

Lesson 20 — Words with /ē/

eat
dream
leap
mean
peach
clean
heat
please

happy
funny
puppy
penny

very
city

1. What words have <u>ea</u> in them?

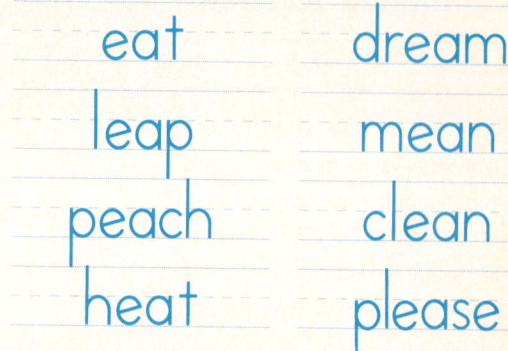

2. What words end in a double consonant and <u>y</u>?

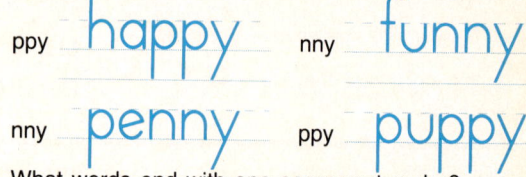

3. What words end with one consonant and <u>y</u>?

I like the puzzles best. Do you?

Yes, but which leg should I write with?

106

Preparation Write /ē/ on the board. Have students say the sound /ē/ as in <u>be</u>. Say these word pairs. Ask students to wave when they hear /ē/.

clam – <u>clean</u>   <u>dream</u> – drum   hit – <u>heat</u>   <u>puppy</u> – puppet   <u>very</u> – veil

Have students look at the spelling words on page 106. Say each word aloud. Then have the students say and spell each word.

Point out the consonant digraph <u>ch</u> at the end of the word <u>peach</u>. Ask the students to pronounce /ch/. Then look at the first group of spelling words. Note that in these eight words, the sound /ē/ is spelled with the letters <u>ea</u>. Have students look at the last group of words. Tell them that the letter <u>y</u> at the end of a word is used as a vowel. Ask them what sound <u>y</u> represents in the word <u>happy</u>. *(/ē/)* Have students identify the other words in which <u>y</u> spells /ē/. *(funny, puppy, penny, very, city)* (See **Note**.)

Have students point to the words as you read each sample sentence.

The Page Do the activities with the students, allowing time for them to write the answers. Then have them spell the words aloud as you write answers on the board for immediate reinforcement.

Follow-Up Ask students how they plan to study the spelling words. Suggest this method: They may spell each word three times—in a whisper, in a normal voice, and then in a loud voice.

Checkpoint

Write a spelling word for each clue.

Then use the Checkpoint Study Plan on page 224.

1. The opposite of sad is ___.

2. My hands are not dirty, they're ___.

3. We moved from the country to the ___.

4. I played in the snow, and my hands got ___ cold.

5. To be polite, say thank-you and ___.

6. Another word for jump is ___.

7. A fruit that is sweet is a ___.

8. What foods do you like to ___?

9. If you are cold, turn up the ___.

10. If something makes you laugh, it's ___.

11. A young dog is a ___.

12. Last night I had a bad ___.

13. One cent is a ___.

14. At first this mystery word meant "shared by everyone." Now the word has many meanings. You may know two meanings of this word. One meaning is "not kind." Guess the mystery word. ___

107

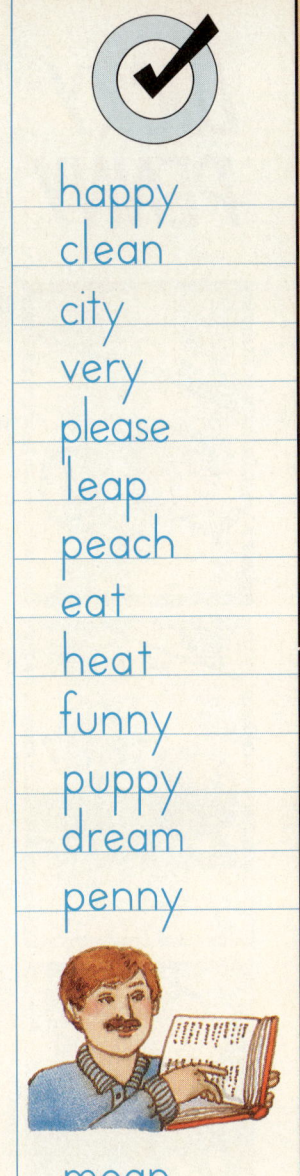

happy
clean
city
very
please
leap
peach
eat
heat
funny
puppy
dream
penny

mean

Objectives

- To write spelling words in response to clues: definitions, synonyms, antonyms, and context.

- To develop the critical thinking skills of classifying, contrasting, and analyzing.

- To understand that the spelling and pronunciation of words in the English language often change over time.

Spelling Strategy

Some students may omit one of the doubled consonants and spell happy, funny, puppy, and penny as hapy, funy, pupy, and peny. In addition to prescribing practice with the **Checkpoint Study Plan**, you may wish to ask students to draw a line between the doubled consonants and quietly pronounce each syllable to themselves as they point to it.

Preparation The clues on this page are like crossword puzzle clues. Explain to students that the response to each clue is a spelling word. Use the following examples to illustrate the types of clues used:

Definition	A young dog is a *(puppy)*.
Synonym	Another word for jump is *(leap)*.
Antonym	The opposite of sad is *(happy)*.
Context	What foods do you like to *(eat)*?

The final clue compares the original meaning of mean with one of its current meanings.

The Page Have students complete page 107 using the words on page 106. When students have finished, have them read each clue and spell the answer aloud. Check each response twice: once for the correct answer and a second time for spelling accuracy.

Follow-Up Guide students in using the **Checkpoint Study Plan** on page 224 to take a self-test. Have them use the plan for independent study.

Objectives

- To write words with /ē/ in continuous text.
- To write each spelling word once.
- To integrate reading with spelling.

LUCKY PENNY

Fill in the blanks with spelling words.

One hot summer day in the _____ city _____ , a penny and a dime were sitting on the sidewalk. They were hoping someone would pick them up. The dime was becoming very grouchy because of the _____ heat _____ .

"No one's ever going to pick you up," the dime said with a laugh.

"Don't be so _____ mean _____ to me," said the penny. "I might make someone happy someday."

"No one wants a _____ penny _____ these days," snapped the dime. "You can't buy an apple or a _____ peach _____ with a penny. You can't buy anything to _____ eat _____ with a penny."

"You can't buy much with a dime either," said the penny in a soft voice. "You can't buy a pet with a dime.

 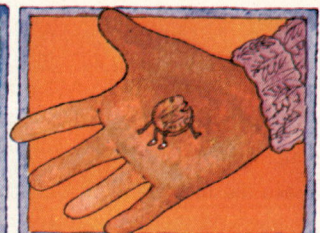 

108

Preparation

Have students turn to pages 108 and 109. Call their attention to the word list. Have the students say the words. Then explain that each spelling word belongs in one of the blanks in the story.

Write the title "Lucky Penny" on the board. Call attention to the pictures. Tell the students that this story is a fantasy about a conversation between a penny and a dime.

The Pages

Read the story aloud, supplying the missing spelling words as students follow along in their texts. When you have finished, you may wish to discuss the story. Ask a student to explain the title of the story. *(The penny felt lucky because it was important to someone.)* Ask students what lesson the penny learned. *(There is something special and important about almost everything.)* What lesson did the dime learn? *(Accept any reasonable response.)*

Then have students complete the story by silently rereading it and writing the correct spelling word for each blank. Then have four volunteers read the story aloud as you read the part of the narrator. The students will read the parts of the penny, the dime, the boy, and his grandmother. Then write the answers on the board so students may check their own work. Be sure to check students' responses for the accurate spelling of each answer.

You can't buy a kitten or a _____puppy_____ with

a dime."

All this talk was making the penny sad. "Some days I

_____dream_____ about being a new penny," it

said. "Once I was shiny and _____clean_____."

Just then the penny had a _____funny_____

feeling. A little boy was squeezing it in his hand.

"Here's an old one!" he cried. "May I _____please_____

keep it, Grandma?"

His grandmother said, "This is a _____very_____ old

penny, Neal. It would be a very good one to collect."

The penny felt its heart _____leap_____ for joy.

Neal put the penny in his pocket and gave the dime to

his grandmother. The penny sang out, "Good-by, Dime.

You see, I do make someone _____happy_____!"

109

eat
dream
leap
mean
peach
clean
heat
please
happy
funny
puppy
penny
very
city

Follow-Up Have students use each of the spelling words they missed in an original sentence.

As an additional follow-up activity, you might have the students draw a cartoon of the conversation between the penny and the dime. Show them how to make dialogue balloons and tell them to write sentences from the story in these balloons. Then ask them to underline any spelling words in the sentences.

Enrichment

If you want to use the blackline activity masters for enrichment and additional practice, assign Lesson 20 activities at this time.

Maintenance and Review

OBJECTIVE

• To review words with /ē/ spelled: e, ee, e-e.

ACTIVITIES

If you want to use the blackline activity masters for maintenance and review, assign Lesson 19 activities at this time.

You can also use the activity below to review Lesson 19 with students:

Write the following words and riddles on the board. Have the students copy the riddles and complete them. Then have volunteers read the riddles and answers aloud so students may check their work. *(Answers are in parentheses.)*

> feet   we   green   three
> street   week

1. From Sunday to Sunday,
   I'm always here!
   I'm a *(week)* .

2. I'm a left and a right.
   I've got ankles and toes.
   I'm your *(feet)* .

3. I'm you and me.
   When you talk about us,
   you call us *(we)* .

4. I'm the place where you live.
   I'm a road for a car.
   I'm a *(street)* .

5. I'm one more than two.
   Guess what!
   I'm *(three)* .

6. I'm the color of a leaf.
   I'm yellow mixed with blue.
   I am *(green)* .

Objectives

- To relate spelling words to a dictionary skill.
- To use guide words.
- To write spelling words in alphabetical order.
- To use the **Spelling Dictionary.**
- To check handwriting for correct letter formation.

a b c d e f g h i j k l m
n o p q r s t u v w x y z

Dictionary

Two <u>guide</u> <u>words</u> are on the top of every dictionary page. The first guide word is the same as the first entry word on the page. The second guide word is the same as the last entry word on the page.

To find a word quickly in a dictionary, look first at the guide words at the top of the page.

dog | elephant

dog /dòg/—*plural* **dogs.** A four-footed anima be used as pets, for hunting, and for doing *Bernie: How do you like my* **dog**? *Ernie: Nice. Is it trained?*

Write these entry words in alphabetical order. Then look up each word in the Spelling Dictionary. Write the guide words for each entry word.

happy	**eat**	**very**	**leap**

	Entry Word		Guide Words	
1.	eat		dot	end
2.	happy		girl	harmful
3.	leap		just	lining
4.	very		van	why

110

Preparation   Have pupils turn to page 199 in the **Spelling Dictionary.** Ask a volunteer to read the two words at the top of the page. *(being, book)* Explain that these words are <u>guide words</u>. Point out that the first guide word is the first entry on the page. Ask students to find the entry for the second guide word. *(at the bottom of the page)* Explain that the rest of the words on the page are in alphabetical order between the two guide words. Dictionaries have guide words at the top of every page to help you locate words.
   Put these guide words on the board: **clean/happy**
Write these words under the guide words: **dream   eat   very**
Ask if the word <u>dream</u> would appear between these guide words. *(Yes, d is between c and h.)* Would <u>eat</u> appear? *(yes)* Would <u>very</u>? *(no)*

The Page   Do page 110 with the students. Remind students to write carefully. Lesson 20 gives practice in formation of the letter <u>p</u>, which can be confused with <u>g</u> or <u>q</u> if written incorrectly. Students should begin the lowercase <u>p</u> at the center of the writing line, bring the tail below the base line, and form the curve to the right.

Follow-Up   Have students write these words in alphabetical order: **mean, peach, funny.** Then have students find them in the **Spelling Dictionary** and write the guide words for each entry word.

WORDS AT WORK

Challenge Yourself

disease　　　**cheap**　　　**cheat**

Use your Spelling Dictionary to answer these questions. Then write sentences. Show that you understand the meaning of each Challenge Word.

1. Would you want your best friend to give you a <u>disease</u> on your birthday?

2. Is a meal <u>cheap</u> if it costs fifty cents?

3. Does your teacher ask you to <u>cheat</u> on your tests?

Write to the Point

In the story "Lucky Penny," a penny and a dime talk. In real life coins cannot talk. Think of two other things that cannot talk in real life. Write a story. Have the two things talk to each other. Use spelling words from this lesson.

Challenge Use one or more of the Challenge Words in your story.

Proofreading

Use the marks to show the mistakes in the sentences below. Write the four misspelled words correctly in the blanks.

⬭	word is misspelled
⊙	period is missing
☰	letter should be capitalized

1. kwan is saving a very old ⬭peny⬭
2. He keeps it bright and ⬭cleen⬭
3. He will take it to the ⬭citty⬭
4. He'll be ⬭hapy⬭ to take it there⊙

1. _____ penny _____
2. _____ clean _____
3. _____ city _____
4. _____ happy _____

111

LESSON 21

Objectives

- To hear and say words with /ī/.
- To write words with /ī/ with attention to letter sequence and sound/symbol relationships.
- To write each spelling word once.
- To recognize that /ī/ may be spelled i_e, eye, and i.

Sample Sentences

1. We took a ride on the downtown bus.
2. When you go away, write to us!
3. Paul learned to ride on a two-wheel bike.
4. This is the side of the record I like.
5. I have five fingers on my hand.
6. There are nine players in the band.
7. Some cats like to hide under the bed.
8. It was warm inside the house.
9. The cat sat on the white picket fence.
10. When I skate on the ice, my cheeks turn red!
11. I like the look of polished floors.
12. That bicycle is mine, not yours!
13. The pirate wore a patch on one eye.
14. It's hard to find a gift to buy.

Note

Words are grouped according to spellings of /ī/:

   i_e
   eye
   i

The sample sentences may be used for pretesting and post-testing.

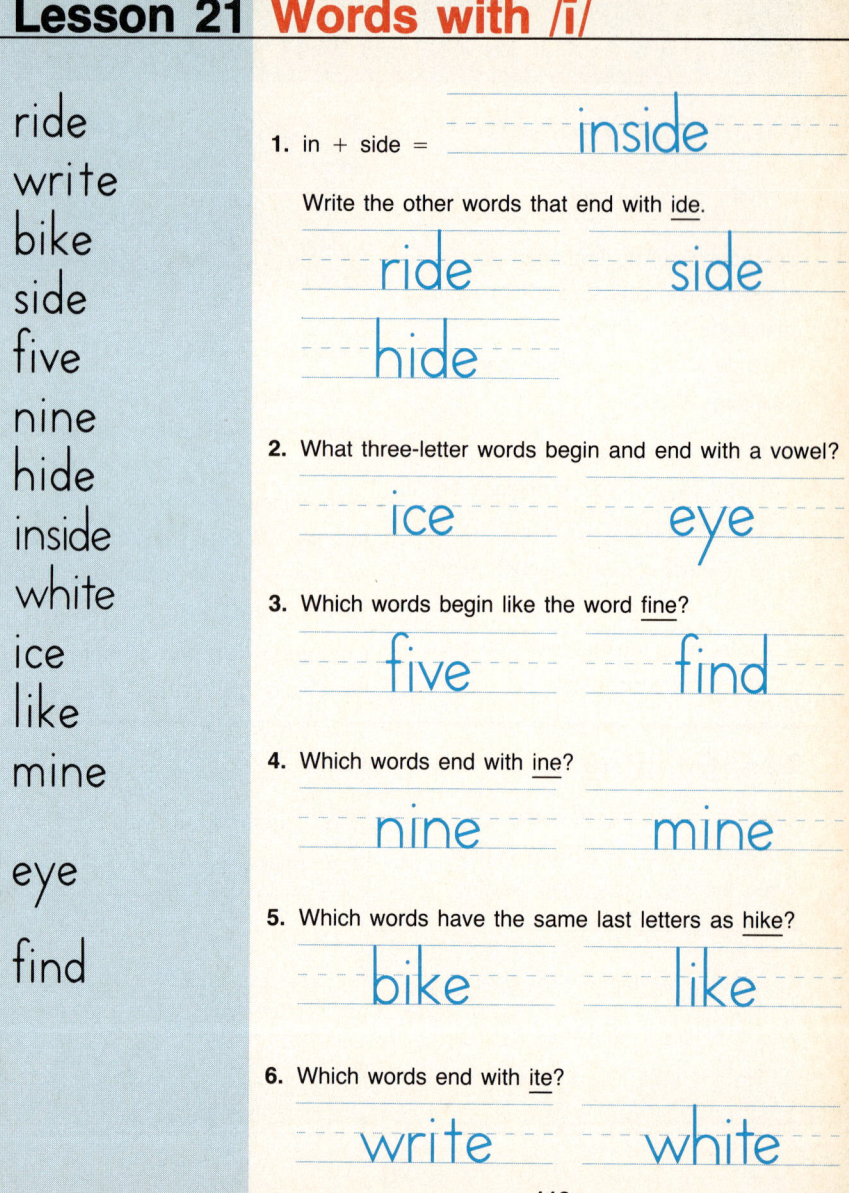

Lesson 21 Words with /ī/

ride
write
bike
side
five
nine
hide
inside
white
ice
like
mine

eye

find

1. in + side = _____ inside

Write the other words that end with ide.

ride   side

hide

2. What three-letter words begin and end with a vowel?

ice   eye

3. Which words begin like the word fine?

five   find

4. Which words end with ine?

nine   mine

5. Which words have the same last letters as hike?

bike   like

6. Which words end with ite?

write   white

112

Preparation Write /ī/ on the chalkboard and have the students repeat the sound /ī/ as in pie. Say the word pairs below. Ask students to raise their right hands when they hear a word with /ī/.

     hide – hid   mine – men   rate – write   it – eye   find – fond

Have students look at the spelling words on page 112. Say each word aloud. Then have the students say and spell each word.

Note the signal e in the first twelve words. Remind students that this e at the end of the word signals the long sound of the preceding vowel. Write the word hid on the board and have someone read it. Ask a volunteer to add a signal e to the word and read the new word. *(hide)* Now direct students' attention to the spelling of the word eye. It has a very unusual spelling of the sound /ī/. Then read the last word on the list. Ask what letter spells /ī/ in find. *(i)* Ask for words that rhyme with find. *(kind, mind, etc.)* (See **Note**.)

Read the sample sentences as students point to corresponding spelling words.

The Page Do page 112. Then have the students spell their words aloud as you write the answers on the board for immediate reinforcement.

Follow-Up Be sure that students have study plans for the week. Suggest that they study words with a partner. First one student will spell a word aloud. Then the partner will say and spell the word.

Checkpoint

Write a spelling word for each clue.

Then use the Checkpoint Study Plan on page 224.

1. What ice cream flavors do you ___?

2. In winter, the pond turns to ___.

3. Another word for bicycle is ___.

4. Cross the bridge to reach the other ___.

5. A word that sounds like kind is ___.

6. The number after eight is ___.

7. My brother is learning to read and ___.

8. Your coat is the same color as ___.

9. My class went for a boat ___.

10. We painted my room ___.

11. When you wink, you close one ___.

12. My cat goes under my bed to ___.

13. The opposite of outside is ___.

14. This mystery word is a number. Long ago, English people used the word <u>fimfi</u> to name the number after four. Years later, the word became <u>fif</u>. Today we say ___.

113

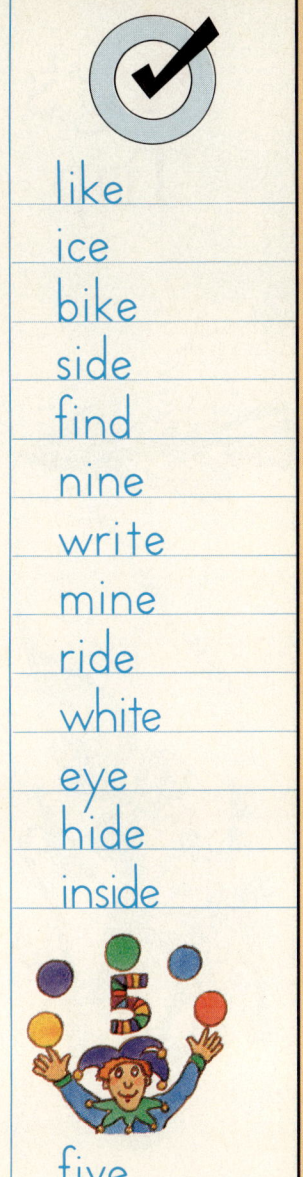

like
ice
bike
side
find
nine
write
mine
ride
white
eye
hide
inside

five

Objectives

- To write spelling words in response to clues: synonyms, antonyms, rhyme, and context.
- To develop the critical thinking skills of sequencing and contrasting.
- To understand that the spelling and pronunciation of words in the English language often change over time.

Spelling Strategy

The <u>wr</u> spelling for an initial /r/ sound is sometimes misspelled <u>r</u>, as in <u>rite</u>. Help students remember the correct spelling of <u>write</u> by having them go to the dictionary and find words that begin with <u>wr</u>. Have them copy any familiar words and underline the <u>wr</u> spelling. You may want to encourage some students to write a short phrase using two or more words that begin with <u>wr</u>, such as "<u>write</u> on the <u>wrapper</u>."

Preparation The clues on this page are like crossword puzzle clues. Explain to students that the response to each clue is a spelling word. Use the following examples to illustrate the types of clues used:

Synonym	Another word for bicycle is *(bike)*.
Antonym	The opposite of outside is *(inside)*.
Rhyme	A word that sounds like kind is *(find)*.
Context	My brother is learning to read and *(write)*.

The final clue explains how the spelling and pronunciation of the word <u>five</u> have changed over time.

The Page Have students complete page 113 using the words on page 112. When students have finished, have them read each clue and spell the answer aloud. Check each response twice: once for the correct answer and a second time for spelling accuracy.

Follow-Up Guide students in using the **Checkpoint Study Plan** on page 224 to take a self-test. Have them use the plan for independent study.

Objectives

- To write words with /ī/ in continuous text and related sentences.
- To write each spelling word once.
- To integrate reading with spelling.

Note

Some of the spelling words will be used twice on these two pages.

114

Finish Meg's diary page with spelling words.

Meg's Trip

December 8

Dear Diary,

Today I want to _____write_____ about a

daydream of _____mine_____. I keep thinking about

being an explorer at the North Pole. I would really

_____like_____ to go to the far far north and

_____ride_____ across all the snow and ice. It would

be lots more fun than riding my _____bike_____ to

school! I would spend more than _____five / nine_____

years looking at every corner. I would ride from one side

right across to the other _____side_____! If I met a

friendly animal, I would say "Hello," and smile at it. Then

it would become a pet and keep me company. If we met

a fierce animal, we could go behind a snowbank and

_____hide_____ from it. My uncle went near the

North Pole about _____nine / five_____ years ago. He

said there was snow as far as the _____eye_____ could

see. I think all that snow and _____ice_____ would be

114

Preparation Have students turn to pages 114 and 115. Call their attention to the word list. Have the students say the words. Then explain that each spelling word belongs in one of the blanks in the story.

Write the title "Meg's Trip" on the board and have a student read it. Then ask the students if they have ever had daydreams about becoming famous. Have them discuss what they think might make them famous. Tell the class that they are going to read another entry from Meg's diary. Have them look back at pages 30 and 31 (Lesson 5). Remind pupils that a diary is a book of a person's special thoughts. This diary entry is about Meg's daydreams.

The Pages Read the diary entry aloud, supplying the missing spelling words as the students follow along in their texts. When you have finished, you may wish to discuss the story by asking these questions:

1. What was Meg's daydream about? (She wrote about being an explorer at the North Pole.)
2. What did Meg think would make her famous? (discovering a piece of land)

Then have students complete the diary entry independently by writing the correct spelling word for each blank. When they have finished, a volunteer may read the diary entry aloud, pausing before each blank. The other students will say the missing spelling word at the appropriate time. Have another volunteer write the answers on the board so students may check their work.

beautiful. I'd really like to _____find_____ one little piece of land that no one else has discovered. Then I would be famous!

I would build a snow house and live in it. I would look out and see miles of _____white_____ snow and ice. If I found a small animal that was hurt, I would bring it _____inside_____ the house. I would take care of it.

Use a spelling word instead of the underlined word in each sentence below.

1. Meg wants to <u>tell</u> about her daydream.

   Meg wants to _____write_____ about her daydream.

2. She wants to <u>slide</u> across the snow.

   She wants to _____ride_____ across the snow.

3. Meg rides a <u>horse</u> to school.

   Meg rides a _____bike_____ to school.

115

ride
write
bike
side
five
nine
hide
inside
white
ice
like
mine
eye
find

Enrichment

If you want to use the blackline activity masters for enrichment and additional practice, assign Lesson 21 activities at this time.

Maintenance and Review

OBJECTIVE

• To review words with /ē/ spelled: <u>ea</u>, <u>y</u>.

ACTIVITIES

If you want to use the blackline activity masters for maintenance and review, assign Lesson 20 activities at this time.

You can also use the activity below to review Lesson 20 with students:

Write the following words and incomplete sentences on the board. Have students copy the sentences and fill in the missing spelling words. *(Answers are in parentheses.)* Then have volunteers read the completed sentences aloud so students may check their work.

happy   puppy   eat   very   leap

1. We just bought a *(puppy)*.
2. He loves to *(eat)*.
3. My puppy is *(happy)*.
4. He is *(very)* nice.
5. My puppy will *(leap)* at me.

Then direct students' attention to page 115 and read the directions aloud. Read each sentence aloud and ask students to identify which word is wrong in the sentence. Have them write the correct spelling word that will complete the sentence correctly. When they have finished, have volunteers write the answers on the board. Be sure to check students' responses for the accurate spelling of each answer.

Follow-Up Have students use each of the spelling words they missed in an original sentence.

As an additional follow-up activity, you may wish to suggest that students write their own diary entry about things that happened to them yesterday.

Objectives

- To relate spelling to another language skill.
- To review the use of the period, the question mark, and the exclamation point.
- To write sentences in correct word order.
- To write spelling words in the context of sentences.
- To check handwriting for correct letter formation.

a b c d e f g h i j k l m
n o p q r s t u v w x y z

Punctuation

Put a period (.) at the end of a sentence that tells something.
Put a question mark (?) at the end of a question.
Put an exclamation point (!) at the end of a sentence that shows strong feeling or surprise.

It is a nice day.   Are you six years old?   I can skate backward!

Unscramble the sentences. Put in end marks.

1. gerbil babies nine Our had

Our gerbil had nine babies!

2. in They hide corners

They hide in corners.

3. mine one is Which

Which one is mine?

4. to write Aunt Berta Please

Please write to Aunt Berta.

5. gerbil like Would she a

Would she like a gerbil?

6. babies five see I more

I see five more babies!

116

Preparation   Write the following sentences on the board and read them:

1. Did you find the letter from Aunt Lily
2. I must write to her today
3. I love getting lots of mail

Have volunteers insert the correct end punctuation marks, paying attention to voice inflection for clues. *(1. question mark; 2. period or exclamation point; 3. exclamation point or period)* Review that a sentence that tells something ends with a period; a sentence that asks something ends with a question mark; and a sentence that shows strong feeling or surprise ends with an exclamation point.

The Page   Do page 116 together. Remind students to form their letters carefully. Pay particular attention to the formation of the letter n in words such as nine and mine. Have students read their unscrambled sentences aloud, noting the spelling word in each one. Write the answers on the board so that the students may check their own work.

Follow-Up   Have students write a sentence for each of these words: **find, eye, ice**. Ask them to use a period to end one sentence, a question mark for another, and an exclamation point for the third.

WORDS AT WORK

Challenge Yourself

license   climate   advice

Decide which Challenge Word fits each clue. Check your Spelling Dictionary to see if you were right. Then write sentences. Show that you understand the meaning of each Challenge Word.

1. You might give this to a friend.
2. You need one to drive a car.
3. The North Pole has a cold one. The desert has a hot one.

Write to the Point

Pretend you are an explorer. Where would you like to go? Write a paragraph. Tell where you want to go and why. Use spelling words from this lesson in your paragraph.

Challenge Use one or more of the Challenge Words in your paragraph.

Proofreading

Use the marks to show the mistakes in the sentences below. Write the four misspelled words correctly in the blanks.

⬭	word is misspelled
⊙	period is missing
⚌	letter should be capitalized

1. At the North Pole, meg will ride a sled over the (ise.)
2. She will be pulled by (wite) dogs⊙
3. Meg must rest after going (fiv) miles.
4. It will be warm (insid) the cabin.

1. _____ice_____
2. _____white_____
3. _____five_____
4. _____inside_____

117

Objectives

- To extend the vowel spellings presented in Lesson 21 to the Challenge Words.
- To use clues and the **Spelling Dictionary** to enlarge students' vocabulary.
- To apply the vowel spellings presented in Lesson 21 in a writing activity.
- To practice proofreading for spelling, punctuation, and capitalization.

Dictation Sentences

1. I will ride my bike today.
2. Can you help me find my black shoe?
3. I like that white dress.
4. The road has ice on it.
5. Three and two are five.
6. My puppy can hide inside the big box.
7. We have nine girls in my class.
8. Please keep an eye on the baby.
9. I will write my name in green.
10. This side of the room is mine.

Challenge Yourself Answers

Possible definitions:

1. advice
2. license
3. climate

Students' sentences will vary.

Test Review these ways to spell /ī/: i_e as in ride; eye; i as in find. Test words with /ī/. Use one of these testing methods: (1) Say the word; read the sample sentence from page 112; say the word; have students write the word. (2) Read each dictation sentence above; have students write the sentence. Correct the test with students.

Challenge Yourself The optional Challenge Words may be assigned to the entire class or limited to those students who do well on the test. Have students note the vowel spellings in the Challenge Words. Responses to this activity should be completed on separate paper. Answers to the questions are provided above.

Write to the Point Have students recall the selection "Meg's Trip" on pages 114 and 115; then assign the paragraph. Remind students that they can make their paragraph more interesting by using describing words. This activity should be completed on separate paper.

Proofreading The proofreading practice includes misspellings of words from this lesson as well as a capitalization error and a punctuation error.

LESSON 22

Objectives

- To hear and say words with /ī/.
- To write words with /ī/ with attention to letter sequence and sound/symbol relationships.
- To write each spelling word once.
- To recognize that /ī/ may be spelled y, ie, i, and igh.

Sample Sentences

1. I don't know why you like to cook.
2. That is my favorite storybook.
3. Please cover your eyes and try.
4. Peeling onions makes us cry.
5. What do you see up in the sky?
6. That baby bird will try to fly.
7. We have a cabin by a lake.
8. I like to lie in the sun and bake!
9. Mom's favorite dessert is apple pie.
10. I bought my dad a yellow tie.
11. The tiger is a jungle cat.
12. Tom Thumb wore a tiny hat.
13. The lion brought food to the cubs.
14. The kite flew high above the trees.

Note

Words are grouped according to spellings of /ī/:

   y
   ie
   i
   igh

The sample sentences may be used for pretesting and post-testing.

Lesson 22 Words with /ī/

why
my
try
cry
sky
fly
by

lie
pie
tie

tiger
tiny
lion

high

1. Which spelling words begin with two consonants?

why   try
cry   sky
fly

2. What words end with y and have only one consonant?

my   by

3. In which words does ie spell /ī/?

lie   pie   tie

4. ti + ny = tiny

5. ti + ger = tiger

6. h + igh = high

7. li + on = lion

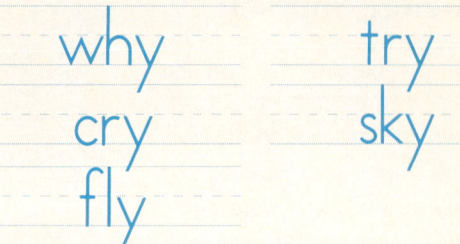

Don't tie up my tiger!!

118

Preparation Write /ī/ on the chalkboard and have students repeat the sound /ī/ as in pie. Say these word pairs. If a word contains /ī/, the students should raise their right hands.

     me – my   pie – pay   tea – tie   tiny – Tony   ski – sky

Have students look at the spelling words on page 118. Say each word aloud. Then have the students say and spell each word.

Note the consonant digraph /hw/ in the word why: /hwī/. Write the sound /hw/ and the letters wh on the board. Have the students say the sound and the word. Point out that some people say why like this: /wī/. Both pronunciations are correct. Then remind the students that y at the end of a word is a vowel. Have them locate the spelling words that contain y as a vowel. *(why, my, try, cry, sky, fly, by, tiny)* Finally, direct students' attention to four spellings of /ī/: y, ie, i, igh (See **Note**.) Read the cartoon and have students identify the three words that illustrate these spellings. *(my, tie, tiger)*

Read sample sentences as students point to the corresponding spelling words.

The Page Do page 118 with the students. Have them spell each word aloud as you write the answers on the board. Help them check their work.

Follow-Up Suggest that students find a quiet place to practice spelling each word aloud. Remind them to check their spelling in the book.

Checkpoint

Write a spelling word for each clue. Then use the Checkpoint Study Plan on page 224.

1. You can bake a cake or a ___.

2. Look up to see the ___.

3. Something that is very, very small is ___.

4. If you hurt yourself, you might ___.

5. At the circus, you might see a ___.

6. Phil wore a red ___.

7. To find out the reason, ask ___.

8. I walked ___ the park.

9. I can't sew well, but I'll ___.

10. A striped wild cat is a ___.

11. The opposite of low is ___.

12. The boy in the story told a ___.

13. I love ___ dog.

14. How would you like to fliugan? That's the Old German word for the mystery word. Long ago, the English word was flēogan. The word tells what birds and airplanes do. Guess the mystery word that comes from fliugan. ___

119

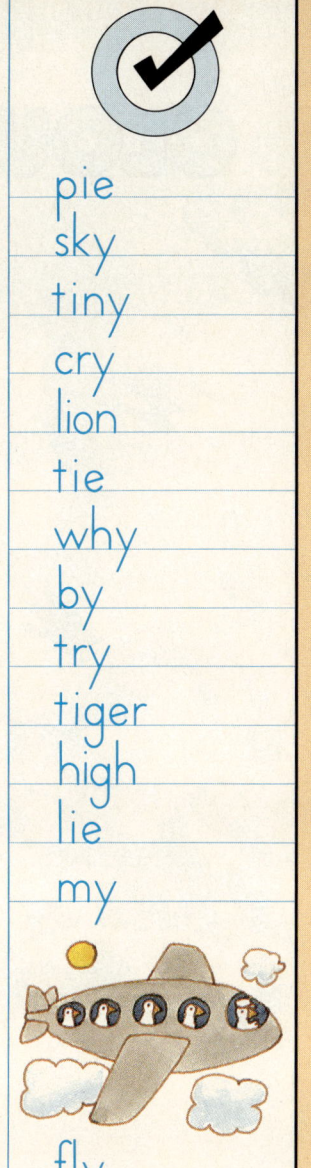

pie
sky
tiny
cry
lion
tie
why
by
try
tiger
high
lie
my

fly

Objectives

- To write spelling words in response to clues: definition, antonym, and context.

- To develop the critical thinking skills of contrasting and predicting outcomes.

- To understand that the spelling and pronunciation of words in the English language often change over time.

Spelling Strategy

Inserting an e in the second syllable of tiny and misspelling the word as tiney is a common spelling error. Remind students that in this lesson the final y in a word is a vowel and therefore does not need an additional a, e, i, o, or u.

Preparation The clues on this page are like crossword puzzle clues. Explain to students that the response to each clue is a spelling word. Use the following examples to illustrate the types of clues used:

Definition Something that is very, very small is *(tiny).*
Antonym The opposite of low is *(high).*
Context I love *(my)* dog.

The final clue traces the evolution of the word fly from Old German to its modern English spelling and meaning.

The Page Have students complete page 119 using the words on page 118. When students have finished, have them read each clue and spell the answer aloud. Check each response twice: once for the correct answer and a second time for spelling accuracy.

Follow-Up Guide students in using the **Checkpoint Study Plan** on page 224 to take a self-test. Have them use the plan for independent study.

Objectives

- To write words with /ī/ in continuous text and related sentences.
- To write each spelling word once.
- To integrate reading with spelling.

Note

Some of the spelling words will be used twice on these two pages.

Fill in the blanks with spelling words.

CLOUD WATCHING

On spring days when it's sunny and windy I like to ___lie___ on my back and watch the clouds in the ___sky___. Clouds might look like big white puffs to you. But if you ___try___ hard you might see some surprises.

Look at the sky today. See that bird ___fly___ past that cloud? Maybe it's trying to get away from the ___tiger___. Watch out, bird!

Over there is a horse with a long tail. The tail is so long it could ___tie___ itself into a knot. Now watch it disappear.

120

Preparation

Have students turn to pages 120 and 121. Call their attention to the word list. Have the students say the words. Then explain that each spelling word belongs in one of the blanks in the story.

Write the title "Cloud Watching" on the board and have a student read it. Ask students if they've ever looked at a cloud and seen a picture of something. Call attention to the illustrations. Do students see any pictures in the clouds on pages 120 and 121? Explain that they are going to read a story about someone who enjoys spotting "cloud pictures" in the sky.

The Pages

Read the story aloud, supplying the missing spelling words as the students follow along in their texts. When you have finished, you may wish to discuss the story. Ask students to describe what they see when they look at clouds.

Then have the students reread the story silently and complete it by writing the correct spelling word for each blank. Ask a volunteer to write the answers on the board so other students may check their own work.

See that cloud way up ___high___? Is that cloud missing a little ___tiny___ bite? Maybe it's a piece of apple ___pie___. What do you think could have sailed ___by___ and nibbled on it?

I can see two lion cubs. See how their mouths are open? I think they are going to ___cry___ for the mother ___lion___. I never feel like crying while I'm cloud watching. I could spend ___my___ whole day looking at clouds. Do you see ___why___ it is a good way to have fun?

121

why
my
try
cry
sky
fly
by
lie
pie
tie
tiger
tiny
lion

Enrichment

If you want to use the blackline activity masters for enrichment and additional practice, assign Lesson 22 activities at this time.

Maintenance and Review

OBJECTIVE

- To review words with /ī/ spelled: i–e, eye, i.

ACTIVITIES

If you want to use the blackline activity masters for maintenance and review, assign Lesson 21 activities at this time.

You can also use the activity below to review Lesson 21 with students:

Write the following on the board. Have the students copy the words and put them in alphabetical order.

ride	find
write	nine
bike	eye
side	ice

(bike, eye, find, ice, nine, ride, side, write)

Follow-Up   Have the students use each of the spelling words they missed in an original sentence.

As an additional follow-up activity, you may wish to have the students illustrate the different cloud pictures described in the story. Ask them to caption each picture with an appropriate sentence from the story and to underline any spelling words.

Objectives

- To relate spelling words to a dictionary skill.
- To recognize the multiple meanings of some spelling words.
- To write spelling words in the context of sentences.
- To use the **Spelling Dictionary**.
- To check handwriting for correct letter formation.

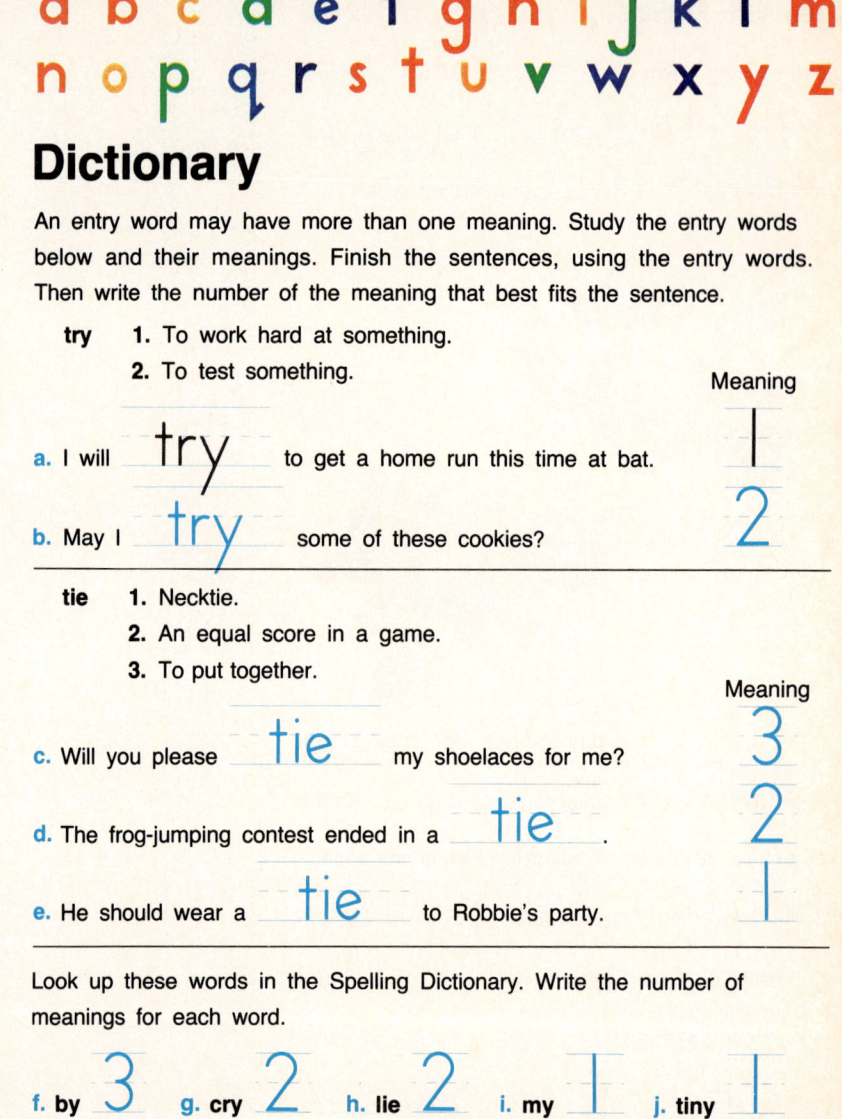

**a b c d e f g h i j k l m
n o p q r s t u v w x y z**

Dictionary

An entry word may have more than one meaning. Study the entry words below and their meanings. Finish the sentences, using the entry words. Then write the number of the meaning that best fits the sentence.

try 1. To work hard at something.
     2. To test something.

Meaning

a. I will _try_ to get a home run this time at bat.   1

b. May I _try_ some of these cookies?   2

tie 1. Necktie.
     2. An equal score in a game.
     3. To put together.

Meaning

c. Will you please _tie_ my shoelaces for me?   3

d. The frog-jumping contest ended in a _tie_.   2

e. He should wear a _tie_ to Robbie's party.   1

Look up these words in the Spelling Dictionary. Write the number of meanings for each word.

f. **by** _3_   g. **cry** _2_   h. **lie** _2_   i. **my** _1_   j. **tiny** _1_

122

Preparation   Ask the students to give you a meaning for the word <u>cry</u>. *(to shed tears* or *to shout)* Explain that if a word has more than one meaning, a dictionary will have each of the meanings. Ask the students to look up <u>cry</u> in their **Spelling Dictionary** and to note its two meanings. *(page 203)* Have volunteers read each meaning and sample sentence. Have other students give sentences for the two meanings of <u>cry</u>.

The Page   Do page 122 with the students. Remind them to write their words carefully. In this lesson, pay particular attention to the formation of the letter <u>r</u>, which, if formed incorrectly, can be confused with an <u>n</u> or a <u>p</u>. Spelling mistakes should not be caused by poor handwriting. When students have finished the activities, review the page by writing the answers on the chalkboard as students read their answers aloud.

Follow-Up   Have students locate the words **fly** and **lie** in the **Spelling Dictionary** and write a sentence for each meaning of each word.

WORDS AT WORK

Challenge Yourself

tying   **rhyme**   **diet**

What do you think each underlined Challenge Word means? Check your Spelling Dictionary to see if you are right. Then write sentences. Show that you understand the meaning of each Challenge Word.

1. Amy is <u>tying</u> her shoestrings.

2. "Pie" <u>rhymes</u> with "my."

3. Some animals are able to live on a <u>diet</u> of fish.

Write to the Point

In "Cloud Watching" the writer tells what he likes to do on a spring day. Write a few sentences telling things that you like to do on a spring day. Use spelling words from this lesson.

Challenge Use one or more of the Challenge Words in your sentences.

Proofreading

Use the marks to show the mistakes in the sentences below. Write the four misspelled words correctly in the blanks.

⬭	word is misspelled
⊙	period is missing
≡	letter should be capitalized

1. The clouds are high in the (skye).   1. ____sky____

2. we (trie) to touch them with a kite.   2. ____try____
   ≡

3. The clouds just (flie) above it.   3. ____fly____

4. Our kite looks (tiney) in the air⊙   4. ____tiny____

123

Objectives

- To extend the vowel spellings presented in Lesson 22 to the Challenge Words.

- To use context and the **Spelling Dictionary** to enlarge students' vocabulary.

- To apply the vowel spellings presented in Lesson 22 in a writing activity.

- To practice proofreading for spelling, punctuation, and capitalization.

Dictation Sentences

1. Maybe you will see a <u>lion</u> and a <u>tiger</u> at the zoo.
2. The jet can <u>fly</u> <u>high</u> in the <u>sky</u>.
3. You can <u>try</u> <u>my</u> new game after lunch.
4. I like to <u>lie</u> in the sun after I swim.
5. <u>Why</u> did the child <u>cry</u>?
6. I just love peach <u>pie</u>.
7. I gave my brother a blue <u>tie</u>.
8. Do you come to school <u>by</u> bus?
9. Did you see that <u>tiny</u> bug land on my hand?

Challenge Yourself Answers

Possible definitions:

1. making a knot or bow in
2. sounds like
3. what an animal or person eats

Students' sentences will vary.

Test   Review these ways to spell /ī/: <u>y</u> as in <u>why</u>; <u>ie</u> as in <u>lie</u>; <u>i</u> as in <u>tiger</u>; <u>igh</u> as in <u>high</u>. Test words with /ī/. Use one of these testing methods: (1) Say the word; read the sample sentence from page 118; say the word; have students write the word. (2) Read each dictation sentence above; have students write the sentence. Correct the test with students.

Challenge Yourself   The optional Challenge Words may be assigned to the entire class or limited to those students who do well on the test. Have students note the vowel spellings in the Challenge Words. Responses to this activity should be completed on separate paper. Answers to the questions are provided above.

Write to the Point   Have students recall the selection "Cloud Watching" on pages 120 and 121; then assign the sentences. This activity should be completed on separate paper.

Proofreading   The proofreading practice includes misspellings of words from this lesson as well as a capitalization error and a punctuation error.

LESSON 23

Objectives

- To hear and say words with the suffixes _ed_ and _ing_.
- To write words with the suffixes _ed_ and _ing_ with attention to letter sequence and sound/symbol relationships.
- To write each spelling word once.
- To recognize when a final consonant must be doubled before the suffix _ed_ or _ing_ is added.

Sample Sentences

1. The dress was <u>dotted</u> kelly green.
2. The <u>spotted</u> leopard was not seen.
3. The rabbit <u>hopped</u> through the gate.
4. He <u>dropped</u> his paperweight.
5. We <u>stopped</u> the car before the sign.
6. We <u>shopped</u> today for a valentine.
7. Today I <u>jogged</u> two miles.
8. The kangaroo is <u>hopping</u> on its hind legs.
9. The farmer is <u>dropping</u> that basket of eggs.
10. The runner is <u>stopping</u> in the middle of the race.
11. We went <u>shopping</u> for curtains of lace.
12. You need a saw for <u>cutting</u> wood.
13. We go <u>running</u> to stay healthy.
14. Many people exercise by <u>jogging</u> in the park.

Note

Another way of explaining the doubling rule is to tell students that in order to keep the short sound of the vowel in a word, you must double the final consonant before adding _ed_ or _ing_. "Double to keep out of trouble!"

Note

The sample sentences may be used for pretesting and post-testing.

Lesson 23 Adding ed and ing

dotted
spotted
hopped
dropped
stopped
shopped
jogged

hopping
dropping
stopping
shopping
cutting
running
jogging

1. Double the final consonant before adding _ed_ to these words: **dot spot**

dotted   spotted

2. Double the final consonant before adding _ing_ to these words:

hop   drop   stop   shop   cut   run

hopping   dropping
stopping   shopping
cutting   running

3. Write the words that have two g's.

jogged   jogging

4. Write the words that end with _ed_, but you hear /t/.

hopped   dropped
stopped   shopped

In these words, double the final consonant before adding _ed_ or _ing_! Like this?

124

Preparation   Write _ed_ and _ing_ on the board and tell the students that they are going to learn to spell more words with these endings. Read the spelling words on page 124 as the students look at, repeat, and spell each word.

Ask students what two things are the same in all the spelling words. _(They all have a short vowel sound. They all have double consonants in the middle.)_ Call attention to the cartoon and tell students that in some words the final consonant must be doubled before _ed_ or _ing_ can be added. Explain that when a one-syllable word ends with one vowel and one consonant, you must double the final consonant before adding the ending.

Write these words on the board: **spot   hop   drop**
Have a student underline the final consonant in each word, double it, and add _ed_. _(spotted, hopped, dropped)_ Follow the same procedure for the _ing_ ending. _(spotting, hopping, dropping)_

Have students point to the spelling word as you read each sample sentence.

The Page   Do page 124 with the students. Then have volunteers spell their answers aloud as others write them on the board for immediate reinforcement.

Follow-Up   Be sure that each student has a study plan for the spelling words. Suggest writing the words on flash cards for individual drill.

Checkpoint

Write a spelling word for each clue.
Then use the Checkpoint Study Plan on page 224.

1. A word that means "letting fall" is ___.

2. The opposite of starting is ___.

3. The glass broke because I ___ it.

4. The light turned red, and the cars ___.

5. The rabbits ___.

6. A way of running is ___.

7. If you are moving like a bunny, you are ___.

8. Don't leave the water ___.

9. I went to the supermarket and ___.

10. A leopard is ___.

11. Something that is marked with dots is ___.

12. When you are buying things, you are ___.

13. I didn't walk to school, I ___.

14. In Iceland long ago, <u>kuta</u> meant "to cut with a knife." What mystery word comes from <u>kuta</u>? Double the final consonant and add <u>ing</u>. What do you get? ___

125

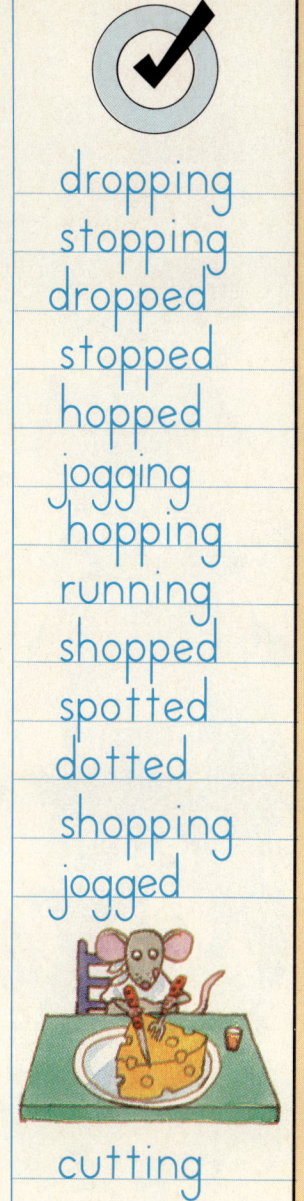

dropping
stopping
dropped
stopped
hopped
jogging
hopping
running
shopped
spotted
dotted
shopping
jogged

cutting

Objectives

- To write spelling words in response to clues: definitions, an antonym, and context.
- To develop the critical thinking skills of making inferences and predicting outcomes.
- To appreciate the diversity of sources of the English language.

Spelling Strategy

Write the root words <u>drop</u> and <u>spot</u> on the board. Point out the /ŏ/ sound of o in each word. Remind students that when they hear this sound in a word, they must double the final consonant before adding the suffix <u>ed</u> or <u>ing</u>. Have students work in pairs. Duplicate and distribute to each pair a list of the root words contained in the spelling words, in the form of equations such as <u>jog</u> + <u>ed</u> = _____. Have pairs work together to add the suffix <u>ed</u> or <u>ing</u> to each root word. Then call on pairs to use each of the spelling words in an oral sentence.

Preparation The clues on this page are like crossword puzzle clues. Explain to students that the response to each clue is a spelling word. Use the following examples to illustrate the types of clues used:

Definition	A way of running is *(jogging).*
Antonym	The opposite of starting is *(stopping).*
Context	The glass broke because I *(dropped)* it.

The final clue explains the origin of the word <u>cut</u>.

The Page Have students complete page 125 using the words on page 124. When students have finished, have them read each clue and spell the answer aloud. Check each response twice: once for the correct answer and a second time for spelling accuracy.

Follow-Up Guide students in using the **Checkpoint Study Plan** on page 224 to take a self-test. Have them use the plan for independent study.

Objectives

- To write words with the suffixes ed and ing in continuous text.
- To write each spelling word once.
- To integrate reading with spelling.

STOP BILLY'S HOPS!

Fill in the blanks with spelling words.

1. Billy's still hopping and ___hopping___.

   He hops and he hops without ___stopping___!

   His friends like his trick,

   How he hops on his stick

   For an hour and a half without

   ___stopping / dropping___.

2. Billy's family went ___shopping___ with Billy.

   His mother said, "Billy looks silly.

   He has hopped and has hopped

   Every time that we've ___shopped___.

   And I fear he will never stop, will he?"

3. Billy doesn't think running's much fun.

   If you run you're just like everyone.

   "When I'm hopping, I'm soaring!

   I think ___running___ is boring,"

   Says Billy while eating a bun.

4. Billy knocks over plants that are potted.

   His living room rug becomes ___spotted___.

126

Preparation Have students turn to pages 126 and 127. Call their attention to the pictures and the word list. Have the students say each word aloud. Then explain that each spelling word belongs in one of the blanks in the seven short poems. Remind the students that poetry is written in separate lines of verse that rhyme. Tell the students that you will read the story aloud, supplying the missing words. Have them listen for rhyming words as you read.

Tell the students that the story is about Billy, a boy who won't stop hopping.

126

"Billy, hop out of doors

Not on these floors.

You have ruined our rug that is _____dotted_____!"

5. Billy's father can't think what to do

With a son like a strange kangaroo.

"It's time that he _____stopped_____!

I want that pogo stick _____dropped_____!

I fear he'll soon live in a zoo."

6. Billy started to hiccup one day,

While happily hopping at play.

The hiccups would stop

When he tried not to hop.

When he _____hopped_____, they

returned right away.

7. Billy's pogo stick rests on the floor.

"I'm afraid I can't hop anymore.

I'm _____cutting_____ this short,

I'll go _____jogging_____ for sport."

And he happily _____jogged_____ out the door.

127

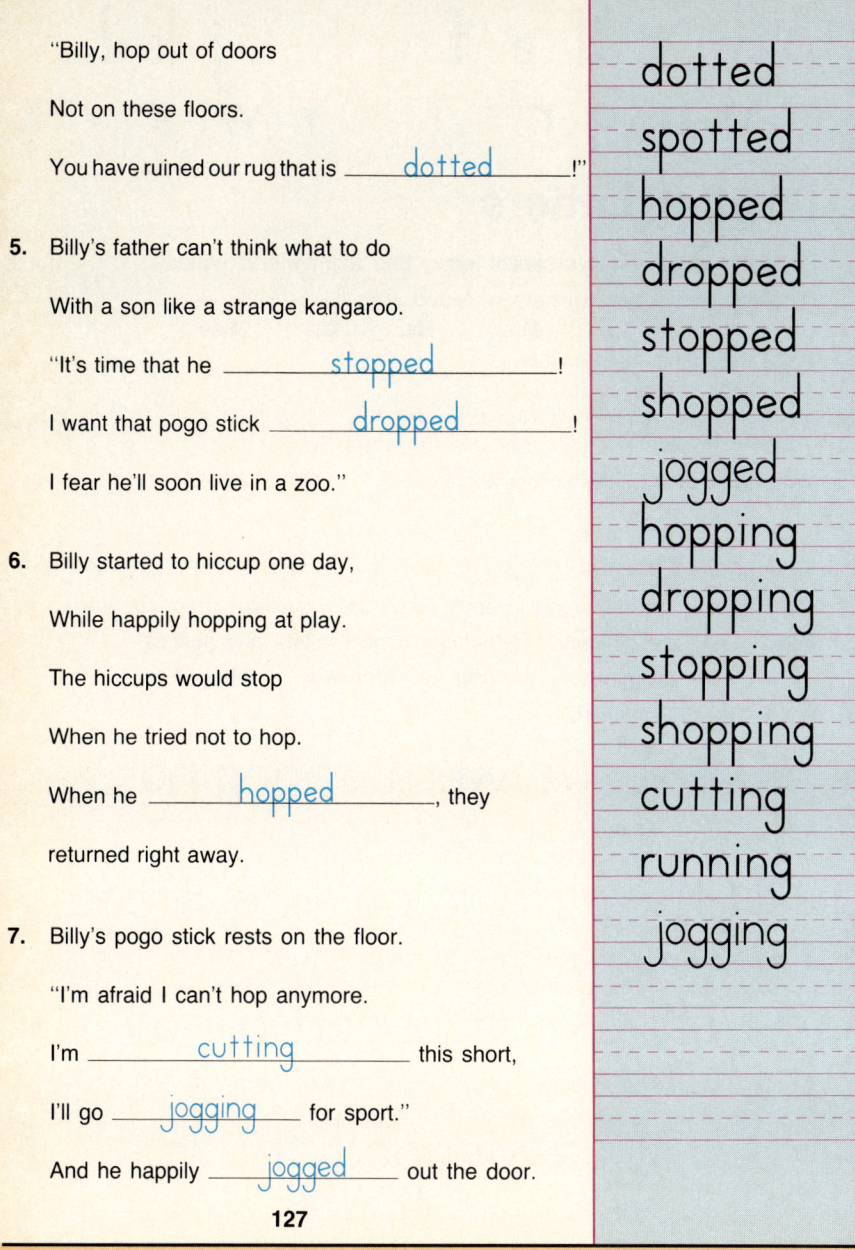

dotted
spotted
hopped
dropped
stopped
shopped
jogged
hopping
dropping
stopping
shopping
cutting
running
jogging

Enrichment

If you want to use the blackline activity masters for enrichment and additional practice, assign Lesson 23 activities at this time.

Maintenance and Review

OBJECTIVE

• To review words with /ī/ spelled: y, ie, i.

ACTIVITIES

If you want to use the blackline activity masters for maintenance and review, assign Lesson 22 activities at this time.

You can also use the activity below to review Lesson 22 with students:

Write the two review words for each sentence on the board. Read the sentence aloud, pausing before each blank so the students can say the missing word aloud. Remind students that words don't have to look alike to sound alike. *(Answers are in parentheses.)*

try   pie
I am going to *(try)* to bake
an apple *(pie)* .

fly   sky
Beth saw a bird *(fly)*
high in the *(sky)* .

why   cry
Can you tell me *(why)*
a baby might *(cry)* ?

Read the following words aloud and have the students volunteer to write them on the board: **tiny, lie, my, tiger, tie, by, lion, high**

The Pages   Read the poem aloud, supplying the missing spelling words as the students follow along in their texts. When you have finished, you may wish to discuss the poem. Ask students what they think of Billy's new sport.

Have the students complete the poem by writing the correct spelling word for each blank. Have the students say and spell the missing spelling words together. Write the answers on the board so students may check their own work.

Follow-Up   Have volunteers make up two rhyming sentences using any two words from the word list. After each student recites the rhyme, have the students spell the words used.

Objectives

- To relate spelling to another language skill.
- To capitalize titles and end them with a period.
- To write spelling words in the context of sentences.
- To practice proofreading.
- To check handwriting for correct letter formation.

a b c d e f g h i j k l m
n o p q r s t u v w x y z

Capital Letters

Begin these titles with a capital letter. End them with a period.
(The title Miss does not have a period after it.)

Mr.   Mrs.   Ms.   Dr.   Miss

Write the name of a teacher.

Write the name of the school principal.

One word is spelled wrong in each sentence. Find the correct spelling below. Write the sentence. Remember capital letters and periods!

dropped   cutting   stopped   shopping

1. dr cruz went shoping.

Dr. Cruz went shopping.

2. mr smith is cuting bread.

Mr. Smith is cutting bread.

3. miss day droped a hat.

Miss Day dropped a hat.

4. ms lea stoped the car.

Ms. Lea stopped the car.

128

Preparation Write these names on the board:

mrs wiggly   dr foot   miss hudson   mr boot   ms merry

Ask the students to tell you what is wrong with the names. *(They need capital letters and periods.)* Tell them that titles before names also need capital letters. All titles, except Miss, end with a period. Have a volunteer come to the board and write each name correctly. *(Mrs. Wiggly, Dr. Foot, Miss Hudson, Mr. Boot, Ms. Merry)*

The Page Do page 128 with the students. Remind them to pay attention to their handwriting. For example, the uppercase M in Miss, Mrs., Mr., and Ms. has a sequence of four strokes and the top of the letter must touch the top writing line. Have students read each sentence aloud as you write it on the board. Ask students to note the spelling word in each sentence.

Follow-Up Put these sentences on the board and have students correct and rewrite the titles and names:

mr laslo baked a cake for ms barker.
mrs meyer gave the keys to dr dewey.

(Mr. Laslo, Ms. Barker, Mrs. Meyer, Dr. Dewey)

128

WORDS AT WORK

Challenge Yourself

admitting   strutting   propped

What do you think each underlined Challenge Word means? Check your Spelling Dictionary to see if you are right. Then write sentences. Show that you understand the meaning of each Challenge Word.

1. <u>Admitting</u> a mistake is hard.

2. The rooster was <u>strutting</u> around the barnyard.

3. I <u>propped</u> my bat against the fence.

Write to the Point

You just read a poem about Billy. He liked to hop and jog. Write a poem about what you like to do for exercise. Use spelling words from this lesson in your poem.

Challenge Use one or more of the Challenge Words in your poem.

Proofreading

Use the marks to show the mistakes in the sentences below. Write the four misspelled words correctly in the blanks.

⬯	word is misspelled
⊙	period is missing
≡	letter should be capitalized

1. Does miguel always go (joging)?

2. I saw him cutting across my yard and (runing) to the store.

3. He (stapped) to buy a drink ⊙

4. Then he (joggd) again.

1. _____jogging_____

2. _____running_____

3. _____stopped_____

4. _____jogged_____

129

Objectives

- To extend the spelling patterns presented in Lesson 23 to the Challenge Words.

- To use context and the **Spelling Dictionary** to enlarge students' vocabulary.

- To apply the spelling patterns presented in Lesson 23 in a writing activity.

- To practice proofreading for spelling, punctuation, and capitalization.

Dictation Sentences

1. I think <u>jogging</u> is fun, but not <u>hopping</u>.
2. Did you see the <u>spotted</u> dog <u>running</u> home?
3. She <u>hopped</u> up the street.
4. She <u>dropped</u> the eggs.
5. We <u>shopped</u> in the city.
6. My baby brother is <u>dropping</u> his food on my coat.
7. The dog keeps <u>stopping</u> when it sees a cat.
8. He <u>jogged</u> home after <u>shopping</u>.
9. He <u>stopped</u> <u>cutting</u> the tree.
10. Her socks were <u>dotted</u> with blue.

Challenge Yourself Answers

Possible definitions:

1. agreeing; making known
2. walking with pride
3. leaned

Students' sentences will vary.

Test Review adding <u>ed</u> and <u>ing</u> to words. Test words ending with <u>ed</u> and <u>ing</u>. Use one of these testing methods: (1) Say the word; read the sample sentence from page 124; say the word; have students write the word. (2) Read each dictation sentence above; have students write the sentence. Correct the test with students.

Challenge Yourself The optional Challenge Words may be assigned to the entire class or limited to those students who do well on the test. Have students note the spelling patterns in the Challenge Words. Responses to this activity should be completed on separate paper. Answers to the questions are provided above.

Write to the Point Have students recall the selection "Stop Billy's Hops" on pages 126 and 127; then assign the poem. This activity should be completed on separate paper.

Proofreading The proofreading practice includes misspellings of words from this lesson as well as a capitalization error and a punctuation error.

LESSON 24

Objectives

- To review and reinforce vowel spellings for /ē/ and /ī/.
- To review and reinforce the suffixes ed and ing.
- To hear, say, spell, and write representative words from Lessons 19–23.
- To write a description using the five steps in the writing process.
- To use a prewriting activity to list sensory details for a description.

Dictation Sentences

1. Do you like being eight years old?
2. The trees along this street are very pretty.
3. I think these books are my favorite ones.
4. I don't think your joke is very funny.
5. My room is always clean.
6. I like to write letters to my friends.
7. Did you find your glove?
8. I don't know why the sky is blue.
9. My little brother can tie his shoes now.
10. That new baby is really tiny.
11. The school bus stopped to pick me up.
12. My dad took me shopping to buy a new coat.

Note

A review test blackline master in standardized format and an answer sheet have been provided on pages T38 and T41 of this Teacher's Edition. The answers to the review test are given below.

1-A	5-D
2-B	6-A
3-D	7-C
4-A	8-B

Lesson 24 Words in Review

A. being
street
these

B. very
clean

C. write
find

D. why
tie
tiny

E. stopped
shopping

1. In Lesson 19 you studied three ways to spell /ē/. Write the words in List A.

being   street   these

2. List B has two more words with /ē/. Write the two words.

very   clean

3. In Lesson 21 you studied words with /ī/. Write the words in List C.

find   write

4. List D has three more words with /ī/. Write the words that end with y.

why   tiny

Write the word in which /ī/ is spelled ie.

tie

5. In Lesson 23 you added ed and ing to some words. Add ed to stop and ing to shop. Use List E to check your words.

stopped   shopping

130

Preparation Tell students that Lesson 24 is a review lesson. Lesson 24 contains several activities that ask them to write some of the words they have studied in Lessons 19–23.

Direct students' attention to the list of words on page 130. Read the words aloud as students look at them. Have students say and spell each word aloud.

Then read the dictation sentences above as students point to each spelling word in their book. Point out that the words in List A are from Lesson 19, words in List B are from Lesson 20, words in List C are from Lesson 21, words in List D are from Lesson 22, and words in List E are from Lesson 23.

The Pages Have students complete the activities on page 130 as a group or independently. Write the answers on the board and have volunteers spell the words aloud for reinforcement of correct spelling.

Test and Study If you wish to test students on the review words, use one of these testing methods: (1) Read the word and the dictation sentence; say the word again; have students write the word. (2) Have students complete the review test blackline master. (See **Note**.)

130

Writer's Workshop

A Description

A description tells about someone or something. The writer uses words that help the reader see, hear, smell, taste, and feel what is being described. Here is part of Nina's description of her tree house.

My Tree House

My tree house has four walls made of wood. The roof is flat and also made of wood. The outside of my tree house is painted dark brown. This makes it hard for people to see it from the ground. The walls inside are green. One wall has a small hole for a window and a big hole for a door. An old green rug covers the rough floor.

To write her description, Nina followed the steps in the writing process. She began with a **Prewriting** activity. She used a senses web to write down all the things about the tree house that she could see and touch. Part of Nina's web is shown here. Study what Nina did.

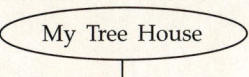

My Tree House

See
wood walls
flat roof made of wood
brown outside
green inside
small hole for window
big hole for door
green rug

It's Your Turn

Get ready to write your own description. You can describe a special place or person. Begin by making a senses web. Then follow the other steps in the writing process—**Writing, Revising, Proofreading,** and **Publishing.**

131

Writer's Workshop Students who have mastered the review words may go on to the **Writer's Workshop** on page 131. Explain that in a description a writer uses words to help the reader see, hear, smell, taste, and feel what the writer is describing. Then read the beginning of the description "My Tree House" with students, noting the sensory details.

Allow students to study the portion of the senses web provided on the pupil's page and guide students to see how this graphic organizer helped Nina prepare to write her description.

It's Your Turn Review the steps in the writing process with students. If students are not satisfied with the result of their prewriting, allow them to revise it as often as necessary or to choose another topic and repeat the prewriting activity.

Process Writing Blackline Masters
• Senses Web, page T50
• Steps in the Writing Process, page T46
• Proofreading Symbols/Checklist, page T47

Note

If students have difficulty deciding on a topic, you may wish to suggest one of the following:

My room
My favorite toy
A friend or relative

LESSON 25

Objectives

- To hear and say words with /ō/.
- To write words with /ō/ with attention to letter sequence and sound/symbol relationships.
- To write each spelling word once.
- To recognize that /ō/ may be spelled o_e, ow, and o.

Sample Sentences

1. Can you jump rope and do a trick?
2. I stay at home when I am sick.
3. The reindeer had a bright red nose.
4. I hope that puppy is the one you chose.
5. A diamond is a beautiful stone.
6. Spot dug a hole and buried a bone.
7. Can you tell a funny joke?
8. An egg's yellow center is the yolk.
9. Plant the bulbs and watch the flowers grow.
10. Do you know how to tie a bow?
11. The snow looks just like drops of lace.
12. Clear the track so we can race!
13. We saw the sleds go down the hills.
14. Can fish breathe if they have no gills?

Note

Words are grouped according to spellings of /ō/:

o_e
ow
o

The sample sentences may be used for pretesting and post-testing.

Lesson 25 Words with /ō/

rope
home
nose
hope
stone
hole
joke

yellow
grow
know
snow

so
go
no

1. Which words have only two letters in them?

so   no   go

2. gr + ow = grow

sn + ow = snow

3. What word has the double consonant ll in the middle?

yellow

4. Which word begins with the sound /n/, spelled kn?

know

Did you know, the e at the end makes the o say its name?
No joke?

5. What words have o and e, but you only hear /ō/?

rope   home

nose   hope

stone   hole

joke

132

Preparation   Write /ō/ on the board and have students repeat the sound /ō/ as in go. Say the word pairs below. Ask students to raise their hands when they hear /ō/ in a word.

rope – ripe   hum – home   know – now   grew – grow   say – so

Call attention to the word list on page 132. Say each word aloud. Then have the students say and spell each word.

Read the cartoon and demonstrate the rule. Write hop on the board and have a student read it. Add an e to the word and have a volunteer read the new word. (hope) Also note that when k and n come together in a word, they make only one sound. Ask a student to find the word that begins with kn and say the beginning sound. (know; /n/) Finally, identify the three ways /ō/ is spelled in this lesson: o_e, ow, and o. (See Note.)

Read the sample sentences as the students point to the corresponding spelling words in their books.

The Page   Do page 132 together. Allow time for students to write the responses. Then ask volunteers to spell the answers aloud while the others write the words on the board. Help the students check their work.

Follow-Up   Ask the students how they plan to study the spelling words. You might suggest that they write the words two times each day.

132

Checkpoint

Write a spelling word for each clue. Then use the Checkpoint Study Plan on page 224.

1. A bird's nest is its ___.

2. See with your eyes, smell with your ___.

3. A small rock is a ___.

4. Bananas and lemons are ___.

5. To make someone laugh, tell a ___.

6. "To wish" means to ___.

7. We tied the big box with a ___.

8. The opposite of yes is ___.

9. Last winter, we had a lot of ___.

10. I hope my bean plant will ___.

11. You need a shovel to dig a ___.

12. The opposite of stop is ___.

13. I like horses ___ much!

14. Many, many years ago, this mystery word was spelled gnōw. You could hear the sound of each letter when the word was said. Today the word does not have the letter g. It has a silent letter instead. Do you know the mystery word? ___

133

home
nose
stone
yellow
joke
hope
rope
no
snow
grow
hole
go
so

know

Objectives

- To write spelling words in response to clues: definitions, antonyms, and context.

- To develop the critical thinking skills of making inferences and contrasting.

- To understand that the spelling and pronunciation of words in the English language often change over time.

Spelling Strategy

The homophones <u>know</u> and <u>no</u> can be the source of a spelling problem. Help students remember which word to use by writing each word on the chalkboard and pointing out that although the words sound alike, they have very different meanings. Discuss the meaning of each word. Then write the sentence <u>The more I grow, the more I know</u> on the chalkboard. Discuss the meaning of the sentence. Then point out the similar sounds and endings of the words <u>grow</u> and <u>know</u>. Urge students to keep this sentence in mind because it will help them to remember the difference between <u>no</u> and <u>know</u>.

Preparation
The clues on this page are like crossword puzzle clues. Explain to students that the response to each clue is a spelling word. Use the following examples to illustrate the types of clues used:

Definition   A small rock is a *(stone)*.
Antonym   The opposite of yes is *(no)*.
Context   We tied the big box with a *(rope)*.

The final clue explains how the spelling and pronunciation of <u>know</u> changed over time.

The Page
Have students complete page 133 using the words on page 132. When students have finished, have them read each clue and spell the answer aloud. Check each response twice: once for the correct answer and a second time for spelling accuracy.

Follow-Up
Guide students in using the **Checkpoint Study Plan** on page 224 to take a self-test. Have them use the plan for independent study.

Objectives

- To write words with /ō/ in continuous text.
- To write each spelling word once.
- To integrate reading with spelling.

Fill in the blanks with spelling words.

Jump Rope Rose

Rose's leg was in a cast. She had been skiing in the

___snow___ and broke her leg. She was wearing

her new ski mask. It covered her mouth and her

___nose___. It also fell over her eyes. When she

started to ___go___ down the hill, she didn't see the

big hard ___stone___ in the trail. Rose fell.

When she stopped, she was sitting in a deep

___hole___.

134

Note

Point out the homophones <u>no</u> and <u>know</u> which appear in this story (see page 136).

Preparation

Have students turn to pages 134 and 135. Call their attention to the illustrations and the word list. Have students say the words. Then explain that each spelling word belongs in one of the blanks in the story.

Write the title "Jump Rope Rose" on the board, and have a student read it. Ask the students if they've ever had to wear a cast on an arm or a leg. Ask what some of the things were that they couldn't do. Explain that this story is about a girl whose leg is in a cast. Have the students use the title as a clue to guess what activity the girl misses most. *(jumping rope)*

The Pages

Read the story aloud, supplying the missing spelling words as the students follow along in their texts. When you have finished, you may wish to discuss the story. Ask a volunteer to explain how Rose broke her leg. *(She was skiing and she fell.)* At the end of the story, why is Rose no longer in a hurry to jump rope? *(Her doctor had broken his leg while jumping rope.)*

At first, being in a cast was fun. Her friends wrote on it. They visited her at ___home___ and told her jokes. Her father brought her a pot of bulbs and she watched them ___grow___ into yellow tulips. But now it was spring and everyone was outside jumping ___rope___. There was ___no___ one coming to see her anymore.

"I ___hope___ my cast will come off today," said Rose to her mother.

"Maybe it will," replied her mother, "but we don't ___know___ for sure."

They went to see Dr. Bradford. There was Dr. Bradford with a big cast on his foot!

"Hello, Rose," he said. "Look what I did jumping rope. Today your cast comes off, but mine just went on!"

Rose felt very sorry for him. She wrote on his cast. She told him a funny ___joke___. The next day she sent him a pot of ___yellow___ tulips. And she wasn't in ___so___ much of a hurry to jump rope herself that spring!

135

rope
home
nose
hope
stone
hole
joke
yellow
grow
know
snow
so
go
no

Enrichment

If you want to use the blackline activity masters for enrichment and additional practice, assign Lesson 25 activities at this time.

Maintenance and Review

OBJECTIVE

- To review words with the suffixes ed and ing.

ACTIVITIES

If you want to use the blackline activity masters for maintenance and review, assign Lesson 23 activities at this time.

You can also use the activity below to review Lesson 23 with students:

Have the students copy the following word equations and complete them. *(Answers are in parentheses.)*

drop	+	p	+	ing	=	*(dropping)*.
jog	+	g	+	ed	=	*(jogged)*.
cut	+	t	+	ing	=	*(cutting)*.
shop	+	p	+	ed	=	*(shopped)*.
spot	+	t	+	ed	=	*(spotted)*.
run	+	n	+	ing	=	*(running)*.
shop	+	p	+	ing	=	*(shopping)*.
dot	+	t	+	ed	=	*(dotted)*.
hop	+	p	+	ing	=	*(hopping)*.
drop	+	p	+	ed	=	*(dropped)*.
hop	+	p	+	ed	=	*(hopped)*.
jog	+	g	+	ing	=	*(jogging)*.
stop	+	p	+	ed	=	*(stopped)*.

Then have the students complete the story independently by writing the correct spelling word for each blank. Ask a student to read the story aloud, pausing before each blank. Have the other students say the missing spelling word at the appropriate time. Ask volunteers to write the answers on the board. Then check students' responses for correct word choice and for the accurate spelling of each answer.

Follow-Up Have students use each of the spelling words they missed in an original sentence.

Objectives

- To relate spelling words to a dictionary skill.
- To identify homophones.
- To check handwriting for correct letter formation.

a b c d e f g h i j k l m
n o p q r s t u v w x y z

Homophones

Sometimes words that sound the same have different spellings and different meanings. These words are called homophones. **Our** and **hour** are homophones.

Choose the correct homophone for each of the sentence pairs below. The Spelling Dictionary will help you.

hole   whole

1. "I can't believe I ate the _whole_ doughnut," said Max.

2. "Don't worry," said Julie. "At least you left the _hole_ !"

nose   knows

3. Max asked Julie how a squirrel _knows_ where it hid its food.

4. Julie told him, "It's the _nose_ that knows!"

so   sew

5. Max: Why did the painter put needles and thread in his brush?

Julie: I give up.

Max: He did it _so_ he could _sew_ on a coat of paint!

136

Preparation Write these words on the board: **our   hour** Have students read them aloud. Ask which word means 60 minutes. *(hour)* Have a student use hour in a sentence. Then ask which word means belonging to us. *(our)* Have students use our in a sentence. Tell the students that when two words sound the same but have different spellings and different meanings, they are called homophones. Explain that homo means same and phone means sound.

Since the spelling of these words determines their meaning, it is especially important to be accurate when spelling them. Have students turn to the story "Jump Rope Rose" on pages 134–135 and locate the homophones no and know.

The Page Have students complete page 136. Remind them to be careful about their handwriting. For example, tell them to be sure they make the w with two points on the base line; the center of the w should come to the middle line. A w should not be confused with the letter v or u. When students have finished the page, have volunteers read each sentence pair, noting the homophone they used by spelling it. You may wish to write the answers on the board so students can check their own work.

Follow-Up Help students to write their own sentences for these pairs of homophones: so – sew, nose – knows, hole – whole.

136

WORDS AT WORK

Challenge Yourself

hopeful   explode   bony

Decide which Challenge Word fits each clue. Check your Spelling Dictionary to see if you were right. Then write sentences. Show that you understand the meaning of each Challenge Word.

1. A very thin horse would be this.

2. You are this when you want something good to happen.

3. Firecrackers do this on the Fourth of July.

Write to the Point

Rose was sad because she could not play outside. Her friends told jokes to keep her from being sad. Write a joke you would tell Rose. Use spelling words from this lesson in your joke.

Challenge Use one or more of the Challenge Words in your joke.

Proofreading

Use the marks to show the mistakes in the sentences below. Write the four misspelled words correctly in the blanks.

◯	word is misspelled
⊙	period is missing
=	letter should be capitalized

1. let's ⟨goe⟩ on a ski trip.
   =

2. The ski trails will be marked with ⟨yello⟩ rope.

3. I hope the ⟨snowe⟩ will be deep⊙

4. Last year I fell over a ⟨ston⟩.

1. _____ go

2. _____ yellow

3. _____ snow

4. _____ stone

137

Objectives

- To extend the vowel spellings presented in Lesson 25 to the Challenge Words.
- To use clues and the **Spelling Dictionary** to enlarge students' vocabulary.
- To apply the vowel spellings presented in Lesson 25 in a writing activity.
- To practice proofreading for spelling, punctuation, and capitalization.

Dictation Sentences

1. Can you jump <u>rope</u>?
2. Our puppy will <u>grow</u> to be a big dog.
3. My <u>nose</u> was red from the cold.
4. I <u>hope</u> it will <u>snow</u> today.
5. This sock has a <u>hole</u> in it.
6. I <u>know</u> a funny <u>joke</u>.
7. This dog has <u>no home</u>, so we will take him with <u>us</u>.
8. I have a ring with a <u>yellow stone</u> in it.
9. I hope you can <u>go</u> fishing with me.

Challenge Yourself Answers

1. bony
2. hopeful
3. explode

Students' sentences will vary.

Test Review these three ways to spell /ō/: o_e as in <u>rope</u>; ow as in <u>yellow</u>; o as in <u>so</u>. Test words with /ō/. Use one of these testing methods: (1) Say the word; read the sample sentence from page 132; say the word; have students write the word. (2) Read each dictation sentence above; have students write the sentence. Correct the test with students.

Challenge Yourself The optional Challenge Words may be assigned to the entire class or limited to those students who do well on the test. Have students note the vowel spellings in the Challenge Words. Responses to this activity should be completed on separate paper. Answers to the questions are provided above.

Write to the Point Have students recall the selection "Jump Rope Rose" on pages 134 and 135; then assign the joke. Remind students to use correct capitalization and punctuation in their joke. This activity should be completed on separate paper.

Proofreading The proofreading practice includes misspellings of words from this lesson as well as a capitalization error and a punctuation error.

LESSON 26

Objectives

- To hear and say words with /ō/.
- To write words with /ō/ with attention to letter sequence and sound/symbol relationships.
- To write each spelling word once.
- To recognize that /ō/ may be spelled <u>o</u> and <u>oa</u>.

Sample Sentences

1. The weather up north is icy and <u>cold</u>.
2. Is your jewelry made of <u>gold</u>?
3. The opposite of young is <u>old</u>.
4. The sign on the lawn said, "This house is <u>sold</u>."
5. They <u>told</u> me the beach has soft, white sand.
6. May I <u>hold</u> the puppy in my hand?
7. Horseback riding is the <u>most</u> fun of all.
8. My gerbil can <u>roll</u> up in a furry ball.
9. When summer is <u>over</u>, the fall begins.
10. If you <u>open</u> that drawer, you'll find needles and pins.
11. We sailed on the lake in a big <u>boat</u>.
12. Is that your new winter <u>coat</u>?
13. A <u>goat</u> gives milk just like a cow.
14. The <u>road</u> to town is closed right now.

Note

Words are grouped according to spellings of /ō/:

o

oa

The sample sentences may be used for pretesting and post-testing.

Lesson 26 Words with /ō/

cold
gold
old
sold
told
hold
most
roll
over
open

boat
coat
goat
road

1. What words begin with the vowel sound /ō/?

over   open

old

2. What word ends with the last two letters in <u>toast</u>?

most

3. What word ends with the double consonant ll?

roll

4. Which words spell /ō/ with <u>oa</u>, as in <u>load</u>?

boat   coat

goat   road

5. Write <u>cold</u>.   cold

Write four more <u>old</u> words.

told   gold

hold   sold

Could I write four <u>old</u> words?

Do as you're <u>told</u>!

138

Preparation   Write /ō/ on the board and have students repeat the sound /ō/ as in <u>go</u>. Say these word pairs. Ask students to shake their heads when they hear a word with /ō/.

<u>hold</u> – held   <u>most</u> – mist   read – <u>road</u>   <u>coat</u> – cot

Call attention to the word list on page 138. Say each word aloud. Then have the students say and spell each word.

Note the surprising spelling of <u>roll</u>: double consonants at the end instead of a signal e. Ask if someone can think of a word that sounds like <u>roll</u> but is spelled differently. Write <u>role</u> on the chalkboard. Tell students that <u>role</u> means a part played by an actor. Ask students to make up sentences for <u>roll</u> and <u>role</u>.

Then have students look at the two groups of spelling words. How is /ō/ spelled in the first group of words? (o) How is it spelled in the other group? (oa) (See **Note**.) Have a student read the cartoon aloud.

Read the sample sentences as students point to the spelling words.

The Page   Do the page together, allowing time for students to write the answers. Check their responses for immediate reinforcement of correct spelling.

Follow-Up   Suggest that two students work in pairs to write spelling words on pieces of paper that are put face down. One player picks a paper and says the word. The other player spells the word. Players take turns.

Checkpoint

Write a spelling word for each clue.
Then use the Checkpoint Study Plan on page 224.

1. What time does the pet store ___?

2. An animal like a sheep is a ___.

3. My dog obeys by doing what he's ___.

4. Of all my cousins, I like Tony the ___.

5. That ring is not silver, it's ___.

6. There were many cars on the ___.

7. The kitten likes me to ___ him.

8. That is not new, it's ___.

9. How many tickets have you ___?

10. The opposite of under is ___.

11. When it's not hot, it's ___.

12. A small ship is a ___.

13. If you're cold, put on your ___.

14. Hundreds of years ago, the word <u>rotulāre</u> was
    used to tell how a wheel moves. Many years later
    in France, <u>rotulāre</u> became <u>roler</u>. What word do
    we use? Guess the mystery word. ___

139

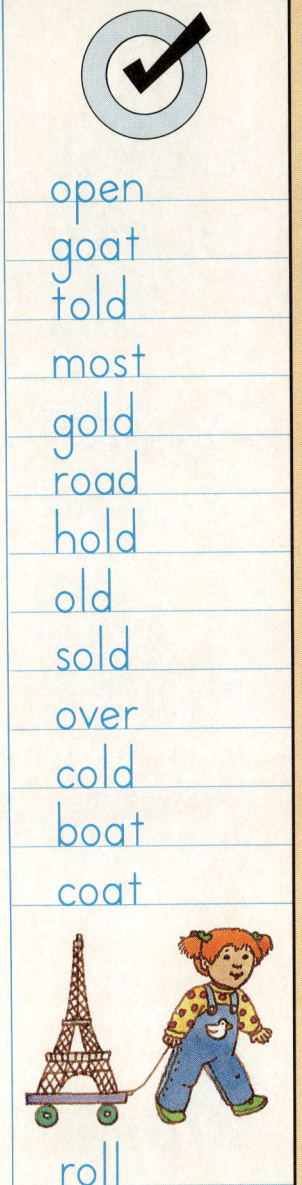

open
goat
told
most
gold
road
hold
old
sold
over
cold
boat
coat

roll

Objectives

- To write spelling words in response to clues: definition, antonyms, and context.
- To develop the critical thinking skills of contrasting and making inferences.
- To understand that the spelling of words often changes over time.

Spelling Strategy

Some students may omit the l in the final consonant blend ld. They may, for example, write <u>gold</u> as <u>god</u>. Have these students practice making new words by replacing the initial consonant, writing the new word, and underlining the final ld. Possible new words from the lesson include <u>cold</u>, <u>sold</u>, <u>hold</u>, and <u>told</u>.

Preparation
The clues on this page are like crossword puzzle clues. Explain to students that the response to each clue is a spelling word. Use the following examples to illustrate the types of clues used:

Definition	A small ship is a *(boat)*.
Antonym	The opposite of under is *(over)*.
Context	The kitten likes me to *(hold)* him.

The final clue traces the origin of the English word <u>roll</u>.

The Page
Have students complete page 139 using the words on page 138. When students have finished, have them read each clue and spell the answer aloud. Check each response twice: once for the correct answer and a second time for spelling accuracy.

Follow-Up
Guide students in using the **Checkpoint Study Plan** on page 224 to take a self-test. Have them use the plan for independent study.

Objectives

- To write words with /ō/ in continuous text.
- To write each spelling word once.
- To integrate reading with spelling.

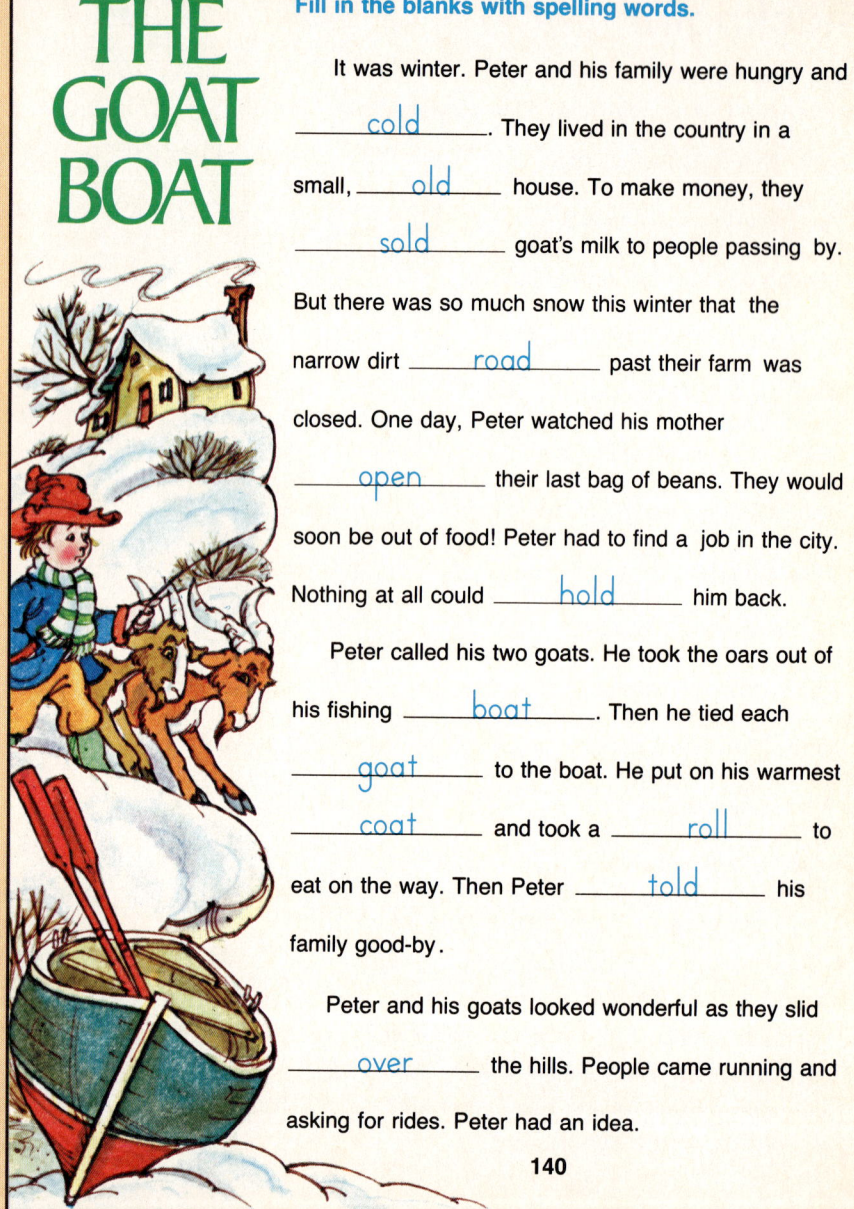

Fill in the blanks with spelling words.

It was winter. Peter and his family were hungry and ___cold___. They lived in the country in a small, ___old___ house. To make money, they ___sold___ goat's milk to people passing by.

But there was so much snow this winter that the narrow dirt ___road___ past their farm was closed. One day, Peter watched his mother ___open___ their last bag of beans. They would soon be out of food! Peter had to find a job in the city. Nothing at all could ___hold___ him back.

Peter called his two goats. He took the oars out of his fishing ___boat___. Then he tied each ___goat___ to the boat. He put on his warmest ___coat___ and took a ___roll___ to eat on the way. Then Peter ___told___ his family good-by.

Peter and his goats looked wonderful as they slid ___over___ the hills. People came running and asking for rides. Peter had an idea.

140

Preparation Have students turn to pages 140 and 141. Call their attention to the pictures and the word list. Have the students say the words. Then explain that each spelling word belongs in one of the blanks in the story.

Write the title "The Goat Boat" on the board and have a student read it. Ask students what they think a goat boat might be. Explain that the story is about a boy who invents the "goat boat."

The Pages Read the story aloud, supplying the missing spelling word as the students follow along in their texts. When you have finished, you may wish to discuss the story. Ask students how Peter got food for his family.

Then have students complete the story by silently rereading it and writing the correct spelling words for each blank. Ask two volunteers to read the story aloud: One student will read the story pausing before each blank; the other one will say the missing spelling word at the appropriate time. Ask another student to write the answers on the board so students may correct their own work. Check students' responses for the accurate spelling of each answer.

"Yes, you may have a ride! But you must pay me, because I have to have money to buy food ."

The people were happy to pay Peter for a ride in his snow boat. It was the ___most___ fun they had ever had!

Peter never got to the city. At the end of the day, Peter went home to his family with a pocket full of ___gold___. Every day he took people for rides. His family was never hungry again.

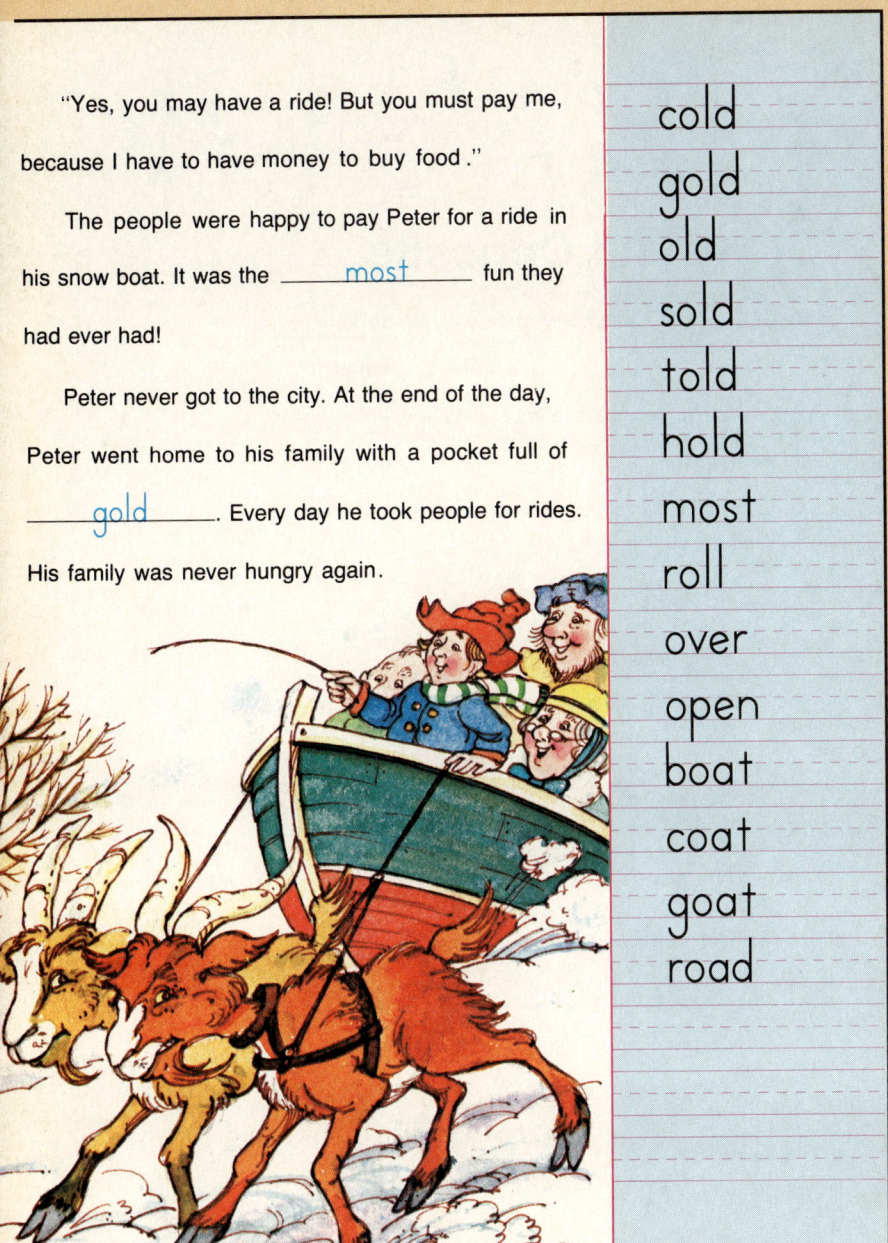

cold
gold
old
sold
told
hold
most
roll
over
open
boat
coat
goat
road

Enrichment

If you want to use the blackline activity masters for enrichment and additional practice, assign Lesson 26 activities at this time.

Maintenance and Review

OBJECTIVE

- To review words with /ō/ spelled: o–e, ow, o.

ACTIVITIES

If you want to use the blackline activity masters for maintenance and review, assign Lesson 25 activities at this time.

You can also use the activity below to review Lesson 25 with students:

Write the following words and riddles on the board. Have the students copy each riddle and complete it with a spelling word. (Answers are in parentheses.)

grow	rope	go	home
	no	yellow	

1. You may hang wet clothes on me.
   I am a _(rope)_ .

2. I am not maybe.
   I am not yes.
   I am _(no)_ .

3. I am the color of a lemon.
   I am _(yellow)_ .

4. I'm a lion's den.
   I'm a person's house.
   I am _(home)_ .

5. I'm people; I'm plants.
   I'm things that get bigger.
   I'm things that _(grow)_ .

6. I'm not stop.
   I'm _(go)_ .

Follow-Up Have students use each of the spelling words they missed in an original sentence.

As an additional follow-up activity, you may ask students to draw an outline of Peter's goat boat. Have them write their spelling words around the outline, making a word picture. Then they may color the picture.

Objectives

- To relate spelling words to a dictionary skill.
- To use synonyms and antonyms.
- To write spelling words in response to synonyms and antonyms.
- To check handwriting for correct letter formation.

a b c d e f g h i j k l m
n o p q r s t u v w x y z

Same and Opposite

Words that have the same meaning are <u>synonyms</u>.

little   small

Words that have opposite meanings are <u>antonyms</u>.

tall   short

Put each of these words with its synonym.
The first one is done for you.

hold   coat   told   road   boat   roll

1. ship   boat   4. bun   roll

2. street   road   5. said   told

3. jacket   coat   6. keep   hold

Put each of these words with its antonym.

over   cold   old   open

7. hot   cold   9. under   over

8. young   old   10. shut   open

142

Preparation

Write these words on the board and read them:

adult   grownup

Explain that these words are synonyms because they have the same meaning. Then write these words on the board: chilly   grasp
Ask a volunteer to find the synonym for <u>chilly</u> in the word list on page 141. *(cold)* Then have students find the synonym for <u>grasp</u>. *(hold)*

Write these words on the board: adult   child
Explain that these words are antonyms because they have opposite meanings. Then write the following words on the board: least   bought
Ask a volunteer to look at the word list on page 141 and find the antonym for <u>least</u>. *(most)* Then have students find the antonym for the word <u>bought</u>. *(sold)*

The Page

Do page 142 together. Tell students to be careful forming the letter <u>l</u>. The <u>l</u> may seem easy to write, but if it doesn't reach the top line, it can look like the letter <u>i</u>. Then have students read their answers aloud while volunteers write them on the board.

Follow-Up

Have the students fold a piece of paper in thirds. Have them copy these words in the first column: **cold, old, over**. Ask them to write a synonym for each word in the second column and an antonym for each word in the last column.

142

WORDS AT WORK

Challenge Yourself

mold   **boulder**   **clover**

Use your Spelling Dictionary to answer these questions. Then write sentences. Show that you understand the meaning of each Challenge Word.

1. Can you put water in a <u>mold</u> to make ice cubes?

2. Can you pick up a <u>boulder</u> with just one hand?

3. Would you look for a four-leaf <u>clover</u> in a field?

Write to the Point

Peter used the gold to help his family. Write a paragraph. Tell someone you would like to help and what you would do to help. Use spelling words from this lesson in your paragraph.

Challenge Use one or more of the Challenge Words in your paragraph.

Proofreading

Use the marks to show the mistakes in the sentences below. Write the four misspelled words correctly in the blanks.

⬭	word is misspelled
⊙	period is missing
≡	letter should be capitalized

1. Wear a heavy ⬭cote⬭ on the ride.

2. <u>hold</u> on as we go down the ⬭rod.⬭

3. Get another ⬭gote⬭ to pull us⊙

4. ⬭Moast⬭ of us want to ride the snow boat again and again.

1. _____ coat
2. _____ road
3. _____ goat
4. _____ most

143

Objectives

- To extend the vowel spellings presented in Lesson 26 to the Challenge Words.
- To use context and the **Spelling Dictionary** to enlarge students' vocabulary.
- To apply the vowel spellings presented in Lesson 26 in a writing activity.
- To practice proofreading for spelling, punctuation, and capitalization.

Dictation Sentences

1. It is <u>cold</u> today.
2. Is your ring made of <u>gold</u>?
3. My brother gave me a very <u>old</u> penny.
4. My cat can <u>roll</u> <u>over</u> and lie on his back.
5. Our class <u>sold</u> food at the game.
6. I did not <u>want</u> to <u>hold</u> the skunk.
7. <u>Most</u> of the children came to see the <u>goat</u>.
8. The men <u>told</u> us that the <u>road</u> was <u>open</u>.
9. We will take a <u>boat</u> ride today.
10. My new <u>coat</u> is <u>black</u> and white.

Challenge Yourself Answers

1. yes
2. no
3. yes

Students' sentences will vary.

Test Review these ways to spell /ō/: <u>o</u> as in <u>cold</u>; <u>oa</u> as in <u>boat</u>. Test words with /ō/. Use one of these testing methods: (1) Say the word; read the sample sentence from page 138; say the word; have students write the word. (2) Read each dictation sentence above; have students write the sentence. Correct the test with students.

Challenge Yourself The optional Challenge Words may be assigned to the entire class or limited to those students who do well on the test. Have students note the vowel spellings in the Challenge Words, especially the following new spelling: <u>ou</u> in <u>boulder</u>. Responses to this activity should be completed on separate paper. Answers to the questions are provided above.

Write to the Point Have students recall the selection "The Goat Boat" on pages 140 and 141; then assign the paragraph. You might want to encourage students to think of creative (nonmonetary) ways in which they might help people, such as raking leaves, washing the dinner dishes, and so on. This activity should be completed on separate paper.

Proofreading The proofreading practice includes misspellings of words from this lesson as well as a capitalization error and a punctuation error.

LESSON 27

Objectives

- To hear and say words with /o͝o/.
- To write words with /o͝o/ with attention to letter sequence and sound/symbol relationships.
- To write each spelling word once.
- To recognize that /o͝o/ may be spelled oo, ou, and u.

Sample Sentences

1. I look in the mirror to comb my hair.
2. I always cook meat medium rare.
3. We took a ride on a passenger train.
4. I read a book when I rode the plane.
5. Joe twisted his foot before the race.
6. I saw a good program about outer space.
7. Chocolate-chip cookies are my favorite snack.
8. My brother and I stood back to back.
9. I wish that we could stay overnight.
10. The teacher says we should never fight.
11. I would like to read a book on cats.
12. The dugout was full of balls and bats.
13. A donkey was used to pull the cart.
14. We put our names on a classroom chart.

Note

Lesson 27 Words with /o͝o/

look
cook
took
book
foot
good
cookies
stood

could
should
would

full
pull
put

1. Write the words that have double o in the middle.

look   cook
took   book
foot   good
cookies   stood

2. Which words have the letter l but no /l/ sound?

could   should
would

3. Which spelling words end with a double consonant?

full   pull

4. Write the word that begins and ends like pat.

put

144

Preparation

Write /o͝o/ on the board. Have the students repeat the sound /o͝o/ as in book. Say these word pairs as the students stand beside their desks. If a word contains /o͝o/, they should stand on one foot.

look – luck   cake – cook   could – can   fill – full

Read the words on page 144 as the students repeat and spell each one.

Note that the sound /k/ is spelled two different ways in the word cook: /ko͝ok/. Ask which letters spell /k/. (c, k) Have students find three words in which /k/ is spelled with the letter c. (cook, cookies, could). In which words is it spelled with a k? (look, cook, took, book, cookies) Then have students read the cartoon aloud. Finally, ask which three words spell the /o͝o/ sound with the letter u. (full, pull, put) Then note the /o͝o/ sound spelled ou in could, would, and should. Ask how /o͝o/ is spelled in the first eight words. (oo) (See Note.)

Have students point to the spelling word as you read each sample sentence.

The Page

Do the page together. Allow time for the students to write the answers. Then write the answers on the board so students may check their own work.

Follow-Up

Suggest that students take turns studying with a partner. One student will spell the word aloud three times. The other will spell it as soon as the partner has finished.

Checkpoint

Write a spelling word for each clue. Then use the Checkpoint Study Plan on page 224.

1. I forgot where I ___ it.

2. A word that sounds just like wood is ___.

3. The opposite of push is ___.

4. There were no chairs in the room, so we ___.

5. I won a prize for the picture I ___.

6. My dad is such a good ___.

7. I'm reading a very funny ___.

8. I didn't want to clean up, but I knew I ___.

9. The opposite of bad is ___.

10. Fill the glass until it's ___.

11. Open your eyes and ___.

12. I asked Mr. Brown if I ___ paint.

13. Carla and I baked ___.

14. In Latin, this mystery word was written <u>ped</u>. In Greek, it was written <u>pod</u>. In Old English, the <u>p</u> was changed to <u>f</u> and the <u>d</u> was changed to <u>t</u>. The word was spelled <u>fōt</u>. It names the part of the leg you stand on. How is it spelled now? ___

145

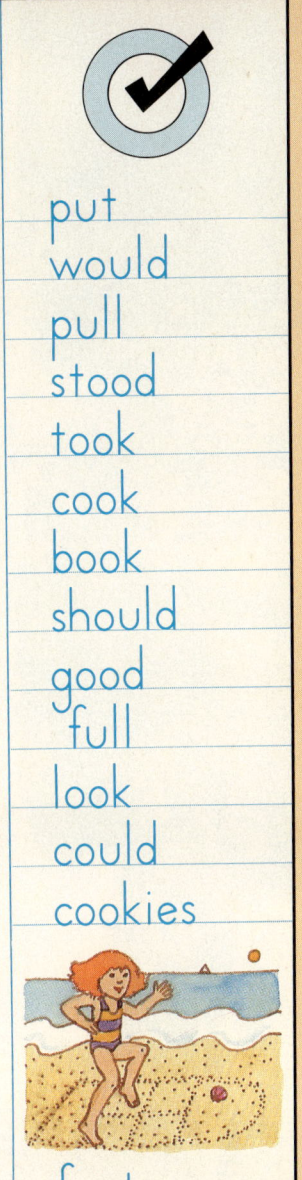

put
would
pull
stood
took
cook
book
should
good
full
look
could
cookies

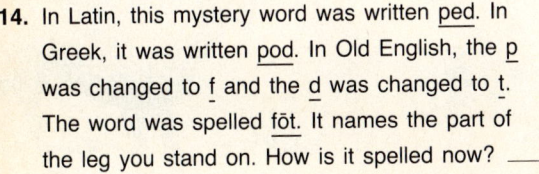

foot

Objectives

- To write spelling words in response to clues: antonyms, homophone, and context.

- To develop the critical thinking skill of analyzing.

- To understand that the spelling of words in the English language often changes over time.

Spelling Strategy

Some students may omit one of the final doubled consonants in <u>pull</u> or <u>full</u>. Remind students that many short, one-syllable words need two l's to spell the /l/ sound at the end of a word. Allow students to make a list of such words on the chalkboard. A number of words can be formed through consonant substitution. Some possible words:

ll		
pull	hill	sell
full	pill	tell
bull	bill	fell

Preparation
The clues on this page are like crossword puzzle clues. Explain to students that the response to each clue is a spelling word. Use the following examples to illustrate the types of clues used:

Antonym	The opposite of bad is (*good*).
Homophone	A word that sounds just like <u>wood</u> is (*would*).
Context	I asked Mr. Brown if I (*could*) paint.

The final clue explains how the spelling of <u>foot</u> has changed over time.

The Page
Have students complete page 145 using the words on page 144. When students have finished, have them read each clue and spell the answer aloud. Check each response twice: once for the correct answer and a second time for spelling accuracy.

Follow-Up
Guide students in using the **Checkpoint Study Plan** on page 224 to take a self-test. Have them use the plan for independent study.

Objectives

- To write words with /o͝o/ in continuous text.
- To write each spelling word once.
- To integrate reading with spelling.

The Fable of the Cookie and Who Ate It

One day, a man bought some cookies. He took them home in a bag. But the bag broke and two cookies fell out.

A peacock found the cookies on the grass. "They smell so good. They must have been baked by a good ___cook___!" said the peacock. He ___took___ them and hopped into a tree.

A dog was passing by. She smelled the chocolate chip ___cookies___. She ___stood___ near the tree and said, "Please, dear peacock, ___pull___ me up in your tree. I will help you eat your cookies."

146

Preparation Have students turn to pages 146 and 147. Call their attention to the word list. Have the students say the words. Then explain that each spelling word belongs in one of the blanks in the story.

Write the title "The Fable of the Cookie and Who Ate It" on the board and have a student read it. Explain that a <u>fable</u> is a story that teaches a lesson. Tell students that this fable is about a dog and a cat who try to play a trick on a peacock.

The Pages Read the story aloud, supplying the missing spelling words as students follow along in their texts. When you have finished reading, you may wish to discuss the fable.

Have students complete the story independently by rereading it and writing the correct spelling word for each blank. Then have three students read the story aloud, taking the roles of the peacock, the cat, and the dog while you read the narrator's role. Have the reader pause before each blank so other students can say the missing spelling word. Ask volunteers to write the words on the board so others may check their own work. Be sure to check students' response for the accurate spelling of each answer.

146

But the peacock ___would___ not help the dog.

The hungry dog began to stamp her ___foot___.

A wise old cat walked by. "Dear cat,

___could___ you help me get the cookies?"

asked the dog.

The cat began to purr, "Dear peacock, please

___put___ the cookies down and fly away so I can

___look___ at your beautiful feathers." But the

peacock would not fly.

The cat said, "I read in my ___book___ that

peacocks are very ___good___ singers. Alas, I

have never heard a peacock sing. Please sing for me."

The peacock opened his mouth to sing. The cookies

fell into the dog's mouth!

As the happy dog ran away, the cat called out,

"Wait, you ___should___ give me a

cookie! I helped you by tricking the peacock." But the

dog kept running.

"We will not have ___full___ stomachs

today," said the cat and the peacock sadly.

147

look
cook
took
book
foot
good
cookies
stood
could
should
would
full
pull
put

Enrichment

If you want to use the blackline activity masters for enrichment and additional practice, assign Lesson 27 activities at this time.

Maintenance and Review

OBJECTIVE

- To review words with /ō/ spelled: o, oa.

ACTIVITIES

If you want to use the blackline activity masters for maintenance and review, assign Lesson 26 activities at this time.

You can also use the activity below to review Lesson 25 with students:

Write the following sentence fragments on the board (without underlining any words). Have the students copy them. Complete each sentence with the students. Write the answers on the board and have students copy them. Then have students underline the spelling word in each sentence.

1. Two things that are made of <u>gold</u> are
2. Five things that grow <u>old</u> are
3. Two things that you can <u>hold</u> are
4. The drink that comes from a <u>goat</u> is
5. A place where you sail a <u>boat</u> is
6. Three things that are <u>cold</u> are

Follow-Up Have students use each of the spelling words they missed in an original sentence that relates to the story.

You may wish to suggest this additional follow-up activity. Have students draw and color pictures of the characters in this fable. Then have them write a spelling word under each picture that relates to what that character did or said.

Objectives

- To relate spelling to another language skill.
- To capitalize abbreviations and end them with a period.
- To write spelling words in the context of sentences.
- To practice proofreading.
- To check handwriting for correct letter formation.

a b c d e f g h i j k l m
n o p q r s t u v w x y z

Abbreviations

Abbreviations are short ways of writing words.   **Mr.   Mrs.   St.   Rd.**

Abbreviations usually begin with a capital letter and end with a period.

Choose the word that is spelled correctly to finish each sentence.
Write the sentence. Add periods and capital letters.

1. mr Roy sells (cookies / coockies) on Bank st

Mr. Roy sells cookies on Bank St.

2. We (stood / stoud) on Elm rd

We stood on Elm Rd.

3. mrs Ryan is a (gud / good) friend.

Mrs. Ryan is a good friend.

4. I (took / tock) mrs Ryan some cookies.

I took Mrs. Ryan some cookies.

5. I wish I (coud / could) cook!

I wish I could cook!

148

Preparation   Write the following sentences on the board and read them:

mrs masters put the book on the shelf.
She works in the library on fleet st

Ask what is wrong with these sentences. *(The names do not have capital letters.)* Remind students that the names of people and streets must be capitalized. Also explain that abbreviations such as Mrs. and St. must be capitalized and end with a period. Have volunteers correct the sentences at the board. *(Mrs. Masters, Fleet St.)*

The Page   Do page 148 with the students, reminding them to be careful about their handwriting. In particular, have them pay attention to the letter t, which is a tall letter with a cross bar right at the center of the writing line. Don't forget to cross the t, or else took will become look. Then have volunteers read each sentence aloud. Others may write the answers on the board, noting both the words to be capitalized and the punctuation. Help students correct their work.

Follow-Up   Have students write sentences using each of these abbreviations: **Mr., Mrs., St., Rd.** Be sure that they use the correct punctuation for each abbreviation.

WORDS AT WORK

Challenge Yourself

bulletin   bushel   cookbook

What do you think each underlined Challenge Word means? Check your Spelling Dictionary to see if you are right. Then write sentences. Show that you understand the meaning of each Challenge Word.

1. The bulletin on the radio told about a bad storm.

2. A bushel of apples will be enough for everyone.

3. Use a cookbook to make bread.

Write to the Point

In "The Fable of the Cookie and Who Ate It," the cat tricked the peacock into dropping the cookies. Write sentences telling another way to get the cookies. Use spelling words from this lesson.

Challenge Use one or more of the Challenge Words in your sentences.

Proofreading

Use the marks to show the mistakes in the sentences below. Write the four misspelled words correctly in the blanks.

⬭	word is misspelled
⊙	period is missing
≡	letter should be capitalized

1. The cat wanted good (cookes)⊙

2. The (cok) who made them had a shop on <u>o</u>ak <u>s</u>treet.

3. The cat (tooke) a walk to the shop⊙

4. The cat (wood) like a treat!

1. _____cookies_____

2. _____cook_____

3. _____took_____

4. _____would_____

149

Objectives

- To extend the vowel spellings presented in Lesson 27 to the Challenge Words.

- To use context and the **Spelling Dictionary** to enlarge students' vocabulary.

- To apply the vowel spellings presented in Lesson 27 in a writing activity.

- To practice proofreading for spelling, punctuation, and capitalization.

Dictation Sentences

1. I <u>look</u> like my father.
2. I <u>could</u> help you clean and <u>cook</u> the fish.
3. I <u>took</u> my cat for a ride today.
4. This is such a <u>good</u> <u>book</u>.
5. I <u>put</u> my <u>foot</u> up on the box.
6. I think we <u>should</u> bake <u>cookies</u>.
7. He <u>stood</u> up and said his name.
8. I <u>would</u> like a peach.
9. The pond was <u>full</u> of fish.
10. Did you see the car <u>pull</u> the boat?

Challenge Yourself Answers

Possible definitions:

1. special announcement
2. a unit of measurement for fruit, grains, and vegetables
3. book of recipes

Students' sentences will vary.

Test Review these three ways to spell /o͝o/: oo as in <u>look</u>; ou as in <u>could</u>; u as in <u>full</u>. Test words with /o͝o/. Use one of these testing methods: (1) Say the word; read the sample sentence from page 144; say the word; have students write the word. (2) Read each dictation sentence above; have students write the sentence. Correct the test with students.

Challenge Yourself The optional Challenge Words may be assigned to the entire class or limited to those students who do well on the test. Have students note the vowel spellings in the Challenge Words. Responses to this activity should be completed on separate paper. Answers to the questions are provided above.

Write to the Point Have students recall the selection "The Fable of the Cookie and Who Ate It" on pages 146 and 147; then assign the sentences. This activity should be completed on separate paper.

Proofreading The proofreading practice includes misspellings of words from this lesson as well as capitalization and punctuation errors.

LESSON 28

Objectives

- To hear and say words with /ōo/.
- To write words with /ōo/ with attention to letter sequence and sound/symbol relationships.
- To write each spelling word once.
- To recognize that /ōo/ may be spelled oo, o, ue, and ew.

Sample Sentences

1. Did you see the animals at the zoo?
2. There is a monkey house and a bird house, too.
3. The dining room is where we eat.
4. Cereal is food made of oats or wheat.
5. We launch rockets to the moon.
6. Will we live there someday soon?
7. The dentist had to drill my tooth.
8. At school we always tell the truth.
9. The monkey likes to scratch its chest.
10. We always try to do our best.
11. Do you know who is on the teams?
12. The jacket has two big seams.
13. On sunny days, the sky is blue.
14. Is that hat old, or is it new?

Note

Words are grouped according to spellings of /ōo/:

oo
o
ue
ew

Point out these homophones: too, to, two. Ask students to define each one.

Note

The sample sentences may be used for pretesting and post-testing.

150

Lesson 28 Words with /ōo/

zoo
too
room
food
moon
soon
tooth
school
to
do
who
two
blue
new

1. Which words end in oo?

zoo   too

2. Which words have double o in the middle?

room   food

moon   soon

tooth   school

3. Which words end with /ōo/ spelled o?

to   do

who   two

4. What word spells /ōo/ with ew, as in grew?

new

5. What word spells /ōo/ with ue, as in glue?

blue

150

Preparation   Write /ōo/ on the board and have students repeat the sound /ōo/ as in boot. Say these word pairs. If a word contains /ōo/, students should hold up two fingers.

tie – too   skull – school   do – done   blow – blue   new – no

Then have students look at the spelling words on page 150. Say each word aloud. Then have the students say and spell each word.

Note the wh spelling of the sound /h/ in who: /hōo/. Remind students that wh can also spell the sound /hw/ as in whale. Then ask students to identify the spelling word that contains the /k/ sound. *(school)* What letters spell /k/? *(ch)* Next, ask students to identify the silent letter in two. *(w)* Finally, read the cartoon together and identify the four ways of spelling /ōo/ in this lesson. (See **Note**.)

Have students point to the spelling word as you read each sample sentence.

The Page   Do the page with the students. When they have finished, have volunteers write the answers on the board so students may check their work.

Follow-Up   Make study plans for the week. Suggest this: Write each word and spell the word as you write it. Then spell it without looking at the word. Check to see if you were correct.

Checkpoint

Write a spelling word for each clue. Then use the Checkpoint Study Plan on page 224.

1. The number after one is ___.

2. The opposite of old is ___.

3. Another word for also is ___.

4. A word that means "what you eat" is ___.

5. At night, we can see the stars and ___.

6. We will eat lunch ___.

7. We saw elephants and camels in the ___.

8. The dentist looked at John's front ___.

9. At nine o'clock, I go ___ bed.

10. I have one more page to ___.

11. Do you know ___ he is?

12. On a clear day, the sky is ___.

13. I moved over to make more ___.

14. Hundreds of years ago, people of Greece liked to spend free time learning. The word for "free time" was <u>skholē</u>. The mystery word comes from <u>skholē</u>. It now names a place where you learn. What is it? ___

151

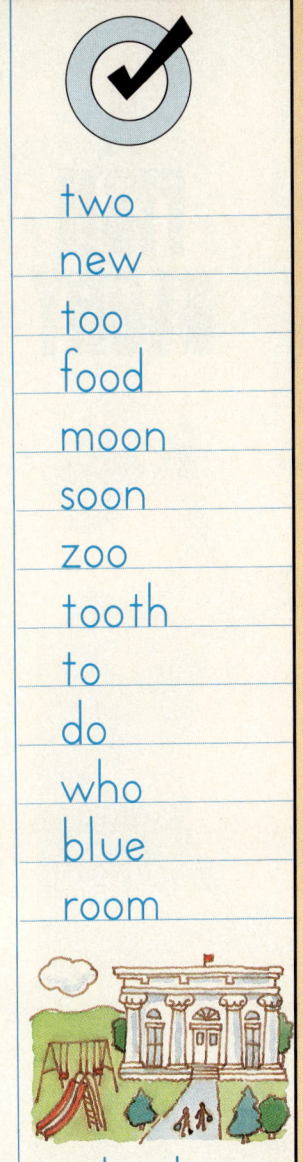

two
new
too
food
moon
soon
zoo
tooth
to
do
who
blue
room

school

Objectives

- To write spelling words in response to clues: definition, synonym, antonym, and context.
- To develop the critical thinking skills of sequencing and comparing.
- To appreciate the diversity of sources of the English language.

Spelling Strategy

The homophones <u>two</u>, <u>too</u>, and <u>to</u> are the source of many spelling errors. Students having difficulty remembering when each of these words should be used might work in pairs to make up sentences showing the correct use of each homophone. Students can then take turns dictating their sentences while their partner writes them.

Preparation The clues on this page are like crossword puzzle clues. Explain to students that the response to each clue is a spelling word. Use the following examples to illustrate the types of clues used:

Definition	A word that means "what you eat" is (*food*).
Synonym	Another word for also is (*too*).
Antonym	The opposite of old is (*new*).
Context	I have one more page to (*do*).

The final clue traces the origin of the English word <u>school</u>.

The Page Have students complete page 151 using the words on page 150. When students have finished, have them read each clue and spell the answer aloud. Check each response twice: once for the correct answer and a second time for spelling accuracy.

Follow-Up Guide students in using the **Checkpoint Study Plan** on page 224 to take a self-test. Have them use the plan for independent study.

Objectives

- To write words with /o͞o/ in continuous text.
- To write each spelling word once.
- To integrate reading with spelling.

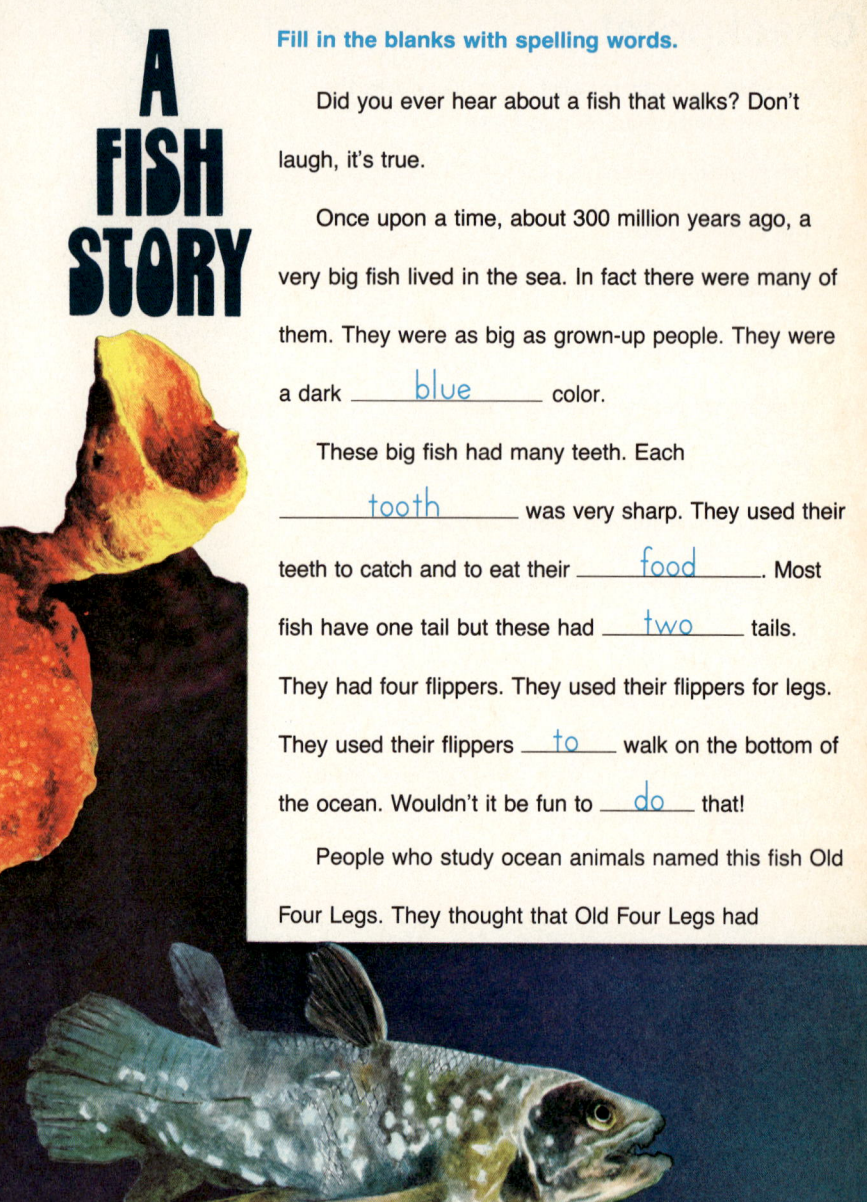

Fill in the blanks with spelling words.

Did you ever hear about a fish that walks? Don't laugh, it's true.

Once upon a time, about 300 million years ago, a very big fish lived in the sea. In fact there were many of them. They were as big as grown-up people. They were a dark ____blue____ color.

These big fish had many teeth. Each ____tooth____ was very sharp. They used their teeth to catch and to eat their ____food____. Most fish have one tail but these had ____two____ tails. They had four flippers. They used their flippers for legs. They used their flippers ____to____ walk on the bottom of the ocean. Wouldn't it be fun to ____do____ that!

People who study ocean animals named this fish Old Four Legs. They thought that Old Four Legs had

Preparation   Have students turn to pages 152 and 153. Call their attention to the word list. Have the students say the words. Then explain that each spelling word belongs in one of the blanks in the story.

Write the title "A Fish Story" on the board and have a student read it. Direct students' attention to the picture on page 152, and tell them that this is a picture of a fish that lived on the earth over 300 million years ago. The scientists believed that this fish, called coelacanth (sē′-lə-kanth), had disappeared forever. Over forty years ago, this very, very old fish showed up again. Tell students that the story tells why this fish is so strange.

The Pages   Read the story aloud, supplying the missing spelling words as students follow along in their texts. When you have finished, you may wish to discuss the story. Ask students what they think should be done with the next coelacanth that is found. *(Answers will vary.)*

disappeared forever, like the dinosaurs. These people were wrong!

In 1938, men ___who___ were fishing caught one. They had never seen such a fish. It was very big. There was hardly enough ___room___ for it in the net. The men thought they had found a new kind of fish.

They asked people who taught in a ___school___ about it. They asked people who studied animals in the ___zoo___ about it. These people told them that they had caught a live coelacanth (sē' - lə - kanth). They had not found a ___new___ kind of fish. They had found a very, very old kind.

People ___soon___ began looking for more walking fish. But it took many years to catch one. One night, by the light of a full ___moon___, another one was caught.

There must be more of these walking fish. Do they live too deep in the sea to be caught?

Or are they ___too___ smart to be caught?

153

zoo
too
room
food
moon
soon
tooth
school
to
do
who
two
blue
new

If you want to use the blackline activity masters for enrichment and additional practice, assign Lesson 28 activities at this time.

Maintenance and Review

OBJECTIVE

- To review words with /o͝o/ spelled: ou, ou, u.

ACTIVITIES

If you want to use the blackline activity masters for maintenance and review, assign Lesson 27 activities at this time.

You can also use the activity below to review Lesson 27 with students:

Write the following spelling words and unfinished phrases on the board. Read the phrases aloud and have volunteers complete them with spelling words. Then have students copy each completed phrase. *(Answers are in parentheses).*

foot	full	stood	look
book	should	cookies	

1. chocolate-chip *(cookies)*
2. a left and a right *(foot)*
3. take a good *(look)*
4. a mystery *(book)*
5. a glass *(full)* of milk
6. *(stood)* under an umbrella
7. of course he *(should)*

Then have students complete the story by silently rereading it and writing the correct spelling word for each blank. Ask a volunteer to read the story aloud, pausing before each blank, while the other students say the missing spelling word at the appropriate time. Write the answers on the board so students may correct their own work. Be sure to check students' responses for the accurate spelling of each answer.

Follow-Up Have students use each of the spelling words they missed in an original sentence.

As an additional follow-up activity, you may wish to ask groups of students to illustrate the story. Have them caption each illustration with sentences from the story and underline any spelling words in their captions.

Objectives

- To relate spelling to another language skill.
- To proofread for correct spelling.
- To write spelling words in the context of a poem.
- To check handwriting for correct letter formation.

a b c d e f g h i j k l m
n o p q r s t u v w x y z

Proofreading

In this poem, eight words are spelled wrong. Find the underlined words and correct them.

food   zoo   blue   who   two   tooth   to   new

WHO'S GOING TO THE ZOO?

1. We're going <u>ta</u> the zoo.

   We'll find hippos and tigers,

   to

2. And a <u>neu</u> baby gnu.

   new

3. He hasn't one <u>toth</u>,

   tooth

4. But he eats enough for <u>twoe</u>!

   two

5. There's a bright <u>bloo</u> parrot

   With a very loud call.

   blue

6. It takes lots of <u>foode</u>

   To feed them all!

   food

7. We're going to the <u>zo</u>.

   zoo

8. <u>Hoo</u> wants to come? DO YOU?

   Who

154

Preparation   Write the following words and poem on the board:

room   moon   soon   school   do

There's plenty to doo at the zoo!
They have a roome full of snakes,
And a rock from the mune
A schol for smart chimps
Oh, let's go there sune!

Read the poem. Then ask volunteers to come to the board, cross out the word that is spelled wrong in each line, and write it correctly. *(do, room, moon, school, soon)* Ask students what they think proofreading is. Explain that when you proofread something, you read to find mistakes and then correct them.

The Page   Have students complete page 154. Remind students to form the <u>z</u> in <u>zoo</u> with three sharp strokes without lifting their pencils off the paper. Have volunteers write the answers on the board for immediate reinforcement of correct spelling.

Follow-Up   Write this sentence on the board: **The zu has blou birds.** Have students proofread it and rewrite it correctly. *(The zoo has blue birds.)*

WORDS AT WORK

Challenge Yourself

cocoon   **bamboo**   **booth**

Decide which Challenge Word fits each clue. Check your Spelling Dictionary to see if you were right. Then write sentences. Show that you understand the meaning of each Challenge Word.

1. This plant makes a good fishing pole or walking stick.

2. This is what a moth grows in.

3. You could sell lemonade at one of these.

Write to the Point

What is the strangest animal you have ever seen? Draw a picture of it. Then write three or four sentences describing it. Use spelling words from this lesson in your sentences.

Challenge Use one or more of the Challenge Words in your sentences.

Proofreading

Use the marks to show the mistakes in the sentences below. Write the four misspelled words correctly in the blanks.

⬭	word is misspelled
⊙	period is missing
≡	letter should be capitalized

1. At first the men didn't know what ⬭too do with the fish.

2. It was too strange to use for ⬭fod ⊙

3. ⬭Whoo would know about it?

4. they ⬭soun found the answer.

1. _____to_____

2. _____food_____

3. _____Who_____

4. _____soon_____

155

Objectives

- To extend the vowel spellings presented in Lesson 28 to the Challenge Words.

- To use clues and the **Spelling Dictionary** to enlarge students' vocabulary.

- To apply the vowel spellings presented in Lesson 28 in a writing activity.

- To practice proofreading for spelling, punctuation, and capitalization.

Dictation Sentences

1. The <u>zoo</u> will open <u>soon</u>.
2. I have <u>two</u> cats and many fish, <u>too</u>.
3. I want <u>to</u> paint my <u>room</u> <u>blue</u>.
4. How much <u>food</u> <u>do</u> we eat in one day?
5. The <u>moon</u> is full.
6. My <u>baby</u> sister has a <u>new</u> <u>tooth</u>.
7. My <u>school</u> is not far from my home.
8. Do <u>you</u> <u>know</u> <u>who</u> has the book?

Challenge Yourself Answers

1. bamboo
2. cocoon
3. booth

Students' sentences will vary.

Test Review these ways to spell /o͞o/: <u>oo</u> as in <u>zoo</u>; <u>o</u> as in <u>to</u>; <u>ue</u> as in <u>blue</u>; <u>ew</u> as in <u>new</u>. Test words with /o͞o/. Use one of these testing methods: (1) Say the word; read the sample sentence from page 150; say the word; have students write the word. (2) Read each dictation sentence above; have students write the sentence. Correct the test with students.

Challenge Yourself The optional Challenge Words may be assigned to the entire class or limited to those students who do well on the test. Have students note the vowel spelling in the Challenge Words. Responses to this activity should be completed on separate paper. Answers to the questions are provided above.

Write to the Point Have students recall the selection "A Fish Story" on pages 152 and 153; then assign the drawing and sentences. Encourage students to use words that describe color and size in their sentences. This activity should be completed on separate paper.

Proofreading The proofreading practice includes misspellings of words from this lesson as well as a capitalization error and a punctuation error.

LESSON 29

Objectives

- To hear and say words with the suffixes ed and ing.
- To write words with the suffixes ed and ing with attention to letter sequence and sound/symbol relationships.
- To write each spelling word once.
- To recognize when a final e must be dropped before adding the suffix ed or ing.

Sample Sentences

1. Jane has a cat named Honeydew.
2. I had hoped I'd get a letter from you.
3. I liked the book about old cars.
4. Mario loved to read about Mars.
5. We baked a cake just for fun!
6. They've always lived in Washington.
7. We biked over to the lake.
8. Now we're baking a lemon cake.
9. My brother is giving me a tie.
10. The mayor's parade is riding by.
11. I'm writing a letter to my friend Dwight.
12. Mom is having dinner guests tonight.
13. The Rogers are living above their store.
14. Her joking made the audience roar.

Lesson 29 Adding ed and ing

named
hoped
liked
loved
baked
lived
biked

baking
giving
riding
writing
having
living
joking

Drop the final e before adding ed or ing to a word.

1. name − e + ed = named

2. joke − e + ing = joking

3. like − e + ed = liked

4. bake − e + ing = baking

5. ride − e + ing = riding

6. bike − e + ed = biked

7. bake − e + ed = baked

8. hope − e + ed = hoped

9. Write the words with the /v/ sound in the middle.

loved   living

having   giving

lived

10. Which word begins with a letter you don't hear?

writing

156

Preparation Write ed and ing on the board. Have students look at the spelling words on page 156. Say each word aloud. Then have students repeat and spell each one.

Ask students what is the same about all the words in the first group. *(They all end with ed.)* Point out that the base word of each word ends with an e that you don't hear: name, hope, etc. Then ask what is the same about all the words in the last group. *(They all end with ing. They all have base words with an e you don't hear.)* Ask what is the base word of giving. *(give)* What letter does give end with? *(an e you don't hear)* Explain that when words end with a silent e, the e must be dropped before adding ed or ing.

Write these words on the board: **hope** **like** **bake** Have a volunteer add ed and ing to hope. *(hoped, hoping)* Have others do the same for like and bake. *(liked, liking, baked, baking)*

Read each sample sentence as students point to the spelling word.

The Page Do the page together. Check students' responses for immediate reinforcement of correct spelling.

Follow-Up Be sure students have study plans for this week's words. Suggest that they write the words on flash cards (or small pieces of paper) with the ed and ing endings traced in red pencil. Then they can use the cards to study.

Checkpoint

Write a spelling word for each clue.
Then use the Checkpoint Study Plan on page 224.

1. The skaters were ___ fun.

2. The opposite of taking is ___.

3. I like reading and ___.

4. My hamster is ___ Chips.

5. Last summer, we hiked and ___.

6. Look in the oven to see what is ___.

7. Tell us where you are ___.

8. Anna likes horseback ___.

9. I was smiling because she was ___.

10. Today you love, yesterday you ___.

11. "Wished for" means ___.

12. Florida is where I once ___.

13. We waited while the cookies ___.

14. Līcian is an Old English word that means "to please." When something pleases you, you enjoy it. The mystery word comes from līcian. It means "enjoyed." Can you guess what the word is? ___

157

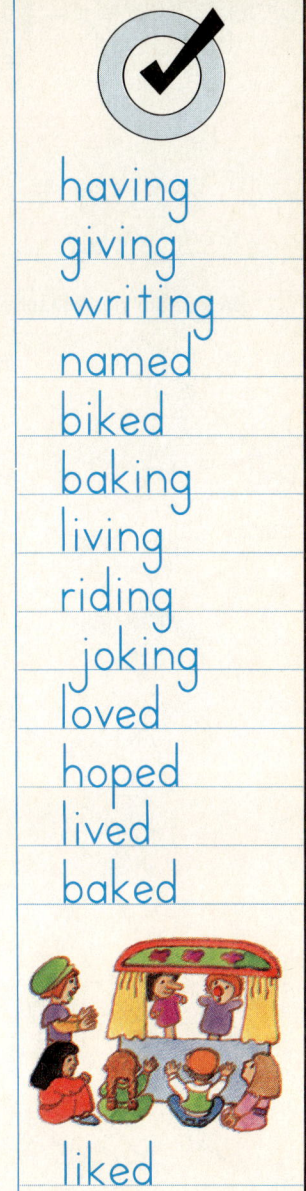

having
giving
writing
named
biked
baking
living
riding
joking
loved
hoped
lived
baked

liked

Objectives

- To write words with the suffixes ed and ing in continuous text.
- To write each spelling word once.
- To integrate reading with spelling.

Fill in the blanks with spelling words.

Mr. Banana's Inventions

Do you know who invented the bicycle and the airplane? A man

_____ named _____ Ralph Banana says he did. I talked with Mr.

Banana for our school paper. I _____ hoped _____ to learn the facts.

Me: How many different countries have you

_____ lived _____ in, Mr. Banana?

Mr. B: Seven, if you count the North Pole. I really

_____ liked / loved _____ living there. It's different from

anywhere else on earth. Are you

_____ having _____ fun talking to me?

Me: Yes, but I'm supposed to ask the questions. How long

have you been _____ living _____ in the

United States?

Mr. B: I moved here right after I invented the airplane.

Me: You must be _____ joking _____! Most

people say the Wright brothers invented the airplane.

Mr. B: Oh, they might have done some work. I invented

the good parts though. Be sure that you are

_____ writing _____ all this down.

158

Note

Bicycle comes from two Latin words: bi meaning two and cyclus meaning circle or wheel.

Preparation Have students turn to pages 158 and 159. Call their attention to the word list. Have the students say the words. Then explain that each spelling word belongs in one of the blanks in the story.

Write the title "Mr. Banana's Inventions" on the board and have a student read it. Ask students what an invention is. *(something new that someone has thought of)* Ask them if they have seen people being interviewed on television. Then ask students to suggest the names of people they would most like to interview if they could choose anyone in the world. This story contains an interview with a man named Ralph Banana.

The Pages Read the story aloud, supplying the missing spelling words as students follow along in their texts. When you have finished reading, you may wish to discuss the interview. Ask someone to explain how Ralph Banana invented the bicycle. *(He said he baked it by accident.)* Ask how many students believe Mr. Banana's story. Ask students for questions they would ask Ralph Banana.

I used to be head baker at the North Pole. One day, my oven blew up. When the smoke had cleared, I saw something that looked like this:

It was as hard as metal! "My wonderful baking oven has _____baked_____ something I can ride," I said to myself. So I added two wheels. I called it a bicycle. I _____biked_____ everywhere. I find riding a bicycle much better exercise than _____riding_____ in a sled. Don't you? Soon I was _____baking_____ lots of bikes, and _____giving_____ them away to everyone at the North Pole. Everybody there _____loved / liked_____ my bicycles! I became a famous baker and inventor.

The next time my oven blew up, I invented the airplane. And this is a true story.

159

named
hoped
liked
loved
baked
lived
biked
baking
giving
riding
writing
having
living
joking

Enrichment

If you want to use the blackline activity masters for enrichment and additional practice, assign Lesson 29 activities at this time.

Maintenance and Review

OBJECTIVE

- To review words with /o͞o/ spelled: oo, o, ue, ew.

ACTIVITIES

If you want to use the blackline activity masters for maintenance and review, assign Lesson 28 activities at this time.

You can also use the activity below to review Lesson 28 with students:

Write the following words on the board. Have the students read the words aloud, copy them, and put them in alphabetical order.

room	who
zoo	blue
food	new
tooth	school

(blue, food, new, room, school, tooth, who, zoo)

Then have students reread the story silently and complete it by writing the correct spelling word for each blank. Have two students read the interview aloud, taking the roles of Ralph Banana and the interviewer. Have them pause before each blank for the other students to say the missing spelling word at the appropriate time. Write the words on the board so students can correct their work. Be sure to check students' responses for the accurate spelling of each answer.

Follow-Up Have students use each of the spelling words they missed in an original sentence.

- To relate spelling words to a dictionary skill.
- To write base words in response to <u>ing</u> words.
- To locate words with the suffixes <u>ed</u> and <u>ing</u> in the **Spelling Dictionary**.
- To check handwriting for correct letter formation.

a b c d e f g h i j k l m
n o p q r s t u v w x y z

Base Words

Many words that end in <u>ed</u> or <u>ing</u> come from other words. For example, **riding** comes from the word **ride**. The word **ride** is a <u>base</u> <u>word</u>.

To find many <u>ed</u> or <u>ing</u> words in a dictionary, look for the base word entry. The <u>ed</u> and <u>ing</u> words are given as part of the base word entry.

Below are six <u>ing</u> words. Write the base word for each one. Look up each word in the Spelling Dictionary and write the page number for each word.

Base + Ending	Base Word	Dictionary Page
1. baking	bake	198
2. giving	give	207
3. having	have	208
4. joking	joke	209
5. living	live	211
6. writing	write	223

160

Preparation Write the following words on the board and have a student read them aloud:

baked   hoped   riding

Explain that the <u>ed</u> and <u>ing</u> forms of words are not listed in separate entries in the dictionary. They are listed within the entry for their base word. Tell students that the base word for <u>baked</u> is <u>bake</u>. Ask students to provide the base words for <u>hoped</u> and <u>riding</u> and write them on the board. *(hope, ride)* Remind students that some words drop the final <u>e</u> before adding <u>ed</u> or <u>ing</u>. Have students locate <u>bake</u>, <u>hope</u>, and <u>ride</u> in the **Spelling Dictionary** and point to the <u>ed</u> and <u>ing</u> forms of the word within each entry.

The Page Do page 160 with the students. Tell them to pay attention to dotting the <u>i</u>. When students have finished, ask volunteers to say and spell the base word and then the spelling word. Write the answers on the board so they may check their own work.

Follow-Up Have students write **named, liked, loved, lived,** and **biked** on cards (or small pieces of paper). On the back of each card, have them write the base word, find the word in the **Spelling Dictionary**, and write the correct page number beside each word.

WORDS AT WORK

Challenge Yourself

amusing   **disliked**   **lining**

What do you think each underlined Challenge Word means? Check your Spelling Dictionary to see if you are right. Then write sentences. Show that you understand the meaning of each Challenge Word.

1. The clowns were <u>amusing</u> the children with funny tricks.

2. Our new kittens <u>disliked</u> getting a bath.

3. The fuzzy <u>lining</u> in my coat keeps me warm.

Write to the Point

Mr. Banana said he invented some important things. Pretend that you are like Mr. Banana. What important thing did you invent? Tell about your important invention in a paragraph. Use spelling words from this lesson in your paragraph.

Challenge Use one or more of the Challenge Words in your paragraph.

Proofreading

Use the marks to show the mistakes in the sentences below. Write the four misspelled words correctly in the blanks.

⬭	word is misspelled
⊙	period is missing
≡	letter should be capitalized

1. I met a man (namd) mr. Banana.

2. He said he (bakked) a bicycle.

3. He (hopped) I liked riding on it.

4. i think he was just (jokking)⊙

1. _____ named

2. _____ baked

3. _____ hoped

4. _____ joking

161

Objectives

- To extend the spelling patterns presented in Lesson 29 to the Challenge Words.

- To use context and the **Spelling Dictionary** to enlarge students' vocabulary.

- To apply the spelling patterns presented in Lesson 29 in a writing activity.

- To practice proofreading for spelling, punctuation, and capitalization.

Dictation Sentences

1. I was the one who <u>named</u> the cat.
2. They <u>hoped</u> to get a puppy soon.
3. We <u>liked baking</u> the pie.
4. I <u>loved riding</u> on the train to the city.
5. My mother is <u>giving</u> us the cookies we <u>baked</u>.
6. They <u>lived</u> up the street from us.
7. We <u>biked</u> to school today.
8. I am <u>having</u> fun <u>writing</u> in school.
9. Who <u>is living</u> there?
10. He is <u>joking</u> with you.

Challenge Yourself Answers

Possible definitions:

1. entertaining
2. did not like
3. inside part of a coat

Students' sentences will vary.

Test Review adding <u>ed</u> and <u>ing</u> to words. Test words with <u>ed</u> and <u>ing</u>. Use one of these testing methods: (1) Say the word; read the sample sentence from page 156; say the word; have students write the word. (2) Read each dictation sentence above; have students write the sentence. Correct the test with students.

Challenge Yourself The optional Challenge Words may be assigned to the entire class or limited to those students who do well on the test. Have students note the spelling patterns in the Challenge Words. Responses to this activity should be completed on separate paper. Answers to the questions are provided above.

Write to the Point Have students recall the selection "Mr. Banana's Inventions" on pages 158 and 159; then assign the paragraph. This activity should be completed on separate paper.

Proofreading The proofreading practice includes misspellings of words from this lesson as well as two capitalization errors and a punctuation error.

LESSON 30

Objectives

- To review and reinforce vowel spellings for /ō/, /o͝o/ and /o͞o/.
- To review and reinforce the suffixes ed and ing.
- To hear, say, spell, and write representative words from Lessons 25–29.
- To write a narrative using the five steps in the writing process.
- To use a prewriting activity to plot the story line in a narrative.

Dictation Sentences

1. Is your answer yes or no?
2. Do you know where he lives?
3. This puppy's nose is cold.
4. My coat is very warm.
5. If you'll open your eyes, you'll see a surprise.
6. I would help you if I could.
7. Aunt May put the flowers in the vase.
8. I loved reading that book.
9. A robin's egg is blue.
10. Did you learn any new games at camp?
11. Those two children are twins.
12. What time do you get home from school?
13. Grandmother has lived in this house for 20 years.
14. I am writing a story about you.

Note

A review test blackline master in standardized format and an answer sheet have been provided on pages T39 and T41 of this Teacher's Edition. The answers to the review test are given below.

1-C	5-A
2-B	6-C
3-D	7-B
4-B	8-D

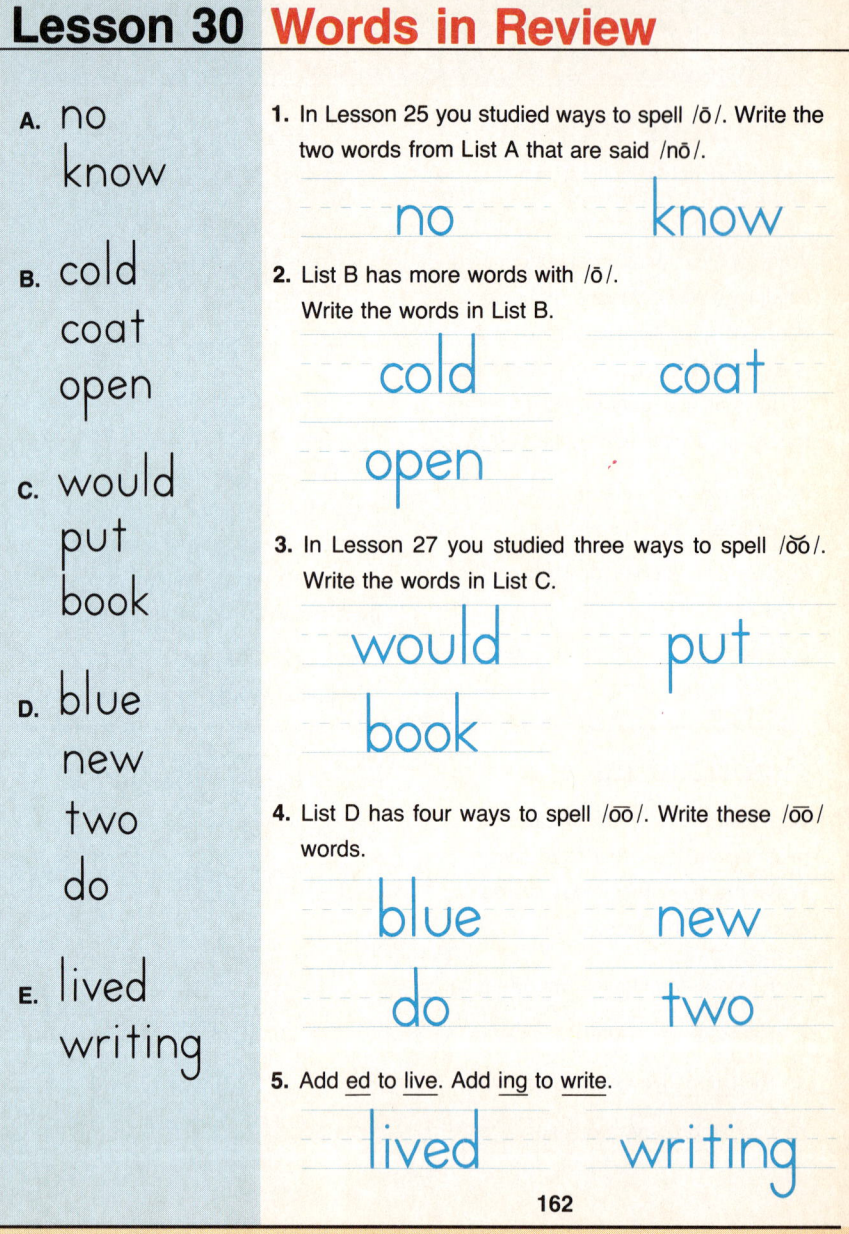

Lesson 30 **Words in Review**

A. no
know

B. cold
coat
open

C. would
put
book

D. blue
new
two
do

E. lived
writing

1. In Lesson 25 you studied ways to spell /ō/. Write the two words from List A that are said /nō/.

no   know

2. List B has more words with /ō/. Write the words in List B.

cold   coat

open

3. In Lesson 27 you studied three ways to spell /o͝o/. Write the words in List C.

would   put

book

4. List D has four ways to spell /o͞o/. Write these /o͞o/ words.

blue   new

do   two

5. Add ed to live. Add ing to write.

lived   writing

162

Preparation

Tell students that Lesson 30 is a review lesson. Lesson 30 contains several activities that ask them to write some of the words they have studied in Lessons 25–29.

Direct students' attention to the list of words on page 162. Read the words aloud as students look at them. Have students say and spell each word aloud.

Then read the dictation sentences above as students point to each spelling word in their book. Point out that the words in List A are from Lesson 25, words in List B are from Lesson 26, words in List C are from Lesson 27, words in List D are from Lesson 28, and words in List E are from Lesson 29.

The Pages

Have students complete the activities on page 162 as a group or independently. Write the answers on the board and have volunteers spell the words aloud for reinforcement of correct spelling.

Test and Study

If you wish to test students on the review words, use one of these testing methods: (1) Read the word and the dictation sentence; say the word again; have students write the word. (2) Have students complete the review test blackline master. (See **Note**.)

Writer's Workshop

A Narrative

You know that a narrative is a story. There are many different kinds of stories. Chen liked to read stories that surprised him. He decided to write a story with a surprise ending. Here is the beginning of Chen's story.

> ### The Surprise Guest
>
> Lee heard a bell tinkle. Someone had come into the restaurant. His father asked Lee to see who was there. Lee was always glad to help. He liked his job. It made him feel big. Lee went out front. No one was there. He opened the door and looked outside. No one except a dog was on the street. Lee thought he had imagined the bell. So he walked back to the kitchen.

Chen followed the steps in the writing process to write his story. He began with a **Prewriting** activity using a story map. It helped him plan what would happen at the beginning, middle, and end of the story. Chen's story map is shown here. Study what Chen did.

Beginning
Lee heard the front doorbell. No one was there.

Middle
This happened all week. Food and other things disappeared.

End
Lee solved the mystery. A dog was taking the food.

It's Your Turn

Get ready to write your own story. Think about the kinds of stories you like to read. Write a story you would enjoy reading. After you have decided what to write about, make a story map. Then follow the other steps in the writing process—**Writing, Revising, Proofreading,** and **Publishing.**

163

Note

If students have difficulty deciding on a topic, you may wish to suggest one of the following:

A story someone else told you
Something that happened at school
Something that you saw on television

Writer's Workshop Students who have mastered the review words may go on to the **Writer's Workshop** on page 163. Explain that writers help readers get to know story characters through the words, thoughts, and actions of the characters. Then read the beginning of the narrative "The Surprise Guest" with students, noting how the writer helps readers get to know the main character by telling us his thoughts and actions.

Allow students to study the story map shown on the pupil's page and guide students to see how this graphic organizer helped Chen prepare to write his narrative.

It's Your Turn Review the steps in the writing process with students. If students are not satisfied with the result of their prewriting, allow them to revise it as often as necessary or to choose another topic and repeat the prewriting activity.

Process Writing Blackline Masters
- Story Map, page T49
- Steps in the Writing Process, page T46
- Proofreading Symbols/Checklist, page T47

LESSON 31

Objectives

- To hear and say words with /ou/.
- To write words with /ou/ with attention to letter sequence and sound/symbol relationships.
- To write each spelling word once.
- To recognize that /ou/ may be spelled ow and ou.

Sample Sentences

1. The owl has feathers of white and brown.
2. A city is bigger than a town.
3. Milk comes from either a goat or a cow.
4. I'd like to hear that story now.
5. The circus clown wears colorful clothes.
6. My favorite flower is a rose.
7. How many ounces are in one pound?
8. Is a football oval, or is it round?
9. The turtle's head came out of its shell.
10. A very loud sound is a shout or a yell!
11. A cat can cause a mouse great harm.
12. There are lots of chores around a farm.
13. I live in a house on Market Street.
14. I found a peach for us to eat.

Note

Words are grouped according to spellings of /ou/:

ow
ou

The sample sentences may be used for pretesting and post-testing.

Lesson 31 Words with /ou/

owl
town
cow
now
clown
flower
how

round
out
sound
mouse
around
house
found

1. Write the words that end with the letters nd.

round   around
found   sound

2. Which words end in the same two letters as down?

town   clown

3. Which word ends like father?

flower

4. Write the spelling words that end like wow.

cow   now
how

5. Which words start with o?

owl   out

6. What words have ou and e, but you hear only /ou/?

mouse   house

164

Preparation

Write /ou/ on the chalkboard and have the students repeat the sound /ou/ as in out. Say these word pairs. If a word contains /ou/, the students should frown.

ton – town   find – found   who – how   around – grind

Have students look at the spelling words on page 164. Say each word aloud. Then have students say and spell each word.

Call attention to the cartoon and note the silent e in the words mouse and house. Then ask what letter the students see but don't hear in how. (w) Ask which other words end with the letter w but don't have /w/. (cow, now) Finally, direct students to look at the way the words are grouped. Have them identify the two ways /ou/ is spelled in this lesson. (See Note.)

Read the sample sentences. Have students point to the spelling word as you read each sentence.

The Page

Do the activities on page 164 as a group. Have students spell the words aloud, write the answers on the board, and check their own work.

Follow-Up

Ask each student if he or she has a plan for studying the spelling words. Suggest that students find a quiet place to spell the words aloud, checking them in their book as they go along.

Checkpoint

Write a spelling word for each clue.
Then use the Checkpoint Study Plan on page 224.

1. A rose is a ___.

2. If it's not too cold, we'll go ___.

3. A bird that hoots at night is an ___.

4. I listened, but I couldn't hear a ___.

5. I can't dive, but soon I'll learn ___.

6. The circus is where you see a ___.

7. Many people live in my apartment ___.

8. A box is square, but a ball is ___.

9. The opposite of lost is ___.

10. My class has a pet ___.

11. Mary's pet followed her all ___.

12. A small city is a ___.

13. I must go home right ___.

14. In Old English words, you often find the letter ū. It had the sound /ou/. We still use many of these words, but we write ow for the sound /ou/. For example, the Old English word hū is our word how. Nū is our word now. Brūn is our word brown. The mystery word was once cū. It names an animal that moos. What is our word? ___

165

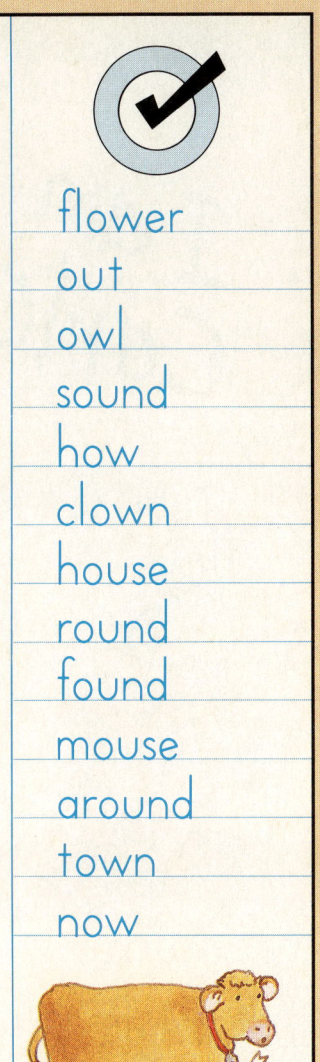

flower
out
owl
sound
how
clown
house
round
found
mouse
around
town
now
cow

Objectives

- To write spelling words in response to clues: definitions, antonyms, and context.
- To develop the critical thinking skills of analyzing and contrasting.
- To understand that the spelling of words in the English language often changes over time.

Spelling Strategy

Because the final syllable of flower does not give a strong sound clue to its spelling, some students may misspell it as ar, or, or ur. Have these students write the word several times and circle the e.

Preparation The clues on this page are like crossword puzzle clues. Explain to students that the response to each clue is a spelling word. Use the following examples to illustrate the types of clues used:

Definition	A small city is a *(town).*
Antonym	The opposite of lost is *(found).*
Context	The circus is where you see a *(clown).*

The final clue explains how the spelling of cow has changed from its Old English spelling.

The Page Have students complete page 165 using the words on page 164. When students have finished, have them read each clue and spell the answer aloud. Check each response twice: once for the correct answer and a second time for spelling accuracy.

Follow-Up Guide students in using the **Checkpoint Study Plan** on page 224 to take a self-test. Have them use the plan for independent study.

Objectives

- To write words with /ou/ in continuous text and related activities.
- To write each spelling word once.
- To integrate reading with spelling.

Finish Jill's story with spelling words.

I am a Cartoonist by Jill

My name is Jill. My favorite thing to do is to draw pictures. People like my pictures because they are funny. When I write my name, instead of a dot for the <u>i</u>, I just use a mouse. It's quite easy to draw a

_____mouse_____. You can see the lines are all

_____round_____ shapes, except for the whiskers

and tail. Right ___now___, I like to draw animals

best. But I know ___how___ to draw lots of other

things. I plan to be a cartoonist.

I also like to play with the kids on my block. It's fun

to go ___out___ and play tag. I have to be careful

when we are running _____around_____. I am

deaf and I can't hear the _____sound_____ of a

car coming.

166

Preparation   Have students turn to pages 166 and 167. Call their attention to the word list. Have the students say the words. Then explain that each spelling word belongs in at least one of the blanks on pages 166 and 167.

Write the title "I am a Cartoonist, by Jill" on the board and have a student read it. What is different about the way that Jill writes her name? *(She dots the i with a mouse!)* Tell students that this story is about a girl who is a cartoonist. Ask students if they have a favorite cartoon or cartoon character. Explain that cartoons are drawn by cartoonists, who are very good artists.

The Page   Read the story aloud, supplying the missing spelling words as students follow along in their texts, or have some or all of the students complete the story without a pre-reading.

When everyone has finished the story, you may wish to discuss it. Ask students what is special about Jill. *(She is a cartoonist. She is deaf.)* Ask them why drawing is important to Jill. *(she is good at it; she enjoys drawing; it helps her "talk" to other people.)* Now ask a student to read the story aloud, pausing before each blank. Have other students say the missing spelling word at the appropriate time. Have a volunteer write the answers on the board so students may check their work.

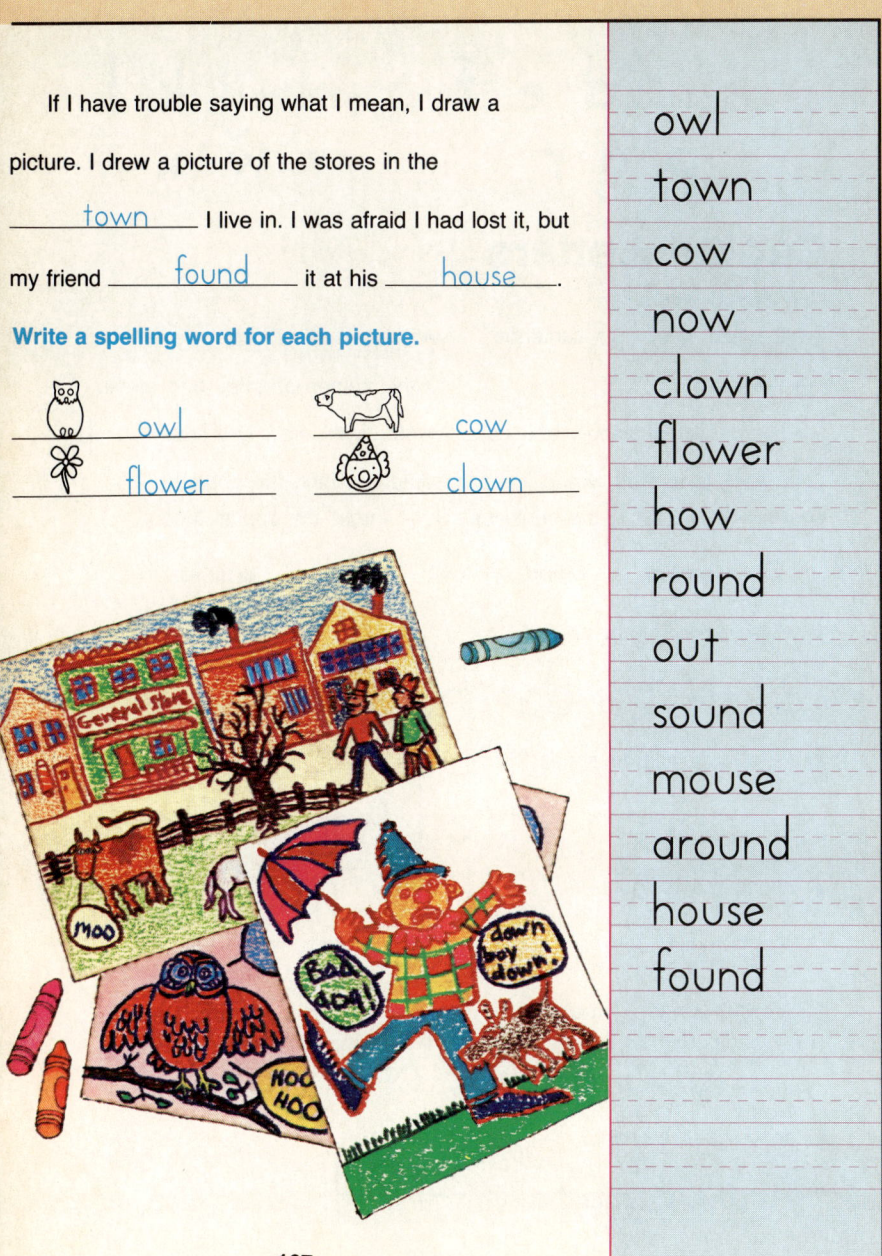

If I have trouble saying what I mean, I draw a picture. I drew a picture of the stores in the _____town_____ I live in. I was afraid I had lost it, but my friend _____found_____ it at his _____house_____ .

Write a spelling word for each picture.

owl

flower

cow

clown

owl
town
cow
now
clown
flower
how
round
out
sound
mouse
around
house
found

167

If you want to use the blackline activity masters for enrichment and additional practice, assign Lesson 31 activities at this time.

Maintenance and Review

OBJECTIVE

- To review words with the suffixes ed and ing.

ACTIVITIES

If you want to use the blackline activity masters for maintenance and review, assign Lesson 29 activities at this time.

You can also use the activity below to review Lesson 29 with students:

Write the following words on the board and have students copy them. Then write the word list for Lesson 29 on the board.

Ask the students to change the underlined letter in each word to make a spelling word from Lesson 29. Have them write the spelling word. *(Answers are in parentheses.)*

1. hiked   *(biked)*
2. hiding   *(riding)*
3. moped   *(hoped)*
4. poking   *(joking)*
5. tamed   *(named)*
6. taking   *(baking).*

Then direct the students' attention to page 167. Explain that these illustrations are some of Jill's drawings. Tell students to write a spelling word for each picture. Be sure to check students' work for correct word choice and for the accurate spelling of each answer.

Follow-Up Ask students to use each of the spelling words they missed in an original sentence.

Objectives

- To relate spelling to another language skill.
- To review capitalization of: the word I, the first word in a sentence, the names of people and pets, the names of streets, the names of cities and states, and title abbreviations.
- To write spelling words in the context of sentences.
- To practice proofreading.
- To check handwriting for correct letter formation.

a b c d e f g h i j k l m
n o p q r s t u v w x y z

Capital Letters

Use capital letters for:

- the first word of a sentence
- the word I
- the names of people and pets
- the names of streets
- the names of cities and states
- Mr., Mrs., Ms., Dr., Miss

One word is spelled wrong in each sentence. Find the correct spelling below. Write the sentence. Don't forget the capital letters!

sound   found   owl   town   around

1. miss sender heard an awl.

Miss Sender heard an owl.

2. its sounde scared agnes the cow.

Its sound scared Agnes the cow.

3. agnes ran to toun!

Agnes ran to town.

4. i fownd agnes on main st.

I found Agnes on Main St.

5. agnes gets aronde!

Agnes gets around!

168

Preparation Review the rules of capitalization previously taught: the word I, the first word in the sentence, names of people and pets, names of streets, names of cities and states, and title abbreviations. Write the following sentences on the board.

we live on tower avenue.
mr. driscoll is my neighbor.
he and i are friends.

Have a volunteer go to the board and circle all the mistakes in capitalization. Ask another student to correct the mistakes. (We live on Tower Avenue. Mr. Driscoll is my neighbor. He and I are friends.)

The Page As your students do the activities on page 168, call attention to formation of the letter u, which begins and ends at the center line and curves at the base. Be sure the top points are separated so u is not confused with o in words such as sound and found. Have volunteers put their sentences on the board so students can check their own work.

Follow-Up Have students write two sentences about the town they live in or a town nearby. They should name the town in the sentences.

WORDS AT WORK

Challenge Yourself

coward   drought   brow

Decide which Challenge Word fits each clue. Check your Spelling Dictionary to see if you were right. Then write sentences. Show that you understand the meaning of each Challenge Word.

1. It is found above your eyes.

2. This is a person who is not brave.

3. A farmer does not like one of these.

Write to the Point

Jill drew a picture of her town. Draw a funny picture of your town. Write words on your picture to name important things. Use as many spelling words from this lesson as you can.

Challenge Use one or more of the Challenge Words in your picture.

Proofreading

Use the marks to show the mistakes in the sentences below. Write the four misspelled words correctly in the blanks.

◯	word is misspelled
⊙	period is missing
≡	letter should be capitalized

1. Jill looks (aroun) town to get
   ideas for pictures⊙

2. once she saw a pretty (flowar.)

3. She tried to draw a (cou.)

4. (Howe) I wish I could draw, too!

1. _____ around _____

2. _____ flower _____

3. _____ cow _____

4. _____ how _____

169

Objectives

- To extend the vowel spellings presented in Lesson 31 to the Challenge Words.

- To use clues and the **Spelling Dictionary** to enlarge students' vocabulary.

- To apply the vowel spellings presented in Lesson 31 in a writing activity.

- To practice proofreading for spelling, punctuation, and capitalization.

Dictation Sentences

1. An <u>owl</u> lived in the hole in the tree.
2. <u>Would</u> you like to live in a city or a <u>town</u>?
3. <u>I found</u> our <u>cow</u> at the pond.
4. Do you want to have lunch <u>now</u>?
5. The <u>clown</u> has a yellow <u>flower</u> on his coat.
6. I know <u>how</u> to ride a bike.
7. I went <u>out</u> to look at the big <u>round</u> moon.
8. The <u>mouse</u> stood up and did not make a <u>sound</u>.
9. The boat went all <u>around</u> the pond.
10. Look at that big <u>house</u>!

Challenge Yourself Answers

1. brow
2. coward
3. drought

Students' sentences will vary.

Test Review these ways to spell /ou/: <u>ow</u> as in <u>town</u>; <u>ou</u> as in <u>round</u>. Test words with /ou/. Use one of these testing methods: (1) Say the word; read the sample sentence from page 164; say the word; have students write the word. (2) Read each dictation sentence above; have students write the sentence. Correct the test with students.

Challenge Yourself The optional Challenge Words may be assigned to the entire class or limited to those students who do well on the test. Have students note the vowel spellings in the Challenge Words. Responses to this activity should be completed on separate paper. Answers to the questions are provided above.

Write to the Point Have students recall the selection "I am a Cartoonist" on pages 166 and 167; then assign the picture. Challenge students to use as many spelling words as they can as labels on their pictures. Encourage them to have fun and to make their pictures funny. This activity should be completed on separate paper.

Proofreading The proofreading practice includes misspellings of words from this lesson as well as a capitalization error and a punctuation error.

LESSON 32

Objectives

- To hear and say words with /ô/.
- To write words with /ô/ with attention to letter sequence and sound/symbol relationships.
- To write each spelling word once.
- To recognize that /ô/ may be spelled a, aw, and o.

Sample Sentences

1. We practiced throwing and catching the ball.
2. I got a long-distance telephone call.
3. The newborn baby was very small.
4. The open-air concert was free to all.
5. A chatterbox likes to talk and talk.
6. Would you like to take a walk?
7. I saw a gorilla at the zoo.
8. I like to paint and draw pictures, too.
9. Our dog barks loudly when he's upset.
10. I'd love a big green frog for a pet.
11. We were tired from the long ride on the train.
12. I lost my umbrella on the plane.
13. The chorus is singing a marching song.
14. Take off your hat and sing along!

Note

Words are grouped according to spellings of /ô/:

a
aw
o

The sample sentences may be used for pretesting and post-testing.

Lesson 32 Words with /ô/

ball
call
small
all
talk
walk

saw
draw

dog
frog
long
lost
song
off

1. Write the spelling words that end in double l.

ball   **call**
small   **all**

2. Which word ends in double f?

off

3. Which words end the same as paw?

saw   **draw**

4. Write the words that end with ng.

long   **song**

5. What words end with the sound /g/?

dog   **frog**

6. What word ends like cost?

lost

7. What words have the letter l but no /l/ sound?

talk   **walk**

Remember the l when you talk, or take a walk!

170

Preparation   Write /ô/ on the board. Have students repeat the sound /ô/ as in paw. Say these word pairs. If the word contains /ô/, students should hold up four fingers.

bell–ball   lost–last   dig–dog   walk–wake   drew–draw

Have students look at the spelling words on page 170. Say each word. Then have the students say and spell each word.

Note the double consonants ff in the word off and ll in ball. Ask the students to locate the other spelling words that contain ll. (call, small, all) Then have students find the spelling words that contain the letter w. (walk, saw, draw) In which of these words do they hear /w/? (walk) Call attention to the cartoon and have students find the words in which they see the letter l but don't hear /l/. (talk, walk) Help students identify the way the words are grouped. (See Note.)

Have students point to each word as you read the sample sentences.

The Page   Complete page 170 with the students. Have volunteers spell the words aloud as others write them on the board. Help students check their work.

Follow-Up   Have students write each word on a piece of paper and put the papers face down. Ask them to pick up one paper at a time, look at the word, spell it aloud, put the paper down, and spell the word again.

Checkpoint

Write a spelling word for each clue. Then use the Checkpoint Study Plan on page 224.

1. The opposite of on is ___.

2. The opposite of found is ___.

3. I had so much work, and I did it ___.

4. You use the telephone to make a ___.

5. To speak is to ___.

6. Let's all sing a funny ___.

7. Our pet snake is twelve inches ___.

8. That is the biggest bird I ever ___.

9. I like to paint and ___.

10. A tadpole grows into a ___.

11. When you go by foot, you ___.

12. A puppy grows into a ___.

13. Something that is not big is ___.

14. Many, many years ago, a round object used in sports was called a bölr. If the word had not changed, you'd be playing basebölr and footbölr. You'd play tennis with a tennis bölr. The mystery word comes from bölr. What is it? ___

171

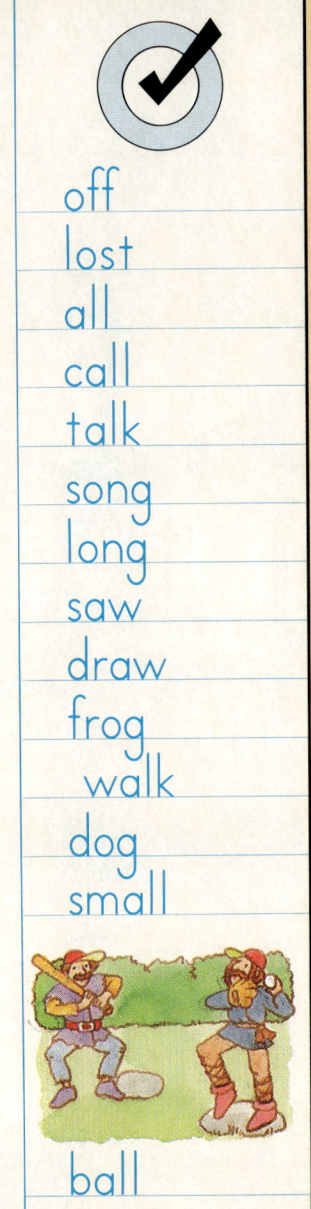

off
lost
all
call
talk
song
long
saw
draw
frog
walk
dog
small
ball

Objectives

- To write spelling words in response to clues: definition, synonym, antonyms, and context.

- To develop the critical thinking skills of comparing, contrasting, and predicting outcomes.

- To learn the source of the English word ball.

Spelling Strategy

The /ô/ sound is often spelled a before an l. Because the /l/ sound is not heard, some students may omit the l when spelling words like walk and talk. Have these students write the spelling words in which /ô/ is spelled a before l, circle the a's, and underline the l's.

Preparation The clues on this page are like crossword puzzle clues. Explain to students that the response to each clue is a spelling word. Use the following examples to illustrate the types of clues used:

Definition	Something that is not big is *(small)*.
Synonym	When you go by foot, you *(walk)*.
Antonym	The opposite of on is *(off)*.
Context	I like to paint and *(draw)*.

The final clue traces the origin of the English word ball.

The Page Have students complete page 171 using the words on page 170. When students have finished, have them read each clue and spell the answer aloud. Check each response twice: once for the correct answer and a second time for spelling accuracy.

Follow-Up Guide students in using the **Checkpoint Study Plan** on page 224 to take a self-test. Have them use the plan for independent study.

Objectives

- To write words with /ô/ in continuous text.
- To write each spelling word once.
- To integrate reading with spelling.

Fill in the blanks with spelling words.

HARVEY, THE PET THAT WASN'T

Last summer, I got bored listening to my friends talk about their pets. That's the only thing they could ever ____talk____ about! Pam's ____dog____ had learned to roll over. Jack's fish tank was too crowded. I had to paint or ____draw____ pictures of animals! I had no pet of my own.

I wanted a pet for a ____long____ time. But my parents don't allow furry animals. Dogs and cats make my brother sneeze. I did have a little turtle once. It ran away and was ____lost____. Then my folks said I could get a fish. A fish didn't seem exciting to me. You can't take a fish for a ____walk____. A fish won't chase a ____ball____. But a fish is better than nothing. Jack said he had a perfect fish for me. It was ____small____, but it had big eyes. I named it Harvey.

Preparation Have students turn to pages 172 and 173. Call their attention to the word list. Have the students say the words. Then explain that each spelling word belongs in one of the blanks in the story.

Write the title "Harvey, the Pet That Wasn't" on the board and have a student read it. Explain that the story is about a boy who wanted a pet. The story will tell students what kind of pet Harvey is—or isn't!

The Pages Read the story aloud, supplying the missing spelling words as students follow along in their texts, or have some or all of the students complete the story without a pre-reading. When everyone has finished the story, you may wish to discuss it. Ask someone to explain the trick that Jack played on his friend. (He gave him a fish that was really a tadpole. Of course, it very quickly became a frog!) Why wouldn't a frog be a good pet? (Frogs need lots of space to jump around. Frogs are noisy at night!)

Now ask a volunteer to read the story aloud, pausing before each blank. Have other students say and spell the missing spelling word at the appropriate time. Help students to check their work for correct word choice and for the accurate spelling of each answer.

It didn't take long to figure out that Harvey wasn't a

fish at ___all___. When I ___saw___ little legs

growing on the sides of my pet I knew I was in trouble!

I could not believe my eyes. I had an about-to-be

___frog___! What would my parents say if they

saw a frog hopping down the hall? What would happen

when they heard Harvey singing that famous frog

___song___, "Ribbit, Ribbit"?

So I took my little tadpole to the pond. I watched him

swim ___off___ to find his friends.

I'm not going to ___call___ Jack for a

while. Not until I have thought of a way to pay him back

for his little joke!

173

ball
call
small
all
talk
walk
saw
draw
dog
frog
long
lost
song
off

Enrichment

If you want to use the blackline activity masters for enrichment and additional practice, assign Lesson 32 activities at this time.

Maintenance and Review

OBJECTIVE

● To review words with /ou/ spelled: <u>ow</u>, <u>ou</u>.

ACTIVITIES

If you want to use the blackline activity masters for maintenance and review, assign Lesson 31 activities at this time.

You can also use the activity below to review Lesson 31 with students:

Write the following words and riddles on the board. Have students write the entire last line of each riddle, completing it with a spelling word. *(Answers are in parentheses).*

flower	now	sound
clown	mouse	

1. I am a funny circus act.
   People laugh at me—that's a fact!
   I am a _(clown)_ .

2. I'm a lilac, a daisy, or a rose.
   I'm part of what your garden grows.
   I'm a _(flower)_ .

3. I'm a rodent and I love cheese.
   Keep cats away from me, if you please!
   I'm a _(mouse)_ .

4. I'm the crash of cymbals,
   or the beat of a drum.
   I'm a yell; I'm a whisper; I'm a hum.
   I'm a _(sound)_ .

5. I am not later; I'm not before.
   I'm at this moment, not what's in store.
   I am right _(now)_ .

Follow-Up Have students use each of the spelling words they missed in an original sentence.

You may wish to suggest this activity as an additional follow-up. Divide the class into teams for a game of leapfrog. Read a spelling word from the list to the first team. If a member spells it correctly, he or she may leap over one teammate. If the word is misspelled, proceed to the next team. Continue through all the spelling words; the team that reaches the finish line first wins.

- To relate spelling to another language skill.
- To recognize compound words.
- To write compound words.
- To check handwriting for correct letter formation.

a b c d e f g h i j k l m
n o p q r s t u v w x y z

Compound Words

FOOT┊BALL

Say the word in the box. There are two smaller words in the word **football**. Football is a <u>compound word</u>. A compound word is two words put together to make one new word. Why would someone choose the name "football" for this game?

Read the words below. Write a compound word using each set of words.

1. base + ball =   baseball

2. song + bird =   songbird

3. draw + bridge =   drawbridge

4. watch + dog =   watchdog

5. leap + frog =   leapfrog

6. side + walk =   sidewalk

7. long + horn =   longhorn

8. see + saw =   seesaw

174

Preparation
Write the following words on the board and have a student read them aloud:

mailbox   bookcase   railroad

Explain that these words are called <u>compound words</u>. A compound word is two words put together to form one new word. What are the two words that form the word <u>mailbox?</u> *(mail, box)* Have a volunteer draw a line between the two words in the compound word. Repeat for <u>bookcase</u> and <u>railroad</u>.

Then write these words on the board:

hay   day   cup   cake   stack   light

Have volunteers match two words to form a compound word. *(haystack, daylight, cupcake)* Ask students to make up sentences using the compound words.

The Page
Do page 174 with the students. Remind them that the letters <u>b</u>, <u>l</u>, <u>d</u>, <u>t</u>, <u>h</u>, <u>f</u>, <u>k</u> must be tall enough to reach the top part of the writing line. Have a few volunteers read the compound words they have written while other volunteers write them on the board so that the students can check their work.

Follow-Up
Discuss the meaning of each of the compound words on page 174. Then have students write a sentence for each compound word.

WORDS AT WORK

Challenge Yourself

false   **haul**   **faucet**

Use your Spelling Dictionary to answer these questions. Then write sentences. Show that you understand the meaning of each Challenge Word.

1. Will people trust you if you say things that are <u>false</u>?

2. Can a truck be used to <u>haul</u> trees and branches to another place?

3. Would you find a <u>faucet</u> in a kitchen?

Write to the Point

Harvey was not a fish at all. He was a frog. What kind of pet would you like to have? Write a paragraph. Tell about the pet you would choose and why you would choose it. Use spelling words from this lesson in your paragraph.

Challenge Use one or more of the Challenge Words in your paragraph.

Proofreading

Use the marks to show the mistakes in the sentences below. Write the four misspelled words correctly in the blanks.

⬭	word is misspelled
⊙	period is missing
☰	letter should be capitalized

1. I have a (smal) dog named Chip.

2. Chip has (longe) black hair⊙

3. <u>i</u> like to take Chip for a (wok)

4. Chip likes to play (bal) with me.

1. _____ small

2. _____ long

3. _____ walk

4. _____ ball

175

Objectives

- To extend the vowel spellings presented in Lesson 32 to the Challenge Words.

- To use context and the **Spelling Dictionary** to enlarge students' vocabulary.

- To apply the vowel spellings presented in Lesson 32 in a writing activity.

- To practice proofreading for spelling, punctuation, and capitalization.

Dictation Sentences

1. The <u>dog</u> lost his <u>ball</u>.
2. My <u>cat</u> will come <u>to</u> me when I <u>call</u> him.
3. Our new puppy is very <u>small</u>.
4. Will <u>all</u> the boys and <u>girls</u> <u>go</u> to the zoo?
5. I like to <u>talk</u> to my pet.
6. My father and I went for a <u>long</u> <u>walk</u>.
7. He <u>saw</u> a <u>frog</u> hopping around the pond.
8. I love to <u>draw</u> and paint.
9. We sang <u>a</u> funny <u>song</u> in school today.
10. I was hot, so I took <u>off</u> my coat.

Challenge Yourself Answers

1. no
2. yes
3. yes

Students' sentences will vary.

Test Review these ways to spell /ô/: a as in <u>ball</u>; aw as in <u>saw</u>; o as in <u>dog</u>. Test words with /ô/. Use one of these testing methods: (1) Say the word; read the sample sentence from page 170; say the word; have students write the word. (2) Read each dictation sentence above; have students write the sentence. Correct the test with students.

Challenge Yourself The optional Challenge Words may be assigned to the entire class or limited to those students who do well on the test. Have students note the vowel spellings in the Challenge Words, especially the following new spelling: <u>au</u> as in <u>faucet</u>. Responses to this activity should be completed on separate paper. Answers to the questions are provided above.

Write to the Point Have students recall the selection "Harvey, the Pet That Wasn't" on pages 172 and 173; then assign the paragraph. This activity should be completed on separate paper.

Proofreading The proofreading practice includes misspellings of words from this lesson as well as a capitalization error and a punctuation error.

LESSON 33

Objectives

- To hear and say words with /ô/.
- To write words with /ô/ with attention to letter sequence and sound/symbol relationships.
- To write each spelling word once.
- To recognize that /ô/ may be spelled o, oo, ou.

Sample Sentences

1. We've lived there for a long time.
2. Do you like lemons or limes?
3. To make orange, mix yellow with red.
4. It's a short walk to our tool shed.
5. A story with a moral is called a fable.
6. Chicken and corn are on the table.
7. The storm left snowdrifts six feet deep.
8. Does a horse lie down to sleep?
9. When you sleep, do you snore?
10. What do you buy in a toy store?
11. When you eat, do you ever want more?
12. How long is our classroom floor?
13. Have you ever seen a revolving door?
14. The number after three is four.

Note

Words are grouped according to spellings of /ô/:

o
oo
ou

Point out these homophones: for, four. Ask students to define each one.

Note

The sample sentences may be used for pretesting and post-testing.

Lesson 33 Words with /ô/

for
or
orange
short
story
corn
storm
horse
snore
store
more

floor
door

four

1. Write the words that begin with the sound /ô/.

or   orange

2. f + or =   for

h + orse =   horse

3. Write the word that ends with the vowel y.

story

4. Write the words that end with two consonants.

short   corn

storm

5. Write the words that end with the letters ore.

snore   store

more

6. Write the words that have double o in the middle.

floor   door

7. Which word has a letter u that you don't hear?

four

176

Preparation

Write /ô/ on the chalkboard. Have students repeat the sound /ô/ as in paw. Say these word pairs. Ask the students to hold up four fingers when they hear /ô/ in any of these words.

storm – steam   house – horse   door – dear   more – much   four – fat

Have students look at the spelling words on page 176. Say each word aloud. Then have the students say and spell each word.

Ask students to identify the words that end with an e they don't hear. (orange, horse, snore, store, more) What word ends with the sound /ē/ but not the letter e? (story: /stôr′ ē/) Call attention to the three spellings of /ô/ in this lesson: o in the first group, oo in the next group, and ou in the last word. (See **Note.**)

Read the sample sentences as students point to the spelling word in each one.

The Page

Do the activities as a group. Then have volunteers spell the answers aloud as others write them on the board so students may check their work.

Follow-Up

Suggest that students study with a partner. One student will spell the word aloud three times while the other student closes his or her eyes and tries to see the word and say it. Partners take turns.

176

Checkpoint

Write a spelling word for each clue. Then use the
Checkpoint Study Plan on page 224.

1. A shop is a ___.

2. The number after three is ___.

3. I spilled my milk all over the ___.

4. A plant that has ears is ___.

5. The color of a pumpkin is ___.

6. The weather is bad during a ___.

7. The opposite of less is ___.

8. The opposite of long is ___.

9. Is this your hat ___ mine?

10. Wake me up if I start to ___.

11. A cowhand rides a ___.

12. There was a loud knock at the ___.

13. What is this tool used ___?

14. This mystery word means "a tale." It comes from
the Latin word historia. In French, the word
became estoire. The mystery word sounds a lot
like both of these words. Can you guess what it
is? ___

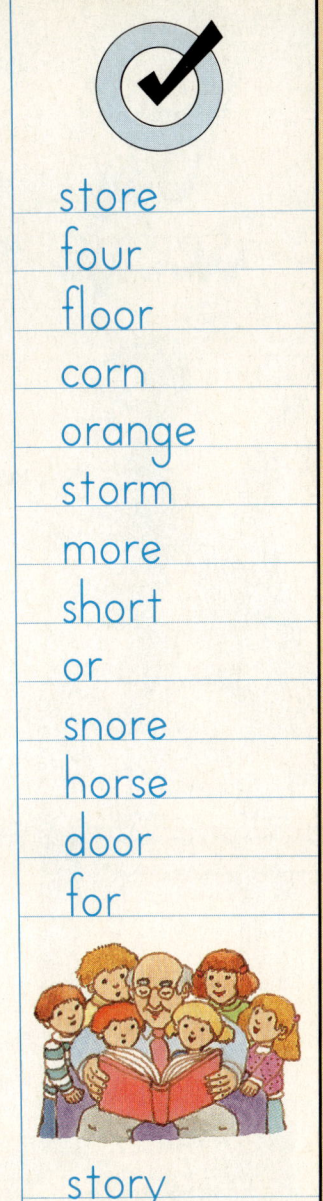

store
four
floor
corn
orange
storm
more
short
or
snore
horse
door
for

story

177

Objectives

- To write spelling words in response
to clues: synonym, antonyms, and
context.

- To develop the critical thinking skills
of comparing, sequencing, and making inferences.

- To appreciate the diversity of sources
of the English language.

Spelling Strategy

Some students may omit the final e in
words like orange. Explain to these
students that a final /j/ sound is
spelled ge. Without the e, the g
becomes a "hard," or /g/, sound.
Demonstrate with orange and rang.
Have students practice writing orange
and circling the final ge.

Preparation The clues on this page are like crossword puzzle clues.
Explain to students that the response to each clue is a spelling word. Use the
following examples to illustrate the types of clues used:

Synonym	A shop is a *(store).*
Antonym	The opposite of less is *(more).*
Context	I spilled my milk all over the *(floor).*

The final clue explains how the word story came into the English language.

The Page Have students complete page 177 using the words on page
176. When students have finished, have them read each clue and spell the
answer aloud. Check each response twice: once for the correct answer and a
second time for spelling accuracy.

Follow-Up Guide students in using the **Checkpoint Study Plan** on page
224 to take a self-test. Have them use the plan for independent study.

Objectives

- To write words with /ô/ in continuous text.
- To write each spelling word once.
- To integrate reading with spelling.

Rainy Day Recipe

Fill in the blanks with spelling words.

It was raining outside. "What shall we do?" Jan asked Nat. "If we had any money, we could go downstairs to the ____store____."

"But we don't have any money," he said. "You could tell me a scary ____story____!"

"Oh, no! I don't know any stories. Let's go down to Burt's until this awful ____storm____ is over."

Burt lived on the ____floor____ below theirs. They locked the ____door____ to their apartment and took the ____short____ elevator ride to Burt's.

Burt, Uncle Ralph, and Chuck were in the kitchen. Chuck was a St. Bernard dog. He was almost as big as a ____horse____! Most St. Bernards are kind of brown and white. Chuck was a beautiful light ____orange____ color. Chuck was asleep.

Note

Here is the recipe for Uncle Ralph's meat pie. You'll need: 2 lbs. hamburger; 1 cup bread crumbs; 1 small can of corn; 1 cup grated cheddar cheese; 1 onion, diced.

Combine hamburger, bread crumbs, corn, cheese, and onion. Form a loaf and place in a baking pan or dish. Bake at 350° for 30 minutes, covered. Bake uncovered 10–15 minutes longer. Serves 6 to 8 people.

Preparation

Have students turn to pages 178 and 179. Call their attention to the word list. Have the students say the words. Then explain that each spelling word belongs in one of the blanks in the story.

Write the title "Rainy Day Recipe" on the board and have a student read it. Then ask students to tell you what they like to do on rainy days. Have the class guess what the children in the story are doing on one particular rainy day.

The Pages

Read the story aloud, supplying the missing spelling words as the students follow along in their texts. Or have some or all of the students complete the story without a pre-reading. When everyone has finished the story, you may wish to discuss it. Then ask a student to read the story aloud, pausing before each blank. Other students will say the missing spelling word at the appropriate time and write it on the board. Check the students' work for correct word choice and for the accurate spelling of each answer. If you wish, you may distribute the recipe for meat pie so the children can take it home and try it. Tell students to cook only when an adult is supervising them.

Now and then Chuck would _____snore_____,

growl, ____or____ bark in his sleep.

"We're going to make a meat pie ____for____

supper," said Uncle Ralph. "Do you want to help? You

can read the list of what we need, Nat."

Nat read out loud from the cookbook:

    2 pounds of hamburger

    1 cup of bread crumbs

    1 small can of ____corn____

    1 cup of grated cheese

    1 onion

Burt started to cut up the onion. The onion made him

cry. He rubbed his eyes. But that made him cry even

____more____. He had to stop for ____four____

or five minutes.

Jan put everything in a bowl. Everyone got a turn at

mixing. Then they put the pie in the oven and waited.

Just as the storm stopped, the pie was ready.

"How do you like that, Chuck?" Nat asked.

"Bow, wow, wow!" barked Chuck.

179

for
or
orange
short
story
corn
storm
horse
snore
store
more
floor
door
four

Enrichment

If you want to use the blackline activity masters for enrichment and additional practice, assign Lesson 33 activities at this time.

Maintenance and Review

OBJECTIVE

- To review words with /ô/ spelled: a, aw, o.

ACTIVITIES

If you want to use the blackline activity masters for maintenance and review, assign Lesson 32 activities at this time.

You can also use the activity below to review Lesson 32 with students:

Write the following CHAINWORDS on the board. Tell the students that two spelling words are hidden in each chainword. Tell them to break each chain and write the two hidden words in each. *(Answers are in parentheses).*

1. ballong	*(ball, long)*	
2. drawalk	*(draw, walk)*	
3. lostalk	*(lost, talk)*	
4. offrog	*(off, frog)*	
5. smallost	*(small, lost)*	
6. call	*(call, all)*	

Follow-Up Have students use each of the spelling words they missed in an original sentence.

You may wish to suggest this activity as an additional follow-up. Divide the class into groups of five. Assign the roles of Jan, Nat, Burt, Ralph, the narrator, and Chuck to each group, and have the students act out "Rainy Day Recipe."

If school facilities permit, try cooking this meat pie and eating it as a class activity.

- To relate spelling to another language skill.
- To review the use of the period, the question mark, and the exclamation point.
- To write spelling words in the context of sentences.
- To check handwriting for correct letter formation.

a b c d e f g h i j k l m
n o p q r s t u v w x y z

Punctuation

At the end of a sentence put:

- a period (.) • a question mark (?) • an exclamation point (!)

Remember to put a period after:

Mr. **Mrs.** **Ms.** **Dr.** **St.** **Rd.**

Choose the correct word to finish each sentence. Then write the sentence. Add marks where they are needed.

1. Did you hear about the ___ (starm storm)

Did you hear about the storm?

2. Snow fell for ___ days (fower four)

Snow fell for four days!

3. Did you ever see ___ snow (more mor)

Did you ever see more snow?

4. Mr Lee didn't open his ___ (door dore)

Mr. Lee didn't open his door.

5. Dr Aaron stayed in ___ days (foar for)

Dr. Aaron stayed in for days!

180

Preparation Remind the students that a sentence that makes a statement ends with a period; a sentence that asks a question ends with a question mark; and a sentence that shows strong feeling ends with an exclamation point. Have students dictate sentences while you write them on the board. Have volunteers come to the board and write the end punctuation marks.

The Page Do the activities on page 180 with the students. Remind them to write carefully. Uppercase letters must be tall enough to reach the top of the writing line. When students have finished, have volunteers read the sentences and spell the list words. Write each sentence on the board and help the students correct their own work.

Follow-Up Write the following sentence fragments on the board. Have students match the sentence parts, copy the completed sentences, and then punctuate them.

Was there	snores
My brother	even hear the rain
I did not	a storm last night

(Was there a storm last night? My brother snores. I did not even hear the rain!)

WORDS AT WORK

Challenge Yourself

torch   **organ**   **orchard**

Use your Spelling Dictionary to answer these questions. Then write sentences. Show that you understand the meaning of each Challenge Word.

1. Does a <u>torch</u> give off light?

2. Could you play an <u>organ</u> while marching in a band?

3. Would you go to an <u>orchard</u> to pick apples?

Write to the Point

Do you know how to make something good to eat? Write four or five sentences telling how to make something good. Use spelling words from this lesson.

Challenge Use one or more of the Challenge Words in your sentences.

Proofreading

Use the marks to show the mistakes in the sentences below. Write the four misspelled words correctly in the blanks.

⬭	word is misspelled
⊙	period is missing
☰	letter should be capitalized

1. We need ⬭fore more things to make our pie⊙

2. ☰it is a ⬭short trip to the store.

3. Put an ⬭orang on your list, too.

4. Leave before the ⬭starm comes!

1. _____four_____

2. _____short_____

3. _____orange_____

4. _____storm_____

181

Objectives

- To extend the vowel spellings presented in Lesson 33 to the Challenge Words.

- To use context and the **Spelling Dictionary** to enlarge students' vocabulary.

- To apply the vowel spellings presented in Lesson 33 in a writing activity.

- To practice proofreading for spelling, punctuation, and capitalization.

Dictation Sentences

1. I went to the <u>store</u> <u>for</u> a can of paint.
2. Do you want <u>more</u> cookies <u>or</u> pie?
3. I will paint an <u>orange</u> flower on my <u>door</u>.
4. I am writing a <u>short</u> <u>story</u>.
5. I love to eat <u>corn</u> in the summer.
6. We could not go out in the <u>storm</u>.
7. This <u>horse</u> can run faster than the other one.
8. Do cats <u>snore</u>?
9. We live on the top <u>floor</u>.
10. I have <u>four</u> brothers and sisters.

Challenge Yourself Answers

1. yes
2. no
3. yes

Students' sentences will vary.

Test Review these ways to spell /ô/: <u>o</u> as in <u>for</u>; <u>oo</u> as in <u>floor</u>; <u>ou</u> as in <u>four</u>. Test words with /ô/. Use one of these testing methods: (1) Say the word; read the sample sentence from page 176; say the word; have students write the word. (2) Read each dictation sentence above; have students write the sentence. Correct the test with students.

Challenge Yourself The optional Challenge Words may be assigned to the entire class or limited to those students who do well on the test. Have students note the vowel spelling in the Challenge Words. Responses to this activity should be completed on separate paper. Answers to the questions are provided above.

Write to the Point Have students recall the selection "Rainy Day Recipe" on pages 178 and 179; then assign the sentences. Remind students that steps should be written in an order that makes sense. This activity should be completed on separate paper.

Proofreading The proofreading practice includes misspellings of words from this lesson as well as a capitalization error and a punctuation error.

LESSON 34

Objectives

- To hear and say words with /ä/.
- To write words with /ä/ with attention to letter sequence and sound/symbol relationships.
- To write each spelling word once.
- To recognize that /ä/ may be spelled a.

Sample Sentences

1. That's the first star to shine tonight.
2. The old red barn was painted white.
3. My cousin Jim lives far away.
4. I broke my arm and cannot play.
5. The farmer hopes that it will rain.
6. The inky pen left a big dark stain.
7. The engine in this car is old.
8. The chicken farm has just been sold.
9. A check mark means you did things well.
10. This art is good enough to sell!
11. We filled the jar with jellybeans.
12. Let's dress for the party and not wear jeans.
13. Carmen and I are good buddies.
14. My father teaches social studies.

Note

The sample sentences may be used for pretesting and post-testing.

Lesson 34 Words with /ä/

star
barn
far
arm
farmer
dark
car
farm
mark
art
jar
party
are
father

1. Write the words that begin with the sound /ä/.

arm   art

are

2. Write the words that end with ar.

star   far

car   jar

3. bar + n = barn

f + arm = farm

4. What word ends with the sound /ē/ and the letter y?

party

5. Which words end in the last two letters of bark?

dark   mark

6. Write the words that end in er.

farmer   father

There is only one r in father. And it comes at the end.

182

Preparation

Write /ä/ on the board. Have students repeat the sound /ä/ as in father. Say these word pairs. If the word contains /ä/, students should raise their hands.

star – stare   firm – farm   are – air   further – father

Have students look at the spelling words on page 182. Say each word aloud. Then have students repeat and spell each word.

Note the sound /ē/ at the end of the word party: /pär′ tē/. Ask the class what letter stands for /ē/ in this word. (y) Also note the sound /k/ at the end of mark: /märk/. Which other word ends with /k/? (dark) Ask which word begins with /k/ but not the letter k. (car: /kär/) Then ask the students to look carefully at all the words and tell you what letter appears after the a in every word but one. (r) What word does not have an r after the a? (father) Read the cartoon with the class.

Read the sample sentences as the students point to each spelling word.

The Page

After the students have completed page 182, have volunteers write the answers on the board. Help students check their own work.

Follow-Up

Be sure that students have study plans for the week. Suggest that they form teams of two and take turns spelling the words aloud.

Checkpoint

Write a spelling word for each clue.
Then use the Checkpoint Study Plan on page 224.

1. Gina's painting was a work of ___.

2. Twinkle, twinkle little ___.

3. A dad is a ___.

4. Does this sentence end with a question ___?

5. A cow lives in a ___.

6. Mom said to be home before ___.

7. If it's not near, it's ___.

8. He grows corn on his ___.

9. Bill is coming to my birthday ___.

10. You find jam in a ___.

11. We are funnier than they ___.

12. Your hand is part of your ___.

13. Someone who grows crops is a ___.

14. This mystery word named the kind of wagon you see in the picture. In some countries, it was spelled <u>carrus</u>. In other countries, it was spelled <u>carre</u>. Today, it's another word for automobile. Write the mystery word. ___

183

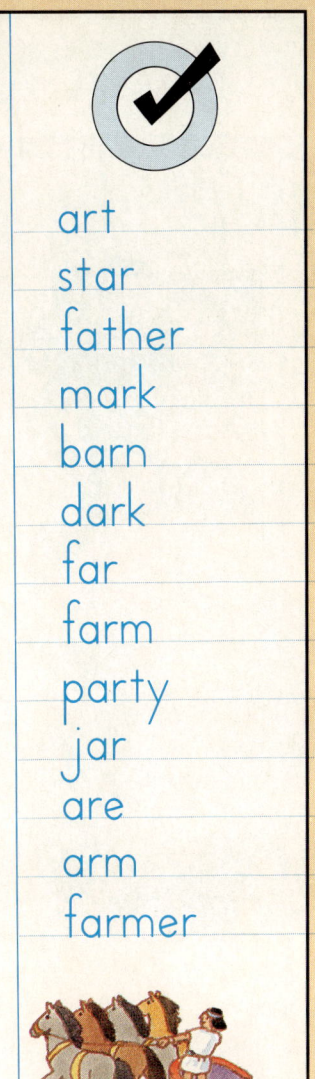

art

star

father

mark

barn

dark

far

farm

party

jar

are

arm

farmer

car

Objectives

- To write words with /ä/ in continuous text.
- To write each spelling word once.
- To integrate reading with spelling.

Fill in the blanks with spelling words.

The Star Party

Four children lived with their parents and

grandmother on a pretty _____farm_____. The

_____farmer_____ and his wife worked hard.

They had many cows in the _____barn_____ to take

care of every day.

One summer night the grandmother was very sad.

"My eyes are bad," she said. "I can't see the stars

anymore."

So, that night after dinner, the mother and

_____father_____ took the children for a ride

in the _____car_____. They made a plan to make the

grandmother happy.

The next night the father said, "Tonight we are

having a star party. The presents _____are_____ all

ready. Let the _____party_____ begin!"

The first child gave the grandmother a kitten. It had a

white _____mark_____ on its face just like a star. The

184

Preparation

Have students turn to pages 184 and 185. Call their attention to the word list. Have the students say the words. Then explain that each spelling word belongs in one of the blanks in the story.

Write the title "The Star Party" on the board and have a student read it. Explain that the story is about a very special party that a family gave for their grandmother. Talk about some presents that a grandmother might appreciate receiving. This grandmother is going to get some very special presents, indeed!

The Pages

Read the story, supplying the missing spelling words as students follow along in their texts, or have some or all of the students complete the story without a pre-reading. When everyone has finished reading, you may wish to discuss the story. Ask students why the children gave their grandmother "star gifts." *(Because her eyesight was poor and she couldn't see the stars in the sky.)*

Then ask a volunteer to read the story, pausing before each blank. Other students will say and spell the missing spelling word at the appropriate time and write it on the board. Check students' work for correct word choice and for the accurate spelling of each answer.

second child had made a bracelet. The grandmother put

it on her ___arm___. It was made of flowers just

like yellow stars. The third child had covered the garden

with a hundred paper stars! It was a work of ___art___.

Then the youngest child put a jar in the

grandmother's hands. It didn't seem to be a

___star___ present at all. He told her to open

the jar in the dark.

Outdoors, the grandmother took the lid off the

___jar___. Everyone smiled. Fireflies flew all

around. They glowed in the ___dark___.

"It's a jar of stars," said the youngest child.

The grandmother said, "I love the stars you gave

me. Now I don't need to see the stars that are so

___far___ away."

185

star
barn
far
arm
farmer
dark
car
farm
mark
art
jar
party
are
father

Enrichment

If you want to use the blackline activity masters for enrichment and additional practice, assign Lesson 34 activities at this time.

Maintenance and Review

OBJECTIVE

• To review words with /ô/ spelled: <u>o</u>, <u>oo</u>, <u>ou</u>.

ACTIVITIES

If you want to use the blackline activity masters for maintenance and review, assign Lesson 33 activities at this time.

You can also use the activity below to review Lesson 33 with students:

Write the following sentences on the board. Have students write each sentence (without underlining any words) and list the items called for. Then ask students to underline the spelling word (or words) in each sentence and to spell it aloud.

1. I can name <u>four</u> things used to clean a <u>floor</u>.
2. I know why a house needs a <u>door</u>.
3. I know the time when people <u>snore</u>.
4. I can name three things you buy in a <u>store</u>.
5. I can name three vegetables other than <u>corn</u>.
6. I know what I'd like to do in a <u>storm</u>.

Follow-Up   Have the students use each of the spelling words they missed in an original sentence.

You may wish to suggest this activity as an additional follow-up. Have the students make a shoe-box film of "The Star Party" and caption each frame with consecutive sentences from the story. The spelling words should be underlined as they appear.

Objectives

- To relate spelling words to a dictionary skill.
- To write spelling words and their sound spellings.
- To use the **Spelling Dictionary**.
- To write spelling words in alphabetical order.
- To check handwriting for correct letter formation.

Dictionary

Look up **star** in the Spelling Dictionary.

Write the pronunciation for **star**. / stär /

Look at the Key on page 196. Does **a** have the same sound in **father** and **star?**

1. Put the words in alphabetical order. Then look up each word and write the pronunciation.

barn   art   mark

Word	Pronunciation
art	/ ärt /
barn	/ bärn /
mark	/ märk /

2. Each picture stands for a spelling word. Write the pronunciation for each.

/ ärm /   / cär /   / jär /

186

Preparation Write these words on the board: last   brave   mark Ask students to locate each word in the **Spelling Dictionary** and have volunteers write the sound spelling beneath each word on the board. Review each of the diacritical marks and the sounds: /ă/ as in last, /ā/ as in brave, and /ä/ as in mark.

Then write these diacritical marks on the board: /ă/   /ā/   /ä/ List these words on the board: **land, cake, place, party, far, van.** Ask students to find these words in the **Spelling Dictionary** and write them under the appropriate diacritical marks. (/ă/: land, van; /ā/: cake, place; /ä/: party, far)

The Page Do page 186 with the students. Review formation of the letter <u>a</u>: a curve to the left attached to a short vertical line on the right. The line must form a tail at the base so an <u>a</u> is not mistaken for an <u>o</u>, or else <u>barn</u> may become <u>born</u>. Then have volunteers write each word and its sound spelling on the board so students may check their work.

Follow-Up Write the following words on the board: **star, arm, party, farm, farmer, dark.** Have the students write the words in alphabetical order. (arm, dark, farm, farmer, party, star) Then have students look them up in the **Spelling Dictionary** and write the sound spelling beside each one.

186

WORDS AT WORK

Challenge Yourself

barber   **depart**   **harmful**

Decide which Challenge Word fits each clue. Check your Spelling Dictionary to see if you were right. Then write sentences. Show that you understand the meaning of each Challenge Word.

1. You do this when you leave for school in the morning.

2. Something that hurts you is this.

3. This person cuts hair.

Write to the Point

Think of another good gift for the star party. Write a paragraph that tells about the gift. Use spelling words from this lesson in your paragraph.

Challenge Use one or more of the Challenge Words in your paragraph.

Proofreading

Use the marks to show the mistakes in the sentences below. Write the four misspelled words correctly in the blanks.

⬭	word is misspelled
⊙	period is missing
≡	letter should be capitalized

1. That night the stars lit up the (daark) sky.

2. The fireflies flew around the (fairm)⊙

3. The father took the grandmother by the (ahrm).

4. she thought it was a great (pardy.)
   ≡

1. _____ dark

2. _____ farm

3. _____ arm

4. _____ party

187

Objectives

- To extend the vowel spellings presented in Lesson 34 to the Challenge Words.
- To use clues and the **Spelling Dictionary** to enlarge students' vocabulary.
- To apply the vowel spellings presented in Lesson 34 in a writing activity.
- To practice proofreading for spelling, punctuation, and capitalization.

Dictation Sentences

1. How far is that star in the sky?
2. Our farm has a red barn.
3. Hold my arm when we walk on the ice.
4. The farmer found a frog in his car.
5. It is too dark to play ball now.
6. She put a mark next to her name.
7. I like to paint in art class.
8. The jar is full of cookies.
9. I will have a party soon.
10. We are helping our father make lunch.

Challenge Yourself Answers

1. depart
2. harmful
3. barber

Students' sentences will vary.

Test Review this way to spell /ä/: <u>a</u> as in st<u>a</u>r. Test words with /ä/. Use one of these testing methods: (1) Say the word; read the sample sentence from page 182; say the word; have students write the word. (2) Read each dictation sentence above; have students write the sentence. Correct the test with students.

Challenge Yourself The optional Challenge Words may be assigned to the entire class or limited to those students who do well on the test. Have students note the vowel spelling in the Challenge Words. Responses to this activity should be completed on separate paper. Answers to the questions are provided above.

Write to the Point Have students recall the selection "The Star Party" on pages 184 and 185; then assign the paragraph. This activity should be completed on separate paper.

Proofreading The proofreading practice includes misspellings of words from this lesson as well as a capitalization error and a punctuation error.

LESSON 35

Objectives

- To hear and say words with the suffix er.
- To write words with the suffix er with attention to letter sequence and sound/symbol relationships.
- To write each spelling word once.

Sample Sentences

1. Does a mouse move <u>faster</u> than a cat?
2. I'm <u>older</u> than my sister.
3. The Arctic is <u>colder</u> than the equator.
4. That snake is <u>longer</u> than an alligator.
5. The <u>helper</u> gave the clerk a hand.
6. The <u>jumper</u> leaped from boat to land.
7. The <u>painter</u> painted our house red.
8. A pancake is <u>flatter</u> than a loaf of bread.
9. I'm <u>bigger</u> than I was before.
10. The <u>shopper</u> runs from store to store.
11. The <u>runner</u> ran around the track.
12. The <u>braver</u> soldiers didn't turn back.
13. The <u>baker</u> made ten apple pies.
14. The <u>writer</u> wrote a book on spies.

faster
older
colder
longer
helper
jumper
painter

flatter
bigger
shopper
runner

braver
baker
writer

When a word ends in two consonants (fast), just add er: faster.

When a word ends in one consonant (flat,), double that consonant before adding er: flatter.

If a word ends in e (brave), drop the e before adding er: braver.

1. Write the words that don't change when er is added.

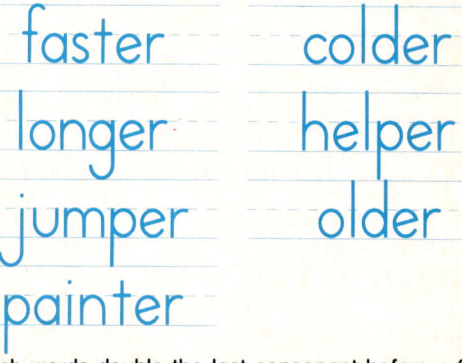

faster   colder

longer   helper

jumper   older

painter

2. Which words double the last consonant before er?

flatter   bigger

shopper   runner

3. Which words drop the final e before adding er?

braver   baker

writer

188

Note

The sample sentences may be used for pretesting and post-testing.

Preparation   Write <u>er</u> on the chalkboard and tell students that they are going to practice adding this ending to words that they have studied. Have students look at the spelling words on page 188. Say each word aloud. Then have students repeat and spell each word.

Write these words on the board: short   big   write
Ask a volunteer to read each word. Then ask someone to add <u>er</u> to <u>short</u>. Tell the students that most of the time when <u>er</u> is added to a word, the base word remains unchanged, like <u>shorter</u>. Then ask someone to add <u>er</u> to <u>big</u>. Remind students to double the last consonant. *(bigger)* Repeat the procedure for <u>write</u>. Note that the signal <u>e</u> must be dropped before the ending <u>er</u>. *(writer)* Have students make up sentences for <u>short</u>, <u>shorter</u>, <u>big</u>, <u>bigger</u>, <u>write</u>, <u>writer</u>.

Have students point to each spelling word as you read its sample sentence.

The Page   Do the activities with the students. Then have them spell their answers aloud as volunteers write them on the board so students may check their own work.

Follow-Up   Be sure that each student has a study plan for the week's words. Suggest that they write each word on a flash card (or small piece of paper) with the base word in red and the <u>er</u> ending in blue.

Checkpoint

Write a spelling word for each clue. Then use the Checkpoint Study Plan on page 224.

1. Which boy is younger and which is ___?

2. If you like the cake, thank the ___.

3. I was a slow swimmer, but now I'm ___.

4. I know an artist who is a ___.

5. If you pull a rubber band, it gets ___.

6. The opposite of warmer is ___.

7. If you help me, you are my ___.

8. A person who shops is a ___.

9. A frog is a good ___.

10. A deer is a fast ___.

11. A person who writes is a ___.

12. My plant is getting ___.

13. He is brave, but I am ___.

14. This mystery word comes from the word flatr. It has not changed very much over the years. It's a word you use to describe a pancake or a tire without air. They are both ___. What word did you use? Now double the final consonant and add er. The word you get is the mystery word. ___

189

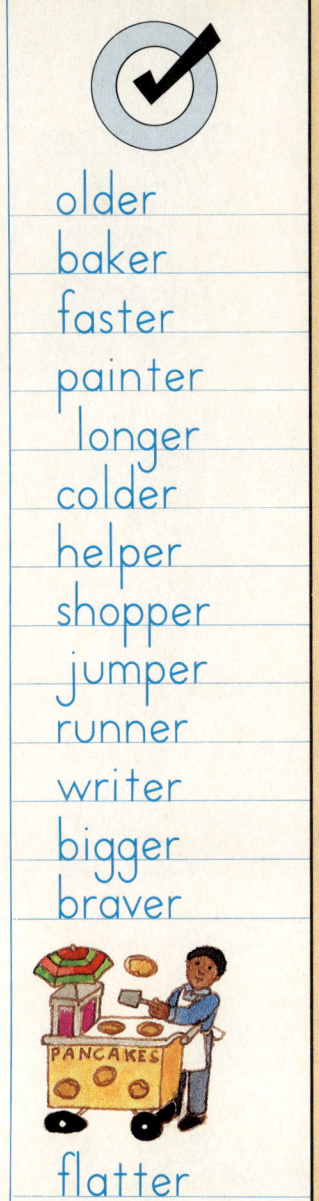

older
baker
faster
painter
longer
colder
helper
shopper
jumper
runner
writer
bigger
braver

flatter

Objectives

- To write words with the suffix <u>er</u> in continuous text.
- To write each spelling word once.
- To integrate reading with spelling.

Remember These Old Friends?

Fill in the blanks with spelling words.

1. Sam must have nails in his driveway. The tires on his van are _____flatter_____ than pancakes!

2. Circus workers are all brave. But I think a lion tamer is _____braver_____ than an acrobat.

3. Alex Tate is big. He is called "Whale." Alex is much _____bigger_____ than his teammates!

4. It's too bad a dragon is too long to mail. A dragon is _____longer_____ than an envelope!

5. Some fast bees caught Robin's grandfather. Those bees went _____faster_____ than he did!

6. Neal found an old penny. It was very old. It was _____older_____ than any coin he had.

7. Meg wants to go to the North Pole. It is _____colder_____ than where she lives.

Preparation   Tell the students that they are now going to read sentences about their old friends, the characters in the stories they have read in this book.

Have students turn to pages 190 and 191. Call their attention to the word list. Have the students say the words. Then explain that each spelling word belongs in one of the blanks on pages 190 and 191.

Write the title "Remember These Old Friends?" on the board and have a student read it.

The Page   Read the story aloud, supplying the missing spelling words as students follow along in their texts, or have some or all of the students complete the story without a pre-reading. When everyone has finished the story, you may wish to discuss it. Ask your students which story in the book they liked the best. Who was their favorite character?

Now have a student read the sentence pairs before each blank. Other students will say and spell the missing spelling word at the appropriate time and write it on the board. Check the students' work for correct word choice and for the accurate spelling of each answer.

8. The ox shopped for his friend. T. Green Frog thanked

him for being a helpful _____ shopper _____.

9. Kristin often writes to her friends. Her letters are

interesting. She is a good _____ writer _____.

10. A rabbit is a faster _____ runner _____

than a turtle. How could a turtle win a race?

11. Billy jumps on a pogo stick and doesn't fall off. Billy

is an amazing _____ jumper _____!

12. Mr. Banana says he baked a bicycle.

Mr. Banana must be a good _____ baker _____!

13. We like to look at Jill's paintings. That's because Jill

is a very good _____ painter _____.

14. Nat helped Uncle Ralph cook dinner. Nat was a

good _____ helper _____.

191

faster
older
colder
longer
helper
jumper
painter
flatter
bigger
shopper
runner
braver
baker
writer

Follow-Up   Ask students to use each of the spelling words they missed in an original sentence.

You may wish to suggest this activity as an additional follow-up. Have the students sketch pictures of any three of the story characters. Then ask them to write a sentence using a word from the word list, describing each character they have drawn. Have them underline the spelling words. Display the pictures with their captions around the room.

Enrichment

Assign the Lesson 35 blackline activity masters for enrichment and additional practice at this time.

Maintenance and Review

OBJECTIVE

• To review words with /ă/ spelled a.

ACTIVITIES

If you want to use the blackline activity masters for maintenance and review, assign Lesson 34 activities at this time.

You can also use the activity below to review Lesson 34 with students:

Write the following poem on the board (without underlining any words). Have students take turns reading each line. Ask readers to identify the spelling words from Lesson 34 by stopping and spelling each one aloud. Then students should write these words. Have students suggest what kind of a birthday present a man from a distant star might bring.

Artie's Lucky Charm
There once was a farmer named Art
Who was very clever and smart.
He traveled by car,
To a faraway star
Where each person was shaped like
  a heart!

Now Art was the father of Artie,
Who wanted a fine birthday party.
Art put into a jar,
From this faraway star,
A guest for his son's birthday party!

On his arm Art did carry the guest,
Who was small and so beautifully
  dressed
The heart-shaped man
Had the name of Dan,
As a present, he sure was
  the best!

Objectives

- To relate spelling words to a dictionary skill.
- To write spelling words in response to base words.
- To locate words with the <u>er</u> ending in the **Spelling Dictionary**.
- To check handwriting for correct letter formation.

a b c d e f g h i j k l m
n o p q r s t u v w x y z

Dictionary

Write these words in alphabetical order. Find the words in your Spelling Dictionary. For example, to find the word **bigger**, look up **big**. Write the Dictionary page number for each.

faster   colder   older   flatter   longer   bigger   braver

	Word	Dictionary Page
1.	bigger	199
2.	braver	200
3.	colder	202
4.	faster	205
5.	flatter	206
6.	longer	211
7.	older	213

192

Preparation Write this word on the board and have it read: **bigger**
Ask students what the base word of <u>bigger</u> is. *(big)* Explain that the <u>er</u> form of a word can often be found under the entry for its base word in a dictionary. Have students find <u>big</u> and point to the word <u>bigger</u> within the entry. *(page 199)* Ask your students to say sentences for <u>big</u> and <u>bigger</u>.

The Page Do page 192 with the students, reminding them to be careful not to make spelling mistakes because of careless handwriting. Then have the students spell the answers aloud as you write them on the board. (You may wish to have students identify and spell each base word.) Help students correct their work.

Follow-Up Have students copy these words and write the base word for each: **baker, helper, writer, painter, shopper.** *(bake, help, write, paint, shop)* Students may then write sentences for any three of the words.

WORDS AT WORK

Challenge Yourself

baby sitter   beginner   dipper

What do you think each underlined Challenge Word means? Check your Spelling Dictionary to see if you are right. Then write sentences. Show that you understand the meaning of each Challenge Word.

1. The baby sitter takes care of Pedro when Mom is at work.

2. Skating is hard for a beginner.

3. Long ago people used a dipper to pour water.

Write to the Point

Look back over the stories in this book. Choose your favorite and write a paragraph. In your paragraph tell what you liked about the story. Use spelling words from this lesson in your paragraph.

Challenge Use one or more of the Challenge Words in your paragraph.

Proofreading

Use the marks to show the mistakes in the sentences below. Write the four misspelled words correctly in the blanks.

⬭	word is misspelled
⊙	period is missing
☰	letter should be capitalized

1. Reading the stories helped me become a better (writter.)

2. One story was about a (runer)⊙

3. Was jill a (bakker) or a jumper?

4. She was a (paintur.)

1. _____writer_____

2. _____runner_____

3. _____baker_____

4. _____painter_____

193

Objectives

- To extend the spelling patterns presented in Lesson 35 to the Challenge Words.

- To use context and the **Spelling Dictionary** to enlarge students' vocabulary.

- To apply the spelling patterns presented in Lesson 35 in a writing activity.

- To practice proofreading for spelling, punctuation, and capitalization.

Dictation Sentences

1. Can a dog run faster than a fox?
2. My older brother is a writer.
3. It is much colder now than it was.
4. How much longer will we ride on this train?
5. The painter has a good helper.
6. My horse is a fast runner and a good jumper.
7. The land is flatter on the other side of the hill.
8. The small dog was braver than the bigger dog.
9. The shopper went to many stores in town.
10. The baker made a peach pie.

Challenge Yourself Answers

Possible definitions:

1. person who takes care of children
2. person who is doing something for the first time
3. cup to dip with

Students' sentences will vary.

Test Review adding er to words. Test words ending with er. Use one of these testing methods: (1) Say the word; read the sample sentence from page 188; say the word; have students write the word. (2) Read each dictation sentence above; have students write the sentence. Correct the test with students.

Challenge Yourself The optional Challenge Words may be assigned to the entire class or limited to those students who do well on the test. Have students note the spelling pattern in the Challenge Words. Responses to this activity should be completed on separate paper. Answers to the questions are provided above.

Write to the Point Have students recall the selection "Remember These Old Friends?" on pages 190 and 191; then assign the paragraph. This activity should be completed on separate paper.

Proofreading The proofreading practice includes misspellings of words from this lesson as well as a capitalization error and a punctuation error.

LESSON 36

Objectives

- To review and reinforce vowel spellings for /ou/, /ô/ and /ä/.
- To review and reinforce the suffix er.
- To hear, say, spell, and write representative words from Lessons 31–35.
- To write a description using the five steps in the writing process.
- To use a prewriting activity to list sensory details for a description.

Dictation Sentences

1. All the children in my town go to this school.
2. Walk around the school to get to the playground.
3. Donna wears her long hair in braids.
4. I saw that movie last week.
5. Tania likes to talk about her frog.
6. The little bird has very small feet.
7. I am too short to reach that shelf.
8. Please bring me a surprise from the store.
9. We sat on the floor and told stories.
10. Your mittens are in your jacket.
11. Mom drives to work in her car.
12. My father and I like to fly kites.
13. This pancake is flatter than a piece of paper.
14. I am a writer of short stories.

Note

A review test blackline master in standardized format and an answer sheet have been provided on pages T40 and T41 of this Teacher's Edition. The answers to the review test are given below.

1-C	5-B
2-B	6-C
3-B	7-B
4-A	8-A

Lesson 36 Words in Review

A. town
around

B. long
saw
talk
small

C. short
store
floor

D. are
car
father

E. flatter
writer

---

1. In Lesson 31, you studied two ways to spell /ou/: ou and ow. Write the words in List A.

town   around

2. Lesson 32 has words with /ô/. Write the words with /ô/ from List B.

long   saw
talk   small

3. In Lesson 33, you studied more words with /ô/. Write the words in List C.

short   store
floor

4. Lesson 34 has words with /ä/. Write the words with /ä/ from List D.

are   car
father

5. Add er to flat and write. Use List E to check your words.

flatter   writer

194

Preparation Tell students that Lesson 36 is a review lesson. Lesson 36 contains several activities that ask them to write some of the words they have studied in Lessons 31–35.

Direct students' attention to the list of words on page 194. Read the words aloud as students look at them. Have students say and spell each word aloud.

Then read the dictation sentences above as students point to each spelling word in their book. Point out that the words in List A are from Lesson 31, words in List B are from Lesson 32, words in List C are from Lesson 33, words in List D are from Lesson 34, and words in List E are from Lesson 35.

The Pages Have students complete the activities on page 194 as a group or independently. Write the answers on the board and have volunteers spell the words aloud for reinforcement of correct spelling.

Test and Study If you wish to test students on the review words, use one of these testing methods: (1) Read the word and dictation sentence; say the word again; have students write the word. (2) Have students complete the review test blackline master. (See **Note**.)

Writer's Workshop

A Description

A description of a person tells how that person looks, moves, and sounds. Writers use details to make the person come alive in the reader's mind. Here is the beginning of Tara's description of her new baby brother.

> ### The Baby
>
> Yesterday Mom and Dad brought Corey home. At first I thought they left the baby at the hospital. The blanket looked empty. Then I saw a tiny pink hand pop out of the blanket. I knew he was in there. I got closer. I could hear little peeps. He sounded like a bird. He even looked like a bird. There was no hair on his little head. His skin was wrinkled.

Tara followed the steps in the writing process to describe her baby brother. She used a senses web as a **Prewriting** activity. On her web she wrote details that told about her baby brother. Part of Tara's web is shown here. Study what Tara did.

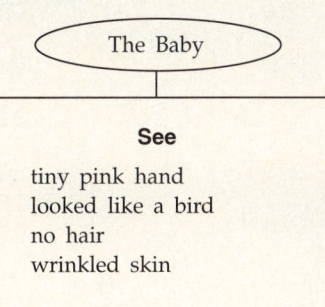

The Baby

See
tiny pink hand
looked like a bird
no hair
wrinkled skin

It's Your Turn

Get ready to write your own description. It may be of a friend or a relative. It may be a person in a story you have read. Like Tara, begin by making a senses web. Then follow the other steps in the writing process—**Writing, Revising, Proofreading,** and **Publishing.**

195

Writer's Workshop Students who have mastered the review words may go on to the **Writer's Workshop** on page 195. Explain that in a description of a person, writers use details that will help readers get to know the person being described. Point out that the writer might include details about the person's looks, speech, movements, and anything else that makes the person come alive for readers. Then read the beginning of the description "The Baby" with students, noting the describing words.

Allow students to study that portion of the senses web shown on the pupil's page and guide students to see how this graphic organizer helped Tara prepare to write her description.

It's Your Turn Review the steps in the writing process with students. If students are not satisfied with the result of their prewriting, allow them to revise it as often as necessary or to choose another topic and repeat the prewriting activity.

Process Writing Blackline Masters
• Senses Web, page T50
• Steps in the Writing Process, page T46
• Proofreading Symbols/Checklist, page T47

SPELLING
Dic·tion·ar·y

Aa Bb Cc Dd Ee Ff Gg

Hh Ii Jj Kk Ll Mm Nn

Oo Pp Qq Rr Ss Tt Uu

Vv Ww Xx Yy Zz

Aa Aa Aa

active | ăk tĭv | —Doing something most of the time; moving around; busy. *My **active** kitten never rests.*

add | ăd | —To put in as something extra. *I will **add** a blue flower to my picture.*

adjust | ə jŭst | —To change so as to make right or better. *She will **adjust** the color on the television.* **adjusted, adjusting**

admit | ăd mĭt | —To say that something is true or a fact. *Did he **admit** that he made a mistake?* **admitted, admitting** *Thank you for **admitting** that you took the wrong jacket.*

adopt | ə dŏpt | —**1.** To take and make one's own. *We will **adopt** the puppy and take it home.* **2.** To take a child born to another person into one's family and raise it as one's own. *My mother and father are going to **adopt** a baby. She will be my sister.*

advice | ăd vīs | —An idea someone else gives of how to fix a problem. *Please give me **advice** on how to win the game.*

after | ăf tər | —At a later time than. *I go to the park **after** school.*

alert | ə lûrt | —To warn. *The bell will **alert** the class to come inside.* **alerted, alerting** *The red light was **alerting** us to stop.*

all | ôl | —**1.** Every one of. ***All** the tadpoles turned into frogs.* **2.** Nothing but. ***All** I could think about was my birthday.*

am | ăm | —*I **am** glad to see you.*

amuse | ə myōōz | —**1.** To entertain. *The puppet show will **amuse** the class.* **2.** To make laugh or smile. *My sister's jokes **amuse** me.* **amused, amusing** *He is **amusing** his father with funny stories.*

an | ăn | —Any, or one. *How do you know when **an** elephant is planning to escape? (You catch it packing up its trunk.)*

and | ănd | —Added to; as well as. *What hides in a tree **and** eats peanuts? (A timid elephant.)*

any | ĕn ē | —One of several, but no special one. *You can take **any** bus to get to my house.*

are | är | —*Why **are** elephants gray? (So you can tell them from bluebirds.)*

arm | ärm | —*plural* **arms**. Part of the body between the hand and shoulder. *Your elbow is in the middle of your **arm**.*

around | ə round | —**1.** All over. *They traveled **around** the country.* **2.** In a circle. *We have a garden **around** our house.*

art | ärt | —*plural* **arts**. Paintings, drawings, or other beautiful things. *My drawings are examples of great **art**.*

ask | ăsk | —To question. ***Ask** me any riddle and I'll tell you the answer.* **asked, asking**

ate | āt | —Had something to eat. *I **ate** a peanut butter sandwich for lunch.* Past of the word **eat**.

athlete | ăth lēt | —*plural* **athletes**. A person who plays sports. *The **athlete** can run fast.*

Bb Bb Bb

baby | bā bē | —*plural* **babies**. A young child or animal. *Brad had fuzz instead of hair when he was a **baby**.*

baby sitter | bā bē sĭt ər | —*plural* **baby sitters**. A person who takes care of children when the parents are not at home. *The **baby sitter** plays games with the children.*

back | băk | —*plural* **backs**. **1.** Opposite of front. *Turn your **back** while I run and hide.* **2.** To a former place. *We go **back** to the lake every summer.*

bacon | bā kən | —Salted and smoked meat that comes from the back and sides of a pig. *I had **bacon** for breakfast today.*

bake | bāk | —To cook in an oven. *Let's **bake** cookies this afternoon.* **baked, baking**

baker | bāk ər | —*plural* **bakers**. Someone who cooks things in an oven. *A very good **baker** made this tasty bread!*

ball | bôl | —*plural* **balls**. Something round that is used in games. *Throw me the **ball**. Hurry!*

bamboo | băm bōō | —*plural* **bamboos**. A tall grass. The long woody parts called stems are empty inside. They are often used to make fishing poles, chairs, and other things. *My chair made out of **bamboo** is light.*

barber | bär bər | —*plural* **barbers**. A person who cuts hair and shaves beards. *The **barber** cuts my hair every six weeks.*

barn | bärn | —*plural* **barns**. A large shed. *Farm animals live in **barns**.*

batch | băch | —*plural* **batches**. A group of things made at one time. *The baker made ten **batches** of cookies today.*

bed | bĕd | —*plural* **beds**. A place to sleep. *How is a **bed** like an elephant? (It has a head and four legs.)*

bee | bē | —*plural* **bees**. An insect with four wings, a hairy body, and usually a sting. *This kind of **bee** makes honey.*

beggar | bĕg ər | —*plural* **beggars**. A person who asks other people for money, food, or clothes in order to live. *My mother gave the **beggar** some money.*

beginner | bĭ gĭn ər | —*plural* **beginners**. A person who is starting to do or learn something for the first time. *Swimming lessons are important for a **beginner** in the water.*

being | bē ĭng | —*Thank you for **being** so helpful.*

belief | bĭ lēf | —*plural* **beliefs. 1.** Trust in someone or something. *I have **belief** in my father.* **2.** Something that one feels sure is true. *My **belief** is that we go to a fine school.*

bell | bĕl | —*plural* **bells.** Something that rings when struck or pressed. *I think I heard the **bell** calling us for dinner.*

best | bĕst | —Most excellent. *It was the **best** movie I'd ever seen.*

big | bĭg | —Large. *Alex ate a **big** dinner after the game.* **bigger, biggest** *He ate a **bigger** dinner than we thought he would. He ate the **biggest** dinner I have ever seen eaten. We ran out of food.*

bike | bīk | —**1.** *plural* **bikes.** Something to ride on that has two wheels; a bicycle. *You move a **bike** by pedaling with your legs.* **2.** To ride a bike. *How far can you **bike** without getting tired?* **biked, biking**

bitter | bĭt ər | —**1.** Having a sharp, biting, or bad taste. *The tea tasted **bitter** without sugar.* **2.** Causing pain; not agreeable. **bitterer, bitterest** *Baking chocolate is **bitterer** than milk chocolate. Today is the **bitterest** day of the winter.*

black | blăk | —The darkest of all colors. *A zebra is **black** and white.*

blank | blăngk | —**1.** *plural* **blanks.** An empty space. *Write your answer in the **blank**.* **2.** Without writing or marks. *I need some **blank** paper.* **3.** Empty. *There is a **blank** spot in the picture.* **blanker, blankest**

blizzard | blĭz ərd | —*plural* **blizzards.** A long, heavy storm of falling snow with very strong winds. *The roads were closed because of the **blizzard**.*

block | blŏk | —*plural* **blocks. 1.** A city section or square. *My best friend lives on my **block**.* **2.** A solid object with flat sides. *A red **block** was missing from the toy box.*

blue | blo͞o | —*plural* **blues.** The color of the clear sky. *If you put a **blue** hat in red punch, what will it be? (Wet.)*

blush | blŭsh | —To become red in the face from feeling ashamed, nervous, or silly. *Sometimes I **blush** when I do not know the answer to a question.* **blushed, blushing**

boat | bōt | —*plural* **boats.** A small ship. *May we borrow your **boat** to go fishing?*

bonnet | bŏn ĭt | —*plural* **bonnets.** A hat that is tied under the chin with ribbons. *The baby looked cute in the white **bonnet**.*

bony | bō nē | —**1.** Made of or like bone. *The dinosaur skeleton is **bony**.* **2.** Full of bones. *The fish we had for dinner was very **bony**.* **3.** Very thin. *The **bony** dog was very hungry.*

book | bŏŏk | —*plural* **books.** Sheets of paper bound together between two covers. *A **book** may have pages of writing, as a storybook. A **book** may have blank pages, as an address book.*

booth | bo͞oth | —*plural* **booths. 1.** A small stall where things are sold or shown. *Our club sold popcorn at our* **booth. 2.** A small closed place. *The telephone* **booth** *is in front of the store.*

boulder | bōl dər | —*plural* **boulders.** A very large rounded rock. *We climbed on top of the* **boulder.**

box | bŏks | —**1.** *plural* **boxes.** Something used to hold things. *Crayons sometimes come in a tin* **box. 2.** To fight with fists as a sport. *You have to be fast on your feet to* **box** *well.* **boxed, boxing**

boy | boi | —*plural* **boys.** A male child. *That* **boy** *with red hair is my brother.*

brave | brāv | —Able to face danger without fear. *The* **brave** *mole protected her babies from the attacking owl.* **braver, bravest** *The little animal was* **braver** *today than yesterday. Animals are* **bravest** *when their babies are being attacked.*

bravery | brā və rē | —Ability to face danger or pain without fear; courage. *Firefighters show their* **bravery** *when they put out fires.*

bring | brĭng | —To carry along with. *Be sure to* **bring** *your lunch to school tomorrow.* **brought, bringing**

brother | brŭth ər | —*plural* **brothers.** A boy or man with the same parents as another person. *Sue and her* **brother** *take good care of their pets.*

brow | brou | —*plural* **brows.** The forehead; the part of the face above the eyes. *His hair covered his* **brow.**

buckle | bŭk əl | —**1.** *plural* **buckles.** Something that fastens together one end of a belt or strap with the other end. *The* **buckle** *on the belt is gold.* **2.** To fasten with a buckle. *I always* **buckle** *my seat belt.* **buckled, buckling**

buddy | bŭd ē | —*plural* **buddies.** A close friend. *My* **buddy** *and I like to go to the zoo.*

bug | bŭg | —*plural* **bugs.** An insect. *Certain* **bugs** *are harmful to trees.*

bulletin | bŏol ĭ tn | —*plural* **bulletins.** A short notice of the latest news on radio, television, or in the newspaper. *The* **bulletin** *on television told us about the flooded streets.*

bus | bŭs | —*plural* **buses** or **busses.** A large car with rows of seats. *The school* **bus** *stops on my corner.*

bushel | bŏosh əl | —*plural* **bushels.** A measure for dry things such as fruit, vegetables, and grain. *We picked a* **bushel** *of apples from our tree.*

but | bŭt | —**1.** Yet, still. *I planted the seeds,* **but** *they never grew.* **2.** Except. *Everyone* **but** *me had a beautiful big garden.*

by | bī | —**1.** Beyond, past. *Marie goes* **by** *my house every day.* **2.** Beside. *My house is right* **by** *the river.* **3.** Not later than. *Be home* **by** *six o'clock, please.*

Cc Cc Cc

call | kôl | —**1.** To cry out. *Mom will call me when it's time for supper. Mom has a loud voice.* **2.** To telephone. *Call her up and see if you can eat here.* **called, calling**

came | kām | —Arrived. *Bob came to my house yesterday.* Past of the word **come.**

cannon | kăn ən | —*plural* **cannons** or **cannon.** A large, heavy gun that is put on wheels or some other base. *They fired a cannon in the park on the Fourth of July.*

car | kär | —*plural* **cars.** An automobile.
Man: *I have no windows in my car.*
Friend: *How do you keep the wind out of your face?*
Man: *I ride the bus.*

cat | kăt | —*plural* **cats.** A small furry animal. *Why is a cat a good pet? (Because it is purr-fect!)*

catch | kăch | —**1.** A game played by throwing a ball. *Let's play catch over in the field.* **2.** To get hold of. *What can you catch but cannot throw? (A cold.)* **caught, catching**

chain | chān | —*plural* **chains.** A number of rings joined together. *The car was fastened to the tow truck by a heavy chain.*

cheap | chēp | —Low in cost. *The candy for one penny is cheap.* **cheaper, cheapest** *It is cheaper to go to the movie in the afternoon. Which toy is the cheapest?*

cheat | chēt | —To act in a way that is not honest or fair. *I will never cheat in school.* **cheated, cheating**

child | chīld | —*plural* **children.** A young boy or girl. *The teacher gave each child a book.*

children | chĭl drən | —Plural of **child.** *There are twenty children in our second grade.*

chop | chŏp | —To cut up into small pieces. *He began to chop the wood into logs.* **chopped, chopping**

city | sĭt ē | —*plural* **cities.** A large and important town. *There are so many places to visit in the city.*

claim | klām | —**1.** To say that something is true. *They claimed that they were the best team.* **2.** To ask for something that is one's own. *I will claim my coat at the door.* **claimed, claiming**

class | klăs | —*plural* **classes.** A group of students. *Our class put on a play for the whole school.*

classmate | klăs māt | —*plural* **classmates.** A person in the same class at school. *My classmate and I have desks next to each other.*

clean | klēn | —**1.** Not dirty. *It is hard to find a clean and shiny penny.* **2.** To take dirt from. *Neal tries to clean all the coins in his collection.* **cleaned, cleaning**

climate | klī mĭt | —*plural* **climates.** The way the weather of a place usually is. The climate includes how hot or cold it is and how much rain falls. *What is the climate in your city?*

clock | klŏk | —*plural* **clocks.** Something that tells the time. *What has a face and two hands but does not speak? (A clock.)*

clover | klō vər | —*plural* **clovers.** A small plant with leaves that have three parts. Clover also has rounded bunches of small white, red, yellow, or purple flowers. *Cows eat clover.*

clown | kloun | —*plural* **clowns.** A person who does funny things to make people laugh. *A circus wouldn't be much fun without the clowns.*

club | klŭb | —*plural* **clubs. 1.** A group of people who like to do the same thing. *Our club is for people who want to learn about insects.* **2.** A stick. *In golf, you use a club to strike the ball.*

coat | kōt | —*plural* **coats.** Clothing with sleeves worn to keep warm. *I will wear a coat today. It is cold out!*

cocoon | kə kōon | —*plural* **cocoons.** The silky case spun by a caterpillar or other young insect that keeps it safe while it is becoming a moth, butterfly, or other adult insect. *The butterfly came out of its cocoon.*

cold | kōld | —Chilly, not hot. *It is so cold today that I had better wear my winter coat.* **colder, coldest** *It is colder than yesterday. It is the coldest day of the year, so far!*

cook | kŏok | —**1.** *plural* **cooks.** A person who prepares food. *Mindy is a good cook. She always has great things to eat!* **2.** To prepare food. *I don't like to cook. I would rather eat at Mindy's house.* **cooked, cooking**

cookbook | kŏok bŏok | —*plural* **cookbooks.** A book that tells how to make and cook food. *The cookbook told how to boil an egg.*

cookies | kŏok ēz | —Small sweet cakes. Plural of **cookie.** *Mindy makes good chocolate chip cookies.*

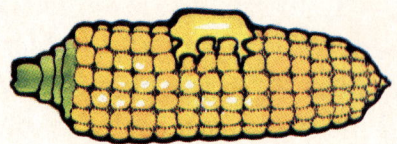

corn | kôrn | —**1.** A plant with large ears of grain. *The corn grows tall in the summer.* **2.** A yellow grain. *Corn is my favorite vegetable.*

could | kŏod | —Was able to. *My pet frog could jump ten feet!* Past of the word **can.**

cow | kou | —*plural* **cows.** A female farm animal that gives milk.
Teacher: *Where is milk stored?*
Student: *In a cow!*

coward | kou ərd | —*plural* **cowards.** A person who is not brave or is afraid to do hard or dangerous things. *Kiesha proved she was not a coward when she got the cat out of the tree.*

craft | krăft | —*plural* **crafts.** Skill in making something with the hands. *Making kites takes craft.*

cry | krī | —**1.** To shed tears. *He fell on his head and began to* **cry**. **2.** To shout. *His friend had to* **cry** *out for help.* **cried, crying**

cut | kŭt | —**1.** *plural* **cuts.** A wound. *Do you have a bandage for the* **cut** *on Lisa's toe?* **2.** To wound. *She* **cut** *herself on Nat's roller skate.* **3.** To slice. *We can* **cut** *a bandage with these scissors.* **cut, cutting**

Dd   Dd   Dd

dainty | dān tē | —Pretty in a small, thin, soft, or light way. *The ring is very* **dainty**. **daintier, daintiest** *This teacup is* **daintier** *than the other one. That is the* **daintiest** *flower I have ever seen.*

dark | därk | —Having no light. *Stars show up well in the* **dark** *night sky.*

delay | dĭ lā | —*plural* **delays. 1.** Time while something is being put off. *There was a* **delay** *in the game.* **2.** To put off. *The teacher will* **delay** *the test.* **delayed, delaying**

deny | dĭ nī | —To say that something is not true. *The children* **deny** *breaking the window.* **denied, denying** *Mark keeps* **denying** *that he is the best player.*

depart | dĭ pärt | —To leave; go away. *The visitors plan to* **depart** *tomorrow morning.* **departed, departing**

desk | dĕsk | —*plural* **desks.** A table on which to write. *Molly keeps 100 crayons in her* **desk!**

diet | dī ĭt | —*plural* **diets.** The things a person or animal eats and drinks most of the time. *Worms may be part of the* **diet** *of birds.*

dipper | dĭp ər | —*plural* **dippers.** A cup with a long handle that is used to lift water, soup, or other liquids. *The* **dipper** *for the cold drinks is next to the glasses.*

disease | dĭ zēz | —*plural* **diseases.** Sickness; illness. *A cold is a* **disease.**

dislike | dĭs līk | —**1.** *plural* **dislikes.** A feeling of not liking something. *I have a* **dislike** *for rainy days.* **2.** To have a feeling of not liking something. *Tanya* **disliked** *the play.* **disliked, disliking**

do | dōō | —To work at a job. **Do** *all the math problems on page 5, please.* **did, doing**

dodge | dŏj | —To miss something by moving away quickly. *Birds* **dodge** *the trees when they fly.* **dodged, dodging**

dog | dôg | —*plural* **dogs.** A four-footed animal. **Dogs** *can be used as pets, for hunting, and for doing work.*
Bernie: *How do you like my* **dog***?*
Ernie: *Nice. Is it trained?*
Bernie: *Sure. When I tell it not to sit up—it doesn't!*

door | dôr | —*plural* **doors.** A piece of wood, metal, or glass that moves to let people in and out. *What goes through a* **door** *but never comes inside? (A key.)*

dot | dŏt | —**1.** *plural* **dots.** A very small round point. *Her best dress is white with red **dots** on it.* **2.** To mark with a round point. *Be sure to **dot** an i when you write it.* **dotted, dotting**

draw | drô | —To make a picture. *Jill will **draw** a picture of you if you ask her.* **drew, drawing**

dream | drēm | —**1.** *plural* **dreams.** Something seen during sleep. *Don't you hate the alarm to wake you up in the middle of a good **dream**?* **2.** To think or see something during sleep. *Children sometimes **dream** about school.* **dreamed, dreaming**

dress | drĕs | —**1.** *plural* **dresses.** Clothing worn by a girl or woman. *May's favorite **dress** has a yellow skirt.* **2.** To put clothes on. *Robbie's little brother can't **dress** himself yet.* **dressed, dressing**

drop | drŏp | —**1.** *plural* **drops.** A round-shaped bit of water or other liquid. *The rain fell in heavy **drops** against the window.* **2.** To let fall. *Kevin was afraid he would **drop** the heavy pail.* **dropped, dropping**

drought | drout | —*plural* **droughts.** A long time with little or no rain. *The plants began to dry up because of the **drought.***

duckling | dŭk lĭng | —*plural* **ducklings.** A baby duck. *The **ducklings** walked in a line behind their mother.*

Ee Ee Ee

eat | ēt | —To swallow food. *A toad will **eat** 100 insects a day—if it can catch them!* **ate, eating**

egg | ĕg | —*plural* **eggs.** A special cell formed in the body of a female animal. *Baby chicks hatch from **eggs.*** Max: *How do you know there is no chicken in that **egg**?* Moe: *Because it is a duck **egg**!*

eight | āt | —*plural* **eights.** The number after seven, written 8. *Many second-grade children are **eight** years old.*

elephant | ĕl ə fənt | —*plural* **elephants.** African or Asian animal with two tusks and a long trunk. *The **elephant** is the largest living land animal.*

end | ĕnd | —**1.** *plural* **ends.** The finish of something. *We go back to school at the **end** of summer.* **2.** To stop. *In June, it seems as if the summer will never **end.*** **ended, ending**

explode | ĭk splōd | —To burst or cause to burst suddenly with a loud noise; blow up. *A balloon might* **explode** *if you put too much air into it.*

eye | ī | —*plural* **eyes.** The part of the body used to see. *The hammerhead shark has one* **eye** *at each end of its head.*

Ff Ff Ff Ff

fade | fād | —**1.** To lose or make to lose color. *The dress may* **fade** *after it is washed.* **2.** To become less fresh. *Flowers* **fade** *if they are not put in water.* **faded, fading**

faithful | fāth fəl | —Able to be trusted and counted on; always there. *His* **faithful** *dog always meets him at the school bus.*

false | fôls | —**1.** Not true or correct; wrong. *His answer was* **false. 2.** Not real. *Some people have* **false** *teeth.* **falser, falsest** *In daylight the flowers looked* **falser** *than I had thought. What is the* **falsest** *story you have ever heard?*

far | fär | —At a distance. *I live* **far** *from school. I have to walk a long way there.*

farm | färm | —*plural* **farms.** Land and buildings in the country. *Crops are grown on a* **farm.** *Animals are raised on* **farms.**

farmer | fär mər | —*plural* **farmers.** A person who grows crops or raises animals. *Why did the* **farmer** *name his pig "Ink"? (Because it kept running out of the pen.)*

fast | făst | —Not slow; speedy. *She ran by so* **fast. faster, fastest** *She is a* **faster** *runner than I. She is the* **fastest** *runner in school.*

father | fä thər | —*plural* **fathers.** Male parent. *Jessie's* **father** *has a beard.*

faucet | fô sĭt | —*plural* **faucets.** A part made for turning on and off water or other liquid from a pipe or sink; tap. *Please be sure to turn the* **faucet** *off when you finish brushing your teeth.*

feet | fēt | —Plural of **foot.**
Dad: *You have your shoes on the wrong* **feet.**
Son: *But they're the only* **feet** *I have!*

fill | fĭl | —To make full. *Please* **fill** *the glass with milk.* **filled, filling**

find | fīnd | —To come upon by chance. *Where do you* **find** *elephants? (Elephants are so big they hardly ever get lost!)* **found, finding**

fish | fĭsh | —**1.** *plural* **fish** or **fishes.** A water animal that has fins and breathes through gills. *The whale shark is the biggest* **fish** *in the sea.* **2.** To catch fish. *This seems to be a good spot to* **fish. fished, fishing**

five | fīv | —*plural* **fives.** The number after four, written 5. *People have five fingers on each hand.*

flat | flăt | —Level. *A flat pan is good for making pancakes.* **flatter, flattest** *A pan is flatter than a bowl. A griddle is the largest, flattest pan of all.*

floor | flôr | —*plural* **floors.** The part of a room that is walked on.
Ned: *What was the hardest thing about roller-skating?*
Ted: *The floor!*

flower | flou ər | —*plural* **flowers.** A blossom. *A tulip is a nice kind of flower.*

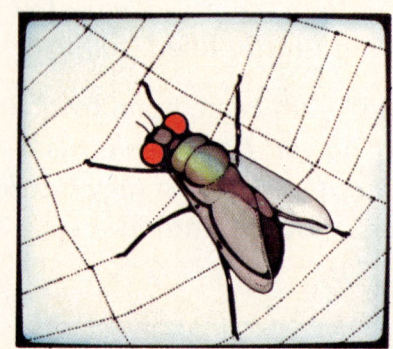

fly | flī | —**1.** *plural* **flies.** An insect with one pair of wings. *A fly would make a nice lunch for a spider.* **2.** To move through the air. *Most birds fly south when winter comes.* **flew, flying**

food | fōod | —*plural* **foods.** Something to eat. *Bring plenty of food to eat at the picnic!*

foot | fŏot | —*plural* **feet.** Part of the leg. *People have five toes on each foot.*

for | fôr | —**1.** Fits the need. *This bike is good for riding long distances.*
2. Helps someone. *I'll get the bike for you.*

found | found | —Came upon by chance. *I found a dime on the way to school.* Past of the word **find.**

four | fôr | —*plural* **fours.** The number after three, written 4. *Every square has four sides.*

freeze | frēz | —To harden from a liquid to a solid because of the cold. *Water will freeze into ice.* **froze, frozen**

frog | frôg | —*plural* **frogs.** A small green animal with webbed feet. *A frog will live near water. Frogs can jump high.*

from | frŭm | or | frŏm | —**1.** Starting at.
Bill: *I just flew in from South America.*
Jill: *Wow! Your arms must be tired!*
2. Out of. *Did you get that from some joke book?*

full | fŏol | —Holding all that it can hold. *When rivers get too full, they sometimes flood.*

fun | fŭn | —A good time. *Everyone had lots of fun at Nat's circus party.*

funny | fŭn ē | —**1.** Causing laughter. *Alice told a funny joke in school today.* **2.** Strange. *Miss Lea gave Alice a funny look.*

Gg Gg Gg

gain | gān | —To increase. *How much weight did your puppy gain?* **gained, gaining**

game | gām | —*plural* **games.** A contest played with rules. *Chess is a game for two people to play.*

gave | gāv | —Handed over. *I gave my brother colored pencils for his birthday.* Past of the word **give.**

girl | gûrl | —*plural* **girls.** A female child. *That girl is my sister.*

give | gĭv | —To hand over. *What do you give an elephant that has a lot of clothes? (Another trunk.)* **gave, giving**

glimpse | glĭmps | —**1.** *plural* **glimpses.** A quick look. *Did you get a glimpse of the pretty bird?* **2.** To get a quick look. *I was able to glimpse the clown in the car.* **glimpsed, glimpsing**

go | gō | —To move from one place to another. *Morris had to go home early. He has chicken pox.* **went, going**

goat | gōt | —*plural* **goats.** An animal with short horns and a beard. *Why is it hard to talk when there is a goat around? (Because it keeps butting in.)*

gold | gōld | —A yellow metal. *Gold is used for making coins and jewelry.*

good | go͝od | —Fine, excellent. *It is a good idea to get to school on time.*

got | gŏt | —Received. *Billy got a pogo stick for his birthday.* Past of the word **get.**

green | grēn | —*plural* **greens.** The color of growing plants. *Why do elephants wear green sneakers? (So they can hide in the grass.)*

grow | grō | —**1.** To get bigger. *Puppies grow into dogs.* **2.** To plant and care for. *We grow tomatoes and lettuce in our garden.* **grew, growing**

guilt | gĭlt | —**1.** A feeling of shame for having done something wrong. *I felt guilt after I hit my friend with a ball.* **2.** The fact of having done something wrong. *He admitted his guilt for telling a lie.*

Hh Hh Hh

habit | hăb ĭt | —*plural* **habits.** Something that a person does so often that it is done without thinking. *I have a habit of brushing my teeth before I go to bed.*

had | hăd | —Owned. *Harry's gerbil had a fancy cage. (But it escaped anyway!)* Past of the word **have.**

hand | hănd | —**1.** *plural* **hands.** The part of the arm below the wrist. *There are four fingers and a thumb on your hand.* **2.** To do something with the hand. *Please hand me a peach.* **handed, handing**

happy | hăp ē | —Glad. *Mike is happy that he found his glove.*

harmful | härm fəl | —Causing hurt; bad for. *Not getting enough exercise can be harmful to a person's health.*

207

has | hăz | —Owns. *What* **has** *four legs and a trunk? (A mouse on vacation.)* Part of the word **have**.

haul | hôl | —**1.** To carry or move from one place to another. *The truck will* **haul** *away the trash.* **2.** To pull or drag something heavy. *We had to* **haul** *the mattress up the stairs.*

have | hăv | —**1.** To own. *Harry and Lou* **have** *four gerbils.* **2.** To go through. *The gerbils* **have** *fun running through the tunnels.* **had, having**

he | hē | —A boy or a man. ***He*** *became the king.*

heat | hēt | —**1.** Warmth. *The* **heat** *from the sun feels good after swimming.* **2.** To warm. *Please* **heat** *the car. I'm freezing!* **heated, heating**

help | hĕlp | —To do something useful. *Would you* **help** *me move these boxes, please?* **helped, helping**

helper | hĕl pər | —*plural* **helpers.** Someone who does something useful. *Mort will work with me teaching swimming. He will be my* **helper.**

her | hûr | —**1.** Belonging to a female. *Janet gave* **her** *brother a red T-shirt.* **2.** A girl, a woman, or a female animal. *I saw* **her** *in the store.*

hid | hĭd | —Put or went out of sight. *They ran and* **hid.** *We couldn't find them anywhere!* Past of the word **hide**.

hide | hīd | —To put or to go out of sight. *Why do elephants* **hide** *behind trees? (To scare ants.)* **hid, hiding**

high | hī | —Far above the ground. *The balloon floated* **high** *up in the sky.*

hill | hĭl | —*plural* **hills.** A raised part of the earth. A mound. *Why do giraffes roll down* **hills**? *(They can't roll up them very well!)*

him | hĭm | —A boy, a man, or a male animal. *Janet gave* **him** *a T-shirt. She told him to wear it to school.*

his | hĭz | —Belonging to a male. *Janet's brother wears* **his** *red shirt all the time.*

hold | hōld | —**1.** To keep back. *We will need a heavy stone to* **hold** *this door open.* **2.** To keep in the hand. *Will you* **hold** *my books while I open the door?* **held, holding**

hole | hōl | —*plural* **holes.** An opening. *A woodchuck lives in a* **hole** *in the ground.*

home | hōm | —*plural* **homes.** The place where a person or animal lives. *A bee's* **home** *is in a hive.*

hop | hŏp | —To move up and down quickly. *We like to* **hop** *over the cracks in the sidewalk.* **hopped, hopping**

hope | hōp | —To wish. *I* **hope** *I remember my spelling words today!* **hoped, hoping**

hopeful | hōp fəl | —Having, feeling, or showing hope. *We are* **hopeful** *that our team will win today.*

horse | hôrs | —*plural* **horses.** A large, strong animal with hoofs. *A horse has very good ears. But horses do not see well.*

hot | hŏt | —Very warm. *There are many hot days in summer.*

house | hous | —*plural* **houses.** A place where people or animals live. *Five people live at my house.*

how | hou | —**1.** In what way? *How do you keep cool at a ball game? (Sit near a fan!)* **2.** For what amount? *How much do these tickets cost?*

Ii Ii Ii Ii Ii Ii

ice | īs | —*plural* **ices.** Frozen water. *In winter, it is fun to skate on the ice on the pond.*

idea | ī dē ə | —*plural* **ideas.** A thought. *I have a good idea for a party. Let's have a square dance!*

important | ĭm pôr tənt | —Serious. *It is important that you know your address.*

inside | ĭn sīd | —Into. *Go inside the house if it rains.*

insult | ĭn sŭlt | —**1.** *plural* **insults.** Rude words or actions that hurt someone's feelings. *It was an insult when you did not wave to me.* **2.** To hurt the feelings of someone by speaking or acting rudely toward that person. *I try not to insult anyone.* **insulted, insulting**

Jj Jj Jj Jj Jj

jar | jär | —*plural* **jars.** A glass with a lid. *Ellie gave us a jar of jam she had made.*

jet | jĕt | —*plural* **jets. 1.** A stream squirted from a small hole. *He got me wet with a jet from his water pistol!* **2.** An aircraft. *I put him on a jet to visit his grandmother.*

job | jŏb | —*plural* **jobs.** Work. *I would like to have a job in an ice cream store.*

jog | jŏg | —To run at a slow, steady trot. *He likes to jog to school.* **jogged, jogging**

joke | jōk | —**1.** *plural* **jokes.** A funny story. *Alice keeps us laughing with her jokes.* **2.** To tell funny stories. *Sometimes Alice jokes too much.* **joked, joking**

jump | jŭmp | —To leap. *The impala is an animal that can jump 30 feet.* **jumped, jumping**

jumper | jŭmp ər | —*plural* **jumpers.** Someone who leaps. *You have to be a good jumper to get across that wide brook.*

209

just | jŭst | —Exactly. *This shirt is just the right size for me.*

Kk   Kk   Kk

keep | kēp | —**1.** To own. *You may keep this toy.* **2.** To stay. *Please keep off the grass.* **3.** To store. *I keep my toys in a chest.* **kept, keeping**

kept | kĕpt | —Continued in the same way. *The children kept playing, even though it was time to go home.*

key | kē | —*plural* **keys.** A piece of metal used to open a lock. *Do you have the key to my toy chest? I can't open it.*

knock | nŏk | —To strike, hit, or rap with the fist or something hard. *Just knock on the door and I will let you in.* **knocked, knocking**

know | nō | —To be sure. *How do you know when there's an elephant in your bathtub? (You can smell the wet peanuts.)* **knew, knowing**

Ll Ll Ll Ll Ll

land | lănd | —**1.** *plural* **lands.** The part of the earth not covered by water. *You cannot see land from the middle of the big lake.* **2.** To arrive by ship or plane. *They will land at the airport at four o'clock.* **landed, landing**

last | lăst | —**1.** Final. *The last letter in the alphabet is z.* **2.** Just before now. *I have been practicing for the last two hours!* **3.** To continue a long time. *I hope my legs last until the race is over.* **lasted, lasting**

leap | lēp | —**1.** *plural* **leaps.** A jump. *That frog took a huge leap and jumped out of the pond!* **2.** To jump. *The salmon is a fish that can leap up waterfalls!* **leaped, leaping**

liberty | lĭb ər tē | —*plural* **liberties.** Freedom. *The whale was given its liberty.*

license | lī səns | —*plural* **licenses.** A paper or card showing that the law says a person may do something. *My sister just got her driver's license.*

lie | lī | —**1.** To be in a flat position. *Why does an elephant lie on its back? (To trip robins that are flying too low.)* **2.** To say something that is not true. *Don't lie to me about elephants!* **lied, lying**

like | līk | —**1.** Almost the same. *People say I look like a movie star.* **2.** To enjoy. *I would like to act in movies.* **liked, liking**

lining | lī nĭng | —*plural* **linings.** A coating or covering for the inside of something. *Often a coat will have a fur lining to make it warmer.*

lion | līˌ ən | —*plural* **lions.** A large, powerful animal related to the cat. *The **lion** stood up and gave a loud roar.*

live | lĭv | —**1.** To be alive. *Fish cannot **live** out of water.* **2.** To stay, as at home. *What would it be like to **live** in a tree house?* **lived, living**

lobster | lŏbˌ stər | —*plural* **lobsters.** A sea animal that has a hard shell and five pairs of legs. The front pair are large claws. *I like to eat **lobster** tail.*

long | lông | —Great in distance, time, or length.
    Boy: *I'd like to buy that dog, but its legs are too short.*
    Clerk: *What do you mean? They're **long** enough to reach the ground.*
    longer, longest *The collie's legs are **longer** than the basset's legs. The greyhound's legs are the **longest** of all these dogs.*

look | lŏok | —To see. ***Look** at that strange bird!* **looked, looking**

lost | lŏst | —Missing. *Ann's pet turtle is **lost**. Have you seen it?*

love | lŭv | —**1.** *plural* **loves.** A strong liking. *Give them my **love**.* **2.** To feel a strong liking. *Burt's uncle **loves** to cook.* **loved, loving**

lunch | lŭnch | —*plural* **lunches.** The meal eaten at midday. *The archer fish gets its **lunch** by shooting bugs with drops of water.*

Mm   Mm   Mm

mail | māl | —*plural* **mails.** Letters and packages sent through the post office. ***Mail** is not delivered on Sundays.*

man | măn | —*plural* **men.** A grown male person. *The **man** with Jessie is her father.*

many | mĕnˌ ē | —A large number. *Brad has **many** friends.*

mark | märk | —*plural* **marks.** **1.** A spot on something. *A wet glass will leave a **mark** on a table.* **2.** A grade given in school. *I got good **marks** on my report card.*

matter | mătˌ ər | —**1.** To be of importance. *It doesn't **matter** if we go sledding before or after lunch.* **2.** Trouble or problem. *What's the **matter** with your foot?*

211

maybe | mā bē | —Perhaps, possibly. *Maybe Miss Lea will forget to give us the math test tomorrow.*

mean | mēn | —**1.** Unkind. *They were* *mean to laugh at Andy's mistakes.* **2.** The idea of. *A dictionary tells what words mean.* **meant, meaning**

melon | mĕl ən | —*plural* **melons.** A large sweet fruit that grows on a vine and has a hard skin. *A watermelon is a kind of melon.*

memory | mĕm ə rē | —*plural* **memories.** **1.** The power to remember things. *Elephants have a good memory.* **2.** Something that is remembered. *One memory I have from this year is the field trip to the zoo.*

men | mĕn | —Plural of **man.** *The men sang loudly in their deep voices.*

method | mĕth əd | —*plural* **methods.** A way of doing something. *I learned a new method of coloring a picture.*

mine | mīn | —Belonging to me. *This sled is mine. I got it for my birthday.*

mold | mōld | —**1.** *plural* **molds.** A form with space inside that is used to make something into a special shape. *Pour water into a mold. The water will take the shape of the mold when it freezes.* **2.** To make into a special shape. *In art we tried to mold clay.*

monster | mŏn stər | —*plural* **monsters.** **1.** A scary creature that is not real. *A picture of the monster was in the book.* **2.** A very large animal, plant, or thing. *The huge shark may seem like a monster to other fish.*

moon | mōōn | —*plural* **moons.** A body that moves around a planet. *Our moon moves around the Earth 13 times in a year.*

more | mōr | —**1.** Greater in amount. *There is more water in the world than there is land.* **2.** An additional amount. *May I have some more milk, please?*

most | most | —Greatest number or amount. *The team that scores the most points wins.*

mother | mŭth ər | —*plural* **mothers.** A female parent. *What did the mother ghost tell her son in the car? (Fasten your sheet belt.)*

mouse | mous | —*plural* **mice.** A small, gray animal with soft fur. *A mouse is about seven inches long. Mice have long, thin tails.*

much | mŭch | —A lot. *Greta is much taller than her twin sister.*

mud | mŭd | —Soft and sticky earth. *Mud on your shoes makes a mess in the house!*

must | mŭst | —**1.** Almost certain to, should. *Her coat is gone, so she must have left.* **2.** Have to. *I must practice the piano every day.*

my | mī | —Belonging to me. *My birthday is in December.*

Nn   Nn   Nn

nail | nāl | —*plural* **nails. 1.** The growth at the end of a finger or toe. *Finger***nails** *protect the ends of your fingers.* **2.** A thin, pointed metal pin. *You can fasten pieces of wood together with a* **nail***.*
Jim: *I hit the* **nail** *with a hammer.*
Dad: *Good work!*
Jim: *No. It was my thumb***nail***.*

name | nām | —**1.** *plural* **names.** A word by which a person or thing is called. *A good* **name** *for a poodle dog is "Curly."* **2.** To give a name to. *What shall we* **name** *our cat?* **named, naming**

napkin | năp kĭn | —*plural* **napkins.** A piece of cloth or paper used at meals to keep clothes clean and to wipe the mouth and hands. *I put my* **napkin** *in my lap to catch spills.*

new | nōō | —**1.** Recently made, grown, or invented. *Every year birds grow* **new** *feathers.* **2.** Never used. *We are going to put up* **new** *birdhouses this spring.*

next | nĕkst | —**1.** Nearest or closest to. *Her puppy slept right* **next** *to her.* **2.** Coming right after. *Turn to the* **next** *page.*

nine | nīn | —*plural* **nines.** The number after eight, written 9. *The number after* **nine** *is ten.*

no | nō | —I do not agree. Opposite of yes. **No,** *thank you. I would not like any more spinach.*

nose | nōz | —*plural* **noses.** The part of the body used for breathing. *The elephant uses its trunk as a* **nose.** *(It is its arm and hand, too!)*

not | nŏt | —No. *Morris is* **not** *in school today. He is at home.*

now | nou | —At the present time. *May we go out and play* **now**? *It has stopped raining.*

numb | nŭm | —Not able to feel or move. *My face is* **numb** *from the cold.* **number, numbest** *My fingers are* **number** *than my toes. My nose is the* **numbest** *of all.*

Oo   Oo   Oo

of | ŭv | or | ŏv | —**1.** Made from. *Many birds live in nests made* **of** *twigs.* **2.** Holding. *May I borrow your box* **of** *crayons?*

off | ôf | —**1.** Away from. *How do you keep a dog* **off** *the road? (Put it in a barking lot!)* **2.** Removed. *Don't take Rusty's collar* **off.** *He may run away.*

old | ōld | —Has lived a long time; not young. *The big elm tree is very* **old.** **older, oldest** *It is* **older** *than the pine tree. It is the* **oldest** *tree in the neighborhood.*

213

on | ŏn | or | ôn |—**1.** Upon, touching. *Please put your coat* **on** *a hanger, not* **on** *the floor!* **2.** Growing upon. *Billy's new sneakers gave him blisters* **on** *his feet.*

one | wŭn |—**1.** *plural* **ones.** The first and the smallest number, written 1. **One** *comes before two.* **2.** Single person or thing. *When two teams play a game, only* **one** *can win.*

open | ō pən |—Opposite of shut. *Why is a piano so hard to* **open***? (All the keys are inside.)* **opened, opening**

or | or |—Word that shows you may choose. *Shall we go to the movies* **or** *stay home?*

orange | ôr ĭnj |—*plural* **oranges. 1.** A round, dark-yellow fruit. *An* **orange** *is good to eat.* **Oranges** *give juice, too.* **2.** The color of this fruit. *My bike is* **orange***. Cars can see me on the road.*

orchard | ôr chərd |—*plural* **orchards.** A place where fruit trees are grown. *My class picked many apples at the apple* **orchard***.*

organ | ôr gən |—*plural* **organs.** A large musical instrument made of long and short pipes. The pipes make sounds when air is blown through them. A person pushes keys and pedals to make the air blow. *It takes hands and feet to play an* **organ***.*

other | ŭth ər |—Different. *She went into the* **other** *room.*

our | our |—Belonging to us. *This is* **our** *garden. We take care of it all summer.*

out | out |—Not inside. *The cat was* **out** *all night.*

over | ō vər |—**1.** Across. *Let's see if we can jump* **over** *the river.* **2.** On top of. *No. Let's put a board* **over** *the water instead.* **3.** Above. *I think the water might be* **over** *our heads!*

owl | oul |—*plural* **owls.** A bird with a flat face and hooked beak. **Owls** *sleep during the day and hunt at night.*

own | ōn |—To have as a belonging. *Do you* **own** *the dog that is barking in the yard, or does she belong to someone else?* **owned, owning**

ox | ŏks |—*plural* **oxen.** A male animal of the cattle family. *A strong* **ox** *is a useful farm animal.*

Pp   Pp   Pp

pail | pāl |—*plural* **pails.** A bucket. *The* **pail** *of water was so heavy that we dropped it.*

paint | pānt |—**1.** *plural* **paints.** Something to color with. *My favorite* **paint** *color is purple.* **2.** To cover something with paint. *Please don't* **paint** *our front porch purple!* **painted, painting**

painter | pān tər |—*plural* **painters.** Someone who puts colors on cloth, paper, or buildings. *The* **painters** *are working on our house. They are* **painting** *it white.*

party | pär tē | —*plural* **parties**. People getting together for fun. *May I invite eight people to my party? Birthday parties are fun!*

peach | pēch | —*plural* **peaches**. A sweet, juicy fruit. *A peach tastes very good.*

pedal | pĕd l | —**1.** *plural* **pedals**. A part that is moved by the foot to work something. *I put a new pedal on my bike.* **2.** To use or work a pedal. *It is hard to pedal up the hill.*

penny | pĕn ē | —*plural* **pennies**. One cent. *A penny is made of copper.*
Granddad: *If you're good, I'll give you a shiny, new penny!*
Girl: *Thanks, but haven't you got a dirty, old dollar, instead?*

people | pē pəl | —Human beings. *Many people watched the parade.*

pick | pĭk | —**1.** To choose. *Did you pick the brown puppy or the black-and-white one?* **2.** To gather. *He went out to the garden to pick flowers.* **picked, picking**

pie | pī | —*plural* **pies**. Fruit, custard, or meat in a crust.
Mom: *There were two pieces of pie. Now there's only one left. Can you explain?*
Son: *I guess I didn't see the other piece.*

play | plā | —**1.** *plural* **plays**. A story acted on a stage. *I hope I get a good part in the play.* **2.** To take part in a game. *It takes 22 people to play football.* **3.** To have fun. *Will you play at my house?* **played, playing**

please | plēz | —Be so kind as to. *Please come to the store with me.*

pond | pŏnd | —*plural* **ponds**. A small body of water. *A pond is a good place to go swimming.*

profit | prŏf ĭt | —*plural* **profits**. The money that a business makes after all its costs are paid. *We spent five dollars on lemonade, cups, and sugar. We made ten dollars selling lemonade. So our profit was five dollars.*

prop | prŏp | —To keep from falling by putting something under or against. *I propped the stuffed bear up with a pillow.* **propped, propping**

pull | pool | —To tug. *A strong engine can pull a long train.* **pulled, pulling**

pupil[1] | pyoo pəl | —*plural* **pupils**. A person who has a teacher. *The pupil learned how to add.*

pupil[2] | pyoo pəl | —*plural* **pupils**. The black opening in the center of the eye where light enters. *The pupil of his eye was wide.*

puppy | pŭp ē | —*plural* **puppies**. A young dog. *What kind of puppy doesn't bark? (A mud puppy. A mud puppy is a kind of lizard.)*

put | poot | —To set something in a place. *Please put the crayons away when you are through drawing.* **put, putting**

215

Rr Rr Rr Rr

rain | rān | —1. *plural* **rains.** Water that falls from clouds. *Animals and plants cannot live without rain.* 2. To fall in drops from clouds. *I wish it would never rain on weekends.* **rained, raining**

recess | rē sĕs | or | rĭ sĕs | —*plural* **recesses.** A short time for rest or play. *Recesses at our school are a lot of fun.*

rest | rĕst | —1. What is left. *If you will wash half the dishes, I will do the rest.* 2. To be still. *After we do the dishes, we can rest.* **rested, resting**

rhyme | rīm | —1. *plural* **rhymes.** Sounds that are alike heard in words or at the ends of lines. *Ball is a rhyme for tall.* 2. To make words sound alike. *Old rhymes with cold.* **rhymed, rhyming**

ride | rīd | —To be carried. *It is exciting to ride on a roller coaster.* **rode, riding**

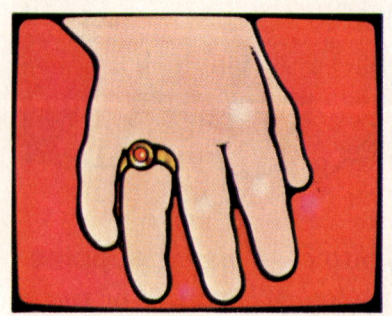

ring | rĭng | —1. *plural* **rings.** Something to wear on a finger. *Clara almost lost her gold ring.* 2. To make a loud, clear sound. *Did the alarm ring?* **rang, ringing**

road | rōd | —*plural* **roads.** A street. *Is this the road to town?*

rock | rŏk | —1. *plural* **rocks.** Solid stone. *Much of the earth is rock.* 2. To move gently back and forth. *A baby goes to sleep when you rock it.* **rocked, rocking**

roll | rōl | —1. *plural* **rolls.** A bun. *These rolls are good. Mindy baked them.* 2. To move by turning over and over. *Catch the ball! It's going to roll down the hill!* **rolled, rolling**

room | rōōm | —*plural* **rooms.** A space in a building. *The best room in the house is my room!*

rope | rōp | —*plural* **ropes.** Heavy string. *We used a rope to tie up our boat during the storm.*

round | round | —Shaped like a ball. *My baby brother is as round as an apple.*

run | rŭn | —To move quickly. *The cheetah is an animal that can run very fast.* **ran, running**

runner | rŭn ər | —*plural* **runners.** Someone who moves quickly. *The best runner will win the race.*

Ss   Ss   Ss

said | sĕd | —Spoke. *I said I would like to come to his party.* Past of the word **say.**

sail | sāl | —1. *plural* **sails.** A piece of cloth spread to catch the wind. *A big sail can make a boat move quickly.* 2. To move smoothly. *Boats look pretty as they sail on the river.* **sailed, sailing**

sang | săng | —Made music by using the voice. *The birds sang at five o'clock and woke me.* Past of the word **sing.**

saw | sô |—Looked at. *Mildred saw her friends coming out of school.* Past of the word **see.**

say | sā |—To speak. *What do you say when you meet a two-headed monster? ("Hello, hello.")* **said, saying**

says | sĕz |—Speaks. *He says the party started an hour ago!* Part of the word **say.**

school | skōol |—*plural* **schools.** A place of teaching and learning.
Mom: *How did you do on your first day of school?*
Child: *Not so well, I guess. I have to go back tomorrow.*

see | sē |—To look at. *Mildred can see the school from her house.* **saw, seeing**

send | sĕnd |—**1.** To mail. *Don't forget to send us a postcard.* **2.** To cause to go. *I'll send Chris to the post office to get the mail.* **sent, sending**

seven | sĕv ən |—*plural* **sevens.** The number after six, written 7. *May was seven years old in May.*

she | shē |—A woman or girl. *Nell says that she will go with us.*

shelf | shĕlf |—*plural* **shelves.** A flat, narrow piece of wood or metal to put things on. *Mimi keeps her tall books on a shelf over her desk.*

ship | shĭp |—*plural* **ships. 1.** A large boat. *My family came to America by ship.* **2.** An airplane or spacecraft. *No one believed Rick had seen a ship from space.*

shop | shŏp |—**1.** *plural* **shops.** A place to buy things. *Sue's favorite place on Main Street is the ice cream shop.* **2.** To look for things in stores. *She likes to shop for birthday presents.* **shopped, shopping**

shopper | shŏp pər |—*plural* **shoppers.** Someone who visits stores. *It is wise to be a careful shopper.*

short | shôrt |—**1.** Not far. *I live near school. It is only a short walk.* **2.** Not tall. *I am too short to reach the top shelf.*

should | shŏŏd |—Have a duty. *People should take good care of their pets.*

side | sīd |—*plural* **sides. 1.** A part of something. *Ed can kick a football to the other side of the field.* **2.** One of two or more groups. *I hope I will be playing on Ed's side in the game.*

sister | sĭs tər |—*plural* **sisters.** A girl or woman with the same parents as another. *Marty has a baby sister.*

six | sĭks | —*plural* **sixes.** The number after five, written 6. *How do you fit **six** elephants in a car? (Two in front, three in back, one in the glove compartment.)*

skunk | skŭnk | —*plural* **skunks.** A small black-and-white striped animal with a bushy tail. *A **skunk** protects itself with a strong, bad-smelling spray.*

sky | skī | —*plural* **skies.** The upper air. *Do those clouds in the **sky** mean rain?*

small | smôl | —Little. *Children start out **small**. Then they grow big!*

snail | snāl | —*plural* **snails.** A slow animal with a soft body and a spiral shell. *We saw a **snail** on the sand at the beach.*

snore | snôr | —*plural* **snores.** A loud noise made while asleep. *If you hear a **snore**, you know that someone is sound asleep.*

snow | snō | —*plural* **snows.** Soft white flakes of frozen water. ***Snow** covered the ground like a white blanket.*

so | sō | —**1.** To such a point. *Alice's joke was **so** funny we could not stop laughing.* **2.** Therefore. *Morris was sick, **so** he missed school today.*

sold | sōld | —Traded for money. *Peter **sold** his car. He needed money for college.* Past of the word **sell.**

song | sông | —*plural* **songs.** A piece of music. *"Jingle Bells" is an easy **song** to sing.*

soon | sōon | —A short time from now. *The clouds are going away. It will stop raining **soon**.*

sound | sound | —*plural* **sounds.** A noise. *An owl can fly without making a **sound**.*

sponge | spŭnj | —*plural* **sponges. 1.** A cleaning pad that soaks up water easily. *I used a **sponge** to clean the tub.* **2.** A water animal with a soft body that has holes and soaks up water. *I have never seen a live **sponge**.*

spot | spŏt | —**1.** *plural* **spots.** A small mark. *What could have made that ugly **spot** on the rug?* **2.** A place. *We always keep our ink in the same **spot** in the desk.* **3.** To make a mark on something. *Nothing **spots** worse than ink!* **spotted, spotting**

spring | sprĭng | —*plural* **springs.** The season between winter and summer. *I love when the flowers bloom in **spring**.*

star | stär | —*plural* **stars. 1.** The sun and other bright heavenly bodies. *The **star** we see the best at night is the North **Star**.* **2.** A leading actor or actress, athlete, or musician. *My brother is a super drummer. I think he will be a rock **star**!*

stay | stā | —To remain in one place, wait. *Please **stay** in your seats until the bell rings.* **stayed, staying**

218

stone | stōn | —*plural* **stones.** A small rock. *Don't trip on that **stone** in the path!*

stood | sto͝od | —Was on his or her feet. *The horses **stood** in the shade.* Past of the word **stand.**

stop | stŏp | —To finish, end. *You may **stop** studying at 7:00.* **stopped, stopping**

store | stôr | —*plural* **stores.** A place where things are sold. *There are many different kinds of **stores** in a city.*

storm | stôrm | —*plural* **storms.** Very bad weather. *It is best to stay inside during a **storm**.*

story | stôr ē | —*plural* **stories.** A tale. *The **story** of "Peter Pan" is exciting.*

street | strēt | —*plural* **streets.** A road in a city or town. *The **street** in front of a house is noisy sometimes.*

strut | strŭt | —To walk like a very important person. *The winners of the game **strut** around the room.* **strutted, strutting** *They **strutted** when they won yesterday. I hope they will not be **strutting** tomorrow.*

such | sŭch | —Very. *Those are **such** pretty flowers.*

summer | sŭm ər | —*plural* **summers.** The season of the year between spring and autumn. *We had fun at the beach last **summer**.*

sun | sŭn | —*plural* **suns.** The closest star to Earth. *Earth and eight other planets move around the **sun**. The **sun** gives them heat and light.*

swim | swĭm | —To move through the water by using arms and legs. *You should know how to **swim** before going out in a boat.* **swam, swimming**

Tt   Tt   Tt   Tt

tail | tāl | —*plural* **tails.** The rear part of something. *The friendly dragon was slow and Lisa stepped on its **tail** by mistake.*

talk | tôk | —To speak words. *What is the best way to **talk** to a monster? (Long distance.)* **talked, talking**

ten | tĕn | —*plural* tens. The number after nine, written 10. ***Ten** pennies equal a dime.*

than | thăn | —Compared with. *Is a pound of books heavier **than** a pound of feathers? (No. They weigh the same!)*

thank | thăngk | —To say that one is grateful. *Don't forget to **thank** Uncle Elroy for the nice orange shirt.* **thanked, thanking**

that | thăt | —**1.** Something or someone at a distance. ***That** man over there is my uncle, not this one.* **2.** Used to connect words in a sentence. *I am afraid **that** he is lost.*

219

the | *thē* | or | *thə* |—A definite thing. *Who broke **the** window? There's a football in **the** living room!*

them | *thĕm* |—People, animals, or things spoken about. *I asked **them** for a ride. I waited for **them** a long time.*

these | *thēz* |—Plural of **this**. ***These** spelling words are certainly easy!*

they | *thā* |—People other than yourself. Al: *How did Jim and Suzie get hurt playing Pin the Tail on the Donkey?* Pal:***They** used a live donkey!*

thing | *thĭng* |—*plural* **things**. An object that may not need to be named. *What is this **thing** used for?*

think | *thĭngk* |—To use the mind. ***Think** about what you are going to say before you say it.* **thought, thinking**

this | *thĭs* |—*plural* **these**. Something here and not there. *Anna, look at **this** spaceship.*

three | *thrē* |—*plural* **threes**. The number after two, written 3. *Two plus one equals **three**.*

tie | *tī* |—**1.** *plural* **ties**. A necktie. *Andy spilled something on his **tie**.* **2.** An equal score. *Andy and Martha's pie-eating contest ended in a **tie**.* **3.** To attach something with string or rope. *Martha tried to **tie** Andy's shoelaces together.* **tied, tying**

tiger | *tī gər* |—*plural* **tigers**. A large wild cat that lives in Asia. ***Tigers** have brown-yellow fur and black stripes.* Will: *What would you do if a man-eating **tiger** were chasing you?* Jill: *Nothing. I'm a girl.*

tiny | *tī nē* |—Very small. *Greta wants a **tiny** piano for her doll house.*

to | *tōō* |—**1.** Toward. *The bus broke down on the way **to** school.* **2.** For. *It is important **to** me.*

today | *tə dā* |—This day. ***Today** is my birthday!*

told | *tōld* |—Said; spoke. *We all **told** about our vacations in school yesterday.* Past of the word **tell**.

too | *tōō* |—Also. *In a thunderstorm, there is rain and lightning. Sometimes there is hail, **too**.*

took | *tŏŏk* |—**1.** Grasped and held. *The bus driver **took** our tickets.* **2.** Traveled on. *We **took** the bus to the ball game.* Past of the word **take**.

tooth | *tōōth* |—*plural* **teeth**. A hard, white bony growth in the mouth. ***Teeth** are used for chewing.* Jenny: *Do you use **tooth**paste?* Benny: *Not unless I have a loose **tooth**.*

top | tŏp | —*plural* **tops.** The highest part. *What time is it when an elephant sits on **top** of a fence? (Time to get a new fence.)*

torch | tôrch | —*plural* **torches. 1.** A burning light on a stick that can be carried. *The parade was at night. Dad carried a **torch**.* **2.** A tool that shoots out fire. *She used a **torch** to make the metal soft.*

town | toun | —*plural* **towns.** A group of houses and stores. *A **town** is larger than a village. **Towns** are smaller than cities.*

train | trān | —**1.** *plural* **trains.** An engine with a line of cars after it. *We take the **train** to visit our cousins.* **2.** To teach. *When you have a dog, you must **train** it to mind you.* **trained, training**

tread | trĕd | —To walk. *Please do not **tread** on the grass.* **trod, trodden** or **trod**

trick | trĭk | —**1.** *plural* **tricks.** A thing that fools someone. *On April Fool's Day, I played a **trick**. (I told my mother there was an elephant in the bathtub.)* **2.** To fool someone. *I will **trick** her again next year. (I will tell her there is a lion in the yard.)* **tricked, tricking**

truck | trŭk | —*plural* **trucks.** A car used to carry heavy loads. *Oranges are sent by **truck** from Florida north to Vermont.*

try | trī | —**1.** To work hard at something. ***Try** not to make a mistake on your spelling test!* **2.** To test something. *Would you like to **try** my bike?* **tried, trying**

two | tōō | —*plural* **twos.** The number after one, written 2. *What **two** things can you never eat at supper? (Breakfast and lunch.)*

tying | tī ĭng | —Fastening with a string or rope. *Eddie is **tying** the string around his finger.* A form of the word **tie.**

Uu   Uu   Uu

under | ŭn dər | --—Beneath. *Pat and I walked **under** my umbrella.*

up | ŭp | —From low to high. *What's red and goes **up** and down? (A tomato in an elevator.)*

us | ŭs | —You and me. *May Roger leave his hamsters with **us** over the summer?*

use | yōōz | —To put into service. *We **use** the subway to get to Mom's office.* **used, using**

van | văn | —*plural* **vans.** A covered truck or wagon. *He took the children to the picnic in his van.*

very | věr ē | —Extremely. *Dinosaurs lived on earth a very long time ago.*

village | vĭl ĭj | —*plural* **villages.** A group of houses and stores in the country. *A village is smaller than a town.*

voice | vois | —*plural* **voices.** The sound that comes from a mouth when you speak or sing. *I think that is Mom's voice calling us for supper.*

wait | wāt | —To stay until something happens. *We had to wait a long time for the movie to begin.* **waited, waiting**

walk | wôk | —To move ahead by foot.
Man: *Do these stairs take you to the third floor?*
Joker: *No. You'll have to walk!*
walked, walking

want | wŏnt | or | wônt | —To wish for. *People want peace in the world.* **wanted, wanting**

was | wŏz | or | wŭz | —*Blackbeard was a famous pirate.*

wash | wŏsh | or | wôsh | —To clean with water or other liquid and often with soap. *You should always wash your hands before you eat.* **washed, washing**

we | wē | —You and I. *We had fun at the circus.*

week | wēk | —*plural* **weeks.** Seven days, starting with Sunday and ending Saturday. *My cousins are going to visit us for a week.*

well | wěl | —**1.** *plural* **wells.** Deep hole dug in the ground. *We get wonderful water from the well in our yard.* **2.** Pleasing, good. *Your homework was done very well.*

went | wěnt | —Moved from one place to another. *Linda went to get the bike.* Past of the word **go.**

whale | wāl | —*plural* **whales.** A large air-breathing sea animal. *A whale is a mammal, not a fish.*

what | wŏt | —Which thing. *What is gray and white and red all over? (A sunburned elephant.)*

when | wěn | —At what time. *When will you be home?*

white | wīt | —The lightest of all colors. *All the trees and houses were covered with white snow.*

who | hōō | —**1.** Which person. *Who is the man ringing our doorbell?* **2.** That. *He is the person who teaches music at school.*

why | wī | —For what reason. *Why do people sneeze? (To get rid of something that could hurt their breathing.)*

will | wĭl |—Going to do something in the future. *I will come to your house after school.*

wind | wĭnd |—*plural* **winds.** Air that blows. *It's fun to fly our kites in the wind.*

wish | wĭsh |—**1.** *plural* **wishes.** A strong desire. *My wish is that it will not rain on Saturday.* **2.** To want. *I wish that we could go to the parade on Saturday.* **wished, wishing**

with | wĭth |—**1.** Having. *My favorite shirt is the one with buttons on the collar.* **2.** In the company of. *Will you come fishing with me?*

would | wŏod |—**1.** Willing to. *Amy, would you get my football out of the bushes?* **2.** Was going to. *Amy said she would return my football after lunch.* Past of the word **will.**

write | rīt |—To make words with pencil, chalk, or other tools. *Meg likes to write in her diary every day.* **wrote, writing**

writer | rī tər |—*plural* **writers.** Someone who writes stories or poems. *I like to read all of Meg's stories. She is a good writer.*

yellow | yĕl ō |—*plural* **yellows.** The color of a ripe lemon. *Owls have big yellow eyes that see in the dark.*

yes | yĕs |—I agree. Opposite of no. *Yes, I would like to go to the circus!*

you | yōō |—Person or persons spoken to. Kate: *How did you get that bump on your head?*
Nate: *Diving.*
Kate: *Where were you diving?*
Nate: *In the bathtub.*

Zz   Zz   Zz

zebra | zē brə |—*plural* **zebras.** A black-and-white striped animal that looks like a horse. *Zebras live in Africa.*

zero | zîr ō | or | zē rō |—*plural* **zeros** or **zeroes.** A number, written 0. *The number zero stands for "nothing." There are three zeros in 1,000.*

zoo | zōo|—*plural* **zoos.** A place where animals are kept. *You can learn a lot about wild animals by visiting a zoo.*

THE CHECKPOINT
Study Plan

When you have finished a Checkpoint page and you know that you have the correct answers, use the Checkpoint page and this Study Plan to test yourself.

★ Cover your answers to the Checkpoint page with a piece of paper. Number the paper 1 through 16. For each spelling clue, do steps 1, 2, and 3.

1 Read the clue and say the answer.

2 Spell the answer aloud.

3 Write the answer.

★ Uncover your first answers and do steps 4, 5, and 6.

4 Check your answers.

5 Circle the number of each misspelled word.

6 Write the correct spelling next to each incorrect word.

★ To study, cover your answers again, and fold the paper so that only the numbers show. For each circled number, repeat steps 1 through 6.

224

Review Test for Lesson 6

Directions: Read each sentence. Choose the correct spelling of the missing word. Mark your answer on the answer sheet by filling in the circle beside the correct letter. Do not write on this test.

Example:

> 1. The ___ barked loudly.
>   A. dawg
>   B. dog
>   C. dogg
>   D. dag

1. What do ___ want?
   A. ewe
   B. yoo
   C. you
   D. yow

2. We visited ___ cousins.
   A. our
   B. hour
   C. owr
   D. ower

3. My ___ has five fingers.
   A. hend
   B. hond
   C. and
   D. hand

4. I ___ only six.
   A. em
   B. im
   C. am
   D. amm

5. Cats ___ kittens.
   A. ave
   B. have
   C. hav
   D. hove

6. Jump over ___ fence.
   A. that
   B. thet
   C. tat
   D. thit

7. The baby ___ funny things.
   A. saiz
   B. sayz
   C. says
   D. sez

8. Mark ___ hello.
   A. said
   B. sed
   C. sead
   D. sad

Review Test for Lesson 12

Directions: Read each sentence. Choose the correct spelling of the missing word. Mark your answer on the answer sheet by filling in the circle beside the correct letter. Do not write on this test.

Example:

1. The monster was ____.
   A. bigg
   B. big
   C. bige
   D. beg

1. A bug has ____ legs.
   A. sicks
   B. sics
   C. six
   D. siks

2. Hold ____ for me.
   A. thiz
   B. this
   C. thes
   D. tis

3. I ____ skating is fun.
   A. tink
   B. thinck
   C. thimk
   D. think

4. Cows ____ milk.
   A. giv
   B. give
   C. gif
   D. geve

5. The deer ____ in the woods.
   A. waz
   B. wuz
   C. wus
   D. was

6. Is that ____ I think it is?
   A. what
   B. wat
   C. wut
   D. whut

7. Do you ____ to play?
   A. wunt
   B. want
   C. wan
   D. wand

8. A ____ sign is red.
   A. sop
   B. stopp
   C. stope
   D. stop

Review Test for Lesson 18

Directions: Read each sentence. Choose the correct spelling of the missing word. Mark your answer sheet by filling in the circle beside the correct letter. Do not write on this test.

Example:

1. Sue ___ an apple.
   A. ait
   B. ate
   C. aet
   D. at

1. I ___ my finger!
   A. cutt
   B. kut
   C. cut
   D. cute

2. Sue got a doll ___ Spain.
   A. from
   B. frum
   C. frun
   D. frome

3. Don't eat too ___.
   A. mush
   B. mutch
   C. moch
   D. much

4. I have only ___ mitten.
   A. won
   B. wun
   C. one
   D. on

5. My ___ is Jennifer.
   A. naim
   B. name
   C. naem
   D. nane

6. Can you ___ a poem?
   A. sai
   B. sae
   C. zay
   D. say

7. A piglet is a ___ pig.
   A. babie
   B. baybe
   C. baby
   D. babe

8. A ___ has many links.
   A. chain
   B. chane
   C. shain
   D. chayn

Review Test for Lesson 24

Directions: Read each sentence. Choose the correct spelling of the missing word. Mark your answer on the answer sheet by filling in the circle beside the correct letter. Do not write on this test.

Example:

> **1.** The fire was ___.
> A. hott
> B. hot
> C. hut
> D. hat

1. You are ___ silly.
A. being
B. bein
C. beeing
D. bing

2. Don't play in the ___.
A. steet
B. street
C. streat
D. strete

3. Who made ___ muffins?
A. thez
B. thes
C. theze
D. these

4. It is ___ cold outside.
A. very
B. berry
C. verry
D. vary

5. The snow was ___ and white.
A. cleen
B. klean
C. clene
D. clean

6. Ann likes to ___ poetry.
A. write
B. rite
C. right
D. writ

7. I want to ___ a treasure.
A. fynd
B. finde
C. find
D. fine

8. Do you know ___ the sky is blue?
A. wie
B. why
C. wye
D. whie

T38

Review Test for Lesson 30

Directions: Read each sentence. Choose the correct spelling of the missing word. Mark your answer on the answer sheet by filling in the circle beside the correct letter. Do not write on this test.

Example:

> 1. The grass is ___.
>   A. grean
>   B. green
>   C. grene
>   D. grein

1. The tree has ___ leaves.
   A. know
   B. noe
   C. no
   D. noo

2. I ___ how to spell.
   A. knowe
   B. know
   C. no
   D. now

3. An ice cube is ___.
   A. code
   B. coald
   C. coled
   D. cold

4. Alice put on her winter ___.
   A. cote
   B. coat
   C. kote
   D. koat

5. The window is ___.
   A. open
   B. oapen
   C. opin
   D. oppen

6. What ___ you like for lunch?
   A. wood
   B. woud
   C. would
   D. wuold

7. He ___ the flowers in a vase.
   A. putt
   B. put
   C. poot
   D. pot

8. What ___ are you reading?
   A. buk
   B. boock
   C. buck
   D. book

Review Test for Lesson 36

Directions: Read each sentence. Choose the correct spelling of the missing word. Mark your answer on the answer sheet by filling in the circle beside the correct letter. Do not write on this test.

Example:

1. The snow is ___.
   A. whyte
   B. white
   C. wite
   D. whiet

1. Mary lives in a small ___.
   A. toun
   B. towne
   C. town
   D. towm

2. My house is ___ the corner.
   A. arownd
   B. around
   C. aound
   D. arount

3. A monkey has a ___ tail.
   A. lawng
   B. long
   C. lung
   D. lomg

4. Al ___ the circus last week.
   A. saw
   B. say
   C. zaw
   D. sow

5. Sue likes to ___ on the phone.
   A. tawlk
   B. talk
   C. tawk
   D. tok

6. The elf was ___.
   A. smoll
   B. smawl
   C. small
   D. smal

7. My slacks are too ___.
   A. shart
   B. short
   C. chort
   D. shored

8. The ___ was closed.
   A. store
   B. stoar
   C. stor
   D. storre

T40

Answer Sheet

Name _____ **Date** _____

Directions: Mark each answer by filling in the circle next to the correct letter. Be sure to fill in only one circle for each number.

Example:

1. A. ○
   B. ●
   C. ○
   D. ○

1. A. ○
   B. ○
   C. ○
   D. ○

2. A. ○
   B. ○
   C. ○
   D. ○

3. A. ○
   B. ○
   C. ○
   D. ○

4. A. ○
   B. ○
   C. ○
   D. ○

5. A. ○
   B. ○
   C. ○
   D. ○

6. A. ○
   B. ○
   C. ○
   D. ○

7. A. ○
   B. ○
   C. ○
   D. ○

8. A. ○
   B. ○
   C. ○
   D. ○

Dear Family of _____ :

    This year your child will be learning to spell and write many new words. It will be exciting for your child to study the sounds and letters, check meanings, and use the new words.

    You can support our classroom work in spelling by asking your child about the words he or she is currently studying and by making the study of words a shared experience at home. Here are some simple but fun ways to help your child build word power.

✔ Keep a list of your child's weekly spelling words handy. Whenever he or she encounters one of the words during the week, put a check mark by it on the list. Count how many times the words are used in daily life.

✔ Together make customized bookmarks for the books your child is reading. Cut a strip of construction paper into the size of a bookmark. Decorate one side with the title of the book and pictures. On the other side write any new words your child finds.

✔ Use your child's spelling words to play a word game. Write the words on slips of paper. Fold the slips in half so that the players cannot see the words. One player choses a word and gives the other player clues until the player identifies the word. Clues might include a pantomine, an illustration, or beginning or ending sounds.

    Activities like these build spelling and vocabulary skills while promoting a lifelong love for learning.

                        Sincerely,

                        Teacher

Estimada familia de _____ :

Este año su hijo(a) aprenderá a deletrear y escribir muchas palabras nuevas. El estudio de los sonidos y de las letras, la verificación de significados y el uso de las nuevas palabras constituirá una fuente de emoción para su hijo(a).

El trabajo de deletreo que realizamos en el salón de clase puede complementarse mediante preguntas a su hijo(a) acerca de las palabras que está estudiando actualmente; así como también al hacer del estudio de palabras una experiencia compartida en el hogar. He aquí algunas maneras simples, mas sin embargo divertidas, de ayudar a su hijo(a) a adquirir habilidades con el uso de palabras.

✔ Mantener a la mano una lista de las palabras semanales de deletreo de su hijo(a). Siempre que él o ella identifique alguna de las palabras durante la semana, poner una marca junto a esa palabra en la lista. Contar cuantas veces se utilizan las palabras en la vida diaria.

✔ Hacer juntos(as) indicadores de página personalizados para los libros que su hijo(a) esté leyendo. Cortar una franja de papel de construcción del tamaño de un indicador de página. Decorar un lado del mismo con el título del libro e ilustraciones. Al otro lado, escribir cualquier palabra nueva que su hijo(a) encuentre.

✔ Utilizar las palabras de deletreo de su hijo(a) para jugar con las palabras. Escribir las palabras en pedacitos de papel. Doblarlos en mitad de manera que los participantes del juego no puedan ver las palabras. Uno de los participantes elige un papelito y da pistas a los demás hasta que uno de ellos identifica la palabra. Las pistas pueden incluir una pantomima, una ilustración, o sonidos del inicio o final de la palabra en cuestión.

Actividades como éstas desarrollan destrezas de vocabulario y de deletreo, al mismo tiempo que fomentan un aprecio por el aprendizaje que dura toda una vida.

Cordialmente,

Maestro(a)

Dear Family of _____ :

This year your child has been learning to spell and write many new words. It is exciting for your child to study the sounds and letters, check meanings, and use the new words.

You can continue to support our classroom work in spelling by asking your child about the words he or she is currently studying and by making the study of words a shared experience at home. Here are some more simple but fun ways to help your child build word power.

✔ Keep a notepad by the phone, on the refrigerator, or in your child's room. Write notes to your child and encourage him or her to write notes back to you.

✔ Play a game using your child's spelling words. Tell your child you are thinking of a word, tell how many letters it has, and give a clue, such as its meaning or something it rhymes with. Have your child spell the word you are thinking of.

✔ Let your child give you a test on his or her spelling words. Checking your answers will help your child to identify the correct spelling of the words.

Activities like these build spelling and vocabulary skills while promoting a lifelong love for learning.

Sincerely,

Teacher

STECK·VAUGHN

Spelling

Estimada familia de _____ :

Este año su hijo(a) ha estado aprendiendo a deletrear y escribir muchas palabras nuevas. El estudio de los sonidos y de las letras, la verificación de significados y el uso de las nuevas palabras constituye una fuente de emoción para su hijo(a).

Se puede continuar apoyando el trabajo de deletreo que realizamos en el salón de clase mediante preguntas a su hijo(a) acerca de las palabras que está estudiando actualmente; así como también al hacer del estudio de palabras una experiencia compartida en el hogar. He aquí algunas maneras simples, mas sin embargo divertidas, de ayudar a su hijo(a) a adquirir habilidades con el uso de palabras.

✔ Mantener una libreta de anotaciones cerca del teléfono, en la refrigeradora, o en la habitación de su hijo(a). Escribir mensajes a su hijo(a) y exhortarle a que le corresponda con mensajes de igual manera.

✔ Participar en un juego que utilice las palabras de deletreo de su hijo(a). Decir a su hijo(a) que usted está pensando en una palabra, decirle cuantas letras tiene y darle una pista, tal como su significado o algo con lo que rima. Haga que su hijo(a) deletree la palabra en la que usted esté pensando.

✔ Dejar que su hijo(a) le haga un examen sobre sus palabras de deletreo. La verificación de sus respuestas ayudará a su hijo(a) a identificar el deletreo correcto de las palabras.

Actividades como éstas desarrollan destrezas de vocabulario y de deletreo, al mismo tiempo que fomentan un aprecio por el aprendizaje que dura toda una vida.

Cordialmente,

Maestro(a)

Steps in the Writing Process

Name _____

1. Prewriting
Think about what you want to say.
- Make sure you know your reason for writing.
- Think about your reader.
- Make a plan.

2. Writing
Use your plan to make a first try.
- Don't worry about mistakes now.
- Add any new ideas you think of while writing.
- Keep your purpose and audience in mind.
- Leave plenty of room between lines so you can make changes later.

3. Revising
Look for ways to improve what you have written.
- Look for places that need more ideas or details.
- Get rid of sentences that don't belong.
- Find places where more colorful or exact words might be used.
- Revise until clear and complete.

4. Proofreading
Review your work for errors.
- Correct any misspelled words.
- Check for other errors.
- Make a clean, final copy.
- Proofread your work again. Make sure you have not made new errors.

5. Publishing
Share what you have written.
- Read it to the class or a friend.
- Add pictures or make a poster.
- Make a recording of your writing.

Proofreading Symbols/Checklist

Name _____

You should always proofread your writing for errors. The chart below shows some proofreading marks and how to use them.

Mark	Meaning	Example
⬭	word is misspelled	I ⬭liek⬭ dogs.
⊙	period is missing	The dog barked⊙
⸙?	question mark is missing	Did the dog bark⸙?
≡	letter should be capitalized	I love my dog b̲uster.

One good way to proofread your writing is to use a checklist.
The checklist below will help you remember things to look for as
you proofread. Place a check mark by each of the following when you
have finished.

☐ 1. I have checked each word to make sure it is spelled
        correctly.

☐ 2. I have used a period or question mark at the end of
        every sentence.

☐ 3. I have started every sentence with a capital letter.

☐ 4. I have capitalized all proper names.

Chain of Events Chart

Name _____ **Date** _____

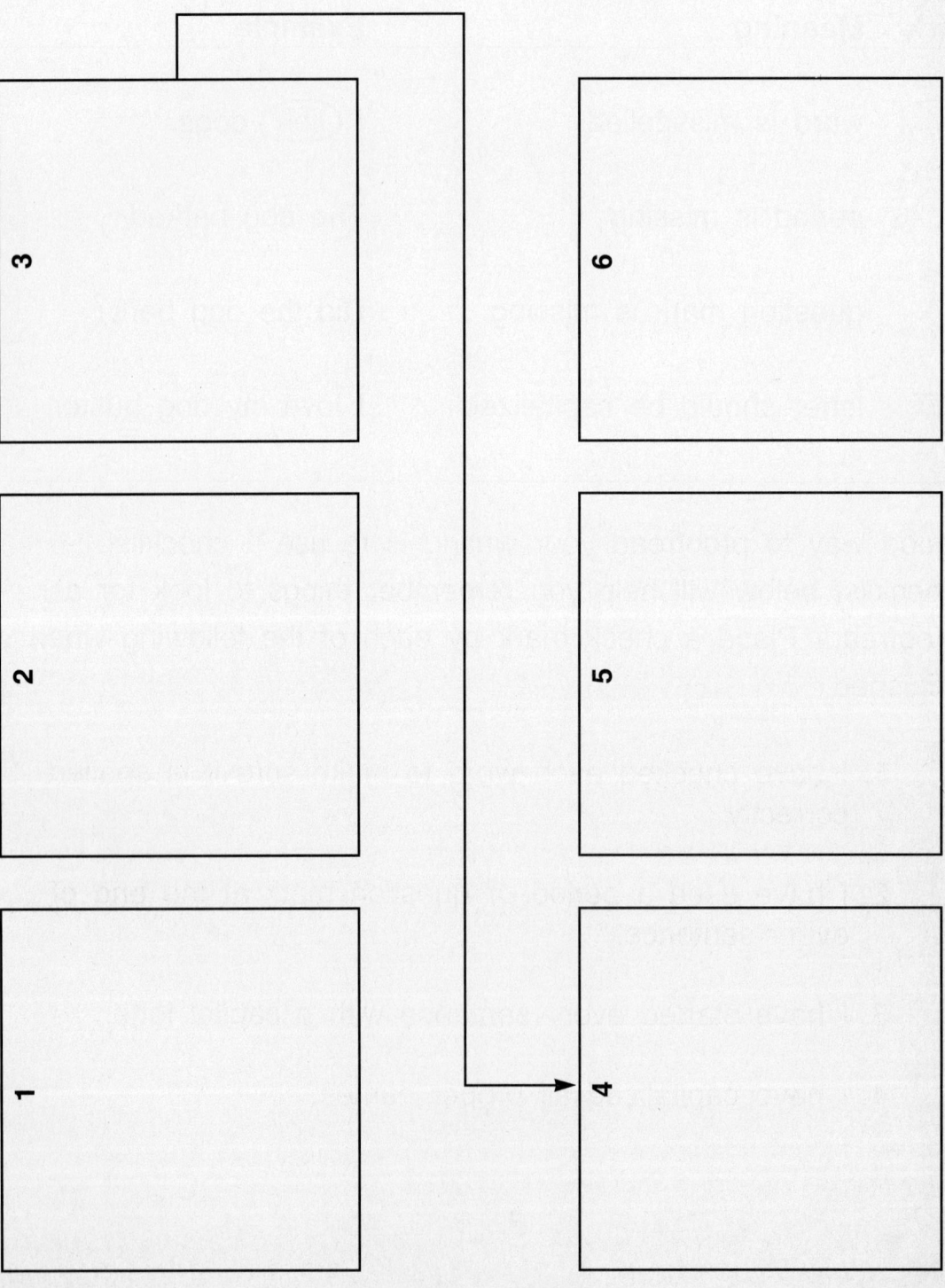

Story Map

Name _____ **Date** _____

Beginning

Middle

End

Senses Web

Name _____ **Date** _____

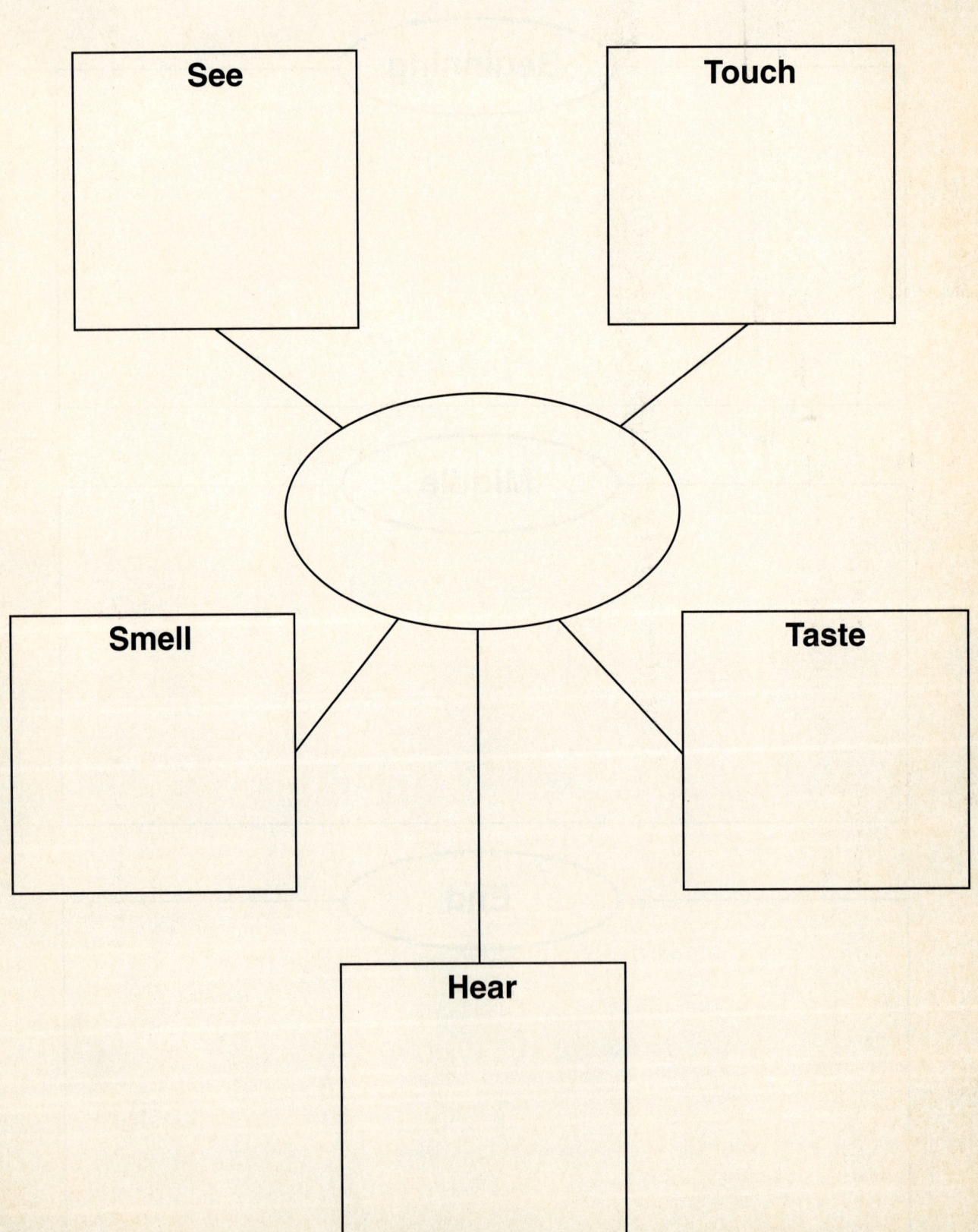

See

Touch

Smell

Taste

Hear